AMERICANS FROM HUNGARY

By the same author

———

THE DANUBE

THE CAULDRON BOILS

MILLIONS OF DICTATORS

TURKEY

CATTLE CAR EXPRESS

DAKAR: OUTPOST OF TWO HEMISPHERES

SIBERIA

NEW DEAL IN EUROPE

HITLER

AMERICA'S ROLE IN WORLD AFFAIRS

AMERICANS
FROM
HUNGARY

—

Emil Lengyel

**THE
PEOPLES
OF AMERICA
SERIES**

Edited by Louis Adamic

J. B. LIPPINCOTT COMPANY
PHILADELPHIA AND NEW YORK

DEDICATED TO THE MEMORIES

OF

PETER ADAM

AND

LAJOS DELEJ

ACKNOWLEDGMENTS

I am under a debt of gratitude to several friends who gave me their help in the preparation of this book. Special thanks are due to Mr. A. S. Pinter who enabled me to read his manuscript study about the history of North American immigration from Hungary during the first three decades of this century. Also to Dr. Géza Schütz whose doctoral thesis about the economic situation of the working classes in pre-war Hungary (1890-1913) prepared for the University of Geneva, Switzerland, was very helpful. Special acknowledgments are given these two works among the "References" at the end of this book.

I am deeply indebted to Mr. Bela Bachkai, formerly of the Political Science Department, University of Indiana, Bloomington, Indiana, and to Professor Michel N. Franck, of the Pacific Lutheran College, Parkland, Washington, for their unfailing kindness and help.

Special thanks are also due to my friends, Messrs. John Forbath, T. G. Kemeny-Harding, Dr. Elizabeth S. Klinger, and Mr. Anthony Seaton for their assistance in preparing this book. Mr. Hugo Kormos was good enough to open up to me a Hungarian settlement which suggested at least one chapter of the book. To Miss Tay Hohoff, who helped with suggestions and criticisms, I extend my heartfelt thanks.

E. L.

THE WARP AND WOOF OF AMERICA

THE DECLARATION OF INDEPENDENCE was more than the birth certificate of a nation. It certified the arrival of a new principle in government, and it hinted in passing at a new kind of population.

The new country not only had a new governmental principle but an unusual population. And although this fact is mentioned only obliquely in the Declaration, it is as much at the core of our history and makeup as the idea of democracy. The fact was recognized by the Founding Fathers. John Adams, Benjamin Franklin and Thomas Jefferson, who were a committee created for the purpose, directly recommended to Congress that the new national emblem of the United States should contain, besides the emblems of the Original Thirteen States, also the national emblems of England, Scotland, Ireland, France, Germany and Holland, as representing "the countries from which these States have been peopled." The committee neglected to mention Africa, from which stemmed about one fifth of the population at that time; and the Indians, and Sweden, Switzerland and a half-dozen other lands whose nationals had come over in small numbers.

The people alive at one time in the United States were never preponderantly of English stock, or German stock, or Dutch or Spanish or Negro stock, or of one religion. The people living here at any period, since European colonization began, came, or descended from people who came, or were brought over, from many different countries. Even the Indians (as will be shown in one of *The Peoples of America* volumes) weren't here always; now they are believed to have crossed the Bering Straits from Siberia between ten and fifteen thousand years ago.

The democratic idea and the exchange, the interflow, within the tremendous variety of national, racial, religious, cultural backgrounds have made this country something unique, something new under the sun. The fabric and texture of the United States is woven of these two factors interacting in a land whose sweep between the Atlantic and the Pacific carries a lavish richness of physical resources. The democratic idea and the mixture of peoples are the warp and woof of America.

If this were a deserted country about which nothing were known,

7

and if archeologists discovered its ruins and tried to find out what it
had been like, they would come across place-names: Dundee, Schuyl-
kill Haven, Prairie du Chien, Holland, Milford, Frenchtown, Tini-
cum, Cambridge, Warsaw, Los Angeles, Dublin, Wichita, Lyndhurst,
New London, Scandia, Berlin, Sevastopol, Traunik, Athens, Tacoma,
San Diego. They would learn what we ate: roast beef, smörgåsbord,
gefüllte fisch, pasta, goulash, corn, corn beef, potatoes, consommé,
borscht, knedliki, strudel, chow mein, wienies, hamburger. They
would read names of people: Lincoln, Roosevelt, Toscanini, Stein-
metz, Brandeis, Chávez, Willkie, Tesla, Kaiser, Benét, LaGuardia,
Pulitzer, Einstein, Paul Robeson, Ingrid Bergman, Maurice Rose,
George Skouras.

From payrolls and army rosters, lists of students and teachers, business and legal documents, the archeologists would discover many
things. They would learn about the labor of the Irish and Chinese
railroad builders, the mixed-strain Paul Bunyan work gangs in the
North Woods, the Cornish and Montenegrin copper miners of Kee-
wenaw and Butte, the Finnish iron miners of Ishpeming, the men of
many stocks who built the boats on Lake Superior and shoveled the
ore of the Mesabi Range into them, the Slavic and Hungarian and
Lithuanian steel workers of Pittsburgh and Gary, the Jewish and
Italian garment workers of Manhattan and Brooklyn, the Russian
and Italian sandhogs under the Hudson River, the Scandinavian and
German farm-pioneers in the Middle West, the dark cotton pickers of
the South, the Hispano sheepmen of the Southwest, the Japanese gar-
deners on the West Coast—

There are an infinite number of historical facts which have been
having a tough time getting into the history books. Nor have they
got into the atmosphere. If they did, I think more and more of us
would incline toward the diversity view of America. We would see
that we are, as Walt Whitman said, "not merely a nation but a teeming
nation of nations." We would see that we are blood relatives of the
whole world; that we are literally the world in miniature.

We would see what unique qualifications our kinship gives us for
living in a world become so small that peoples can no longer ignore
or antagonize each other, but must learn about one another and learn
to get along together in order to survive.

LOUIS ADAMIC

Milford, New Jersey,
Thanksgiving 1947.

CONTENTS

Part 1   A People out of Asia

I   THE LONG SHADOW OF THE PAST   13

Part 2   People on the Move

II   EARLY HUNGARIANS IN AMERICA—FACT AND FABLE   19

III   SOLDIERS AND TRAVELERS   26

IV   THE SOUND OF DISTANT THUNDER   37

V   KOSSUTH'S PEOPLE   47

VI   "BEHOLD, ALIVE THE SACRED BAND. . . ."   65

VII   HUNGARIANS IN THE CIVIL WAR   73

VIII   A MAN TO POWER BORN   84

Part 3   The Pull and Push

IX   THE HIGH TIDE OF IMMIGRATION   94

X   RIDING THE HIGH TIDE   123

XI   *Öreg Amerikás*   135

Part 4   Little Hungary in America

XII   STRENGTH IN UNITY   156

XIII   RELIGION IN LITTLE HUNGARY   179

XIV   PRINT IN THE NATIVE TONGUE   194

Part 5 *A Hungarian Intermezzo*

XV   THE BIRTH OF AN INDUSTRY   206

Part 6 *A New Wave*

XVI   AN END AND A BEGINNING   216

XVII   LIFE IS SCIENCE   236

XVIII   LITERATI AND ILLUMINATI   255

XIX   MELODIES AND COLORS   274

XX   ABOUT LEADERS OF MEN AND OTHER PIONEERS   292

XXI   THE DRUMS AND AN EPILOGUE   302

REFERENCES   307

INDEX   311

AMERICANS FROM HUNGARY

Part 1

A PEOPLE OUT OF ASIA

I

THE LONG SHADOW OF THE PAST

TWILIGHT HOURS ON the Hungarian plains perform a magic. As the huge red hoop of the sun touches the horizon, the sweep of the draw-well is turned into the reflection of an apocalyptic sign, which is cut from its moorings. It races across the earth, bent on escaping the shadow's death as the sun drops below the soil. Then the darkness rushes out of the East and is shattered into tiny fragments.

The shadow of the past is very long on the Hungarian plains, as it is long elsewhere in Hungary too. People have so few tangible possessions that they attach themselves to intangibles. The past is precious because it is not the present, and the taste of yesterday is sweet because it is a memory of dreams.

The Eastern European is far more attached to the past than the Western European, even though the latter occasionally turns to the consecrated forms of convention. England's royal formalism is merely an anointed substitute for the essence of tradition. But the Western European is more tied down to the past than the American who trusts the present, is confident of the future and uncomprehending in the sight of the tradition-bound East.

Those who came to America from Hungary are creatures of the past. Their children may be redeemed, but their own natures are fixed in inexorable casts. Hungary's Árpád the Conqueror and the Mohács Disaster have molded their lives, even though their historical knowledge is slim.

The folk memory of the Hungarian is more oriental than his present site. Scholars spent lifetimes seeking out Hungary's ancestors, assisted only a little by legends. Two warriors—valiant as only reflections of the past can make them—once graced the Eastern world. They were

Hunor and Magor, and out of their loins have sprung the Hungarians and Huns. The former call themselves Magyars to this day, and the outside world transformed their name into Ungar and Hungarian.

In search of clues, scholars penetrated into the least-known regions of Asia, looking for the Magyars' ancestral home at the foot of the Himalayas, in the Gobi Desert, in the wastes and steppes of Central Asia, in the Altay range of the great Asiatic *massif,* beyond Lake Baikal, in Chinese Turkestan and even in Tibet.

A nomadic tribe must have been like a stream into which many tributaries fell. Some of the wandering ancestors of the Hungarians must have emerged from the mysterious East. But today many scholars incline more to the view that the main tributary of the Magyar group —which gave it many words—had its indigenous abode on the European side of the Urals. That region is watered by the Kama, Vjatka, Belaya and Volga.

Hungarian history began only when the Magyar hosts crossed the Carpathian range across the Verecke pass in 895 or 896, under the leadership of Árpád the Conqueror. Hungarian *"Mayflower* ancestors" are the horsemen crossing the pass, setting their eyes on the lush valley at the foot of the hills. The picture is so much like that of Moses on Mount Nebo that its authenticity has been questioned. In those distant days a grain of history was wrapped in a generous wad of foil.

It was the Middle Danube valley that the Hungarians found and settled. It had been crossed by many wandering tribes that marched onward, dazzled by the fame of the Romes of East and West. Some of the tribes had attempted to settle there, counting on the protective mountains all around. But mountains are not impediments to nomads in search of bread and life, and so the Middle Danube was soaked with blood. The Hungarians seem to have arrived at a psychological moment, when the previous occupants had fought one another to exhaustion. Held by a half-mythical Slavic overlord, the site of present-day Hungary was a no man's land. Thus the Magyars came into possession of a rich country and also of Pandora's box.

In an unsettled world, constantly in flux, in a world of war, the Magyars tried to seal off their newly acquired possession by gaining control of the strategic gap in the mountains, where the Vienna of today is situated. Beyond that they tried to obtain control of a natural staging area, a glacis, on the western slopes of the hills, all the way into Bavaria.

The conquerors' desperate drive projected them into the Germans' land. The West was on the point of being crystallized, reconciled to the Christian creed. It was to give peace to the peaceless world, fashioning the universal kingdom of the earth upon the universal kingdom of heaven. As there was one God, so there was to be one ruler in a new Roman Empire sanctified by its consecration to the only creed. The Magyars disturbed these attempts at unification. They were the outsiders, cast out by the parched East, bent on taking roots in the blessed West. Their frustration was a triumph of agricultural over pastoral pursuits.

The West repelled the intruders, as it had repelled many previous intruders. The Magyars were flung back into the Middle Danube region, unable to seal that mountain gate in the west. Their failure was to cast its long shadow into the future. The lot of hundreds of thousands of Hungarians in future centuries was then and there decided. Wreathed around by the mountains, Hungary seemed to be a perfect geographic unit, but it was not, because of that gap in the hills, and because, in the opposite direction, the East kept on exerting its pressure upon the Middle Danubian land.

Hungary became an independent country under her native Árpád dynasty, but that independence was not to last long. Even then, small peoples were at the mercy of mighty dynasties, and of predatory hunger. In the early thirteenth century, hunger burst its bounds in Eastern Asia, as the Tatars broke from the steppes into the lands of the Sown.

The Danube saw the Tatars' hordes. The Hungarian plain was seared by their ferocity. But they had overextended themselves and had to clear out not because they met their equals, but because they had spent too much of their substance in the global march. When the tide receded, the Magyars' countryside was depopulated, at the mercy of other marauders. It was then that Hungary's rulers turned to the nomadic Cumans, who had been biding their time beyond the hills. That was a precedent many rulers were to follow, and soon the long shadow of minority conflicts could be perceived.

Hungary was not able to recover from the Tatar blow. The days of her native dynasty were numbered and at the turn of the fourteenth century it was gone.

In a land of historic memories, fourteenth century politics furnishes the documentation of many twentieth century events, among them the immigration to the United States. Dynasties followed one another in quick succession. The dominant aristocracy may have been still mainly native, but the candidates for the crown were outlanders. They needed the help of Magyar nabobs to fight rivals. They promised increased power to the magnates in exchange for the crown. This arrangement suited both the rulers and their mighty backers. The "common man" had to foot the bill.

That part of the world was not yet stabilized. Out of the East threatened another danger, no less formidable than that of the Tatars three centuries before. This time it was the Ottoman Turks who menaced Western Europe and their way lay across Hungary. The Magyars formed the first line of defense. A great emergency created great opportunities and great opportunities created great men. One of them reached European stature with his heroic resistance to the Turk—János Hunyadi, known to his contemporaries as the Turk-Beater, and claimed by two other peoples besides the Magyars.

He was a great leader, who knew how to inspire his forces with a desperate creed and firm belief in their Christian mission against the Moslem. But the Turks also were imbued with a feeling of their own mission, and constant pressure in their Asiatic home had forced them to become a fighting machine. They introduced the system of a whole people at war, and thus anticipated the modern total conflict. Christendom was hopelessly split by a tragic dissension. On the banks of the Danube, near the town of Mohács, the Hungarians lost a crucial battle in 1526—the year of the Mohács Disaster. Hungary was lost and Christendom faced doomsday.

Turkish pashas ruled over most of Hungary. In a small strip of the western marches of the land, momentarily out of Turkey's advance, dissident nobles turned to the Habsburg neighbor for help and elected Ferdinand I King of Hungary. His realm was a hope, far more than a reality.

The Turkish victory turned out to be ephemeral. Architects of effective military machines, the Turks were not architects of peace plans. Success spoiled them, inducing them to sit on their laurels and those laurels were prickly. As Turkish strength ebbed away, the remaining Hungarian nobility jockeyed itself into position, playing off one side against the other. By the end of the seventeenth century, the Ottoman Empire was about to become a realm in agony. Now the Habsburgs were in the saddle, backed by the Magyar nobles. From the West colonists were invited to till the rich soil which had been neglected so long. The native Hungarian stock was thinning, and the question of nationalities became acute.

Serfdom was on its way out in Western Europe, but not in Hungary. There it was on its way in. The Ottoman Empire had completely eradicated the aristocracy in the adjacent Balkans, but not in Hungary where it could not obtain a foothold on all of the land. Now the local lords were back, eager to make up for lost time. They reduced the working people to pariahs, *misera plebs contribuens,* miserable tax-paying masses. The Habsburgs, aliens in the land, had to introduce an indirect regime. Their henchmen were the lords of the manor who acted on their estates as sovereign powers. The *aulic,* aristocracy—so called because it was attached to the Vienna Court, *aula*—lost contact with the people, which it despised as uncouth and uncivilized. The people spoke Hungarian, while the lords spoke Latin. Nationalities were pitted against one another, the lords became pawns in the imperial game, and the peasant became a beast of burden, not credited with human feelings or a soul of his own.

The incubation period of the new age was long. It was from the West that the call came: "All men are created equal!" and the notion that man is never the instrument—always the end. These were words that meant nothing to the tillers of the soil, too deeply submerged in ignorance to be able to comprehend abstract ideas.

But there were people in Hungary to whom these words made sense. Some of them were aristocrats, who had the advantage of higher education. Others were members of the lower nobility. Those members of the privileged classes who responded to the Western call were decried by their privileged fellow citizens as heretics and traitors. But name-calling could not halt the march of ideas.

The Hungarian messiah of the mid-nineteenth century awakening was magnetic, eloquent Lajos Kossuth, who was to play an important rôle in the history of emigration from Hungary. He was the leader of the revolt against the Habsburgs, which was also a revolt against the old order, since history is indivisible. How much was the common man to profit from the success of the revolution? It would be hard to say, since it failed. Probably it would have been a triumph for the middle classes, as was the case with contemporary revolution in the West.

The revolution failed, but some of its ideas were marked for triumph. The peasant gained his freedom from serfdom. The Habsburgs made their peace with Hungary in 1867, the year of the historic Compromise. *Ausgleich.* Austria and Hungary were to become partners—more or less—in the Austro-Hungarian Monarchy under the rule of the

House of Habsburg and Lorraine. The head of the House was Austria's Emperor and Hungary's King. Foreign affairs, defense and finances relating to both, were to be matters of joint concern.

K.u.k. the new monarchical institutions were called, *kaiserlich und koeniglich,* imperial and royal. Austria was more populous, larger, far more advanced, more prosperous. Her influence predominated. Many Hungarian young men found the German language of the "joint" army distasteful. It was not Hungary's, it was not their army. Many sneaked across the boundary on their way to the United States.

In foreign affairs, again, Austria called the tune. Some Hungarian statesmen played important parts, but they became *aulic,* dazzled by the Court. Spokesmen of the Habsburgs, these statesmen soon forgot their native Hungary.

Hungary was "free" and so was the Hungarian peasant. At any rate, he was no longer legally a serf. The redemption fees of the former feudal lands were high and many peasants could not afford to pay them. Besides, what good was a farm without tools and animals? The peasant swelled the army of the *nincstelenek,* people without nothing. He knew the truth of the proverb: *Szegény embert még az ág is huzza.* Even the thorn pricks the poor man. The schoolbooks maintained that feudalism was dead in Europe. Was it really dead in Hungary?

Part 2

PEOPLE ON THE MOVE

II

Early Hungarians in America—Fact and Fable

No Hungarians sailed on the *Mayflower,* but one Hungarian may have trod on American soil centuries before the arrival of that famous boat. He was Tyrker, a companion of Leif Ericson.

Leif was the son of Eric the Red, founder of the earliest Scandinavian settlement in Greenland. From there Leif proceeded to the court of King Olaf Tryggvason of Norway who appointed him his official Christian missionary in Greenland. On his return, Leif was driven off his course and saw lands "of which he had previously had no knowledge," land of "self-sown wheat" and vines and *"mösur"* wood. It was in the year 1000.

Where was that blessed land? Could it have been Nova Scotia, as some thought? But one would not expect to come across wild grapes there. Could it have been northern New England, Rhode Island's Mount Hope or the estuary of the Hudson River? Is Eric's tale fact or fiction?

Serious historians today are inclined to accept Leif as an early Scandinavian discoverer of America. The story is related in near-contemporary manuscripts, including *The Saga of Eric the Red,* but Leif's companion, Tyrker, entered the saga at a later time, in the *Heimskringla or Lives of the Norse Kings,* by Snorri Sturluson,[1] and this is the story told there.

The expedition first touched land in a region abounding in bare rocks, and hence called *Helullaland* (*hella*-naked), Land of the Naked Rock. It may have been Labrador. Sailing with thirty-five men, Leif's boat hugged the coast, rounded a huge promontory, reaching a region well protected against northern winds, called *Markland,* Land of the Forest (*mark*). It may have been somewhere near Newfoundland.

Again they set sail for the south and after a time the crew found a land of grass. There Leif decided to make a halt.

It came to pass one evening that a member of the crew was missing. He was from the South Country, named Tyrker, "small in stature and ugly," but "dexterous in all feats." Tyrker was a person who enjoyed a special position, since he was Leif's foster-father. Understandably, the leader of the expedition was worried, he upbraided his men for having let his foster-father run into danger, and organized a search party. They had gone but a short way when they came upon Tyrker and the joy was great on all sides. Leif observed that Tyrker was very merry, and he thus spoke to him:

"Why art thou so late, foster-father, and why didst thou leave thy comrades?"

Thereupon, according to the record, Tryker rolled his eyes, frowned, and "babbled in Turkish," uncomprehended by his Scandinavian companions. He became aware of their incomprehension and now spoke in Norse:

"Wines and grapes I have found. I come from a land in which wines and grapes are abundant."

So Lief Ericson, offspring of Eric the Red of Brattlid, called the place *Vinland*.

At this point begins the controversy which has raged around the incident. Dr. Eugene Piváný, a Hungarian scholar,[2] mentions the supposition, first of all, that Tyrker was not the man's real name, but was a sobriquet, meaning Turk or Turkish, for in the Constantinople of those days the Hungarians were called Turks and the Northmen of the Middle Ages were in frequent intercourse with Magyars. This fact had been noted by the eighteenth century historian Schjoeningius, commissioned to prepare a critical analysis of the *Heimskringla*. Dr. Piváný further points out that the early Hungarians were called "Turks" even by Byzantine authors, such as Constantine Porphyrogenietus and Leo the Philosopher, and the royal crown which the Eastern Roman Emperor Michael Ducas dispatched to King Geiza I of Hungary in the eleventh century, forming the lower portion of Hungary's "holy crown," contains the Greek inscription: "To Geiza, King of *Turkia*." (Until recent times it was assumed that Hungarian was a Turkic tongue.)

Dr. Piváný calls attention to the fact that wine was grown in Pannonia, which later became part of Hungary, from the days of the Roman Emperor Probus.

How did Tyrker, the "Hungarian," get in touch with Leif, the son of Eric? The Hungarians of the tenth century, the Hungarian scholar continues, were in touch with the Rurik dynasty, Norse founders of the Principality of Kiev. The Prince of Kiev, Sviatoslav, had a Slavic name and Northman blood, and he fought Constantinople with a host of Northmen-Varangian subjects and Hungarian and Petcheneg mercenaries. "The war ended disastrously for Sviatoslav. He had to agree to humiliating peace terms, and on his homeward march the Petchenegs turned on him and killed him. There were many Hungarians among the fleeing Norse-Russian soldiers, so that it was likely that some *Tyrker* got with them to the North of Russia and thence to Norway and even to Iceland. Bravery and love of adventure having been characteristics common to Northmen and Hungarian, there was little in the way of understanding each other."

This is convincing so far, but the Danish scholar, Charles Rafn,[3] for instance, contended that Tyrker might have been a German, his name being a contraction of *Thythverskir Menn,* a *thythversku* meaning German. He is mentioned as a German in later literature.

Several Slavonic nations and the Rumanians have also claimed Tyrker as their own. While Homer was claimed only by seven cities, the obscure Tyrker has been claimed by at least seven countries. Many Americans of Hungarian birth cling to their Tyrker, as if they wanted to go one better than the numerous descendants of the *Mayflower* passengers. Their pride in Tyrker is necessarily academic, as they could not have failed to notice that stringent quota restrictions apply also to the countrymen of Columbus.

It is also believed by many Americans—again supported by Dr. Pivány—that the name "America" is of Hungarian origin, derived from Emericus, the Hungarian princely saint, son of St. Stephen, King of Hungary. St. Emeric was highly popular in mid-fifteenth century Florence, when Amerigo Vespucci, son of Nastaggio, the notary, was born. Amerigo is the Italianized form of Emeric.[4]

Some scholars believe that Vespucci was the first to set foot on the American continent. His statement to this effect was contained in a letter he wrote to Lorenzo Piero Francesco de' Medici. The letter was publicized in 1507 by Martin Waldseemüller (Hylacomylus), professor of cosmography at the St. Dié University in Lorraine. It was this professor who suggested that the newly found part of the globe should be called "America because Americus discovered it." The learned Pivány adds that it would have been more correct to spell America's name as *Emerica*.

A Hungarian did play a part in one of the earliest attempts to settle America from England. The sixteenth century British geographer, Richard Hakluyt, told the story in *The Principal Navigations, Voyages, Traffiques and Discoveries of the English Nation*.

In 1578 Sir Humphrey Gilbert, step-brother of Sir Walter Raleigh, obtained letters patent from Queen Elizabeth for the "inhabiting and planting of our people in America." The patent was to run for six years, giving Sir Humphrey and his heirs liberty to "discover, finde, search out and view such remote, hethen and barbarous countrys and territories not actually possessed by any Christian prince or people," to have, hold and occupy "such regions with all their commodities, jurisdictions and royalties both by sea and land." The Queen was to receive one-fifth of the silver and gold ore of the newly discovered regions, in addition to sovereignty over redeemed human souls, which should have weighed more in the scale than even gold.

It was the navigator's fixed idea that if he sailed in a northwesterly direction he would find the fabulous land of spice and gems, *Cataia*. It was his object to find the Northwest Passage. However, before engaging in that venture, Sir Humphrey wanted to gain possession of a part of America for the purpose of colonization.

He tried and failed, then tried again in the summer of 1583. This time he assembled a fleet of five ships, manned by 260 men, gentlemen, adventurers and rovers. In order to beguile the savage heathens of the New World, they had "musick of good variety," Morris dancers, and hobby horses.

One of the members of this expedition was a Hungarian: Stephen Parmenius of Buda (Stephanus Parmenius Budaeus). He was born of Protestant parents at Buda, during the occupation of the Turks, in mid-sixteenth century. He studied in England for three years, and seems to have made such a good impression on the famous geographer Richard Hakluyt—who was to tell his story—that he introduced him to Sir Humphrey. Parmenius, conversant with the foibles of the great, composed a paen in praise of that noble navigator, and Sir Humphrey appointed him the official chronicler of the expedition. It was the task of the Hungarian poet to describe its feats in elegant Latin, then the *lingua franca* of intellectual Europe.

Parmenius sailed on the flagship of the flotilla, the *Delight*. They sighted Newfoundland in July and cast anchor at St. John's, held by

English merchant adventurers. The English residents were suspicious of the visitors' designs and it was only after protracted negotiations that they displayed the "welcome" sign. In a letter dated August sixth, which Parmenius dispatched to Hakluyt, the Hungarian scholar expressed keen disappointment that the land was cold and barren and that the natives were out of sight. He wrote that he had seen bears, whose fur was grey, and they were not so large as Europe's brown beasts.

After a stay of several days, they set sail again, now for Cape Breton. They saw no land for days. On August 29 a violent storm arose. Near Cape Sable the *Delight* ran on a sandbank and sank with a loss of a hundred men. Among them perished Parmenius, the poet. Thus ended a noble enterprise and a promising career.

A worthy memorial to the Hungarian poet was penned in a letter of Captain Haie:

"This was a heavy and grievous event, to lose at one blow our chiefe shippe fraighted with great provision, gathered together with much travell, care, long time and difficultie. But more was the losse of our men, which perished to the number of a hundred soules. Amongst whom was a learned man, an Hungarian, borne in the citie of Buda, called thereof Budaeus, who of pitie and zeal of good attempts, adventured in this action, minding the record in the Latin tongue, the gests and things worthy of remembrance, happening in this discoverie, to the honour of our nation, the same being adorned with the eloquent stile of this Orator and rare Poet of our time." [5]

At the turn of the seventeenth century, Hungary entered American history through one of the principal founders of Virginia, John Smith. That enterprising person reached the west coast of the Atlantic after paying a visit to Hungary and several other European countries, including the Netherlands, France, Austria, Wallachia and Russia.

As he tells the story, he offered his strong young arms to the Austrian ruler trying to stem the Ottoman tide, which then threatened to overwhelm Western civilization. He fought the Turks in Hungary and Transylvania. He tells us that he invented the "fiery dragons," shells filled with explosives dropped into the enemy's camp; and another device which was an anticipation of long-distance signals, the transmission of code with torches.

He tells us that he killed three Turkish lords in single combat, for which he received his coat of arms of three Turkish heads. Badly wounded in a battle, he was taken prisoner by a "Lord Turbishaw," who turned him over to his favorite mistress, Charatza, as her slave. She fell in love with him and the pasha sold him on the slave market. Tired of maltreatment, John Smith killed the slave overseer and escaped, finally reaching a crossroads where, he tells us, a picture of the sun indicated the road to China, a black man full of white spots showed the way to Persia, a half-moon the road to Tartary, and a cross the way to Russia. He chose the cross and found himself on the River Don, where the Russians gave him a great welcome.

A free man again, he traversed Hungary and German-speaking countries, reached England and, at the beginning of the seventeenth century, put the colony of Virginia on the map. Fantastic as Smith's stories sound, history corroborates the essential part, so that we may accept his Hungarian interlude as part of the record of that remarkable man.

The resistance of the untamed continent was now about to be broken and America was open to settlers. Word spread in Europe that in parts of the New World all could worship God in their own ways. Whittier wrote about one of the first who came from Hungary:

> Painful Kelpius from his hermit den
> By Wissahickon, maddest of good men . . .

The "maddest of good men" was John Kelp, known in Latin as Johannes Kelpius, a native of Transylvania's Szász-Dalla, presumably of Saxon parentage. His education was in the contemporary peripatetic way, first in his native Transylvania, then in Germany's Thuringia, and in Leipzig. In Germany he established contact with the founder of Pietism, Philipp Jakob Spener, under whose influence he made a vow to live according to Christian precepts, not merely pay lip service to them. Religious feuds swept the German lands in those days and Kelpius' living Christianity found the environment too agitated. Britain beckoned him but even there he did not tarry long. Soon he was on his way to the Wissahickon, near Philadelphia, conducting a group of German settlers to Penn's colony. In his new home he dedicated himself to the service of God, spending his time in prayer, meditation, and the performance of good deeds. He led a hermit's life, and the district in which he lived became known as "Hermitage," later incorporated in Philadelphia. He also gave his name to a street in suburban Roxborough.[6]

A contemporary of Kelpius, Hungarian-born Izsák Nándor de

Sárossy, led a far from godly life. He, too, had a German education. In the classical secondary school—gymnasium—of the German town of Windsheim he acted as an assistant to another native of Hungary, Professor Tobias Schumberg. Sárossy's conduct was bad, and some townsmen induced him to try his luck overseas, in the colony of Francis Daniel Pastorius, who had settled near Philadelphia with some German families, giving the new settlement its name of Germanopolis, Germantown. Sárossy insisted that if he was to spread the word of the Lord he must have an agreed compensation. The devout Pastorius interpreted this as a "sign of a lack of faith in God." The Hungarian thereupon wrote a farewell letter to Pastorius, informing him that he was headed for Maryland. No more was heard of him.

In far-off New Mexico and in California, Hungarian Jesuits were at work long before those regions became States of the Union. One of them was Baron John Rátkay, sent to Mexico by the Society of Jesus in 1760. The Indians murdered him four years later.

Another was Father Ferdinand Konsag or Konschak, former professor at Buda, sent to America in the twenties of the eighteenth century. He became head of the mission of St. Ignatius in California and, later, visitor of all California missions. "He was a pioneer, and explorer, traveling over territory then mostly unknown, and drew a map of California in 1749. He died there in 1759." The Hungarians are not the only ones to claim him as their own. The Croatians also claim him as theirs.[7]

III

Soldiers and Travelers

George Washington did not sleep in every bed, but every nation likes to boast of a general attached to George Washington's staff. Few had the luck to produce a Marquis de Lafayette, or a Count Pulaski. But there was a Hungarian officer who played a distinguished part in Washington's army. His elusive fame had fascinated workers in the field of Hungarian Americana, and one of them, a judge in the Budapest Patent Office, Aladár Póka-Pivny, spent years in tracking down incidents in his hero's life.

The name of this officer was Michael Kovats, or de Kovats, or Kowatch, Kovach, Kowacz, Cowatch. . . . He himself preferred to sign his name as "Kovats." The common spelling in today's Hungary is Kovács, meaning Smith.

Michael Kovats was born at Karczag-Ujszálás, now Karczag, on the Hungarian plains, of Calvinist stock. The year was 1724. Military tradition was strong in the region peopled largely by descendants of Cuman warriors who had terrorized Eastern Europe centuries before. Young Kovats joined the *huszárs,* mounted troops, and had an adventurous life in Europe. One luckless day, however, he found himself in the Habsburg capital, Vienna, an unemployed hero. A disloyal servant had stolen his mounts and Kovats set out to catch him. Hot on the servant's trail, he reached Bohemia's Prague, and thence proceeded northward.

Frederick the Great was then Prussia's ruler, warring against a large part of the world. In great need of soldiers, he was not very scrupulous as to how he got them. No sooner was Kovats inside Prussia than he was impressed into the Prussian army by the King's men, in spite of the fact that he was a foreign subject. This type of service was, evidently, to the liking of our Hungarian, however; he fought for Frederick for sixteen years, won his promotion as a captain, and had command of a body of men known as *Kovats'sches Corps.*[8] He was wounded several times. One of Frederick's enemies was Queen Maria

Theresa of Hungary, Kovats' own sovereign. During an engagement the Hungarian *huszár* was captured by the troops of the Queen. Fighting one's own country today would be high treason, but in those days the dividing lines were not so sharp, and Captain Kovats talked himself out of trouble. Again unemployed, and finding nothing better to do, he returned to his native Hungary. But word had reached him about the fight of the American colonists for independence and he decided to try his luck overseas. By way of Venice and Genoa, he reached Bordeaux and there he offered his services to America in a letter to Benjamin Franklin in Paris.

Franklin was one of the three commissioners the Continental Congress had dispatched to France to negotiate a treaty of alliance, amity and commerce with the French government, and to obtain supplies, military and naval assistance. His fellow commissioner, Silas Deane, had concluded a contract with the far-famed champion of Polish liberty, Count Casimir Pulaski, to fight for the freedom of America. Kovats, therefore, approached the right people. However, we have no record of any answer from any of the commissioners.

If America did not want him, that did not mean that he did not want America. He set out for himself, arrived in America, sought and obtained an interview with Pulaski, who must have found him to his liking. The Count wrote to Washington on behalf of Kovats on January 9, 1778, that the new cavalry formations which it was contemplated to set up "must be exercised and taught the service from Col⁰· to private. Col⁰· Kovats is a man of great merit and deserves the charge of Master of Exercises; he is an officer worthy of research and exclusive of a thorough knowledge of his abilities I request his being employed by your Excellʸ. I can recommend him and assure your Excellʸ· will never have reason to repent your confidence in him, if this proposal should be agreeable to your Excellʸ. The sooner I am informed the better, as he will be of infinite service to the Cavalry this winter in Quarters."

No reply was forthcoming from Washington's headquarters. A few weeks later the Count wrote again, this time from Trenton, "about the commission for Colonel Kovats with authority to command a detachment as a Colonel." Still no reply, and he dispatched another letter to George Washington in mid-March: "I would propose for my subaltern, an experienced officer, by name Kovats, formerly partisan in Prussian service."

A few days later the authorization did come for the formation of the Pulaski Legion, sixty-eight horse and two hundred foot, and in mid-April Colonel Kovats was appointed Colonel Commandant of the Pulaski Legion. By that time word had got around about the Hungarian ex-*huszár* and we hear him described as "that famous Colonel Kovatz," and "the well-known Kovats, Prussian officer in the last war."

Pulaski's Legion was ordered to Sussex Court House, then to Cale's Fort, where it wintered, defending New Jersey against the Indians. In February 1779 it received orders to join General Benjamin Lincoln in South Carolina, and reached Charlestown (now Charleston) in May. The town was defended by General William Moultrie. His plight was so hopeless that civilian authorities urged him to surrender. At that strategic moment the Pulaski Legion arrived. While not a large force, the commander knew how to make it appear impressive. The British forces were commanded by General Augustine Prevost.

On May 11, Pulaski and Kovats attacked General Prevost with 120 men, and met an overwhelming force. In the very first onslaught, Kovats was mortally wounded. "The British buried him where he fell," Dr. Joseph Johnson, Charleston physician, recorded in his *Traditions and Reminiscences*[9] "on the west side of the road, in the land now owned and enclosed by John Margart, at the corner of Huger Street. He was an officer of great merit," the physician added, "a Hungarian by birth . . ."

The Pulaski Legion was the "best cavalry the rebels ever had," wrote Major F. Skelly, brigade major of the English forces at Charleston.

The commander of the Legion, Count Pulaski, met his death at the siege of Savannah, on October 9 of the same year. These losses so weakened the Legion that it was disbanded. Its colors were preserved in the Maryland Historical Society at Baltimore.

"The news of Kovats' death seems to have reached Hungary very quickly, for a report dated September 28, 1779, from the Buda Fortress Command to the Hungarian General Headquarters speaks of his wife as a widow. She herself, unable to visit her gallant husband's grave, erected a small memorial chapel to his memory near the church of Szinne. There it stands to this day, surrounded by century-old lime trees, recalling the memory of the Hungarian officer of hussars who died in action for the liberty of the United States of America. . . ."[10]

Were there other Hungarians in the American revolutionary armies? Not in the Continental army itself, says Dr. Eugene Piványi, but there were Hungarians in the French army sent to the assistance of the infant republic.

"When the King of France entered into a treaty of alliance with the United States and sent a large army to America under the command of General Count Rochambeau, the Duke of Lauzun was given, as part of that army, a legion of 800 foot and 400 horse"—as he writes in his memoirs (*Mémoires du Duc de Lauzun* /1747-1783/, publié par Louis Lacour, Paris, 1858, on p. 253)—"*sous la dénomination de volontaires étrangers de Lauzun, dont je serois colonel-propriétaire inspecteur*," i.e. under the name of Lauzun's Foreign Volunteers, of which he will be the colonel-proprietor inspector.[11] The cavalry of the Foreign Volunteers consisted of a squadron each of lancers and *huszárs*. At that time the *huszárs* in French service were Hungarians and so, "it may be asserted with absolute certainty," Piványi writes, "that the squadron of *huszárs* in Lauzun's Legion, viz. without officers 140 men, were Hungarians."

The major of Lauzun's Polish Lancers was John Polereczky, grandson of Major Matthias Polereczky, who had lost his life in the eighteenth century Hungarian War of Independence led by Prince Ferenc Rákóczi. After the American War of Independence, John moved to the State of Maine where he served as town clerk of Dresden for fifteen years.

The other Hungarian officer in Lauzun's Legion in America was Ferenc Benyowsky, younger brother of Count Maurice Augustus Benyowsky. Ferenc died in America in 1789.

Count Maurice Benyowsky (also spelled Benyovszky) was only fifteen when he fought in the Seven Years' War. After he had done his fighting there he joined the Poles in their struggle against the Russian Czars. He was captured by the Russians, taken across Siberia, and interned in Kamchatka, the dreariest spot in the dreariest region of Asia. It was such a fearful place that even the strongest were broken in body and spirit. The Count was not broken, however. On the contrary, he was so active that he led a revolt of the prisoners against the guards. He managed to escape from captivity and, braving the elements of that awful country, got out of Siberia. He reached France, after traveling half around the globe, where he tried to persuade the Paris government to place the island of Madagascar under French protection. He found ready ears and did indeed make an attempt to carry out his plan. Just then the French throne changed occupants and King Louis XVI, the indolent new ruler, withdrew his support.

Then the Count turned up at Philadelphia with a letter of recommendation from Benjamin Franklin which he transmitted to General Washington through Baron Frederick von Steuben, offering his blood, skill and courage to America. This was in 1782.

General Washington replied with consummate courtesy:

"I sincerely lament that your arrival in America was not at an earlier period, when this country could have employed you in a manner suitable to your rank, and thereby received essential benefit from that military experience, which a length of service must have given you."

The Count was not a man to be so easily discouraged. He continued to pursue his aim through the French Minister in the United States and conceived a grandiose scheme. He would raise an army of 3,483 men in Germany (the odd figure is not explained), clothe, arm and transport it into the United States, all for the sum of 518,000 livres. America would agree to pay his men monthly stipends and provide them with grants of land.

Congress referred the plan to a committee headed by James Madison, which reported back to the legislature: "The zeal for the American plan, which the author of it professes, and which the generous terms of the plan evince, have not failed to inspire a just esteem for his character and a disposition to favour his wishes. Considerations, however, which in no respect derogate from this esteem or this disposition, render it expedient for Congress to decline the offer which has been made."

Having failed to persuade the American government to set up an army, Count Benyowsky returned to his idea about Madagascar, which he thought potentially the richest land on the globe. He turned the full force of his galvanic eloquence on two Baltimore merchants, Messrs. Meisonnier and Zolihoffer. They placed a 500-ton boat, the *Intrepid,* at his disposal for the Madagascar expedition. He reached the island safely.

The natives had no use for trading companies and had acquired the habit of massacring white settlers. Count Benyowsky was one they slaughtered. He had left his wife in America and she remained here for a time. Their son found death on the Mexican frontier some years later. Soon the entire family of the adventurous Count was lost to sight.

Three centuries after the physical discovery of America, the continent was still largely a blank spot on the map of human knowledge. Even Voltaire knew so little about the New World that he called France's vast North American possessions *quelques arpents de neige,* a few acres of snow. In such a landlocked country as Hungary, America was far less known. Nobody could foresee that America, but recently independent, would show the way to the realization of a society in which the individual was not confined by a caste system, and was encouraged to do his utmost for his spiritual and physical betterment. This, indeed, was a new experiment in human society, bound to succeed beyond all expectations.

Hungary was still deeply mired in the feudal system; the contrast with American society was tremendous. Would Hungarians be able to learn from the experiment of the New World? Word of American events did penetrate into Hungary and the call was answered by some perceptive travelers.

One was Sándor Bölöni Farkas, who came to America in 1831 as the secretary of Count Ferenc Béldy. He covered 2,450 miles in this country, and wrote an instructive book about his experiences, *Utazás Éjszak-Amerikában (Journey in North America)* published in Kolozsvár in 1835. It reached two editions in a short time. The author painted contrasting pictures of the American and Hungarian ways, and told of meeting several new Americans of Hungarian birth, as well as other Hungarians traveling in the United States.

One day he observed a young fellow passenger following him like a shadow. After a while, the young man summoned enough courage to introduce himself. He was Ferenc Mueller, formerly of Pozsony, Hungary. Bölöni Farkas gave his name. "Thank God," the young man exulted, "that you are a Hungarian. I thought as much because of your moustache and Latin accent." Mueller was a traveling salesman for his relative, Martin Bock, for sixteen years a New Orleans trader in furs. He was now homeward-bound, down the Mississippi. His Hungarian was broken, but he insisted on speaking it, delighted to have a companion with whom to talk about Hungary. He exclaimed ecstatically that no country would be happier than Hungary if she could gain benefits such as derived from the American Constitution.

Our author said farewell to the young man, and headed for Philadelphia. There he met a Hungarian-born importer, a Mr. Leimer, who complained that twice he had tried to import Hungarian wines into America and each time the wine turned sour. So had the importer, evidently, and he insisted now that Hungarian wine was no match for the French in quality and price.

At Baltimore Bölöni Farkas met an interesting ex-countryman of his, from Hungary's famous wine district, Tokaj. At home he was called Király—Hungarian for King—and that was the name he assumed in the United States. The meeting was particularly instructive because of the contrast it provided between the American and Hungarian ways. Mr. King launched into a tirade against Hungarian autocrats, particularly a certain Gyuri Jozsa, whose name he mangled into "Gijuri Josha." This man must have been the terror of the countryside. Once he summoned Király into his exalted presence. Displeased with him he issued orders to the beadle: "Get out the bench, beadle! Get on it, Király! Twenty-five strokes."

Rubbing his flanks, Mr. King exulted: "No whipping bench in America, and no twenty-five strokes." The author added that the wearer of the name now looked every inch a King.

Bölöni Farkas found Philadelphia attractive and distinguished; he likened it to classical Rome. He described many of its houses as being built of granite and marble. He observed incredulously that there was no police force in evidence at the Mint. He confided to the director that every single person in such a place in Europe would be watched by three persons. "We trust people," the director replied simply.

Our author attended the Maryland Jockey Club ball and looked it over with critical eyes. "The music of the colored citizens was poor," he observed, "mostly *contre-danse* and sometimes waltz. An envoy of a European court appeared, Mr. XY, his chest covered with decorations. People stole sly glances at him, smiling inwardly."

Visiting Washington, he and his employer called at the White House as a matter of routine courtesy, thinking that they would sign their names in the visitors' book and let the matter rest at that. The attendant was kind and inquired if they would like to see President Jackson. They answered in the affirmative, believing that the audience would never be granted. But it was granted, not later than eleven o'clock next morning. "In came Mr. Jackson," the author records, "a tall, gay, friendly oldster, wearing a black business suit, without any badge of office."

Back at Boston, Bölöni Farkas remarked that his host's table was appointed with as much luxury as that of a European aristocrat. He marveled at how school-minded Americans were. There was a school for every New England family. "While Americans do not like to pay taxes," he observed, "they readily tax themselves to support their schools."

In every town, no matter how small, he found public libraries. For the book-minded Hungarian visitor, this was Utopia, indeed. He inquired about wages and was told that unskilled labor was paid as much as a dollar and sometimes two dollars a day. In comparison with the pittance passing for wages in Hungary, this was fabulous.

He was struck by the eagerness of Americans to learn about his native land. He was greatly embarrassed, he tells us, since he was reluctant to tell his hosts about the backwardness of the land of his birth.

The keynote of his book is that America is a happy land, while Hungary is unhappy, America is progressive, while Hungary is backward, America is young, Hungary is old, and yet the young could teach the old. As his 500-ton boat, *Albania,* set sail for Europe, he exclaimed: "Farewell, glorious country. Keep on being the eternal defender of man's rights. Keep on being the inspiration of the oppressed."

Another Hungarian, not many years later, also found an America he had never expected to find and wrote a book about his experiences. This man was Agoston Mokcsai Haraszthy, author of the two-volume book *Utazás Éjszakamerikában* (*Journey in North America*) published by Gustav Heckenast in Pest in 1844.

"The attempt to do justice to the greatness of the North American States," the author writes, "is doomed to failure in advance. Where one was hunting but a few years ago, a city may have sprouted. Where the visitor may have been looking at a swamp, a railway may be running now. The European never stops marveling at America, the enchanted land. The Hungarian is even more amazed, since he has been entertaining the illusion that his is a perfect country beyond whose boundaries life is intolerable. . . .

"Nothing daunts the American and no impediments can halt him in carrying out his design. The boundless energy and self-assurance characterizing the American above all other nationals are truly breathtaking. He seems to live twice the span of others and to accomplish a hundred times more. Early he rises and without delay he begins his work. He reads his paper while having his breakfast, so as to waste no time. . . .

"Lunchtime comes and all appear at the table at the sound of the gong. They sit down to eat, lose no time while talking and lunch is over in no more than twenty minutes. Nor are the State legislatures, courts and Congress exceptions. On the contrary, they dispatch their business with even greater speed. They meet from nine to noon, and continue after dinner sometimes as late as the midnight hour. The American is extremely thrifty with his time, and nowhere in the world can one find so few idle hands."

Conditions in Congress may have changed since those days, or the author's enthusiasm may have carried him away. Other observations of Haraszthy indicate that his observations may not always have been meticulous or that America showed a different face in his day. He found American women attractive only between sixteen and twenty-five, while beyond that age feminine beauty was rare. "Beauty is more evanescent in America than in Europe." Students were allowed no time for sports, so that young people appeared to be wan, as if recovering from grave maladies.

Haraszthy translated his admiration for America into deeds. He bought a tract of ten thousand acres from the government in the Wisconsin Territory, twenty miles from Madison, in partnership with a certain Mr. Bryant, an Englishman. They founded a town, called Széptáj—Hungarian for Belleview—changed it to Haraszthy, then to Westfield and eventually it became Sauk City.

Haraszthy's family was still in Hungary, and now he returned home, wound up his affairs, then brought back his parents, wife and children. Through one of those children—his name was Agoston, too —he entered American history.

The two Agostons had commanding presence and their neighbors called the elder Haraszthy, "General" and the younger one, "Count." "Count" Haraszthy tried his hand at many things in his Wisconsin backwoods pioneer settlement. He operated a ferry on the Wisconsin and a steamboat on the Mississippi. He built a restaurant as well as a school. He became head of an immigrant association that tried to settle the vacant land by bringing pioneer colonists from Switzerland, England and Germany. His interest in local lore was great and twice he was elected Vice President of the Wisconsin Historical Society.

The "Count" ran into debt, was forced to sell his share in Sauk City and struck out for the promising West with his family, pioneer fashion. Their goal was California, and their prairie schooner trip took nine months. In January 1850 they finally reached their western destination and there Haraszthy was among the first to notice the great wine-growing potentialities of California. The eighteenth century

Franciscans had already laid out vineyards and the missions had their wineries. Haraszthy decided to work on that foundation.

In 1851 he introduced cuttings of the Muscat Alexandria grape, which "founded California's huge raisin-growing industry," in the words of the State's official chroniclers. He also introduced the Zinfandel red wine grape and later imported two hundred thousand wine cuttings, including the most important European varieties. He founded Buena Vista (it is still Széptáj, Belleview, but now in Spanish) in Sonoma County, and from there the industry spread to Napa and Alameda Counties. Fortified sweet wines were to come from the great vineyards of the Lodi region, from Fresno and San Bernardino County. Hungary's own Tokaj, the Pinot of Burgundy, Cabarnet of the Gironde, Riesling and Traminer of the Moselle and the Rhine were acclimatized. Due largely to Haraszthy's initiative, California was to produce most of the nation's wine. He pioneered in an industry that was to have an investment of half a billion dollars and employ directly and indirectly some 125,000 persons. Half a million California acres were to be turned over to viticulture, second only to orange growing in the State's agricultural economy.[12] Haraszthy became California's State Commissioner of Viticulture. In 1862 he published a valuable book on the subject closest to his heart.

He was a restless man, with adventurer's blood in his veins. He and two other Hungarians, "Count" Wass and Captain Urnay, opened a bank, an exchange office, a melting and refining plant. It was said that all three became very rich, perhaps millionaires. He began to play politics, too, and was elected a member of the California legislature in Sacramento. He gambled with fortune, and lost. Again he was on the move and this time he took his family all the way to Nicaragua. He acquired a large plantation near Corinto and called it Hacienda San Antonio.

From all accounts, he was doing well. Besides his plantation work, he went into the food-processing industry and had his own mills. On July 22, 1869, he mounted his horse in order to inspect his mills. Later on, the horse and his coat were found on the opposite bank of the river from his plantation. What fate befell him no one knows. He may have committed suicide or fallen into the river which was infested with alligators. The same year, his old father, the "General," took a boat at Corinto for San Francisco which, however, he never reached. He found his end on the high seas.

The pioneer books of Bölöni Farkas and of the elder Haraszthy did for Hungarians what the classic volume of Alexis de Tocqueville, *De la Démocratie en Amérique,* did for the world at large. They discovered the United States for Hungarian readers.

Apart from their literary qualities, there was a great difference between the Tocqueville masterpiece and the two Hungarian books. The French aristocrat was the product of a civilization that had acquired a deep insight into the nature of social changes, a civilization nurtured on Voltaire and Rousseau, with a nostalgic attachment to certain features of the *ancien régime.* Particularly, he could not detach himself from the belief in the intellectual supremacy of the elite, as distinguished from "common clay." He saw America from the lofty observation tower of a privileged member of a privileged country, France.

The Frenchman was highly critical of what he saw in America, although he saw many features that held a strong appeal for him. The two Hungarian authors were admirers, not critics. How could they be otherwise? They came from a country in which the highest merit was birth and in which traditions were petrified into molds that only a political earthquake could break.

IV

The Sound of Distant Thunder

THAT POLITICAL EARTHQUAKE did come as Hungary's people rose—the people of Lajos Kossuth, leader of the revolution of 1848, crucial date in Hungarian history. The day of the outbreak of the revolution, March 15, the Ides of March, became Hungary's Fourth of July, her great national holiday.

It was a revolt against oppression, against the feudal system, against the Habsburg dynasty, in favor of freedom, the emancipation of the serfs, and independence.

The American people were stirred, themselves products of a revolution, champions of liberty. Congressman Sweetser of Ohio cried: "If I was authorized to speak for the whole American people, and had the voice of *articulate thunder,* I would tell the despotic governments of Europe that henceforth in contests for liberty . . . there must be no such interference as there has been in the past."

President Zachary Taylor issued special instructions to an American diplomat then in Europe, A. Dudley Mann, to proceed to Hungary and hold out to the revolutionary government assurances of recognition if such a step seemed warranted. And Daniel Webster, Secretary of State, wrote one of his strong notes in answer to that of the Austrian Chargé in Washington, Chevalier Hülsemann, who had protested against this seeming interference in the affairs of the Habsburg realm:

"The power of this republic at the present moment is spread over a region one of the richest and most fertile on the globe, and of an extent in comparison with which the possessions of the House of Habsburg are but as a patch on the earth's surface." And this led the New York *Herald* to declare: "We question if any document that ever emanated from the State Department gave more general satisfaction than the reply . . . to the insolent and supercilious letter of the Austrian Minister." [13]

The Hon. Abraham Lincoln, Representative from Springfield, Illinois, in Congress, presented a resolution of sympathy with the cause of Magyar freedom to a mass meeting on September 12, 1849:

"Resolved, that in their present glorious struggle for liberty, the Hungarians command our highest admiration and have our warmest sympathy.

"Resolved that they have our most ardent prayers for their speedy triumph and final success.

"Resolved that the government of the United States should acknowledge the independence of Hungary as a nation of freemen at the very earliest moment consistent with our amicable relations with the government against which they are contending.

"Resolved that in the opinion of this meeting, the immediate acknowledgment of the independence of Hungary by our government is due from American freemen to their struggling brethren, to the general cause of republican liberty, and not violative of the just rights of any nation or people."

Lajos Kossuth fought the Habsburgs to a point where that mighty dynasty had to invoke Russian help. Then only was the Hungarian revolution beaten.

In September 1851 the "Hungarian George Washington" was on his way from his Turkish exile to the United States aboard the American warship *Mississippi*. Turkey could no longer guarantee security to the great exile. The Ottoman Empire was the "sick man of Europe," and the Habsburgs exerted strong pressure on it to deliver the Hungarian patriot to their tender mercies.

If Hungarians ever had a hero it was Kossuth. At the head of an oppressed small nation he dared to challenge the might of a dynasty that was still thought to be one of the strongest in the Old World. Kossuth had much courage. He was supremely self-confident, trusting in his lucky star. He was temperamental, impetuous—a human whirlwind, as his admirers saw him. He was dashing, full of fire, a man of heart. His eloquence held audiences spellbound. In a foreign language, English, he was hailed as one of the greatest orators of the age. He was vain, too, and conceited, but could he have become the darling of the masses without those qualities?

The Hungarians' admiration of Lajos Kossuth was shared by the outside world. "He is most certainly a phenomenon," England's Richard Cobden wrote. "Not only is he the first orator of the age, but he combines the rare attributes of a first-rate administrator, high moral qualities and unswerving courage. This is more than can be said of Demosthenes or Cicero." Chauncey M. Depew, the United States Senator and railway attorney, was to say of Kossuth: "It was easy to see after listening to him, how he had united Hungary. . . . Though a foreigner, he spoke to us in our own majestic tongue, of which he was a master. . . . There was no repetition, though his theme was always the same. Each oration stood by itself, a sustained and superb argument and appeal for the rights of man and the liberty of Hungary.

"There are few scattered moments in a life, when the heights and depths of the significance of the occasion become too great for utterance, when the thrill of electric sympathy touches the whole country at once, and brings its inhabitants to their feet with a spiritual shock. Three of these have happened in my time—the surrender at Appomattox, the assassination of Abraham Lincoln and the landing of Kossuth." [14]

Ralph Waldo Emerson was thus to greet Kossuth: "We please ourselves that in you we meet one whose temper was long since tried in fire, and made equal to all events, a man so truly in love with the greatest future that he cannot be diverted to any less. We only see in you the angel of freedom, crossing the sea and land, crossing parties, nationalities, private interests and self-esteems, dividing populations where you go and drawing to your heart only the good." [15]

"I remember," said Charles Sumner, the anti-slavery champion, in a Boston address, "the landing of Kossuth. The admiration, the enthusiasm and the love of the people which had been gathering force and momentum during the voyage across the Atlantic, gave him an ovation which only two men had ever received—Washington and Lafayette."

On his way from Turkey to the United States, Kossuth and his party stopped off at England, where he spent three weeks. The supposedly phlegmatic British could not be demonstrative enough in their manifestations of affection for him.

December 5, 1851, the day on which Kossuth set foot on Manhattan was historic not merely for Hungarian immigration, for New York, but for all America.

As the boat bearing the former Governor of Hungary came within sight of Governor's Island, thirty-one cannon shots were fired for each of the States then composing the Union. The square in front of Castle Garden, where the boat was to dock, was black with excited humanity. The health officer who boarded the vessel, as told by an eminent American historian,[16] pitched his address of welcome in an appropriate key:

"Noble Magyar! Illustrious Kossuth! We greet you from the New

World. Welcome to the land of free speech and action. Welcome to the American republic, which demonstrates successfully to the world man's capacity for self-government. Thrice welcome to our infant country, the hope and trust of the friends of liberty in every nation and clime."

The Mayor of New York welcomed Kossuth as the "spokesman of Hungarian independence, champion of human progress, representative of the freedom of the world." Professor Bailey entitles his account of the great Hungarian's stay in America "The Kossuth Craze," [17] and mentions the fact that in New York one burst of cheering lasted without interruption for fifteen minutes. He quotes Henry W. Longfellow that people had gone "*clean* daft." "No foreign visitor since Lafayette's triumphal tour had received such an ovation. . . . Meanwhile the Kossuth infatuation was running its course. Hungarian history, music, dances and wine became popular; Kossuth clubs were organized, immense crowds turned out and shed tears while the eloquent Magyar addressed them in flawless English."

Kossuth replied that he came to the United States to bespeak its sympathy and crave assistance for Hungarian independence. Then he mounted a black steed and passed twenty thousand troops in review. The soldiers greeted him ardently, whirling their caps on their musket muzzles.

It was afternoon when the procession got started up Broadway, the great highway of New York gala receptions. About three hundred thousand people hailed him, a large number for those days. Streamers across the avenues greeted the great Magyar in his native tongue: *Éljen Kossuth!* Long Live Kossuth! and *Isten Hozta,* Hearty Welcome!

After New York came a triumphal march across much of the United States. His itinerary included Philadelphia, Baltimore, Washington, Annapolis, Harrisburg, Pittsburgh, Cleveland, Columbus, Springfield, Dayton, Cincinnati, Madison, Indianapolis, Louisville, St. Louis, New Orleans, Mobile, Montgomery, Concord, Albany, Buffalo, Syracuse, Utica and back again to New York.

America fell in love with Kossuth. All that had been said about his eloquence in the English language was eclipsed by the actual performance. The dashing Hungarian was, indeed, one of the greatest speakers in the English language. The conditions under which he mastered the language became widely known.

The Habsburgs had imprisoned him for years before the revolution.

Shakespeare and the English translation of the Bible were among his most faithful companions in prison, and from them he learned the living language he handled with such consummate mastery. The slightly archaic flavor of his phraseology was explained.

Dozens of books, hundreds of pamphlets, thousands of editorials were written about him—a Kossuth literature. Streets, squares, cities and counties were named after him. To this very day Iowa has a Kossuth County and there is a Kossuth in Pennsylvania, in Ohio and in Mississippi. There are Kossuth Avenues and Kossuth Streets. Kossuth hats became the rage and Kossuth beards the fashion. The Kossuth tricolor, with the Hungarian national colors of red, white and green, was at every hand. Children were named after him. There was a gentleman in Cleveland whose full name was E. K. Willcox— Eljen (Long Live) Kossuth Willcox. Victory arcades were set up in the great Hungarian's honor throughout the land.

The distinguished visitor had two principal aims in America. He wanted to collect funds to raise a well-supplied army so that he could resume his fight against the Habsburg tyrants, who were now oppressing Hungary more than ever. And he wanted the official backing of the United States for his enterprise.

It is thought by some historians that he had only the first aim in mind when he landed. The remarkable success of his trip induced him to harness American public opinion in the service of the democratic revival of his native land. The United States had introduced a new way of political life. A few years later a great American was to say that a country could not exist half free and half slave. It may have occurred to Kossuth to suggest that the world could not live partly free and mostly slave.

Now that the people of America had spoken their delirious welcome, would the nation's capital hear their voice? It was with great expectation that Kossuth looked forward to his Washington trip.

On New Year's Eve, 1851, Lajos Kossuth, former Governor of Hungary, was escorted to the White House, by the Secretary of State, Daniel Webster. The rules of diplomatic etiquette required that a foreign visitor should be introduced to the Chief Executive by the envoy of his country. But the representative of Austria considered Kossuth a common criminal (there was a price on his head), while Kossuth regarded the envoy as the representative of a mass-murderer and usurper. No such introduction, therefore, could take place. The State Department and the White House created a precedent for a man whom the American people had taken to their hearts. This appeared to be a good omen, from which Kossuth expected the best results.

President Fillmore was cordial enough in shaking his visitor's hand, but his words of welcome were disappointing. If your country is destined to be free, he told his guest, then God should help you reach your nation safely, but if, on the other hand, it was not fated to be free then he besought the blessing of heaven for Kossuth wherever he might be. He uttered no word of official recognition of the justice of Hungary's cause, nor did he hold out hope that the United States would support that gallant small country in its fight against despotism. After the formal reception, the President and the former Governor of Hungary had a conversation, reported by the chronicler of the trip, Károly László. Fillmore revealed complete ignorance of Hungary and her cause, according to the report. It was an unsatisfactory conversation and an anti-climax to the magnificent reception by the people themselves.

Kossuth now pinned his hope on Congress. The Senate put the motion to a vote whether the Hungarian patriot should be invited to appear there, and the vote was 123 in favor and 54 against the invitation.

On January 5, Kossuth appeared on the rostrum of the Senate, and was introduced by the presiding officer. The senators filed in front of him and he shook hands with each. He was not asked to address the Senate and that was a bitter disappointment to him. Two days later he was invited into the House of Representatives, which he addressed. But the House had little to say about foreign affairs.

Kossuth was to learn later something about the background of his reception. The government of the United States had to employ the official protocol. Austria was one of the major powers of Europe. It would have been impossible for the government to do more for Kossuth without creating a diplomatic incident in our relations with a country that lived at peace with us.

There was another problem to be considered. When Kossuth spoke about smiting off the tyrant's chains, his northern audiences went into a frenzy. Were they thinking only of Hungary's freedom, which was his concern, or were they also thinking of something else—an issue which was to divide the nation in years to come? Several senators—those especially who voted against his being invited into the Upper Chamber—must have been thinking of that other issue, slavery.

Secretary of State Webster, speaking at a banquet on January 7, 1852, struck a keynote which aroused hopes in the guest of honor, Lajos Kossuth.

"We shall rejoice," Daniel Webster said, "to see our American model upon the Lower Danube and on the mountains of Hungary. . . . I limit my aspirations for Hungary, for the present, to that single and simple point,—Hungarian independence, Hungarian self-government, Hungarian control of Hungarian destinies."

The Austrian government was so deeply offended by this statement that it instructed its representative to have no further dealings with Webster, and relations remained strained until he died in October 1852.[18]

Kossuth decided now to take his fight to the people themselves, in the hope that public opinion might exert pressure on the government.

"You excellent people of America," he wrote, "who were chosen by the Almighty as an example to show the world how to deserve freedom, how to win it and how to use it—you will allow that the Hungarians, though weaker and less fortunate than you, through the decaying influence of the old European society, are not unworthy to be your imitators and that you would be pleased to see the stars of your glorious flag emblazon the double cross of the Hungarian coat of arms. When despotism hurled defiance at us, and began the bloody war, your inspiring example upheaved the nation as one man, and legions, with all the means of war, appeared to rise from nothing, as the tender grass shoots up after spring showers. . . .

"The Hungarians, more fortunate than I, who were able to reach the shores of the New World, were received by the people and government of the United States in the most generous manner—yes, like brothers. With one hand they hurled anathemas at the despots and with the other they welcomed the humble exiles to partake of that glorious American liberty more to be valued than the glitter of the crowns. Our hearts were filled with emotion to see this great nation extend its sympathy and aid to every Hungarian who was so fortunate as to arrive in America."

The triumphant march continued. A hundred thousand people met Kossuth upon his arrival at Cincinnati. A group was formed in that city, calling itself "Friends of Hungary." The enthusiastic receptions continued throughout the Middle West and he was welcomed by governors, and introduced to the legislatures. The contemporary chronicler reported that all sought to see and hear him, to touch his hands and even his clothes. "No mortal man has ever received so much affection, sympathy, such ardent and colorful reception."

Kossuth now set out to accomplish the first part of his program. He had to carry on the fight and he needed financial means. He ordered forty thousand muskets for two dollars each. He appealed to his audiences to help the cause of freedom by contributions. His followers had medals struck in his honor: "Lajos Kossuth, the Washington of Hungary," and those medals were for sale. Kossuth banknotes, known among Hungarians as *Kossuth bankó,* of five and ten dollar denominations, were printed to be sold. They were promissory notes, the bonds of an exile, to be redeemed with interest after the liberation of Hungary.

Time was running short and he had much to do. Now he was in the heart of new America, the pioneer land, where people understood the meaning of his mission even more than in the East. He sailed down the Ohio River in a boat which, ironically, was called *Emperor.* At St. Louis the crush was so frightening that, we are told, his very life was in danger and only a flying wedge saved him from being trampled. The pioneer backwoods country sent a delegation of Hungarians bent on prevailing upon him to remain in the United States and here to build up a New Hungary until the Old Country could be cleaned of the poison of tyranny. He was told that a strong Hungarian immigrant body could exert effective pressure upon the Congress and the State Department.

From St. Louis the Kossuth party sailed into the slave-holding South. There he became acquainted with the great American problem that was soon to rend the nation. At the landing place of New Orleans there were no enthusiastic crowds, nor delegations. Kossuth was undaunted and smelt a fight, which he liked. Trouble was expected at the mass meeting announced to take place on the main square. A protective wall was formed around the stand by a band of loyal followers. He spoke about the freedom of Hungary and the freedom of man to a sullen crowd. But Kossuth's eloquence was irresistible and that inexplicable magnetism of his did the rest. The crowd became very friendly in the end.

Kossuth had a chance to demonstrate one of his prodigious gifts at New Orleans that night. A delegation of several nationalities called at his lodgings in order to welcome him in their native tongues, which included French, Italian and Polish, besides German and Hungarian. Kossuth addressed the delegations in German, French, and Italian. To the Poles he spoke in Slovak, which he employed as a substitute for Polish which he had not mastered. The Poles as well as all the rest were highly satisfied.

Now Kossuth had covered most of the populated areas of the country, with the exception of New England which he was to visit on his way back. Before going there, however, he wanted to stop off again in the nation's capital. Now that the people of the country had spoken so unmistakably, would the government of the United States also speak? Would the White House accept the verdict of public opinion?

Climaxing his tour, he arrived at Washington on April 13, 1852. He learned that some senators had delivered addresses on the subject of Hungarian freedom, appealing to America's conscience, and likening him to George Washington. But the White House kept mum.

His triumphal march continued in New England. When he arrived at New Haven cannon boomed and bells tolled. The train taking him to Boston was bedecked with the colors of the United States and Hungary. Troops escorted him to the State House, where the Governor of Massachusetts gave him a hearty welcome. He addressed a mass meeting in the Cradle of Liberty, Faneuil Hall, and afterwards nine hundred guests attended a banquet in his honor.

From New England he returned to New York, on his way back to Europe. This was the time to take stock of the results. He found that the money he had collected would not have been sufficient to wage war against the Habsburgs even for a few days. What had he accomplished, then?

Among the Hungarian exiles jealousy raised its head. He was accused of having misappropriated funds collected on the tour. Not a word of it was true, of course, but the very thought that people could stoop so low almost broke his heart. He did not want to see too many Hungarian émigrés now. Public curiosity having been satisfied, he was no longer the hero of the age. Only his wife and some close friends formed the party that was to set sail for Britain aboard the steamboat *Africa*. His luggage was marked: "Mr. Smith." They put to sea on July fourteenth.

He had received more applause than any statesman before him, except Washington and Lafayette. As far as tangible results were concerned, his trip was a failure. The United States had her own "manifest destiny" in the historic march across the land. Then, too, the "irreppressible conflict" was about to explode. It was not Kossuth's

fault that he could not divert part of America's energy into a struggle
for Danubian independence.

Some Hungarians remained in America, even though Kossuth had
returned to Europe. Among them were his three sisters, Susannah,
Emilia and Louise. Susannah married a Mr. Meszlényi and opened a
lace shop in Boston. Her heart was weak and she lived only two
years after her arrival in America. Emilia's husband was a Pole, a
Mr. Zulavsky. He vanished, leaving her alone with three children. An
admirer of Kossuth, a Boston merchant, presented her with a farm in
New Jersey's Orange County. Her children seem to have inherited
their Polish father's restless blood and they, too, were lost to sight.
Eight years after her arrival in America, Emilia died and was buried
in Brooklyn. The third sister, Mrs. Louise Ruttkay, arrived in the
United States a year after her sisters. She opened a rural boarding
house on the Hudson, and moved to Brooklyn from there. After her
brother had settled in Northern Italy, Turin, she joined him, later
returning to New York; then back again to Turin. She spent her life
with Lajos Kossuth until death claimed him in 1894.

V

KOSSUTH'S PEOPLE

AMERICA WAS ON the march, across the hills, over the prairies, across the land of the sagebrush and cactus, across the mountains towards the sea. Democracy was found in hearts and not in books, in nature and not in airless rooms. Character counted and ingenuity. One could not be selfish on the frontier, since that would have been the end of the frontier and the end of America, the end of the dream that a man was as good as his worth and that every man must have a chance to prove his worth.

It was into this America that Kossuth's soldiers came. Some of those fighters had ended their lives on the gallows, treated as rebels, not as men fighting for freedom. Some escaped, to find sanctuary in the land of the "heathen" Turk. America beckoned to the homeless as the realization of what they had been fighting for. The first wave of Hungarian immigrants came as the aftermath of the abortive Danubian War of Independence of 1848, the year of the great revolutions, the year of great dreams.

Some had preceded Kossuth to the New World, some accompanied him. Others came to the United States after his return to Europe. Some of these followers were rainbow chasers, Utopians, who wanted to build a Hungarian New Jerusalem on the untamed soil of America. Others were practical people who wanted to live and die as free men, as part of the American way of life.

Among the first group was László Ujházy, former Lord Lieutenant of County Sáros, and ex-government commissioner of the Danubian fortress of Komárom, which played an important part in the War of Independence. He conceived the plan of taking a group of Hungarian officers to America, to settle there. In execution of this plan he called upon the American Minister at London. Through the Minister he addressed a petition to President Zachary Taylor, bespeaking his help in granting asylum to the band of former warriors.

President Taylor's reply was cordial. The citizens of the United

States, he informed the Hungarian, had followed the fate of the Hungarian champions of freedom with great sympathy, and he believed he was speaking in the name of all Americans in offering them the benefits and protection of a free country, and in welcoming them to American soil.

Ujházy and his group arrived at New York two years before Kossuth, in December 1849. It was a festive occasion. A committee rented a "Hungarian House" on Bond Street and was on hand to welcome the new-comers. They were given heart-warming receptions by the city and State. Already here was former *Honvéd* Major Kornél Fornet, probably the first of the Hungarian fighters to arrive in New York.[19]

The United States Congress invited the new arrivals to visit the national capital. In response, a seven-man delegation, consisting of Kornél Fornet, Imre Havassy, Imre Radnich, Ede Reményi, László and Tivadar Ujházy and Samu Wass left for Washington early in 1850. Their trip turned out to be a prelude to Kossuth's triumphal march.

In Philadelphia they were given a torchlight serenade. The crowd in front of their quarters, Washington Palace, wanted not only to see but to hear them. Thereupon László Ujházy, who had made a great success in New York by talking to the people in Hungarian—although few people understood the language—decided to speak in German, the only "world language" he knew. Again few understood him, but the crowd decided it must be wonderful and he received a big hand.

Stopping off at larger towns and being fêted all around consumed much time and they reached Washington by the middle of March. President Taylor invited them to a White House gala dinner, where the ministers accredited to Washington were present, with the conspicuous exception of the envoys of Austria and Russia.

Their presence in the national capital inspired Congress to a spirited manifestation in favor of freedom for Europe's oppressed nations. The venerable Senator, General Lewis Cass, former Democratic presidential candidate, took the floor in the Hungarian delegates' presence and in a voice vibrant with emotion proposed that the United States sever diplomatic links with the Habsburgs who were trampling human rights underfoot. The Austrian Chargé d'Affaires in Washington, Chevalier Hülsemann, protested against this "interference with the internal affairs of a friendly country." The Senate debate had to be dropped, but it did serve a useful purpose. The pro-Habsburg Colonel

Webb was not confirmed in the Senate as American Minister to the Court of the Habsburgs at Vienna.

On the wave of popular enthusiasm, Senators Cass and William H. Seward submitted a bill providing that the Hungarian émigrés be granted free land in recognition of their great services for human freedom. Although the bill failed of passage, this was a noble gesture and it made a great impression upon the Hungarian émigrés.

The Hungarian exiles in America were much encouraged by these signs of popular favor. They took a step that was unique in the history of Hungarian immigration to the United States. Their action took the shape of a formal proclamation in which they solemnly deposed the Habsburg dynasty as the rulers of Hungary. Speaking "in the name of the Hungarian people," they issued the proclamation on February 20, 1850.

"We, the undersigned," the preamble read, "natives of the Kingdom of Hungary, do hereby proclaim, in the name of God the Eternal and Just, Protector and Revenger of Truth, fully convinced that we are giving voice to the sentiments of the entire Hungarian nation, and in the sight of all civilized countries . . ." that neither Franz Joseph, then ruling, nor any other member of the House of Habsburg and Lorraine had any right to the Hungarian crown. Therefore, the signatories declared: "Franz Joseph is a usurper, despot and traitor." In view of this fact, they warned all countries that his actions in Hungary were not binding. Hungarians who recognized the deeds of that illegal government and who "entered into agreements with, accepted offices, ranks, emoluments and donations from Franz Joseph, would be prosecuted and punished."

The proclamation was signed by Major Kornél Fornet, Major Imre Havassy, Major Edward Danburghy, Captain Imre Radnich, Colonel János Prágay, Colonel László Szálay, and G. A. Wimmer, former Hungarian Chargé d'Affaires to the Prussian Court.

The much harassed Chevalier Hülsemann answered with a strong statement that it was inadmissible for Hungarian subjects to commit such overt acts of hostility against the government of a country with which the United States maintained normal diplomatic relations.

The proclamation was, naturally, a mere gesture, but many wondered whether it served any useful purpose. Where was the mandate of these Hungarian ex-officers to speak in the name of the entire Hungarian nation? Whom did they expect to impress with their threats?

Was it right for them, guests in America, to strain relations between the host country and Austria?

The atmosphere around the overheated exiles began to chill. The group now broke up. The most rhapsodic member, László Ujházy, was attracted by the lure of untamed America in the Middle West. With his family and a handful of friends, he headed in that direction. They reached Chicago, and from there they traveled by easy stages to Decatur County in south central Iowa, not far from Davis City. The distance was covered in a month. Rhapsodically, Ujházy greeted the site of the home they choose:

"We reached the banks of the chosen stream and the bewitching view made us forget the hardships of our trip. Deeply moved, my head uncovered, I prostrated myself on the blessed soil, thanking Providence that it permitted us to reach the goal. Here we were at last, my heart at rest, in silent solitude, far from vanity and guile."

The Hungarian settlement was founded some 110 miles from the Missouri, in a fertile basin fringed by meadows and woods. Ujházy himself bought twelve sections of the land, and a small Hungarian colony of five families was soon established. They called their home New Buda, in remembrance of the capital of their old country. Ujházy was appointed postmaster with a minimum annual salary of two hundred dollars. Hungarian voices resounded in the log cabins of the distant land.

It was soon thereafter that a document reached Ujházy, which read: "I, the undersigned Governor of Hungary, herewith appoint László Ujházy, Lord Lieutenant of County Sáros, and Civil Governor of Komárom, as envoy plenipotentiary and representative of the Hungarian nation in the United States of North America, investing him with full authority to represent the Hungarian nation in accordance with instructions at the place of government of that high-minded and generous nation. Kossuth, Governor of Hungary."

Lajos Kossuth was then still an exile in Turkey. Thus he appointed László Ujházy, pioneer farmer of the American frontier, to represent the Hungarian nation, which was then non-existent, at the seat of the American government, weeks away from Iowa's Decatur County. Political exiles are often afflicted with delusions.

Ujházy made no attempt to have his "credentials" accepted, but he definitely did think of turning New Buda into New Hungary. It was he and some of his followers who tried to persuade Kossuth a year later to move to the Iowa New Hungary and help build up a large

Hungarian community which, by its votes, would exert a pressure on Washington to back the Kossuth solution of the Hungarian problem. The plan did not appeal to Kossuth.

New Hungary was represented to the outside world as an important settlement. The log cabins had grown into magnificent palaces by the time word of them reached Europe. To encourage Hungarian settlements in Iowa, an "American Society" and a "Hungarian Committee" were founded in London.

Some famous Hungarians were attracted to Iowa, such as revolutionary Hungary's Minister of Police, a hot-blooded youth of the Kossuth era, László Madarász, who later returned to his native country and lived to be a hundred years old. The ex-revolutionary, Ferenc Varga, was taken aback by the sight of the rude log cabins, instead of the expected palaces, but he adjusted himself to his new environment quickly.

The pioneer life was too much for Mrs. Ujházy. She died and her passing was a terrible blow to her husband. He now decided to try his luck elsewhere. He trekked deep down into the South, traversed the huge body of Texas, all the way to the Gulf. Near Corpus Christi Bay he founded another place he thought would become his home. He went back to New Buda for the body of his wife, on the way selling his Iowa place to German settlers for eight hundred dollars. Back in sub-tropical Texas, with his wife's coffin and his meager belongings, he built his new cabin and called the place Sirmező, Grave Meadow.

He seems to have maintained some political links with Washington. President Lincoln appointed him Consul of the United States at Ancona, the Italian port city on the Adriatic Sea. From 1861 to 1864 he lived there, presumably having little to do, and then returned to Sirmező, a broken man. His was the tragedy of the dynamic person who could live dangerously or not at all. He committed suicide.

New Buda carried on, even though its original inspiration was gone. Other Hungarian émigrés bought Ujházy's place from the German settlers and it became a modest community center. Homesick pioneers met there to reminisce about the past, to read their mail and newspapers from Hungary, the land they loved, although it had cast them out.

One was a poet, Paul Kerényi, in quest of peace and inspiration. He lived in the clouds, which seem to have carried him away, as he was never seen again. Then there was an exile with a double personality.

In the growing season he was farmer Ignatius Hainer, and the grain he grew was good. Outside of the season, he was Professor Ignatius Hainer, teacher of modern languages. One of his sons, Eugene, was later elected to Congress. Farmer-Professor Hainer took deep roots in the rich country. He also became the county treasurer.

Most persistent of the local frontiersmen was Stephen Radnich, who tilled his soil for fully fifty years. The Croatians also claim him, but there is no shortage in claimants for American frontiersmen.

In spite of these efforts, Iowa's official historian recorded some years later: "No trace remains of the original Hungarian settlement." Building the City of God in America may have been the dream of many veterans of Hungary's War of Independence, but between dream and reality there stood the forbidding presence of the untamed and unspoiled wilderness. A great statesman or strong general was not necessarily a good frontiersman. The nerves of political exiles are notoriously taut. They had played for the grand prize and received an obscure living, if that. Men who have been featured players once, want to be featured players always. But here the stage was missing and the obscurity of their rôle was galling.

All followers of Kossuth did not congregate in New Buda. Some struck out for themselves to live in other pioneer settlements. One of these, Captain John Prágay, is remembered as the author of the first book on Hungary's 1848 War of Independence to be translated into English. He had gone South, attempted to found a colony in the heart of Texas, but found no congenial company to help him. He continued to New Orleans, following the fata morgana which lured on so many men of his ilk. There, too, he met indifferent luck and obscurity. His overstimulated nature craved the excitement that not even the American frontier farm could offer.

He and eight Hungarian companions set sail for Cuba, where the political earth was trembling and disaffection was on the march. Cuba belonged to Spain and the Spanish royal house was related to the Habsburgs. The Spanish regime in Cuba was under the fire of the stalwarts of Narciso Lopez, Venezuelan-born filibuster, who had led several revolutionary expeditions to the island. Prágay became Lopez's chief of staff with the rank of a "general." The uprising failed, the leader was captured and shot at Havana. Prágay committed suicide in order to escape a similar fate.

Kornél Fornet, whose name we have already met, sowed his American wild oats during the great gold rush days of the West. As restless as many other Hungarian exiles, he visited the Sandwich Islands, later named Hawaii. For a short time he returned to Europe to see if there was anything doing there. Already, America was in his blood and he came back, settled in New Jersey and worked an experimental farm. A patriotic American, he named one of his children Washington Béla Fornet. Kornél's name will appear again in the Civil War.

Where one Hungarian obtained a foothold, several others often followed suit. The plains of the United States spoke a language many of them, reared on the Hungarian plains, understood. For several of them Davenport in Iowa became an important settlement.[20]

The magnet that attracted several Hungarians to Davenport was Miklós Fejérváry. That name had a familiar ring in Hungary, and soon it was to be familiar in the nascent Middle West. As an early settler he was signally successful. His sandstone house became known locally as the Castle, probably because it had the pretentious air of a European mansion about it. He worked hard, played hard, and succeeded. When he died, he left a sizable estate, part of which was bequeathed to the city itself, which commemorated his name by giving it to Fejervary Park.

Another settler was Miklós Percel, known to his countrymen as the "hero of Schwechat," and defender of the fort of Arad in Hungary's War of Independence. A former grandee of his country, Baron Joseph Majtényi, was still another settler. He delivered milk to the customers himself and, according to all accounts, his dairy business flourished. He appears to have been a sensible man and was happier as a dairy farmer than he had been as a mighty lord.

Another was Albert Anselm, a major in the army of Kossuth. He become a lieutenant colonel in the Union army of General Franz Sigel, was wounded at Wilson's Creek, and subsequently became chief of staff of General John Charles Frémont, when in command of the Mountain Department in West Virginia.

A physician in Kossuth's army, Dr. Ignac Langer, also turned farmer. In the American Civil War he served as a physician with the Army of the Potomac and gained such distinction that the State and War Departments gave him high citations.

Samuel Hirschl, the first Hungarian Jewish settler in Davenport, opened a store. He had a large family, the members of which could not agree on their choice of land. With six children he returned to Europe, while five remained in Davenport. One of them, Felix, became one of the richest men of the town.

The story of Jakob Janos Wunderlich, another veteran of Kossuth's army, was sad at first and gay later on. It was sad because he was a tavern-keeper in a Michigan community which was strongly in favor of temperance, and which virtually ran him out of town. Whereupon he joined a band of German colonists and settled with them in the South. There, however, slavery was rampant and he recalled that once he fought for human freedom. He complained bitterly: "In the North it's temperance, in the South it's chains." He tried the West and found Davenport to his liking. He plunged into local politics, as he was not opposed to the limelight. His fellow citizens deemed him public-spirited and elected him to public positions, junior grade: highway commissioner, alderman, and sanitation chief.

The American career of one of the famous generals of the Hungarian War of Independence, Lázár Mészáros, was full of contrasting shadows and lights. He became an immortal in Hungary not so much because of his valor in battle—which was great—but because of his insistence that even revolutionary soldiers must wear ties. One of his men was Hungary's greatest poet, Sándor Petőfi, a young man of extremely strong views. He disliked ties and never wore one. But ties formed part of the soldiers' outfit and General Mészáros decided that, poet or no poet, they must be worn. This brush between genius and disciplinarian gave birth to a poem that has made generations of Hungarians chuckle. "Soldiers without ties," the poet sang, "off with you. Only those who wear ties can qualify as heroes."

Petőfi was lost in battle, but Mészáros was not. First, he shared Kossuth's Turkish exile, then moved to France, England, and finally, the United States. He was highly accomplished, a master of many languages, Latin, modern Greek, English, French, German, Italian, Serbian, Slovak and Turkish. He was so many-sided that he could not make up his mind at first what occupation to choose. A gifted horseman, he could have opened a riding school, or done well as a veterinarian. Finally, he decided upon an occupation where his horsemanship and knowledge of languages were of little avail—farming. He called his place in New Jersey, Hungarian Farm, and there he worked with his two aides-de-camp of the past, ex-Captain Lajos Dáncz, a farm hand, wood cutter and cook, and ex-Colonel Miklós Katona, coachman, gardener and stableboy. The farm was consumed by fire and their promising enterprise failed. The ex-General now had to think about his other gifts and accepted a post in a wealthy Long Island home as a tutor, instructing four children in German at an

annual salary of three hundred dollars, plus board and lodging. Mészáros dreamed of the time he could visit his native town. An amnesty had been proclaimed in Hungary. First he would become an
American citizen and then he would pay that visit to his native land.
He did become a citizen of the United States and set out for the long
trip in the fall of 1858. But he never reached the Danube. Death
overtook him in London, on the banks of the Thames.

To venture into the pathless unknown was the fate of only a few
Hungarian settlers. Most remarkable of these was János Xántus. He
might have become a Hungarian country lawyer if the cataclysm of
the Hungarian Revolution had not cast him out of his country. He
had been merely a first lieutenant in Kossuth's army and his obscurity
saved him from the hangman's noose. The victorious Austrians
stripped him of his rank and impressed him into the Habsburgs' service as a private. He escaped, went to England and from there sailed
to the United States in 1850. In this country began his adventurous
life about which he wrote two enthralling, not too dependable, books.[21]
He had only seven dollars upon arrival in the United States and began
to make his living by digging ditches. His American apprenticeship
over, he got a job to help survey the land across which the rails were
laid from the Middle West to California. He received two dollars a
day for his pains.

He wrote tender letters to his mother: *"Kedves, édes anyám,"* My
dear, beloved mother. He told her he was getting ahead in the strange
American world and that he was now in charge of sixty-four men. "I
magyarized the stomachs of the esteemed gang," he wrote, "with
paprika fish soup and *gulyás.*" As the gang pierced the secrets of the
virgin land, swarms of birds were flushed, and he saw "milliards" of
wild fowl, turkeys and pheasants, also countless buffaloes and elks. In
the midst of this tremendous animal wealth, the huntsman was defeated, shooting at random in his greed and thereby giving the warning signal. On one occasion, Xántus was introduced to a Seminole
chief as an overseas visitor compelled to flee his home because he had
been robbed of his country. Thereupon the Indian worthy remarked
that the Hungarian was his *nekam,* bosom friend, because he, too, had
been robbed of his land. As a token of his abiding friendship for
Xántus he offered him a pair of slippers and his daughter. Our Hungarian thanked him warmly, accepted the slippers and asked for time
to think over the daughter.

Trouble arose, as two other lines put in claims for the railroad's right of way and Xántus' company abandoned its claim. Xántus turned to New Orleans, where there was a Hungarian colony, from which he hoped to obtain work. His hopes were disappointed, and he turned north again, headed for St. Louis, taking passage on a Mississippi steamer. They were approaching Natchez when he learned, to his consternation, that the captain of their boat was racing another vessel for a $25,000 purse. The strain on the steamer was too great and not very far from Natchez the boat was blown apart, the passengers were hurled into the water, and several lost their lives. Xántus swam ashore and found himself in a wilderness. Apprehensive about the creeping creatures of the earth, he nestled on a treetop, to which he lashed himself, spending a most uncomfortable night, exposed to myriads of mosquitoes. Next morning he did not recognize his own face.

In St. Louis, too, adversity dogged his steps. The northern winter was inclement and he was out of work. In the South at least he would not be cold. Again he returned to New Orleans, determined to await the turn of his fortune this time. Luck was with him, indeed, as he made friends with a Congressman who used his "pull" to have him appointed Professor of Latin, Greek and Spanish at the University of New Orleans for an annual stipend of nine hundred dollars and lodging. That was not bad pay in those days and he could afford to live in style.

Xántus kept on reporting the incidents of his daily life to his mother in Hungary. He wrote that although the distance between them was no less than six thousand miles, it took no more than four weeks for his letters to reach their destination. He commented with some acerbity that it took no longer for one of his letters to reach Hungary than for a letter to cross Hungary from end to end, some four hundred leagues.

The difference in the treatment of domestics at home and in the United States struck him forcefully. In his native land they were delivered to their masters' tender mercies. In America the masters were frequently delivered to their domestics' tender mercies. He had a man, Patrick, who received a monthly wage of twenty dollars, as against as many pennies in Hungary. One morning Patrick sauntered into Xántus' room, his shoes shined to a fault, a fat cigar sitting in a corner of his mouth, to inform him grandly that he was off to a party that might last throughout the night. His boss should get a helper to clean his room. Xántus also reported that a New Orleans lady had so far forgotten herself as to tap her maid's face with her fan. The maid complained to the magistrate, who set a high bail for the lady, and then fined her the enormous sum of a thousand dollars. The newspapers gave full coverage to the incident, thereby aggravating the lady's sorry plight.

In the summer of 1853 yellow fever struck New Orleans. Xántus himself contracted the dread malady, but recovered, so that he was in a position to give an account of life in the afflicted town. The number of dead bodies was large and the heat intense. The churchyards were clogged with open coffins and the bodies decomposed quickly. It was gruesome to see the covers of the coffins rise slowly, pushed into the air by the gases of decomposition. The smell was so noisome that many people could not stand it and tried to disperse into the surrounding countryside. There was a great shortage of gravediggers and the town fathers offered volunteers the princely sum of ten dollars an hour for the work. The guards forced the Negroes to bury their own dead. Hundreds of bodies were piled high on the Place des Armes, covered with fish oil and pitch, to which the torch was applied. It was awful to hear the screams of kinsmen trying to snatch their dead from the flames. Cannon burst everywhere, as physicians employed this method to "cleanse" the air.

Restless as always, Xántus could not stay at New Orleans indefinitely. He applied for a post as a member of the United States Survey Expedition commissioned to explore the Kansas Territory, with headquarters at Fort Riley in Texas. He received the appointment, with orders to lead his gang of twenty-nine men into prescribed regions of southern Kansas. Work was started in 1855 and was to last for two years.

The team crossed the Komancho and Kiovay Indian lands. Xántus gave the name of Hungarian Creek to one of the brooks they encountered and Frémont Creek to another. They reached the source of the Arkansas River after unspeakable hardships, then traveled across wild country for five weeks. Finally, they returned to Fort Riley with a large haul of minerals as well as fauna and flora. Their booty included three hundred different snakes in twenty-six parcels consigned to the Smithsonian Institution.

Xántus' name was becoming known in scientific circles. President Buchanan received him in the spring of 1857 and asked him about his explorations and, naturally, about Kossuth. Xántus wrote to his mother that the President kept open house every Friday. On those days it was the privilege of every "gentleman" to appear at the White House. It was customary for guests to come after eight and leave before ten.

The United States Department of the Interior now appointed him a member of the United States Coast Survey. In order to reach his destination he would have to go to the West Coast, which was a long trip. He took a boat to Panama, and crossed the isthmus in a jungle train. On the Pacific side, he took a steamer for San Francisco. He commented that this long trip took him no more than a stage coach journey across Hungary.

Life in San Francisco in those days was described vividly in Xántus' letters. The contents of the local newspapers mirrored the hectic ways of the gold rush. About a third of the contents was devoted to quotations of gold, one-half to advertisements of the needs of the diggers of gold, and the rest to news, mostly dealing with murders for gold. World events commanded hardly any attention. The cosmopolitan nature of the gold diggers was shown by the fact that three of the papers were printed in German, three in French, and two, each, in Spanish and Chinese. The number of English-language papers was seventeen.

His headquarters were the frontier forts of southern California. He took his team into the Mojave Desert, the San Bernardino and Sierra Nevada country, to the Camino del Diablo. He collected many specimens of the local fauna and flora, kept his eyes open for native ways and wrote entertainingly about the results of his explorations in his *Journey in the Southern Parts of California*. Never a man of understatement, sometimes he may have overdrawn his pictures.

He was unable to keep quiet. Nostalgia was strong in him and he decided to pay a visit to Hungary, but did not appear to be happy at home. Evidently, the comparisons—for which he had a sharp eye—did not favor the native land. He returned to the United States and received an appointment as a consul of the United States in the Pacific Coast city of Manzanillo, in southern Mexico. He was not happy there either and applied for a government position as a member of a government-sponsored scientific expedition into the Far East.

He was deteriorating very rapidly, as all could see. The zeal that had carried him into distant regions was now transmuted into fantasmagorias. His eyes grew vacant as he told anyone who would listen that it lay in his power to make all mankind rich. He would need do no more than turn solid rock into solid gold, and that he could do.

He would distribute the gold among all the poor of the earth. Again he returned to Hungary and there the sad end overwhelmed him at Pest. Few knew about his death and even fewer cared.

One of Kossuth's ex-officers, Márton Koszta, gave his name to a *cause célèbre* in American diplomatic history. He had been a captain in Hungary's revolutionary army, captured by the Austrians, and sentenced by them to death, according to an unverifiable account. Somehow he got out of the country, found his way into the Ottoman Empire, where he joined several ex-comrades. Evidently, he did not like life there and he asked the Ottoman authorities to permit him to leave. This request was granted on the condition that he would not return to the Ottoman Empire. This, at least, was the contention of the Austrian government in the famous case.

Koszta made his way to the United States and probably filed an application for American citizenship. But he was not an American citizen when he returned to Turkey on a business trip in 1853. In spite of the alleged promise not to return, the Ottoman authorities granted him a *tezkereh,* safe conduct. His business affairs took him to the Aegean coastal town of Smyrna. To be on the safe side, there he called at the United States consulate and placed himself under its protection. Most foreigners enjoyed special rights in the Ottoman Empire and it was customary for them to signalize their presence to the representative of their country. This Koszta could not do, since he was a marked man in Austria. But as a prospective American citizen he invoked the assistance of the United States.

As he was strolling near the port of Smyrna one evening, footpads overpowered him and tossed him into the sea. A boat standing near by picked him up forthwith, delivered him to the Austrian brig-of-war *Huszár,* and he was placed in irons. It was brought out subsequently that the Austrian Consul at Smyrna, Herr M. D. Weckbecker, had something to do with this. The footpads and the Austrian ship were participants in a plot. Koszta was considered an Austrian subject, a "criminal," and was to be taken to the Austrian Adriatic port of Trieste. Since Austrian subjects did not belong to Ottoman jurisdiction, the Austrian Consul in town felt sure that international law was on his side.

But he did not reckon with the United States. Hearing about the incident, the United States Consul went aboard the Austrian boat and declaring that Koszta was under American protection, demanded that he be set free. The captain informed him that according to the statement of his prisoner he was not a citizen of the United States, but an Austrian subject, covered by Austrian laws in the Ottoman Empire, that he had broken his pledge not to return to Turkey, and that he was a "criminal traitor."

History has not transmitted the exact words of the American Consul but it does tell us that at that very time the U.S. sloop-of-war, *St. Louis,* entered Smyrna harbor, Captain Nathan Duncan Ingraham in command.

The Austrians were willing to compromise and the proposal was made to the United States Consul that Koszta should be handed to the Consul General of France at Smyrna, a neutral in this case, until the diplomatic incident was settled between the two powers. In answer to this proposal Captain Ingraham maneuvered the *St. Louis* next to the *Huszár,* uncovered her guns, had the battle stations manned and a lifeboat lowered. The boat headed straight for the Austrian brig, and an American naval officer in full uniform went aboard, asked to be shown to the commander and told him:

"We are informed that you are holding an American citizen."

"The person in question," the Austrian replied, "is not an American citizen. He is an Austrian subject of Hungarian nationality, and he is wanted by the Austrian authorities."

"That man is under the protection of the United States. Are you ready to release him?"

"By no means," was the answer.

"Then I am in duty bound to inform you on behalf of the commanding officer of the *St. Louis* that unless he is on board our ship within the next thirty minutes we'll be compelled to take action."

In less than thirty minutes Koszta was aboard the *St. Louis.*

The American press reported the incident fully. Captain Ingraham was shown on the bridge of his ship, watch in hand. "Had Captain Ingraham sunk the Austrian vessel," Horace Greeley wrote in *The New York Tribune,* "he would have become the next President of the United States."

The Koszta incident did not end with the release of the famous prisoner. The overworked Austrian Chargé, Chevalier Hülsemann, sought to prove to the American government that the law of nations had been violated, that Koszta himself did not claim American citizenship, but on the contrary had exclaimed in the presence of Austrian witnesses that he was a Hungarian and would die a Hungarian. The

American Secretary of State, William Learned Marcy, replied that although Koszta had not acquired American citizenship rights, he had acquired nationality rights, owing to the fact that he was a legally admitted resident of the United States. It was the law of God and man, the United States government enunciated, to deal with others as one wished to be dealt with. Everyone was in duty bound to protect the weak and those whose lives were endangered. Koszta had been the victim of grave injustice and was therefore under the protection of all those who were able to extend it to him. Such action was pre-scribed not by international law but by the law of humanity.

The country applauded and *The New York Evening Post* wrote that Secretary Marcy's reply was "one of the ablest state papers that ever emanated from Washington." It has also been suggested that "Secre-tary Marcy . . . desired the Democratic presidential nomination and . . . doubtless aimed at appealing to the large immigrant vote." [22]

President Franklin Pierce took up the matter in his Message to Con-gress, declaring that the principles and policy employed by the United States in this case would be employed in every case when opportunity presented itself. The "Koszta Affair" was hailed as a significant action of President Pierce's Administration, mentioned together with Com-modore Matthew Calbraith Perry's historic mission to Japan in the same year.

A picture of the famous ex-prisoner fell into the hands of a lady plantation-owner in Guatemala, who took a fancy to him. Determined to see the original, she paid a visit to New York. Evidently, the origi-nal pleased her no less than the picture for they went to Guatemala as husband and wife. We may assume that they lived happily ever after and the *affaire* had a happy end. Koszta's name was perpetuated in the name of the town of Koszta, Iowa, not far from Cedar Rapids.

Viennese spies reported to the Austrian government that some 158 Hungarian revolutionary exiles had crossed the Atlantic up to the fall of 1851. Sixty-nine of the prominent exiles lived in New York. Chi-cago was next with twenty-one, then followed Boston and Philadel-phia with seven each, St. Louis, six, Albany, four, and the West and South had the rest. Some were lost to sight without a trace, while others prospered. It was natural that the "American Athens," Boston, should attract some of the Magyar celebrities. The New England Brahmin, George Luther Stearns, became the high priest of the Hun-garian cult there. He opened his Medford house to the exiles and it became known as the "Magyar Club." The far-famed Protestant minister, Gedeon Ács, was one of the members. Others were ex-Colonel Thoult, and ex-Captains István Kinizsi and Kalapsza. Another was the virtuoso Károly Zerdahelyi. He had tasted fame in Europe, and in Boston also his music was liked. It was sad, Hungarian music and Zerdahelyi was a sad, Hungarian musician. The small Hungarian colony began to melt away and Zerdahelyi found himself the last survivor. He married a waitress and doors that had been hospitably open to him, were now closed to the couple. He craved applause, but could not get it. Later, he applied for service in the Union army but was rejected as physically unfit. The couple then moved to Philadelphia, but could never reach solid ground. He died a sad old man, a casualty of fate, an exile who remained an exile all his life.

More immigrants came from Hungary, scattering over much of settled America, making bids for modest fame or only for a living, succeeding and failing. One was Anthony Vallas, whom the Habsburgs had deprived of his chair as professor of mathematics at Pest. He settled at New Orleans, one of the larger Hungarian colonies, and eventually became president of the New Orleans Academy of Science. He was elected professor of mathematics and natural history at the Seminary of Learning of the State of Louisiana, which soon became the land-grant Louisiana State University at Baton Rouge. The sympathies of Vallas were with the Union cause and he lost his chair.

Another New Orleans college professor was Alexander Kocsis. He took an interest in the Indians and began to travel in North and Central America. He held the view that the American Indians were not aborigines but descendants of Eastern Asiatic natives, mostly Mongolians, anticipating the noted anthropologist, Aleš Hrdlička. Many held the view then that the Hungarians were also descendants of Eastern Asiatic natives, mostly Mongolians. Therefore, Hungarians and Indians were related. Professor Kocsis set out to establish that link by studying Indian idioms and comparing them with the Hungarian tongue.

An émigré of those days founded the first Hungarian-language newspaper in the United States, *Magyar Számüzöttek Lapja* (*Journal of the Hungarian Exiles*). Charles Kornis Tothvárady was less interested in news than in broadcasting his esoteric views. His readers, however, preferred news and the paper did not last long. Besides, there were not enough Hungarian exiles to support a newspaper of their own.

Former senior officers in the Hungarian army gradually sank into the obscurity of humdrum life. Some became tavern-keepers, artisans and gold-miners. Antal Dembinszky opened a cigar store. His heart was good, his sense of charity strong and quickly he went on the rocks. Sensing the trend of the expanding country, Ignac Babri went into the real estate business, Gábor Koenigsberg opened a store in California's Oakland, ex-Colonel Ödön Kozlay became a lawyer, Cornel Beniczky a photographer. He thus broke ground in a field which was later favored by arrivals from Hungary. Jakab János Loewenthal became a professional chess-player, Ernő Szemelényi a teacher of music, ex-Major János Dömötör a store attendant, Anton Vurglics a shoemaker, Lajos Kosztka a goldsmith, Sándor Szabó a councilman, and Manó Lulley a Department of Justice secret service agent.

The United States was past her revolutionary *élan*. It was no longer a land of romantic dreams, but of hard pioneer work. One of Kossuth's former followers, a certain Hennigsen, devised an interesting scheme to keep ex-Hungarian revolutionaries in training. Life in the United States was too placid to suit their taste, therefore they should go to turbulent Santo Domingo, working as guards on American-owned mahogany plantations, standing by for the long-awaited call from Hungary. Should the revolution against the Habsburgs break out there anew, they could be sent home on short notice.

In Hungary the idea began to take root that the United States could become the staging area for revolutionary patriots. Emigration from the Habsburg realm to the United States was still small. In the entire year of 1857 not more than 868 Habsburg subjects left Europe via Hamburg, the main exit gate, for the United States. Empire subjects were permitted to sail for America only with special Chancery permits from Vienna, which were seldom granted. It was then suggested that instead of placing obstacles in the way of rebellious-minded Hungarians, they should be encouraged to leave the country. The Hungarians, generally, were considered rebels and troublemakers by the imperial Court.

The Habsburgs appeared to be favorable to the scheme of ridding their realm of potential revolutionaries, but they disliked the idea of letting them go to the United States, a country conceived in the sin of rebellion and still entertaining such rebellious ideas as the one about all men being created equal. Vienna would have preferred sending no-good Hungarians to a "good" country, such as Brazil, but the plan failed to materialize, as did so many other plans in the Habsburg realm.

Finally Hungarian immigrants began to arrive whose coming was not related to Kossuth and the War of Independence. One of these was Bernát Bettelheim, a Hungarian Jewish lad from Pozsony, in northwestern Hungary. First he had gone to Italy and qualified as a physician in Padua. There he embraced Christianity. Then he turned up in London, struck with the idea that while a physician could save the life of one person at a time, a missionary could save many. He attended missionary school with the famous Dr. David Livingstone.

He set sail for Far Eastern waters and reached the Japanese archipelago in 1846, about a decade before that mysterious empire was pried open by Americans. He settled on an island of the Ryukyu chain, translating the Bible into the vernacular, performing his missionary work, while, at the same time, curing the sick. He was there when the "Black Ships" of Commodore Perry appeared before Japan's reluctant gates, and Dr. Bettelheim served as the interpreter of the American commander. He sailed for the United States on one of those black ships, and settled in the recently founded pioneer community of Brookfield, Missouri, writing religious tracts in English, and serving as an army doctor in the Civil War. Fifteen years after his landing in America he died. About half a century after his death it was reported in a roundabout way [23] that the Japanese had erected a statue in his honor on the Ryukyus. The story was fantastic but, then, so had been his life.

VI

"BEHOLD, ALIVE THE SACRED BAND. . . ."

THEY CAME FROM Hungary in the middle of the last century and have fructified America's intellectual soil ever since. Some of the most inspiring pages of Hungarian immigrant history have been written by them. Not only the social scientist, but also the eugenist should be interested in their remarkable gifts. Curiously, they have drawn kindred gifts unto themselves through marriage. This is the story of the Heilprin family.[24]

The forefathers' names may be traced in Hebrew lore from the middle of the sixteenth century. Michael Heilprin, one of the most creative members of the family, was not born in Hungary, but he spent his formative years there, became a Hungarian, considered himself a Hungarian, and played a part as a cultural leader of the Hungarian-born in the United States.

Michael was born in 1823, in Piotrkow, an old town in which Poland's Kings had been elected and Polish Diets had met in the fifteenth and sixteenth centuries. Michael's father was Phineas Mendel, tradesman and Talmudic scholar. Even in his early years Michael gave promise of great gifts. He was his own hard taskmaster and in his ardent desire to do justice to his work, he rose with the summer sun, to study Latin, Greek and French.

That part of the Polish settlement was under the rule of the Russian Czars and the Heilprins were irked by the tyrannical rule. They made up their minds to find greater freedom in the lovely country of Hungary beyond the Carpathian mountain range, setting out on their journey in 1842. At that time Hungarian intellectuals were under the influence of the French champions of human liberties. Contrary to all that the Czarist regime held to be sacred and true, these dangerous thinkers maintained that the common man was a creature of God and that he, too, was entitled to a share in the benefits of life. The Heilprins found the atmosphere stimulating.

Promptly, Michael Heilprin set out to master the Hungarian tongue, certainly no easy task, considering that it is not related to Germanic or Slav. But he had unusual gifts and soon he not merely spoke and wrote it, but also composed poetry in it. Attracted to the world of letters and compelled to make a living, he combined necessity with personal predilection, and opened a bookstore in the town of Miskolc. There he and his wife, Henrietta, found a congenial circle of friends, ardent apostles of the age of *Aufklaerung,* enlightenment. She, too, was a remarkable person. Among her other gifts, she spoke English, German, Hungarian, and Polish, and read French. In Miskolc their eldest son, Louis, was born, who was to amaze his contemporaries with his genius.

Class distinctions persisted in Miskolc, in spite of the *Aufklaerung*— the force of traditions was too strong. Yet the local club of the nobility invited Michael Heilprin, a storekeeper, to become a member. Even the Hungarian government took notice of the remarkable tradesman and invited him into the Ministry of the Interior to occupy a post in the secretariat of the literature department.

The Revolution of 1848 was the great dividing line in the life of Hungary and it was a dividing line also in the Heilprins' life. The revolution was broken, and Michael had been too close to progressive thought to escape the vigilance of the political secret service. They no longer felt safe in Hungary and in the darkness of the night they crossed her frontier. France was then the land of light in Continental Europe and thither the Heilprins moved. But the reaction against the revolutionary upheaval of 1848 was gathering strength there, too. Besides, the Heilprins had no livelihood there, and so they had to move again. Where should they go this time? Heilprin had become a Hungarian in mind and heart. His rôle in the Hungarian revolution had been trifling and would probably be forgotten by now. They decided to return to Hungary.

Indeed, they were not molested. They settled in the town of Sátoraljaujhely, where he taught school. At the age of thirty, he began to study English and he selected, probably, the best master: *The Decline and Fall of the Roman Empire.* The Hungary of everyday reality was entirely different from the Hungary of Heilprin's dreams. The hand of oppression lay heavy on the land. Liberal thoughts were persecuted as contrary to the command of God and King. The atmosphere was suffocating and the Heilprins decided again to leave the land of their choice.

They went to London where they met the legendary "Governor," Kossuth, who gave them letters of introduction to prominent Ameri-

cans. The United States should thus be their goal. They arrived here
in 1856, in time to witness the epic explosion, as the slave controversy
was reaching its climax.

Two years passed before Michael found his place in American
society. Then he had an opportunity to reveal his remarkable gifts to
the full. He was employed to edit and revise the historical, biographical and geographical articles in *Appleton's New American Cyclopaedia*. He not merely edited the encyclopaedia, but he wrote a large
number of articles which reveal the phenomenal range of his interests,
his voracious intellectual appetite and a type of erudition that seems to
be no longer of this world.

Eventually the Heilprins moved from Philadelphia to Brooklyn
where their house became a center for local Hungarians. There they
entertained the Kossuth sisters, Emilia and Lujza, General Sándor
Asboth, whom we shall meet again, Major Stahel (Számvald), and
Colonel Károly Zágonyi, Hero of Springfield, whose names will also
appear later.

In 1863 Heilprin moved to Washington and there opened a bookstore. He became an intellectual but never a financial success. Word
of the encyclopaedic bookseller quickly spread and he acquired a distinguished clientele, including Senator Charles Sumner, the anti-slavery
champion, Charles A. Dana, the newspaper editor and Assistant Secretary of War, and United States Secretary of State William Henry
Seward.

It was in Washington that Heilprin began his work for *The Nation*
which was to last to the end of his days. Also, he became a correspondent of Colonel Forney's *Chronicle,* thought to be President
Lincoln's mouthpiece. His work for *The Nation* was truly remarkable
for range and erudition. It would be easier to enumerate the international problems he did not treat, than the ones he did. Many of his
articles probed very deep into the backgrounds of men and events,
as when he discussed Pan-Slavism, the ideological changes of nationalism, de Tocqueville, and Napoleon.

One of the gifts which the amazingly gifted Michael Heilprin did
not possess was business ability. He had to close his store in Washington. He tried his hand at publishing a magazine, *Balance,* in which
he issued eager warnings to the North to be lenient with the South
in the true spirit of the work of the martyred President, Abraham
Lincoln.

The Heilprin family moved back to New York and there Michael resumed his work on the *Cyclopaedia*. It was then that his beloved Hungary concluded the *Ausgleich*, the Compromise, with the Habsburgs and expected to look forward to a more auspicious future. It was with true delight that Heilprin greeted the father of the pact, Ferenc Deák, whom his countrymen honored by calling the Sage of the Fatherland.

In 1881 the Russian Czarist government launched a violent anti-Semitic campaign in order to divert attention from its own mistakes and misdeeds. The pogroms wrought havoc among the Jewish communities and the number of victims was large. Many Jewish survivors fled to America. Heilprin was not a pious Jew, he was not a member of the synagogue. But he was a religious human being. He had taken a hand in the cause of emancipation and now he took a hand in settling Russian Jews in the United States. He was active in the Montefiore Agricultural Society, engaged in the task of colonizing Jewish refugees in the Middle East and on the Pacific Coast. He put all his heart into the work. The strain must have been too great. It was while working on that problem that he died in the spring of 1888.

The Unitarian clergyman, the Rev. John W. Chadwick, wrote an eloquent obituary: "Mr. Heilprin's knowledge of history was nothing less than an epitome of its universal course. . . . His command of dates was by tens of thousands. His accuracy was equal to his range. He would run his eyes along the pages of a dictionary of dates and make corrections by the half-dozen or dozen upon every page. The time and place of the 600 battles and engagements of our Civil War were all at his tongue's end. . . . His confidence in his memory was great, and he wrote the most elaborate historical reviews without a particle of special preparation. . . . His apprehension of the philosophy of history was not less vivid than his apprehension of the concreter elements. He was satisfied with no 'disconnection dull and spiritless.' . . . His intellectual enthusiasm was immense, and swept along his hearers in a tumultuous flood. He had a reading knowledge of eighteen different languages, having acquired Rumanian in the last few weeks of his life. . . . Withal he was extremely modest. . . . He made it easy for those who knew little to talk with him."

Michael Heilprin's younger son, Angelo, was the most gifted member of that highly gifted family. He was born in Hungary—in Sátoraljaujhely—in 1853, and was three when his parents brought him to the United States. A great American, he was always conscious of his origin, attached to the memory of the country of his birth. At an early age he revealed great interest in animals and rocks. Beyond that, he was also a good painter. As a boy of ten he requested permission to to copy the painting, "Marriage of Pocahontas," in the Capitol Building of Washington. At the age of twelve he helped his father edit the encyclopaedia, and at the same time he was a messenger boy in a hardware store. When other children of his age were absorbed in marbles, he took an interest in invertebrate palaeontology. As a young boy he was sent to Europe to study in England's Royal School of Mines and Vienna's Imperial Geological Institute. He also visited his Hungarian homeland and the Poland of his forebears.

Back again in America, he continued his studies at the Academy of Natural Sciences of Philadelphia. He was twenty-seven when invited to occupy the chair of invertebrate palaeontology at the Academy. He held it for fifteen years and then exchanged it for the chair of geology. He wrote books and monographs of scholarly value, such as *The Geological Evidences of Evolution, The Earth and Its Story, Town Geology, Tertiary Geology and Palaeontology of the United States, The Lesson of the Philadelphia Rocks, Explorations of the West Coast of Florida, Okeechobee Wilderness, The Geographical and Geological Distribution of Animals, The Animal Life of Our Sea-Shore, The Bermuda Islands, Principles of Geology*. Angelo wrote not merely as a scholar but as an artist. Highly technical subjects came to life in his talented hands.

In the late eighties Angelo Heilprin began the explorations that gave him fame beyond the learned circles. He explored the Florida Everglades, cleared up several obscure problems about Mexican Gulf coral reefs and Yucatan geology and made a study of the geology of Bermuda. From the tropics he turned to the Arctic and played an important part in Robert E. Peary's explorations. He was in Peary's North Greenland expedition in 1891 and led the relief expedition the following year. On their homeward trip, in southern Greenland a Danish official welcomed them in his home. Heilprin was invited to play on a new piano recently received from Europe. "Without a moment's hesitation," an eyewitness reported, "Heilprin sat down and entertained us for an hour with selections from the works of Rubinstein and other composers, all executed with the power and expression of an artist. Never before or since, I venture to say, had those bleak shores heard such harmonies."

In his account of the expedition, *Northward Over the Great Ice,*

Peary thus summed up Heilprin's contribution to his work: "The Philadelphia Academy was the first Institution to which my project was presented, and the first to endorse and commend it, which it did in warm and unequivocal terms. . . . To the personal interest, friendship and intense energy of Professor Angelo Heilprin, Curator of the Academy, I was indebted more than to any other person, not only for the official action of the Academy, but for the unofficial interest and efforts of its members, which assured the balance of the funds necessary to make the affair a success."

A few years later Heilprin was exploring in Morocco, Algeria and Tunisia, climbing the Atlas rocks in search of ancient glaciation. Then again he turned up in the Arctic, in Alaska, and returned with his brilliant book, *Alaska and the Klondike.*

In May 1902 the world was shocked by news of the outbreak of the Mount Pelée volcano on the French island of Martinique, in the Caribbean, wiping out the capital, St. Pierre, with an estimated loss of some forty thousand human lives. "Not since the days of Pompeii," a contemporary account grieved, "has mankind seen such a volcanic eruption." Heilprin decided to observe the volcano at work while it was still rumbling, its lava flowing. He ascended the mist-shrouded mountain, and took snapshots, which are among the most dramatic of their kind, and he studied the volcano in action. For days he was completely absorbed in his work and no word came from him. The world was on the point of giving him up as lost. He came back, unaware of the stir he had created, a famous man, without having sought fame.

Heilprin's work had been an important factor in the decision to build a canal across Panama, in preference to Nicaragua. When he spoke on the subject, his voice was heard: "The facts all prove the broad reach of the volcanic force, and that reliance for the protection of the canal running through a volcanic country like Nicaragua, on the localization of the volcanic force, its assumed dormancy or the resistability of the canal to its destructive force, is absurd."

He helped his brother Louis re-edit *Lippincott's Gazetteer of the World,* discoursed on education and, particularly, on the project of an international university where world-minded persons would be trained. That project was especially close to his heart. In the midst of all his labors, in 1907, when he was but fifty-four, death overtook him.

The creative vein in the Heilprins was uncommonly rich. Angelo's brother, Louis, also turned out to be a remarkable man, but in a different way. He, too, was born in Hungary, in the town of Miskolc, and his native land left a deep impression on the child of five, the age at which he was brought to America. A precocious child, like his brother, Louis was interested in drawing, painting, and geology. He reached full intellectual stature at an early age and was an accomplished scholar at twenty-two. At that time he assisted his father in revising the *American Cyclopaedia.* He wrote a contribution on the Thirty Years' War, which was scholarship at its best—meticulously accurate, well documented and good reading.

Louis is thought to have mastered as many languages as his father, but he was too modest to speak about them. Difficulties which overwhelmed others, made no impression on him. Toward the end of his life, he decided to study Japanese. He explained, almost apologetically, that one had to do that if one wanted to penetrate into the secrets of an important country of the East.

A man of phenomenal memory, Louis compiled a historical reference book, combining a chronological dictionary of universal history with a biographical dictionary. A contemporary described it as a "standard manual of unrivaled accuracy." In the course of his work Heilprin found how carelessly dates were handled even by scholars of repute. His great passion was to hunt up exact data on historic events and he devoted endless care to the task. It was a matter of enormous importance to him to find out if an event occurred on the fourteenth or fifteenth of a month many centuries ago. His matchless memory in retaining numbers, names and events were of great help to him.

Next he was invited to edit the *New International Encyclopaedia* then in proof. His memory was so prodigious that he detected inconsistencies several hundred pages apart. Then he turned his attention to *Lippincott's Gazetteer.* It was in that connection that his biographer wrote: "It was for him not merely a question of writing and rewriting. His memory was ever on the alert for changes that were going on while the proof-sheets were passing through his hands. Minnesota was outstripping Michigan in the output of iron, Germany outstripping Great Britain in this or that industry, Ontario establishing a new record in the supply of nickel, a new lieutenant governor was created in the British possession of Eastern Bengal; the Jungfrau railroad was approaching completion—all these and a thousand other facts had to be thought of, and none escaped his vigilance."

His talents were not merely those of memory acrobatics. He deduced the radius of the curvature of the parabole by reasoning that it was essentially identical with that of the differential calculus. "Indeed," a newspaper obituary commented, "his analytical power in many domains of thought, including political economy, was as remarkable as his prodigious and accurate memory of facts."

He needed that remarkable memory, as he was almost blind. His relatives took turns in reading to him, and he hoarded the treasures of those precious moments with indefatigable zeal. He died in 1912. *The New York Evening Post* wrote: "His extraordinary modesty and a certain shrinking, due partly to the circumstances of his extreme nearsightedness, held him back from activities of the highest kind, for which his mental qualities fitted him."

The creative force of the Heilprins was far from exhausted. The Heilprin brothers had several sisters. One of them, Celia, married Walter Pollak, author of the story of Michael Heilprin and his sons, and of other books, such as the notable *Hygiene of the Soul: The Memoirs of a Physician and Philosopher*.

Walter Heilprin Pollak, son of Celia, became a prominent lawyer in the United States. He was counsel in the famous Scottsboro Case in the Supreme Court at Washington, involving Negro boys accused of having raped white women and sentenced to death, and won his appeal.

Adassa Heilprin married Adolph Loveman, and they were the parents of Amy Loveman, for many years associate editor of the *Saturday Review of Literature* and head of the editorial department of the Book-of-the-Month Club.

A nephew of Michael Heilprin was Fabian Franklin, born in Eger, Hungary, who achieved great reputation as a mathematician and writer, professor at Johns Hopkins University for many years, editor of such leading newspapers as *The Baltimore News* and *The New York Evening Post,* author of books on economics, such as *Plain Talks on Economics*. His wife, Christine Ladd-Franklin, made a name for herself as a psychologist and logician, author of an original method for reducing syllogism to a single formula, and of an original theory accounting for the development of man's color sense. A member of a collateral line of the Heilprin family was Michael A. Heilperin (the spelling is different), an economist, who was on the faculty of the Graduate Institute of International Studies at Geneva, and a professor at the Academy of International Law, before he came to the United States. He established his reputation with his works on international trade, money and gold.

VII

Hungarians in the Civil War

MANY AMERICAN-HUNGARIANS had fought tyranny in their native land. Now a good cause invited them in the country of their adoption. The tyrant was slavery, and they offered their arms to strike it down.

The problem appeared in a somewhat different light to President Lincoln: "My paramount struggle is to save the Union and is neither to save or destroy slavery. . . . What I do about slavery and the colored race, I do because I believe it helps to save the Union, and what I forbear, I forbear because I do not believe it would help to save the Union." He believed that slavery would be gone eventually. The abolition he contemplated "would come gently as the dews of heaven, not rending or wrecking anything."

"For my part," Lincoln said, "I consider the central idea pervading this struggle is the necessity that is upon us of proving that a popular government is not an absurdity. We must settle this question now, whether, in a free government, the minority have the right to break up the government, whenever they choose. If we fail, it will go far to prove the incapability of the people to govern themselves."

On these grounds, this was no more than a constitutional debate, of little interest to Hungarian ex-revolutionaries. However, the way they saw the conflict was an anticipation of a later Lincoln—the man who held that a country could not live half free and half slave.

The Hungarian exiles were electrified by the fire of the shell that burst in Charleston harbor in the morning of April 12, 1861. "That first gun at Sumter," James Russell Lowell, the American poet, essayist and diplomat, wrote, "brought all the free States to their feet as one man." Twenty-two States in the North aligned themselves against eleven in the South. The odds in manpower were overwhelming, twenty-two million against a mere nine, but the smaller number were fighting in their own backyards for what they thought was the right of free people to keep slaves.

"Historians say rhetorically," one of Lincoln's biographers, John T.

Morse, wrote, "that the North sprang to arms, and it really would have done so if there had been any arms to spring to." They had no arms and they had no military minds. Americans have never been a warlike people. On the other hand, several of the Magyar exiles in the United States were seasoned fighters, veterans of Hungary's War of Independence. Some were veterans of other wars, from Danubia to Crimea, from the Adriatic to the Baltic Sea. By that time there were approximately four thousand Hungarians and Americans of Hungarian descent in the United States. Their number was not large, but the ratio of those who volunteered for war service—about eight hundred —was considerable.[25] Such a high ratio of soldiers to the total number was not reached by any other group in the United States and it is explained by the Hungarians' fighting background. About a hundred of the eight hundred were officers.

Two of the Hungarians became major generals and five reached the rank of brigadier general. Major General Julius H. Stahel (Számvald) commanded an army corps, and Major General Asboth a division and was in charge of a district. Brigadier General Albin Schoepf commanded a division and a fort, Brigadier Generals Frederick Knefler (Knoepfler), Eugene Kozlay, Charles Mundee (Mandy) and George Pomucz as well as Colonel Ladislaus Zsulavszky were commanders of brigades. Besides, the Hungarian-born furnished the Union armies with fifteen colonels, two lieutenant colonels, fourteen majors, fifteen captains, a number of subaltern officers and several surgeons. Some of the military camps were named after Civil War officers of Hungarian descent. Hungarian officers were particularly active in Missouri. There was a Camp Zagony, a Camp Asboth, a Camp Utassy and a Camp Rombauer.[26] Fort Mihalotzy on Cameron Hill, Chattanooga, Tennessee, was named after Colonel Géza Mihalotzy, of the Twenty-fourth Volunteer Infantry Regiment, who had been fired upon from ambush and killed. Many Hungarians served in the Lincoln Riflemen, formed by Hungarian and Czech units even before the days of Fort Sumter. On February 4, 1861, Géza Mihalotzy wrote to President Lincoln: "We have organized a company of Militia in this city [Chicago] composed of men of Hungarian, Bohemian and Sclavonic origin. Being the first company in the United States of said nationalities, we respectfully ask leave of your Excellency to entitle ourselves 'Lincoln Riflemen' of Sclavonic origin.

"If you will kindly sanction our use of your name, we will endeavor to do honor to it, whenever we may be called to perform active service."

To which Lincoln replied: "I cheerfully grant the request above made."

Later the company was merged with the 24th Illinois Volunteer Infantry Regiment, of which Mihalotzy became the colonel.

The Lincoln Riflemen were among the first to respond to the call to arms. Its artillery support was formed at Cairo, Illinois, by a former major of the *Honvéd* army, and former fellow exile of Kossuth in Turkey, Colonel Gustav Wagner.

The Garibaldi Guard or Thirty-ninth New York Infantry Regiment, also had a large Hungarian-born contingent. Nearly one-half of the troops had come from Hungary, many of the others from Italy. A Hungarian, Frederick George Utassy, was the first colonel of the Guard. It received an American, a Hungarian and a Garibaldi flag. The men's uniform resembled that of the Italian *bersaglieri*.

The Hungarian-born played an important part in the Western Department, comprising Missouri, Kansas, Illinois and Kentucky, under the command of General John C. Frémont. His chief-of-staff was a Hungarian, Brigadier General Alexander Asboth. Three of his aides were also Hungarians; the commander of Frémont's Body Guard, Major Charles Zagonyi, his chief topographical engineer and his chief of ordnance. Native American officers were scarce on his western front, and Frémont was partial to the foreign-born because, he held, fighting was in their blood. Frémont attracted the Hungarians, too. He was the "brave pathfinder," who had planted the American flag on the highest Rocky Mountain peaks. A bold fighter, he was the presidential candidate of the young Republican Party in 1856, and he lost. But he remained the hero of large masses of people. Like the dashing Hungarians on his staff, he was temperamental. Discretion was not his chief virtue. He declared the slaves of disloyal owners in Missouri free men. This was ahead of Lincoln's more cautious policy, and the gesture must have impressed his Hungarian followers greatly. They were loyal to him unto death.

General George B. McClellan, commander of the Army of the Potomac, and later in command of the Union forces, was also partial to the Hungarians.[27] During Hungary's War of Independence, in his early twenties, he asked Secretary of State John M. Clayton to appoint him to the post of military observer in Hungary. Six days later the Hungarian army surrendered, and McClellan remained at home.

Major General Julius H. Stahel (Számvald) occupied the highest position among all the Hungarian-born Union commanders. He had had a bookstore in Szeged, Hungary's second largest town, and it was to him that Hungary's greatest poet, Petőfi, addressed one of his famous poems: *Egy Könyvárus Emlékkönyvébe*, (For a Bookseller's Souvenir Book). He, too, joined the Hungarian army of independence and fled abroad after its defeat. He made his way to London. His name had been Gyula Számvald, but in England he changed it to Julius H. Stahel. It is thought that his middle initial stands for "Hungarian." He came to the United States in the middle fifties and turned to journalism, contributing articles to the *Illustrated News* and *Belletristische Zeitung*. When Lincoln issued his call, Stahel helped to organize the Eighth Infantry Regiment. He became a lieutenant colonel.

The first Battle of Bull Run was one of his first engagements. It was also one of the Union's major defeats, which could have easily been turned into a rout, endangering the safety of Washington, if certain units had not held their ground. One of those units was Stahel's.

He distinguished himself at the Battle of Piedmont, Virginia, in the summer of 1864. He was wounded, received first aid, returned to battle, and led his cavalry in another charge. General David Hunter, the commander, wrote to General H. W. Halleck: "It is but justice to Major General Stahel to state that in the recent engagements he displayed excellent qualities of coolness and gallantry, and that for the final happy result the country is much indebted to his services." Stahel received the Congressional Medal of Honor twenty-seven years later.

His wound incapacitated General Stahel for further military service. Until the end of the war he was president of the military court. After the war he was attached to the American consular service in the Far East. He died at a ripe age in 1912, and was buried in the Arlington National Cemetery, where a granite obelisk was to mark the grave of the Hungarian bookseller who became an American hero.

Major General Asboth had a highly impressive presence, with flowing moustache, penetrating eyes and tall, spare frame. In his youth he wanted to become a mining engineer. After the failure of the Hungarian War of Independence, he followed Kossuth into his Turkish exile, and arrived in the United States aboard the American man-of-war *Mississippi* which had called for the ex-Governor of Hungary.

Kossuth came and went, but Asboth remained in America. However, he retained contact with Kossuth.

Asboth appears to have been a jack-of-all-trades. We are told, although no evidence of it may be found, that he made a living as an engineer in Syracuse and New York, and that his fertile mind was engaged in the work of drawing up plans for Washington Heights and a large city park. We are not told what happened to those plans.

The Civil War struck a sympathetic chord in his freedom-loving heart, and he promptly set about organizing a regiment of volunteers in the nationality sections of the eastern States. He does not appear to have been successful and so he went West and there joined Frémont's staff. Asboth's rise in service was spectacular. He turned out to be a born soldier, fearless, uninhibited, bold in action, yet not recklessly so. He took part in several campaigns in Missouri and Arkansas and gave such good account of himself that he was appointed brigadier general in a short time. It is recorded of him that although wounded he continued in the saddle. The Missouri campaign over, he was transferred to Kentucky and was eventually entrusted with the command of the West Florida Department. At the battle of Marianna in Florida his left arm suffered a double fracture and a bullet entered his right cheek. On March 13, 1865, he resigned from active service. In recognition of his gallant actions and meritorious services, the President conferred upon him the rank of major general by brevet, by and with the advice and consent of the Senate.

The career of General Asboth was not over as yet. President U. S. Grant appointed him American Minister to Argentina and Paraguay. Before assuming his office in South America, he sailed to France, where he had the bullet extracted from his face. He resumed his journey to Argentina where he was given a most cordial welcome. The gaunt American Minister walking his huge dog was a common sight in the streets of Buenos Aires, but not for long. On a rainy January day in 1868, another big dog set on his animal. Straining to pull them apart, Asboth lost his balance and fell to the pavement in such a way that his skull was fractured. He who had sought danger in war, lost his life in a quiet South American street.

Brigadier General Albin Schoepf was of Austrian-Polish origin. Poles were well represented in the Hungarian War of Independence. Many of them had found sanctuary in Hungary and were grateful. The Habsburgs were their enemies, too, and fighting them on the Hungarian front was an indirect way of fighting for their own lost independence. Schoepf escaped the Austrians' punitive hands, and found refuge in Turkey. From Turkey he came to the United States with a group of fellow émigrés. At first luck shunned him. He tried to make a modest living as a hotel porter in Washington. The Civil War changed his fortune. He, too, was a born soldier and his superior officers were quick to see what a good fighting man they had found. He played a part in the Battle of Mill Spring in Kentucky, where the Confederates suffered serious reverses.

Brought up in Continental European military ways, he thought that American troops lacked discipline. He made an attempt to transplant European military ways to America, but was not particularly successful. The outcome of the war should have convinced him that formal discipline is not a condition of victory. After the war he was appointed principal examiner in the Washington Patent Office. We may assume that he acquitted himself of his work conscientiously.

Brigadier General Frederick Knefler was of Hungarian Jewish descent. His father, called Knoepfler at home, practised medicine which was then little more than routine work in his part of the Hungarian countryside. Frederick was a mere boy of fifteen when he enlisted in Kossuth's army. Two years later, in 1850, the family came to the United States. Here Frederick worked as a carpenter by day and studied law by night. Early in the Civil War he enlisted as a private in the Eleventh Indiana Volunteer Regiment. General Lewis (Lew) Wallace, world-famous author of *Ben-Hur,* appointed Knefler his aide-de-camp. In the West they had a hand in taking Fort Donelson, which was a major victory. Knefler remained with Wallace until the Seventy-ninth Indiana Volunteer Regiment was organized, and he became its colonel. We are told that he had an unusually stimulating effect upon his men.[28] He appeared to be concerned only with the welfare of his troops even under the most withering fire and always retained his composure. "He never slept in the house or outside of his camp, when his men had to stay without shelter, and always demanded the best provisions and quarters for his soldiers." At the end of the war he was honored by an appointment as a brigadier general by brevet.

For a time after the war he practised law and worked on the committee appointed to erect memorials to Civil War soldiers and sailors. He died in 1901, and the *Indianapolis Journal* wrote. "He was one of the first to enlist, taking whatever place came to him, serving faithfully and tirelessly in the positions to which he was assigned, useful in a high degree because of instruction in Europe when a mere boy, but more useful through intense devotion to his adopted country. During his four years spent at the front in doing duties assigned to him he won the regard of subordinates and the confidence of superiors. No better, braver soldier than he ever buckled on a sword."

Charles Zagonyi came to the United States with a romantic reputation. Stories were current about how he had saved the life of one of the most picturesque revolutionary heroes of Hungary, *Bem Apó*, Father Bem, whose real name was General Jozef Bem who was of Polish origin, and who carried on against the Austrian forces as if he were to win the war single-handed. He defeated the Austrians, and when the Russians came he defeated them as well. Finally, he was defeated by far superior forces. The further fate of Bem Apó is characteristic of that fantastic age. He escaped to Turkey, embraced Islam and became a pasha. It was in connection with the legendary Bem that Zagonyi himself had become a semi-mythical person.

There was nothing mythical about Zagonyi, however, when he came to America. His debut in this country was singularly lacking in "romance." Since he had to eat, Zagonyi had to accept the only job that was offered him—that of a house-painter's apprentice. Evidently, he learned the tricks of the trade, and became a master house-painter, but success eluded him. Stephen Thoult, the former Hungarian officer, needed a competent riding master in Boston, and Zagonyi applied for the job, obtained it and stuck to it until the outbreak of the war. He volunteered to join the Union forces in the East but was not accepted. He went West and introduced himself to General Frémont, who commissioned him to organize his cavalry guard, Frémont's Body Guard, with the rank of major. Within a few days Zagonyi organized the first company and then three more companies in quick succession. He himself designed the uniforms which showed a trace of the Hungarian *huszár* dash. An expert on horses, he selected the mounts himself.

The most important event in Zagonyi's military career took place in Springfield, Missouri. The Confederates were entrenched on a strategic hill near the town, and quick action was imperative to dislodge them. General Frémont, in command, believed the hill was held by some three hundred troops and gave permission to Zagonyi to attack with a corresponding force. The General learned at the last moment that the enemy forces on the hill numbered much closer to two thousand than three hundred, and countermanded the attack, while calling for reinforcements. Zagonyi did not want to call off the attack now that he and his men had braced themselves for the engagement. He explained to his soldiers how matters stood and ordered those who wanted to take on no such odds to stay behind. "Not a man flinched," Captain James L. Foley reported, "when Zagonyi addressed the column, giving permission to any man who so desired to drop out before the fray began. Queer proposition for a foreign-born officer to make to an American soldier under arms in defense of his country. Later this officer learned, as the world has, that the American soldier is not given to dropping out in the presence of the enemy." [29]

The cavalry did attack the hill and the foe was routed. Springfield was cleaned out. "It had a much-needed bracing effect all the country over. Had the attack failed, Zagonyi would have been the subject of a court martial charge, since he acted against orders. Now that it succeeded, he became a hero." General Frémont compared his deed with the "Charge of the Light Brigade" at the Battle of Balaklava in the Crimean War, a few years before. In American-Hungarian lore the charge became known as "Zagonyi's Death Ride."

General Frémont was entrusted with the command of the Mountain Department, and Zagonyi, a colonel, became his chief of cavalry. His subsequent record is not clear. We do not know why he withdrew from active service in the summer of 1862, and why he resigned a year later. The mercurial Zagonyi may have been too much even for Frémont. After the war, Zagonyi's name remained in circulation for a time. He seems to have played a part in the foundation of the *Magyar Egylet* (Hungarian Association). Beyond a point, his record became increasingly blurred. He informed a friend that he was a member of the board of directors of a railway line, that it was his hope to be able to retire on his capital and spend the last years of his life in his native country. Later, he informed the same friend that he had lost his fortune and had to abandon the idea of transferring to Hungary until he succeeded in recouping his losses. It does not seem that he ever did. Judging by the silence which enshrouds him from that time on he became a casualty of American-Hungarian life.

The life of Kornél Fornet has already engaged our attention. General Frémont appointed Fornet a major of engineers. When the Civil War was over, Fornet availed himself of the offer of amnesty by the rulers of his native country to return to Hungary. He settled in a small town on the Danube as a minor government official. He died in 1894 and was buried in Budapest. The United States Military Commission on the Allied Control Commission in Hungary honored the memory of the American Civil War veteran at a solemn service in 1946.

A minor but interesting rôle was played in the Civil War by Fülöp Figyelmessy. He was of German extraction with the family name of Merk, but became a patriotic Hungarian, fighting on Kossuth's side in the defense of the Danubian fort of Komárom. When it surrendered, he was one of those who received immunity from prosecution on his promise that he would not engage in politics and would obey the laws of the Habsburgs. He did not take that promise quite literally because he helped political prisoners escape the country. He would have got into trouble on that score if he himself had not been successful in escaping. First he joined Hungarian exile "headquarters" in Kutahia, Turkey. Some of the émigrés conceived the idea of transforming wooded, hilly Transylvania into a "redoubt" from which to continue the struggle. Figyelmessy was chosen to be a member of the "underground" to promote public sentiment in favor of Kossuth, and thus stir up trouble for the Habsburgs. Woods and hills were the plotters' friends, but the Austrian police was extremely vigilant. The proposed conspiracy was discovered, and several participants were captured and hanged. Figyelmessy, an expert at eluding pursuers, again managed to escape the noose. He was an adventurous and bold man, who had now got into the habit of opposing tyranny, especially if the tyrant's name was Habsburg. Figyelmessy went to Italy, obtained a colonelcy from King Victor Emmanuel II, fought the Austrians in the War of 1859-1861, and was hailed by Giuseppe Garibaldi, the Italian patriot, as a "hero of heroes." His work accomplished, Figyelmessy returned to England. Kossuth gave him a letter of introduction to Secretary of State William H. Seward. In Washington he received the offer of a colonelcy in a body of volunteers which, however, he rejected on the grounds that he was not an "amateur." He, too, made his way to the "Little Hungary" at General Frémont's headquarters, and was appointed inspector general at Wheeling, West Virginia, a thoroughly "professional" job. He took part in several engagements, and was wounded on two occasions.

Consulships in out-of-the-way places were political plums for deserving Civil War veterans in those days, and Figyelmessy was appointed American Consul at tropical Georgetown (Demerara) in British Guiana, South America. The erstwhile daredevil stayed at his steaming tropical post for twenty years. He was himself an octogenarian when the Hungarian National Federation sent a flag to the

American Hungarians shortly after the turn of the twentieth century. In the return visit of the American Hungarians aged Figyelmessy was a member of the delegation and it is recorded that he delivered two stirring addresses in Hungary. He lived in Philadelphia until 1907, and when he died he was eighty-seven years old. The inscription on his tombstone read: *"To the Champion of Liberty.* Hungarian American Federation."

Hungarian émigrés appear to have been successful in raising colored regiments during the Civil War. One of these émigrés was László Zsulavszky, a nephew of Kossuth, who organized the Eighty-second Colored Regiment, of which he was appointed the colonel. He became the commander of the Fifty-first Colored Regiment. Serving with General Asboth in Major General Gordon Granger's division, he commanded the First Brigade of the District of West Florida, to which the Twenty-fifth, Eighty-second and Eighty-sixth Colored Regiments belonged. His brothers, Emil and Zsigmond, also served as officers of the Eighty-second Colored Regiment.

Péter Pál Dobozy was General Asboth's aide-de-camp. He organized and commanded the Fourth Colored Heavy Artillery Regiment at Fort Columbus, Kentucky. After the war he moved into Arkansas in order to raise cotton. He made his home in the Ozark country where he became known as a public-spirited citizen. He was something of a local miracle and a contemporary newspaper account mentioned the fact that besides English and Hungarian he also spoke Turkish, German and Italian.

At the seventy-fifth anniversary of the Battle of Gettysburg in 1938, the oldest living Civil War veteran of Hungarian origin was discovered in the person of Charles Barothy, of Omaha, Nebraska. At the age of eighteen, he joined an Omaha regiment, and was mustered out two years later, having remained a private throughout the war.

So far we have mentioned only Union men of Hungarian descent. Were there no Hungarians on the Confederate side? Obviously, the sympathies of the Hungarians in this country were with the Union forces, fighters for the emancipation of slaves, but a few Hungarians did join the Southern camp. The only one of them known to hold a commission was Béla Estván, a typical soldier of fortune with a positive genius for taking the wrong side. In Europe he had fought for the Austrians and Russians. He came to America, settled in Richmond. In an "aristocratic" world he fell in line quickly and claimed that he belonged to the old nobility and that he had the title of "Count." He saw service in the Confederate army as a colonel. After the war he sailed for Europe and, for unknown reasons, was arrested while proceeding eastward, to Vienna. Then and there he dropped out of sight.

VIII

A Man to Power Born

The town of Makó is famous for the grain and onions of the surrounding fertile Hungarian plains. Fülöp Politzer, known to the
neighbors as "Red" Politzer, because of his red hair, was famous for
his success in the grain and onion trade. It was to Fülöp Politzer and
Lujza Berger that Providence presented József who, under the name
of Joseph Pulitzer, was destined to make history in the newspaper
world of the United States.

Even though the soil of Makó's environs was rich, trade in grain
and onions had its ups and downs, and so it happened that Red Politzer one day went bankrupt. Not a man to resign himself to the
blows of fate, he decided to move to the Hungarian capital, Pest, still
under Austrian rule, before the Compromise of 1867. The official
language of the capital was then German, for it was only after the
conclusion of the Compromise that its inhabitants turned to the Hungarian tongue, so that German was Joseph's native tongue. What
would have happened if Red Politzer had lived we do not know, but
he died. Joseph's mother grieved over her loss and then she married
another tradesman, by the name of Max Blau.

It was Max Blau who, indirectly, gave Joseph to America. It seems
that he behaved toward the boy as old-fashioned step-fathers were said
to behave. Besides, family finances were far from promising, and there
was that confined air in oppressed Hungary that induced so many of
her sons to try their luck outside. A boy in his middle-teens, Joseph
was already mature, bent on making a career. It was a period of un-
rest and it was not unnatural that this young Hungarian should dream
of being a soldier. His eyesight was very poor and he was physically
weak, so that his desire to become a fighting man was even more
natural. Even though that age was not yet familiar with the term
"compensation," there was such a thing.

Joseph left home and struck out for himself in the wide world. He
had the advantage of speaking German, a language which was under-

stood over much of Europe. At the time, one of the dynastic wars was being waged for the possession of Schleswig-Holstein, to the south of Denmark, with the Austrians and Prussians lined up on the same side, against a much weaker dynasty. A "noble cause" was not involved—it was merely a looting expedition. Yet Joseph volunteered for the Austrian forces, not because he favored aggression, but because he was keen on joining an army and Hungarians were Austrian subjects. The Austrians could not have been very hard up for manpower because his application was unceremoniously rejected.

The time was the spring of 1864, Joseph was seventeen, and, in spite of past reverses, he still felt very warlike. The world was agog over events in Mexico, where the former Austrian Archduke, Maximilian, became Emperor with the active help of the ruler of the French, Napoleon III. The Mexicans resisted the usurper under the leadership of Benito Pablo Juárez. Joseph traveled to France and applied for admission in the Foreign Legion, in the hope that he might be sent to Mexico; but was again rejected.

There was always trouble in India and the British would surely need a young man with a tremendous will power, even though his arms were not overly strong. So he went to London and offered his arms to the British for service in India. By that time he should have got used to reverses. . . .

Ready, at last, to admit defeat, he returned to the Continent, penniless, humiliated, defeated. Now he thought only of finding his way home, but he had no money. He reached Hamburg and there he found a boat on which he could work his way closer home, to Fiume, the Adriatic port nearest to the Hungarian capital.

He was roaming the waterfront when a recruiting agent of the Union army of the United States came across him. The agent had to fill his quota of recruits and he was more interested in quantity than in quality. He signed up the young man and put him aboard a boat which set sail for Boston. One evening the boat cast anchor in Boston harbor, and the following morning Joseph and a companion were to be assigned to a regiment. The idea did not appeal to him. He wanted to join the fighting forces, but as a free agent, so the two young men lowered themselves into the water and swam ashore.

We do not know what happened to the other young man, but Joseph went straight to New York and enlisted in the First New York Cavalry Regiment which contained a goodly number of Hungarians and other foreigners. His name appeared on the regimental lists as

"Politzer" and "Poulitzes." He changed it to Pulitzer and under that name he entered American history.

Several times his regiment was transferred up and down the Hudson, and was finally assigned to the Army of the Potomac. He served under General P. H. Sheridan, hero of the ride from Winchester, and under George Armstrong Custer, who was to acquire immortal fame in his fight against the Indians. The Civil War was drawing to its close and Pulitzer's units participated only in minor engagements.

At the age of eighteen he was a war veteran, mustered out of service in July 1865. He had his severance pay, ignorance of English, a frail body and great will power. With that baggage he faced his future in the New World.

He still wanted to show his mettle in hazardous work. The fantastic idea came to him to seek service on board a whaling boat, so he set out for New Bedford, the center of the whaling industry of America. When he arrived, he learned that the Civil War had ruined the industry, and that it was doubtful whether it would ever regain its former status. Whether it would or not, young Pulitzer could not bide his time in that New England town.

The great concentration-place of the foreign-born was New York, and Pulitzer returned there. He lived in Austrian, Hungarian and Polish slums, associating with Central Europeans, physically in the United States, but spiritually outside of it, on the margins of American life. His companions were fodder for America's new industries, for the sweatshops. How could they ever rise to the full stature of Americans? Their children might be admitted into the Promised Land, but as for them, they were neither here nor there. . . .

Where was the real America Joseph had dreamed about? The call sounded: "Go West, young man!" A friend suggested he should go all the way to St. Louis on the Mississippi River, most American of all American streams. There he would not live in a foreign ghetto.

His severance pay was giving out and he had to sell the few belongings he possessed to have enough money to reach the West. The railway took him only to the left bank of the river. In the distance he saw the skyline of the town. Between him and St. Louis there was a ferry, and he did not have the fare. He went to the ferry and poured out his heart to a deckhand who knew German. The fellow was friendly and told him they needed a stoker and that he would probably be hired for the job. He was hired promptly. The furnace was on the deck and the night was cold. Roasted by the furnace on one side and chilled by the cold wind on the other, he worked his way across the last barrier to Canaan. For him it turned out to be a promised land.

At first, he was faced with the huge problem of how to make enough money for his food and lodging. He got odd jobs, and in his free time and periods of unemployment he spent his time in the public library. When the librarian arrived to open the place, Pulitzer was already waiting on the step, and he was the last one to leave at night. This was his formal education.

The local German newspaper, *Westliche Post,* needed a reporter, and Pulitzer was engaged. He found his vocation in journalism. In him burned the zeal of a prophet. Words meant much to him only when accompanied by action. As a reporter he had to write routine stories, but not for very long. He threw himself into his work with fanatic zeal, wanting to see all, do all. His frail body was of steel. Joseph Pulitzer had found himself.

This was the age of phenomenal expansion in that part of the West. The opportunities were great for honest work and also for political corruption. Ethical standards were blunted. In the great chase for money people were disposed to forgive others, so that they, in turn, might be forgiven. Jobbery was rampant. The judiciary was not always beyond the grasp of evil influences. The police had a hand in keeping open gamblers' dens and disorderly houses. In other words the time was ripe for a man with a great capacity for indignation and the strength to engage in a bitter and possibly dangerous fight.

Joseph Pulitzer was the man. But he saw that as a reporter his freedom of movement was greatly circumscribed. He must own the paper. Good journalists are not always good business men, but Pulitzer was both. He was the type of man who could command money, and he bought the paper. As the owner he made his own editorial policy, resulting in exposés which provided good reading for a public trained on "safe" reading. Pulitzer never forgot the lesson he learned in the offices of a German-language paper in St. Louis.

Flaming eyes, a reformer's ardor, ability to command attention, aroused interest in some friends of clean government. They proposed that he should run for the Missouri legislature. He had a gauche appearance and his English was broken, but when they heard him fight for a cause the voters overlooked these defects. He was only twenty-two when they elected him.

The Missouri legislature was no place for a reformer. The majority was against him, and it was easy to keep him quiet. Every time he wanted to speak, somebody else also wanted the floor. By a curious coincidence, the presiding officer saw only the other man, never Pulitzer. This would have cured most hardy souls of the desire to champion honesty, but Pulitzer was not a man who could be discouraged. The police were corrupt, therefore he must get a top job on the force. He was elected one of the three police commissioners.

He kept on fighting there and in his paper. He realized, however, that the influence of a foreign-language newspaper—although the city had a large German-speaking population—was limited. *Westliche Post* was doing so well that he sold his share in it for $30,000—a tidy sum in those days—and before doing anything further, he took a trip to Europe.

He fell in love with the French Riviera, and it was an abiding affection. Pulitzer also paid a visit to his native Hungary. Here was a perfect story of Local-boy-makes-good, but Hungary did not look at his achievements with favorable eyes. He was not noticed in Hungary, then nor later, in spite of the fact that he continued to have Hungarian friends in the United States and judging by some of his actions it should have been easy to enroll his help in matters of common interest to American-Hungarians.

When he returned to the United States, he knew one thing definitely —his place was in St. Louis. But now he was not sure whether he would return to publishing. He began to study law. In his native country a young man in doubt about his future turned to the study of law, a key to open many doors. Law fascinated him; his mind was orderly, and law was order. But what could he do with the cases he received—mostly the collection of bad debts?

In 1878 *The St. Louis Dispatch* was to be sold at the sheriff's auction on the stairs of the courthouse. The paper had seen better times, but its circulation had dwindled to the vanishing point and now was no more than a thousand. Was it on an impulse or by design that Joseph Pulitzer acted? The purchase price was low—he would try his hand now at an English-language newspaper. In order to bolster circulation, he eventually bought the *Post* and founded *The St. Louis Post-Dispatch*.

In those days American journalism was under the influence of James Gordon Bennett, of *The New York Herald,* and of the late Horace Greeley, of the *Tribune.* These two great figures of American journalism had turned the press of the United States into something unique

—events were no longer lifelessly recorded but humanized, so they became living dramas. Newspapers began to take an active interest in the life of the community and the country, espousing worthy and rejecting unworthy causes, taking a hand in the shaping of events. Pulitzer learned from these great masters, but he went beyond their teachings. Being of immigrant stock, he was far more conscious than they of the great change the United States was undergoing as a result of the tidal wave of immigration. America was filling up, to a large extent, with new Americans. Pulitzer observed the immigrants' influence on American life. Millions who had never read papers in their native lands might here be turned into newspaper readers, to become acquainted with the institutions of their new country through the press. The newspapers could make good or bad Americans. The newspaper must become livelier, and "human interest" must be assigned a more prominent place. Abstract events are of little interest to people not used to reading. But man is always interested in his own kind. He is encouraged by the success of others to try his luck, and warned by failures. The battle of ideas can best be presented to the masses through the battle of personalities. The newspaper must become a fighting instrument, an integral part of community and national life. It must champion good causes and wage war on dangerous ones. Corruption must be ferreted out. Sensationalism is an unpleasant word, but it is an inevitable by-product of constructive journalistic work in pursuit of honest government. People will read a paper that does not mince words. Great issues should be presented to the readers. Debates in print should be stimulating. "Are you in favor of national divorce laws?" was one of the numerous problems Pulitzer broached.

ACCURACY, TERSENESS, ACCURACY was the motto he announced to his staff on posters throughout the editorial rooms. The best story is the accurate one. Lack of accuracy destroys the credit of the paper and shakes the foundation of journalism. The press was not merely private enterprise but also a public trust.

The action headline was one of Pulitzer's innovations. It must be so arresting as to beguile the reluctant reader into following the story. The busy reader should have enough information in the first paragraph, to be acquainted with the substance of the story, if he lacked the time to go on. Every single story should be a bid for the reader's attention. Pulitzer's enemies charged that he was the founder of the yellow press, in which sensation rated high and gossip dominated the editorial rooms. He was the founder of the popular press, it is true, but he had no patience with the yellow press. He chided one of his editors for having allotted too much space to a story of bigamy. It lowered the standards of the press, Pulitzer warned him.

The Post-Dispatch began to flourish like the desert after a spring shower. Here was a new tone in American journalism. Here was an example of the popular press, addressed not merely to the select, but to the broad masses of the people. Here was a mighty medium of political education, one of the potent weapons of democracy.

Workers in the dark recesses of politics did not like this type of journalism because it called attention to their misdeeds. Pulitzer raised a flock of enemies, devoured by hatred. They distorted his motives and represented him as a danger to the citizenry. The crusader's life in St. Louis was no bed of roses.

In 1883 he moved to New York. The notorious railway operator, Jay Gould, was then the owner of *The New York World*, which had lost public confidence, was running downhill rapidly and had a circulation of a mere twelve thousand. Pulitzer saw great potentialities in that newspaper and bought it for $346,000. How was he to forge ahead in that competitive field? He soon found the answer. While other dailies were selling for three and four cents, he reduced the price of a copy of the *World* to two cents. The circulation bounded upward. That cent made a big difference to the "little man" whom Pulitzer wanted to reach.

In New York's strategic location, Pulitzer was in his element. The city certainly needed good government. It needed the stimulating effect of a man like Pulitzer. He drew up an ambitious program of national policy. The *World* waged a campaign to have large incomes taxed. Income tax was known to the North during the Civil War, but it was a wartime measure. In the eighties of the last century it was a bold proposal and not at all popular with influential people. Pulitzer's own income was large, and he would have been one of the taxpayers. Almost a decade went by before the campaign he conducted ripened into action and a federal income tax law was passed. It was declared unconstitutional, and a Constitutional Amendment was necessary to make it a part of the American scheme.

That was the era when mammoth corporations were born. The dominant idea then was that free enterprise was a part of freedom in general and that interfering with trusts and other forms of big business was equal to tampering with freedom. Pulitzer held the view that monopolistic practices interfered with freedom by denying the opportunities of free competition to others. The *World* dared to espouse ideas that ran counter to deeply rooted interests. Protective tariff was supposed to be part of the American system. Pulitzer advocated tariff for revenue only and not for "protection." In a mature economy, there was no place for protection. If business wanted to be free it must stand on its own feet and making the consuming public pay the tax on imports was not part of free enterprise. Civil service reform continued to engage Pulitzer's attention. Democracy and corruption were incompatible. As a matter of fact, corruption was a denial of democracy, no matter under what guise it paraded. Jobbery deprived the people of their right of self-government as effectively as autocracy.

Pulitzer was not content with waging his crusades merely in print. He carried them to the floor of the national legislature. He was a member of the House of Representatives from New York in 1885-1886, but he was not at his best in Washington. He ran into the difficulties usually prepared for people stamped as "social reformers."

He became one of America's most effective newspaper publishers. In 1887 he founded *The New York Evening World* and now he had key dailies in both the morning and afternoon fields. He set up machinery to run his organizations and they became semi-automatic.

It was at that time that the French Republic presented to the people of the United States the Statue of Liberty, a copper statue weighing 225 tons, 151 feet high, created by Frederic Auguste Bartholdi and named by him *"Liberté Éclairant le Monde,"* Liberty Enlightening the World, to be placed in New York's harbor, to greet the millions of immigrants seeking a freer life in the New World. A vast pedestal was needed for the statue, to cost a quarter of a million dollars which, however, was not available until Joseph Pulitzer launched a campaign, and collected $280,000.

In 1886 America was visited by the greatest living Hungarian painter, Mihály Munkácsy, considered by many the greatest Hungarian painter of all ages. Pulitzer served as the toastmaster at a New York banquet given in Munkácsy's honor, and took that occasion to pay homage to the country of his birth.

"We welcome Munkácsy," Pulitzer said, "not merely because he is an artist, but also because he is a Hungarian. We welcome him, too, as the representative of the two most beautiful countries of the world, France, where he has his home, and Hungary, the country of his birth." It was the ex-Hungarian immigrant who spoke. He was now an American institution, an important part of the American way of life, yet he never denied his Hungarian origin and contributed to Hungarian causes. Still the Hungarian government failed to notice him, and American-Hungarian "society" made no attempt to bring him closer to itself.

In 1903 Pulitzer founded the School of Journalism at Columbia University, one of the most famous institutions of its kind, and established the Pulitzer Prizes which are among the most coveted distinctions of writers and artists all over the United States.

The prizes are awarded "for the encouragement of public service, public morals, American literature and the advancement of education." Each year prizes are given for the most distinguished meritorious service rendered by an American newspaper throughout the year, and for the best example of a reporter's work—the test being strict accuracy and terseness—preference being given to news stories prepared under the pressure of edition time that redound to the credit of the profession of journalism. Other awards are for distinguished service as a Washington or foreign correspondent and distinguished editorial writing, the test of excellence being clearness of style, moral purpose, sound reasoning and power to influence public opinion. Prizes are also awarded for original American plays, performed in New York, which best represent the educational value and power of the stage, dealing preferably with American life, by an American author; for distinguished books about the history of the United States; for the best American biography teaching patriotic and unselfish service to the American people.

Pulitzer bequeathed a considerable sum to the Philharmonic Society of New York for the performance of his favorite music, which he specified as Liszt—the great Hungarian composer—as well as Beethoven and Wagner. He also bequeathed a large amount to the Metropolitan Museum of New York. He set aside a sum in his will for the building of fountains "like those at the *Place de la Concorde*" of Paris, which materialized in the fountain at the Plaza entrance to Central Park on Fifth Avenue.

His last years were tragic. He became a nervous invalid and—catastrophe of catastrophies—almost totally blind. Like the Dutchman of folklore, he found no peace anywhere and sailed from port to port. From his youth he had had a deep affection for the French Riviera and, later, he took a liking to the maritime South of the United States. His luxurious yacht, which he named *Liberty,* became his floating home and hospital.

The *Liberty* left her New York pier on October 20, 1911 for a West Indies cruise with Joseph Pulitzer, one of his sons, his readers and household help on board. In five days the yacht cast anchor in Charleston harbor. The editor of the *Charleston Courier*, Mr. Lathan, came aboard to pay his respects to the *doyen* of American newspaper publishers. The yacht set sail again for the south four days later. Pulitzer's attendant was reading to him about Louis XI of France. Slowly Pulitzer closed his unseeing eyes and whispered: *"Leise, leise,"* softly, softly. They were his last words.

$Part$ 3

THE PULL AND PUSH

———

IX

The High Tide of Immigration

HISTORY HAD WITNESSED many migrations, but never anything like this. It had seen much of desert Asia pouring into fertile Europe during the turbulent centuries of the *Voelkerwanderung*. It had seen the stampede of the Mongolians out of their parched steppes toward the East and the West, and the bursting of the dam by the Turks, as they tore westward in their irresistible advance that took them to the very ramparts of Vienna, while all Christianity watched with unspeakable fear. Swiss mountaineers had scaled their native crags and descended into remote valleys in quest of bread and life. The Germans had marched toward the steppes of Russia, the banks of the Volga, the warped soil of the Crimea, the valleys and woods of Transylvania, the Bánát and Bácska. Hungary, too, had been sought out by immigrants from across the Carpathians, Poles in search of bread and freedom, Polish Jews in search of tolerance.

The migration to America was on an even more gigantic scale. In a century and a quarter, from 1820 to 1945, it brought to these shores nearly thirty-nine million people. In the first decade of the twentieth century alone 8,795,811 people came to the United States. Originally they had come from the British Isles and Western Europe, where the sea broadened horizons. Then they came from Central and Northern Europe, seized by the fever of migration, possessed of the hope of nobler goals for man. Now, however, conditions at home had changed. Manchester and Sheffield, the towns of the Clyde, sold their goods to the entire world—hands were needed at home. In Central and Northern Europe, too, indigenous industries sprang into life, and the sooty Eldorado of the worker was close at hand. The new immigration at the turn of the century came from farther east and south—Austria,

Hungary and Italy and from Poland which was not Poland in anything but the dreams of her inhabitants.

Strong muscles were needed to stand the heat of the furnaces, and bear the backbreaking work of the mines. Strong wills and patience were needed to bear the toil of the sweatshop with its endless hours of soul-killing work. Little skill was needed in the machine civilization of the new age. The machine did most of the work, and man served as its attendant. "From ship to shop" was the immigrants' motto.

Why did the immigrant leave his native country, and particularly why did the Hungarian leave home? He was unlike the immigrant of a previous generation, the Western and Central European. His horizon was not the alluring sea. His country was locked in the continent of Europe. His horizon was limited and definite, reaching only to the end of the wheatfields of the near-by estate. His only landmark was the church steeple of his village. Not merely physically but mentally he was mired in the native soil. "Good enough for the forebear, good enough for me." Centuries of training in the service of alien interests had rendered him suspicious of change and motion. "Don't stick your neck out." It was safest not to be seen or heard. Otherwise, you are too conspicuous and somebody will get after you. Hibernate in your mud throughout life.

Then, all of a sudden, the Hungarian immigrant decided to leave the protective shadow of the church steeple, the familiarity of the native wheat, the security of his own language, and entrust himself to the tender mercies of an ocean-going steamer floating on an element that was full of unfathomable uncertainties.

In some of the older immigrations loyalty to one's creed was the dominant motive; faith was the essence of life and without it was death. Religion was not the motive—with few exceptions—for the high tide of Hungarian emigration. Most of the emigrants were Catholics, the dominant religion in Hungary. Others were Protestants. Jews were not persecuted in Hungary then.

Political persecution was important—the followers of Lajos Kossuth were political refugees. But their number was not very large. In discussing political conditions at the high tide of Hungarian emigration we shall see the impact of those conditions upon this mass movement.

The easiest way to explain the emigration from Hungary was to blame it on the travel agents. It is true that their number was large, as we shall see, in certain places and at certain times. But on-the-spot investigation failed to link mass emigration to the agent. He was what his designation implies: an instrument and not a cause. The emigrant's mind was already made up when he turned to the travel agent. Such "explanations" are too superficial to be considered seriously.

Romantic persons had romantic explanations. Hungarian-born Max Nordau, who wrote his numerous notable books in German, attributed emigration to a deep human craving he called *ein geheimes Weh,* a secret malady. He himself became a globe-trotter who went in search of human frailties and conventions in many parts of the globe. Possibly he was driven by the "secret malady" of the restless Gypsy, and explained the mass movement of emigration in terms he best understood. A similar explanation was given by the French philosopher, Pierre Paul Leroy-Beaulieu, who attributed migration to a basic trait of man. V. d. Goltz formulated a "Law of Migration" (*Gesetz der Stroemung*) saying that population moves from higher to lower social pressure along the line of least resistance. Pressure was meant in the broadest sense, embracing such social factors as economic and political causes. Some observers of the phenomena of migration found that it was the result of irrepressible economic laws. Others were more specific [30] in stating that while the most compelling force of migrations was the economic motive, it was accompanied by numerous subsidiary causes, such as religious and political persecution, racial discrimination and love of adventure. If reason had ruled in social relations, it was shown, there would have been far less need for mass migration. Speculating on how many people the earth could sustain, scientists reached different conclusions. The present population of the globe is about 2,200,000,000. The noted German-born English cartographer, Ernst Georg Ravenstein, held that the earth could sustain five billion people with ease, while von Fircks went a long step further in maintaining that the number could be increased to nine billion.

Professor Franz Oppenheimer [31] showed that conditions differed in countries where land holdings were small and in countries where they were large. In the former it was possible to accommodate the population increase—and even more. The difficulty arose in the countries of large estates. There the surplus population presents a great problem of which one solution is to redress the balance through the highly unsatisfactory means of "vice and misery" which decimate the population. Another answer is to apply "moral restraint" or tolerate social means to exterminate the surplus. No doubt Thomas Malthus was no stranger to these thoughts. Finally, the third way is to drain off the surplus through migration. In England, and later in Germany, a dynamic industrial life created the cities that absorbed the rural surplus, so that after a time there was no need for overseas migration. In Hungary, however, there were few large industries and, consequently, hardly any large cities outside of the capital. Hence, the surplus rural proletariat had to go to cities where it would be assimilated—mostly in America.

The most satisfactory explanation of overseas migration is that of "push and pull." Conditions—largely economic—pushed the emigrant outside his native land, and conditions—again mainly economic— pulled him toward his new home. The effect of the pull appears to have been stronger than that of the push. When conditions were very bad at home and not particularly favorable in the prospective new home, migration was not at high tide. But it did increase greatly in response to improved economic conditions in the receiving land. The high-water marks of Hungarian emigration did not coincide with especially unfavorable economic conditions there, but occurred during periods when some improvement had set in, as shown by national income and wages. On the other hand, years of increased emigration from Hungary followed shortly after some dramatic increase in earning possibilities in the United States.

When the misery was gravest in Hungary—and no doubt in other similarly situated countries—emigration was almost at a standstill. There can be such a low level of economic conditions that the prospective emigrant is unable to leave home. A bunk in the steerage cost thirty dollars, but to him it was a huge fortune. If he had no kinsmen in America, he was doomed to live out his miserable life at home. He fell into apathy and became little more than a beast of burden with no thought for anything but the filling of his simplest requirements. It may sound paradoxical, but it is a fact that the Hungarian peasant matured for emigration when his condition bettered. Then he dared to conceive the bold idea of turning his back on his native land, the only land he knew, the only world he knew, ruled over by the only God he knew, the God that understood his language. Then he dared to contemplate the idea of striking out for himself in an alien civilization—alien and therefore strange—strange and therefore unfriendly.

In line with what has just been said, peaks of immigration in the United States were in 1854, 1873, 1882, 1907 and 1914. "The passage of some time is required before the full effect of a change in employment is felt upon immigration." [32] Sometimes an economic slump overtook the unwary immigrant by the time he reached these shores. The flood tide of immigration into the United States began in 1882, the beginning of the "golden age" of iron and steel, with our own industrial revolution in full swing and industries expanding. The maturity of the American industrial civilization was marked by the creation of vast combinations—monopolies—deriving great benefits from the accumulation of capital and managerial ability. For a few years immigration receded again, as if it had overreached itself. A new high-water mark was reached in 1903, when the United States was fully established as the new industrial giant and as the Eldorado of Europe's underprivileged millions. In that year 857,000 immigrants entered this country. Three years later the number had risen still higher, to 1,100,-000, and in 1907 it reached the all-time peak of 1,285,000. Then the tide receded slightly, only to rise again, reaching 1,197,000 in 1913 and 1,218,000 in 1914, only a little below the high-water mark.

America was short of labor. That is why the institution of the indentured servant flourished in the early days. The South tried to solve its problem in its own way and the devil was to pay in due time. The economist speaks of factors of production. One of them—land— was in such abundance in the United States that it was freely given away to prospective farmers in one period of our national history. American enterprise, another factor, was also abundant, drawing upon the boldest and most adventurous people of many lands. Under such conditions, capital was created, soon to grow to enormous proportions. First, the land had to be tamed, and then the stage was set for America's industrial revolution. But there was a shortage of working hands.

The early immigrants from England brought with them much of the inventive genius of Old England. The first American industrial establishment on a large scale was the textile mill of the English immigrant Samuel Slater, Pawtucket, Rhode Island. Nine children tending textile machines were America's first industrial workers. Deeper into the heart of the industrial frontier penetrated Francis Cabot Lowell, with his cotton spinning and weaving mill, aided by the indestructible Paul Moody. Milestones on the road toward industrial maturity were marked by the cotton gin of Ely Whitney and the sewing machine of Elias Howe.

In the fires of war industrial America was tempered. England had been the forge of the United States, but it was of no use when the two countries were at grips. That was the situation confronting this country in 1812. The United States was thrown upon its own native resources and it met the challenge. When peace came, the United States was no longer an industrial amateur. True, England was still in the van, but this country had learned to depend upon its own resources more and more. Improvements of the plow were of great importance, since agriculture was still the main national industry. The first steel plow was invented by blacksmith John Lane. The first American cast-iron plow was patented by Charles Newbold. The process for manufacturing hard-faced plows was invented by James Oliver. New England established tin and brass industries, went into the production of jewelry, novelties and clocks. William Kelly invented the converter for making steel through the Bessemer process. Since labor was scarce, requiring careful husbanding, standardization—America's contribution to industry—was called upon to reduce the need for hand labor.

"The old America was a nation of farmers, artisans and small-scale business men, transporting their goods by wagons, river steamers or canal boats; the new America still had its millions of farmers, but it was now more and more characterized by its industrial proletariat massed in cities, its capitalists and big business men, its consolidation of industry, its enormous factories, and its far-flung railroad system." [33]

When the War Between the States broke out America had four hundred steel mills; twenty years later their number had risen to close to a thousand, and the value of their products to $300,000,000. The Civil War was one of the causes of this remarkable industrial expansion. Arms plants mushroomed, the woolen industry grew by leaps and bounds, meat packing became one of the nation's main industrial occupations. Modern refrigeration was invented, canning was used more widely, as the world became the meat market of America. Petroleum began to lubricate the civilization of the machine. In the late fifties, Edwin Drake sank the first oil well, in northeastern Pennsylvania, which produced twenty-five barrels a day, and neighbors called it Drake's Folly. Mass production needed masses of raw materials, masses of producers and masses of consumers. It required industrial leaders with boldness and vision, love of adventure, risk and, above all, push.

In 1859 the value of American manufactured products amounted to $1,886,000,000 and forty years later to $11,886,000,000. In 1849 the number of industrial workers in the United States was 957,000 and forty years later 4,252,000. In 1854 about 400,000 immigrants entered the United States, and in 1882 their number reached 789,000.

These are my earliest memories of Hungarian emigration as a child and youth. Every so often, with a heavy load of tin plates, wires and some mysterious instruments the first "American" I ever saw would appear in our house at Budapest. He was a *drótostót,* soldering Slovak. In Hungary damaged pots were not thrown on the scrap-heap, but were mended, and to do that was the job of the itinerant potter and solderer.

This man was a Slovak from one of the hilly counties of Hungary's North. He spoke a broken Hungarian, so that I could not understand much of what he said. But I do recall his having told us about America, where he once had lived. I am sure he did not talk about literature and art in the United States. But he did tell us, in his plaintive singsong: "Meat, plenty of meat in America."

At home, only potatoes, and an itinerant Slovak needed meat to make him strong for his hard work. And then the potato crop failed and the devil was to pay. Belts had to be tightened, and soon they would embrace mere shadows. For a long time I could not forget that plaintive voice: "Meat, plenty of meat."

Why had he returned to Hungary? Such things are hard to explain. An atavistic urge may have pulled him back to his native land. With the soot of the Pennsylvania coal town in his nostrils, he may have been overwhelmed by a craving for the scented air of his mountain home. He may have been pulled by a desire to see his old parents. He may have failed to save enough to pay the fare of wife and child, and so he returned to begin his life of involuntary servitude anew: working the potato patch in warm weather and repairing pots in cold. Every penny not needed for immediate necessities was saved, and one great day the entire family would be on its way to port. He dropped out of sight. Once or twice we thought of him when we needed an itinerant Slovak, and then we thought of him no more.

Perhaps a decade later, on the eve of World War I, an uncle took me to a seaside resort in neighboring Austria, my first trip abroad. We were near Fiume, Hungary's only seaport, and the officially authorized port of embarkation for Hungarian emigrants bound overseas. We were to take an early morning train for Trieste, the Austrian port at the western end of the peninsula. The rural railway station was deserted but for one person. He was a tall young man, and he looked furtive. We spoke Hungarian and it was impossible not to see that he was interested. He moved up to us and there I met a person such as I had heard about but never met until then.

During the night he had crossed the Hungarian frontier on his way to a German port of embarkation for the United States. Why not Fiume, the official port? The question was not asked, since the answer was obvious. That was the port for "authorized" emigrants and obviously this tall young man was not one of them. He was of pre-military service age, and his leaving the country was not permitted in the normal way. Besides, steamer fares at Fiume were high, as the Hungarian government received a share. Here was an "illegal" emigrant, sturdy and strong, the type of man an agrarian country needs. But the use Hungary had for strong and sturdy young men like this one was far more an abuse. Unless he belonged to the fortunate few that battered their way to the peasant's very modest peak, he would be doomed to waste himself in the hardest imaginable work for the barest livelihood.

Hungary is a predominantly agricultural country and was even more so at the flood tide of her great emigration movement before the First World War. The country is part of the great Central-Eastern European peasant belt and part of pre-war Hungary belonged to the southeastern black-belt, the humus region. Little of the country could not be cultivated one way or another. Hungary was rich in agrarian resources.

Only 22 per cent of the population lived in urban areas in 1910. In an agrarian country, the nature of land division is of the utmost importance for emigration, as Professor Oppenheimer has shown. What was the division of land in Hungary?

Taking the landowners into consideration, the year 1895 presented this picture: more than one-half of the land-owning population—53 per cent—owned holdings of less than five *jochs* (one *joch* is a trifle more than one acre—1.07 acres) and 6.15 per cent of the area. This did not include the lowest level of peasants, as we shall see. On the highest level, owners of holdings in excess of a thousand *jochs* formed only 0.16 per cent of the total owners, while their holdings covered an area of 31.19 per cent.[34] This is a typical picture of a latifundium-ridden land, in which there is bound to be a surplus population because of the predominance of the large estates. In accordance with the thesis formulated by Franz Oppenheimer, the surplus seeks to find its livelihood in industrial urban areas and failing those—as in the case of Hungary—it seeks its livelihood abroad.

One could not live on land of less than five acres, especially not in a region of extensive cultivation. (Holland produced two and a half times as much wheat from an acre as Hungary.)

Altogether, 87 per cent of the peasants had fewer than 10 *jochs*. Gyula Rácz, quoted by Pinter,[35] showed on the basis of the 1900 census that out of Hungary's thirteen million agriculturists not fewer than ten million were landlack proletarians, and he did not include one-*joch* "property owners." According to his calculation, only 4 per cent of the total had enough land to live decently. A family required at least ten *jochs* for a living, whereas, as we have seen, more than half of the peasant population had less than five *jochs*.

The real landlack peasants were the farm workers and farm servants. The former comprised about one-fourth of the total population toward the close of the last century. Some may have had tiny pieces of land, but about 1,500,000 had absolutely nothing.

What made the situation particularly tragic was the fact that the condition of the small farmer deteriorated in the course of time, instead of improving. He fell into arrears with the payment of his mortgage, interest charges were heavy, and the competition of the economically stronger estates fatal. With the increase of the population, tiny holdings were atomized even more. The beneficiary of this trend was the large estate. The following few figures tell a story of misery, social injustice and emigration. They tell the story of the approaching end of a hardy peasant population that survived the devastating onslaughts of Tatar and Turk, but was going down in defeat in the hopeless fight against the selfish and unimaginative rule of Hungary's ruling classes. In 1895 the total area of land holdings of fewer than 100 *jochs* amounted to 54.6 per cent, in 1913 only 45.6 per cent. On the other hand, the corresponding figures for large estates of over 1,000 *jochs* were 31.2 and 40 per cent.[36]

While millions had either nothing or next to nothing of the rich soil of their country, a few had vast estates. The Eszterházy family owned half a million acres; the Counts Schoenborn had a quarter of a million. Count Mihály Károlyi—who later distributed his estate among the peasants—had 186,000, a Count Pálffy had 112,000 and a Count Pallavicini had 75,000 acres.

The small peasant could buy land only with the greatest difficulties, if at all. In certain regions he might have been working for years in the hope of calling a piece of soil his own, only to find that his hopes were dashed. This was the case in regions where the "dead hand" held the land in its rigid grasp. These mortmain estates might belong

to the treasury, churches, religious foundations, individuals, family
estates or trust funds. It was this system of the entailed land that Lajos
Kossuth denounced as a "monstrous institution." And monstrous, indeed, it was, since no grass ever grew for the peasant in the shadow of
the entailed estate. At the turn of the century about twenty-five million acres of Hungarian soil were entailed. Entire villages became
deserted and, in due time, their populations headed for America.

How did the farmers live in one of the bread-baskets of the world?
An independent investigation showed in 1910 that total earnings of
an entire farm family of five amounted to $60—300 kronen. This
amounted to three cents a day per person for work which during the
season lasted for what the peasant called *vakulástól vakulásig,* from
blindness to blindness—from blind darkness to blind darkness.

A letter from Count Bertalan Széchenyi to his "faithful servants," in
Hungary's golden age around the turn of the century, is significant:
"I had occasion this year to notice your industry, loyalty and the way
you resisted the advances of irresponsible agitators. Although there was
some talk in the servants' quarters about stopping work and requesting
wages, you kept on working hard, trusting to your master to help you
in case of need. Your trust in me will not be disappointed. I shall
keep on affording help to those who need it, as in the past. But this
year I want to do more, making it memorable for you, by giving you
great joy—a bonus on New Year's Eve. To each farm worker and
servant who had five years of service with me I am going to give five
kronen [$1] a year, repeating it six times at five-year intervals, so that
those who serve me thirty years will receive a bonus totaling 30 kronen
[$5]. This is a large sum of money, but I give it away gladly . . ." [37]

The fate of the farm worker was more bitter than that of the small
farmer. In many places he was forced to perform unpaid work for
the lord, which looked very much like the notorious *corvée* of the
ancien régime in France or the *robot,* forced labor, in feudal Hungary.
Although serfdom was no longer legal, some of its phases lingered on.
"Discretionary work" was the name attached to this type of work
servitude and that rendered it legal. The worker in hiring himself out
to the estate owner undertook to perform so many days of unpaid
work. In some cases the contract provided that he must provision the
landlord's larder with fresh-killed chicken and eggs. Sometimes his
wife had to serve as unpaid domestic help for a specified number of
days a year; if ill health, or any other reason interfered, the contract
stipulated that a certain amount should be deducted from her hus-

band's wages for every day she missed.[38] In one of western Hungary's more "advanced" counties, Sopron, the average farm servant's annual wages amounted to a cash payment of $16 at the turn of the century. However, these were the gross wages, out of which the employer was entitled to deduct $6.40 for lodging, $4 for damages caused by the employee, and 60 cents for taxes, leaving an annual net of five to six dollars. In later years conditions improved somewhat, so that it was calculated that the farm servant actually received a payment of $12.80 a year, besides his food computed at $67.

A typical weekday bill of fare for a family of farm workers, during the period February 1-7, 1911, as reported by an investigator [39] was as follows: *Wednesday morning*—cabbage with sausage; *noon*—noodle soup; *evening*—nothing. The Sunday fare: *morning*—bread and bacon; *noon*—stuffed cabbage; *evening*—noodle soup. In poorer districts the farm servants' fare often consisted of no more than a piece of bread on weekdays, with some shreds of meat on holidays, and whatever else they might have been able to pick up for themselves. In County Liptó—northern Hungary—the record speaks of bread and noodles as the farm servants' typical fare. Even during the harvest season when the worker needed more food so as to have more strength, County Bereg's farm-servant population received no more than corn-bread, potatoes and some vegetables. It is recorded that by the end of the autumn season many lacked even a little salt. Necessity was turned into a virtue by some of the peasants who fasted for days on end, breaking the fast only to eat some crumbs.

Living conditions of the peasant of his district were described by twenty-five-year-old Sándor Csizmadia, himself of peasant origin, charged with inciting to violence in 1895: "I have watched the family life of estate servants, three or four families, sometimes of as many as twenty to twenty-five persons, living in a one-room hut. I have seen men collapsing on the richest soil of the country because of starvation and I have also seen men being virtually drowned in their own fat. Families of the *puszta* [steppe] are working for 15 *krajcár* [less than a dime] from three in the morning till ten at night."

Tuberculosis was called the "Hungarian malady" and hunger typhus was endemic in parts of the land in the late nineteenth century. Health was impaired by such vitamin-deficiency diseases as pellagra. Insanity induced by hunger was reported in Transylvania and the North Hungarian hills. Half the babies died before the age of five. For every

3,496 persons in rural Hungary there was one physician. On the other hand every 1,851 had a Roman Catholic priest.[40]

The 1898 domestic servant law provided that one separate room should be built for every family affected by the law. But the legislature allowed ten years for compliance with this provision and it never set up effective controls. At the Mezőhegyes State estate, which was supposed to be a model farm, laborers lived in thatched huts, completely dilapidated, in which one square meter of living space cost half the price of a square meter of stable. Taking the entire country, and not merely the more backward rural areas, the conservative social scientist-statesman Gustav Gratz pointed out that Hungary in those pre-First World War days spent one-third more for race horse prizes than for sanitation. The peasants spent much of their time in the taverns, low-ceilinged, smoke-filled, evil-smelling dens, but far more desirable than their "homes." An investigator, selecting a parochial school at random, found there was only one child out of 136 who did not know alcohol and 86 of them drank *pálinka*, the favorite Hungarian "hard drink," daily, probably because that was one of the few things the parents could give to them and because, in their deep ignorance, many may not have even known that it was harmful.

Investigating a Hungarian "Middletown," the village of Oros, Béla Bosnyák found that for the six classes of the Roman Catholic and six classes of the Greek Catholic schools one room and one teacher had to do. Both the government and influential organizations expressed doubts about the desirability of giving children too much education, presumably on the ground that education would make the peasants think and thinking might lead to action. In those days there were many officials who evidently thought that *büdös paraszt,* stinking peasant, was one word. Everything in connection with the peasant was *büdös.* The "public servant," who acted as a public master, would shout at him: *"Fogd be a büdös pofádat!"* Shut your stinking mouth! A contemporary observer said that the Chinese coolie lived no worse than some Hungarian peasants. One of the Hungarian magnates— whose name deserves to be forgotten—made the proposal that Chinese coolies should be imported into Hungary in view of the fact that peasants at home received too "high" wages.

Conditions were favorable for assuring the Hungarian farmer a better life. The population of Western Europe increased by leaps and bounds and its needs for grain were great. The production of Hungarian wheat—and Hungary was predominantly a wheat-producing country—did increase between 1848 and 1880. This increase was due to several causes. In 1848 the serfs were freed. Serf labor was highly inefficient, the work of human beasts of burden with no vestige of incentive. The antediluvian wooden plows were largely exchanged for iron ones.

Wheat farming becomes profitable in modern times mostly if it is done on a large enough scale. America's open-air "bread factories" are the best illustration of this fact. The soil of Hungary is such that diversified farming would have been possible. The country had considerable fruit farming and it was a boon to the peasantry. Truck farming would have been just as profitable, if not more so. This was shown by the success of independent Bulgarian truck farmers on the outskirts of the capital and some of the larger towns. There is more money in that type of farming for the small peasant, as compared with small grain lots. Transformation of wheat land into truck farms would have required either the farmers' own co-operative effort or government aid. The first was impossible in view of the fact that the peasants had no capital and were not trained in co-operation. As to the government, it was in the hands of the large estate owners, who did not want to change the existing pattern.

Originally, Hungary and the adjacent countries had the advantage of proximity in providing parts of Europe with wheat. But transportation costs were reduced in due time and overseas bread factories went into production in the fourth quarter of the last century. By 1880 overseas wheat sold cheaper than Hungarian wheat. Until then Hungarian wheat prices had been determined in the world market. Hungary ceased to be an exporting land, except for special uses.

What did the government do? It imposed wheat duties with the result that in the very center of Europe's breadbasket a ton of wheat cost from one to two dollars more than in London. Pinter points out [41] that this was the unique case where a country courted an unfavorable trade balance and indebtedness. As prices increased in a protected market the landowners could realize higher profits. High food prices raised the general price levels, and the cost of industrial production increased. This created favorable conditions for industrial imports from Germany, England and France.

The estate owners of Hungary found it more profitable to increase their acreage than their labor force. They introduced farm machinery and that reduced farm employment. Farming is mentioned in books as a classical example of perfect competition, since the contribution of each producer to the total product forms only a small part of the grand total. That was not the case in Hungary, however, where the large owners were able to defy the laws of economics and create conditions that looked very much like a farm monopoly.

The taxation system of the government and its subdivisions also discriminated against the small farmer and favored the land magnates. In the Western world we take progressive taxation for granted. The rate of taxes increases progressively with the taxpayers' ability to pay. In the Hungray of those days we can observe the operation of a tax system which was regressive in its effects. The lower the ability of the taxpayer to pay, the higher were his taxes. In the village of Oros, for instance, estates between 500 and 1,000 *jochs* paid taxes at the rate of 1.31 kronen, land between 100 and 500 *jochs* paid 1.49 and less than 100 *jochs* paid 3.76 kronen. This was mostly the result of the system of assessment, which worked to the disadvantage of the small farmer. The assessing officials were completely beholden to the magnates' interests.

Consumption taxes are also considered regressive in their effects, since persons with small incomes must spend a larger part of their total revenue than persons with larger incomes. In Hungary, indirect taxes amounted to one billion kronen in 1911, against 270 million kronen in direct taxes. The tax on sugar rose some 3,400 per cent in the four decades up to 1910. Although the 1848 revolution emancipated the peasants, they remained taxpaying beasts of burden, *misera plebs contribuens.*

Internal colonization might have been a partial answer. Czarist Russia, surely not a shining light of progress, experimented with that solution. The land of the State and public corporations alone comprised some sixteen million acres, which could have been distributed among the small and landlack peasantry. Thus a million and a half peasants could have obtained a livelihood, extremely modest to be sure, but a livelihood just the same. Such a move would have increased farm wages and the national income. It would have created a domestic market for Hungary's own industries. A considerable increase in the standard of living would have been possible through industrialization.

In 1903, a minister of Agriculture did submit a bill of settlement to parliament. To head off land baron opposition to the bill the Minister specified in its motivation that all he wanted was to help peasants supplement their earnings as employees by cultivating a small plot of land of their own. It almost sounded as if he had told the employers:

"Look here, you can pay low wages, perhaps even lower than now, if you permit these poor devils to dig their own gardens." He did officially state: "The creation of labor settlements does not signify that we desire to settle laborers there with a view to turning them into independent farmers."

If this was the condition of the land-owning peasantry, what was the plight of the *nincstelenek,* landlack masses? Their massed strength would have carried weight—since their number ran into millions—if parliament had been responsive to it. And it is considered the aim of the legislature to represent the people's will. Parliament, however, in a law of 1876 provided that employers were not subject to prosecution in their treatment of employees. Also, the authorities had the right to employ force in making agrarian laborers fulfil their obligations under contracts.

The First Agrarian Congress, which opened in Budapest on January 31, 1897, proposed very moderate reforms. It asked that the workday be reduced to twelve hours, that farm workers be protected by minimum daily wages, state employment offices and rural health service. At next harvest time, tens of thousands of farm workers went on strike. Thereupon the government drafted strikebreakers on the State farms and had thousands of strikers thrown into jails. As a result of this, estate owners intensified their efforts to introduce seasonal workers—underfed Slovaks and Ruthenians—from the northern countries.

In 1898 the Hungarian parliament passed "A Law Regulating Legal Relations Between Employers and Agricultural Workers," which the peasants called the "Slave Law." It declared combinations of farm workers illegal, meted out punishment to those attempting to found farm labor unions of any kind, even those who merely participated in farm workers' meetings or placed meeting places at their disposal. The "Slave Law" turned a civil contract into a public act, which the State had the right to enforce.

It was customary for agents of estates to visit the hunger-ridden farm-workers' section of the country, carrying with them some food and, in some instances, a little money. The poor wretches would have signed away their souls for a little food for themselves and their families to the very devil. The devil was the agent, who offered the farm worker some food in one hand and the labor contract in the other. The peasant sometimes could not read at all or if he could, was unable to understand the complicated legal language of the contract.

Under normal conditions, the farm worker could have pleaded misrepresentation or duress, but not under the Slave Law. He had to live up to the letter of that obligation, and that was not the worst of it; if for some reason he could not or would not do it a private contract became a public obligation. The authorities had the right to throw the farm laborer into prison for non-fulfilment of his contract. If he failed to appear at his place of work, he was a "fugitive," just as his forebears were in serfdom days. Then the dreaded gendarmes went into action.

In 1905 the workers of a district struck for a daily wage which was the equivalent of a nickel. The gendarmes were augmented by regular troops, and some of the strikers were killed. It was then that the suggestion was made to introduce Chinese coolie labor into Hungary. It was then that an observer remarked: "Coolie ordinances are more liberal than the Hungarian law. The coolie is exempted from work on days of rest, while the Hungarian farm worker has neither religious nor any other holidays. The coolie's workday lasts only ten hours, while the Hungarian's lasts from sunrise to sunset. . . . Indeed, the Hungarian farm worker has every reason to envy the Chinese coolie."

Farm servants—household workers—were brought under even more stringent rules under a law of 1907, which provided that their standard contract must run for a period of at least a year, and that, barring a few exceptions, they lost the right to leave their employment. If they refused to work, they were liable to fine and jail—up to sixty days in the workhouse. They also rendered themselves liable for damages caused by their "negligence" and "disobediance," which, naturally, were determined by their employers. This was involuntary servitude in everything but name. Sometimes there were not enough jails for agrarian workers and barns had to be transformed into places of detention.

There were some public-spirited people on the opposite side of the fence, who were outspoken in their condemnation of these conditions. An attorney for the Hungarian National Association of Manufacturers (*Gyáriparosok Országos Szövetsége*), Dávid Papp, stated: "Laws such as the Domestic Servants' Act and the language employed in parliament in regard to these classes of people are doing far more damage (from the point of view of emigration) than the travel agents." In the Hungarian Chamber of Peers Count J. de Mailáth said: "Three out of ten emigrants will tell you: 'I am leaving the country because there is no justice here.' Our government is Asiatic."

The Hungarian landowners had a strong organization, the O.M.
G.E., National Hungarian Landowners' Association, a super-lobby, an
unofficial government. Preaching patriotism and calling everybody a
"Socialist" (the term "Communist" was not yet known) who disagreed
with its extreme measures, it was indefatigable in bringing about the
social revolution which took the form of mass emigration.

The labor-protecting provisions in the laws were very few. The
government, eventually, set up a farm employment service and made
provisions for farmers to buy tools. It also lent its help to farm worker
co-operatives. The Ministry of Agriculture set up a free legal advice
bureau for farm workers.

Hungary had a parliament and legislatures operate through the party
system, but was there a peasant party in Hungary? After all, it was
and still is mainly a peasant country. Yet there was no such party until
the beginning of this century. Then one came into existence but it was
little more than a one-man affair. Its name was "Independent Socialist
Peasant Party" and its "leader"—and largely, follower—was András
Achim, who had a seat in parliament. Achim's program was extremely
moderate: universal secret ballot, reform of the public administration,
progressive taxation, freedom of speech and press, social legislation for
the peasantry. He was cautious about land reform and asked merely
that estates in excess of ten thousand acres should be distributed among
small farmers and the landless peasants.

Achim was not subtle and he knew it. "More refined people," he
said, "may employ subtler ways. The geese of the Capitol of Rome
could not utter as lovely sounds as the nightingales and yet it was the
geese that saved eternal Rome. The Romans heeded the warning, and
did not mind the voice." Talking about the status of the Hungarian
nation, he charged: "The prevailing order is designed for birth, privilege and wealth. Inferior brains rule the land, while competent heads
are wasted in foul workshops." He was denounced as a rabble-rouser
and a traitor to the country. "The ruling classes have instigated a
political hunt against me to keep me—a man of the people—from
speaking about the sufferings of the masses and the sinful negligence
of the ruling classes—the real cause of emigration." He was a violent
person, and he had a violent end—he was murdered, although not for
political reasons.

The Socialist Party in Hungary also fought for the rights of man.
But it could not penetrate the domain over which the gendarmes

watched. It concentrated largely on the problems of the industrial proletariat, also virgin soil.

What was the peasant to do? Industrial work might have provided the answer, if Hungary had had more industries. And those of the peasants who migrated to the towns? Were they better off than their neighbors who stayed at home? We shall see.

Hungary was not a country of large industries, with the exception of some large flour mills and sugar factories. Before the First World War, Budapest was the largest flour milling center in Europe, and the second largest in the world, next to Minneapolis. At the turn of the century sixteen per cent of the population was engaged in industry, transportation, trade and mining. The census spoke of half a million industrial enterprises, but that was a grandiloquent statement, since about two-thirds of these "enterprises" employed one worker each; not more than one-half of one per cent employed more than twenty workers. One-fifth of the industrial enterprises were classified as restaurants and cafés. In 1890 Hungary's industrial population amounted to 776,-000, which increased to 992,000 in 1890 and to 1,297,000 in 1910.

Hungary's industries were young and should have been modern and social-minded, since they were not burdened with the heritage of a long tradition. Western industrial workers had achieved a human status by the time Hungarian industries began to work. We have the testimony of a shrewd Hungarian observer about the plight of the Hungarian industrial worker early this century. Samuel Gompers, for several decades head of the American Federation of Labor, studied labor conditions in Europe in 1909, visited Hungary, and wrote a book about his observations.[42]

"In few civilized countries," he wrote, "are the trade unions weaker than in Hungary. There are only about 100,000 members." The country then had a population of about twenty million, including Croatia. He went on to point out that with at least four million who under manhood suffrage could guide the State democratically, only 800,000 had the franchise. In the trade unions not one man in twenty had the right to vote. "With regard to landed property," he was told by one of his informants, "we are in the condition of France before her revolution. With regard to child-labor, we are in the position of England prior to 1830." The Social Democratic Party, he observed, had not a single member in parliament. When the railway train of his party passed a penitentiary, a Hungarian said: "In that building are robbers, murderers and Socialists."

By way of comparison, American labor's "Grand Old Man" mentioned the fact that the New York hod-carrier earned as much a day as a hod-carrier in Hungary was paid for an entire week. In Hungary's leading industry, milling, wages ran from fifty-five to eighty-five cents a day. Unlike most of the other trades, the printing trade was 95 per cent organized, but it was not permitted to collect strike funds. The union sought to evade this injunction by collecting five dollars a year from its members for the subscription of a union newspaper, a very modest sheet, worth only a fraction of this amount. The rest of the money was set aside as an unauthorized strike fund.

"Such squalor, such composites of all things to be classed as dirt, such indiscriminate heaping together of human beings," Gompers wrote, "I have never seen elsewhere. . . . Places cost the miserable poor occupants more per square foot of space than were paid by a prosperous artisan in an American city for his home, with all its civilized accommodations." Gompers quoted an informant as saying that a million Hungarians were in America at that time and that they gave their support to the fight against reaction at home.

Let us examine now the status of Hungarian industrial workers as seen by Hungarian eyes and presented in Hungarian publications. The country lacked several essentials for a fair degree of industrialization. It had coal, but mostly of inferior grade. It did not have enough iron ore. It lacked capital, adequate domestic consumption and industrially skilled labor. Things in the Austro-Hungarian Monarchy were so arranged that certain regions of the Austrian part of the country specialized in industrial activities, while Hungary looked after agriculture. This was in line with the interests of the leading Hungarian agrarians who opposed the industrialization of the country as likely to raise wages.

The average weekly wage of the better paid industrial worker was four dollars a week. Early this century 40 per cent of the industrial establishments began work at six in the winter and five in the summer. Less than 6 per cent began their working day at 7:30. Quitting time was 6 P.M. in more than 60 per cent of the establishments, while 21 per cent closed at seven in the summer and 13 per cent in the winter.

Official inspectors noted the following conditions: "Employers have no understanding of the necessity of employee protection and the authorities themselves are not strict enough regarding violations. . . .

In certain plants there is not even a toilet. . . . Medical help is inadequate. . . . Authorities do not bother to inquire into the causes of
accidents. . . . Few employers are humane." [43]

The basic industrial employment act was passed in 1884 and it for-
bade the employment of minors under sixteen in industries injurious
to health, prohibited employers to work women at night and for four
weeks after confinement. The working day was not to begin before
5 A.M. or end after 9 P.M. Half-hour periods of rest were to be given
workers in the forenoon and afternoon. The lunch period was one
hour. Hungary followed the example of Germany by introducing
sickness and accident insurance for industrial workers. This she did
as far back as 1891.

Theoretically, unions were legal, but had to be authorized by the
government before starting to operate, and were placed under strict
regulations. Strikes were forbidden if they appeared to be in violation
of labor contracts, and unions were forbidden to accord financial aid
to strikers. Violence and intimidation in industrial disputes were pun-
ishable offenses. Those who refused to work without legal sanction
in railway labor disputes, were subject to punishment. The authorities
were invested with the right of supervising union activities, opening
their books and attending their meetings.

It is clear that the laws governing the activities of industrial workers
were less drastic than the laws relating to farm labor. Hungarian industry was not strong and the landed interests looked askance at the
industrialists. Only land ownership gave "status." The government
was in the hands of the large estates. At the same time, the regime
could not afford to liberalize industrial worker laws too much, for fear
of creating a precedent for farm labor.

How did the industrial worker live? He spent forty cents a week
on his lodging, if single, and what a lodging it was! At the Eighth
International Congress of Hygiene and Sanitation in 1896 one of the
French delegates told his Hungarian hosts that "among all the large
European cities the worst conditions prevailed in Budapest."

The Hungarian capital was one of the most beautiful cities of
Europe, if not the most beautiful. The magnificence of some of its
public buildings was unsurpassed. Some of the best-dressed people of
Europe thronged its fashionable streets. The Danube Embankment
was a dream and Margareten Island had no peer. But behind this
beautiful façade misery was rampant. In 1890 one-quarter of the population of the capital lived in cellars. More than ten per cent of the

lodgings had no kitchen, so that living quarters had to be used for cooking. More than forty per cent lived in lodgings inhabited by more than five persons per room. At the turn of the century nearly sixty per cent of Budapest flats consisted of only one room and kitchen, and even two decades later the percentage was fifty-three. Four-room flats were described in official bulletins as large. It was common practice in Budapest to let beds out for the night to the *ágyrajáró,* bed-goer.

Conditions were even worse outside of the capital. For years after the end of World War I, there were troglodytes on the outskirts of Budapest where industrial workers actually lived in caves. In the country's second largest city, Szeged, it was reported at the turn of the century that 72 per cent of the flats had only one room. In the supposedly rich city of Kecskemét, in the heart of the country, the ratio of such flats was 76 per cent, and the corresponding figures were 81 and 86 in the industrial suburbs of the capital, Ujpest and Erzsébetfalva.

A computation shows that the weekly breakfast bill of the industrial worker came to thirty-five cents, his lunch to eighty-five cents and his supper to seventy cents. These expenditures, together with his rent, almost exhausted his weekly wages. He also needed money for transportation, clothing, the payment of debts and taxes, not to speak of entertainment. How did he manage? Perhaps he did not. Perhaps he supplemented his frugal fare with foraging expeditions to rural kinsfolk, or his wife and some of his children may have worked. It was a very hard struggle. Most of the amenities of life, taken for granted by the western worker, were not available to the Hungarian. He carried on as long as he could, and when he reached the end of his rope, he tried to leave the country. If he could not scrape together the steamship fare, he just hoped for a windfall, such as extra work or the lottery.

"The President is Mister and I am Mister, too." Even today you can hear this in the Hungarian settlements of the United States. It is not just a phrase lightly uttered, but a thought deeply felt. Man craves social recognition, he wants "status." The lack of status in Hungary was not the main cause of mass emigration, but it was a factor, and an important one.

The social structure of Hungary before the First World War was highly stratified. Each group had its place and was supposed to know its place. It would not be correct to compare the Hungarian social system with the Indian caste system, usually taken as a norm of one extreme. Within certain limits, it was possible in Hungary to batter down the dividing walls between certain classes, given a strong will, great ability and more than the average measure of good luck.

But the Hungarian social system was unique in Europe. An immigrant from France, Scandinavia, or Switzerland would never think of boasting: "The President is Mister, I am Mister, too." The social structure among Hungary's neighbors was also entirely different from that of the land of the Magyars. One would expect that peoples in that corner of Europe would display similar social traits. After all, for centuries they shared a common fate and all of them are suffering from too much history. Among Hungary's next-door neighbors, the Serbians, there was very little social stratification. The Serbian farmer may have been as poor as a church mouse and yet he had an air of human dignity. He certainly was not one to scrape and bow in the presence of the city man or even his King. The Serbian's Balkan neighbors, the Bulgarians, had no aristocracy, and therefore no social stratification. The explanation for this phenomenon is not far to seek. For many centuries these people had been under the Ottoman rule and those clever but indolent masters knew that the way to keep their Balkan subjects true to them could best be achieved by exterminating their ruling classes, the potential leaders. After that, they took the best human material into their own service. Hungary's eastern neighbor, Rumania, also had far less social stratification than Hungary. It had many other drawbacks, but a strong native aristocracy was not one of them. Social stratification was stronger in the regions to the West, in Austria, the Germanic and Italian countries, but was nowhere as penetrating and enervating as in Hungary.

This seems to be inexplicable, since much of Hungary was under Ottoman Turkish rule for a century and a half, long enough to exterminate the native ruling seed. But the class system was perpetuated in the "free" region. As soon as the Turks were out, the country was again overrun by the aristocracy. In many cases it was not even native stock. The new rulers were the Habsburgs who found it convenient to impose their rule upon the Hungarians by delegating power to the aristocracy, which found it advantageous to make common cause with the House of Austria. Thus this unique social stratification came into existence, the like of which cannot be found anywhere else in Europe.

At the top of the social pyramid stood the House of Austria, the Habsburgs, of Swiss-German origin in early medieval times, German-speaking, but supposedly a-national, because of the multiplicity of nations within the Monarchy. In a world ruled by national sentiment and interests, the Habsburgs stood above nations. In the social scale they stood between man and tribal deity. Magic rites were employed in approaching them. They were addressed in the third person, as if the second person were too personal, irreverent. Petitions to them had to be drawn up in an awe-inspired tone—*alleruntertaenigst,* most submissively. They themselves never spoke in the first person, but employed the *pluralis majestatis.*

A long way behind the semi-divine ruling House stood the aristocracy. The ruling House was the sun around which the great *aulic,* court, dynasties of the aristocracy revolved. To the outsider the closed circle of the aristocrats looked like a unit. In reality the stratification within was extreme. Members knew their places, prescribed by rigid social custom. The true aristocrat would not besmirch his hands with honest work. Playing at the gambling table was considered a noble occupation and legends were told about bluebloods who lost a fortune at baccarat in a few hours without batting an eye. It was proper for the aristocrat to serve at court, in the highest level of diplomacy and certain branches of the armed services, particularly cavalry. It was all right to be a gentleman farmer, since it required no physical work. The aristocrat was forgiven if he accepted a top government position —prime ministership, for instance—although not all the titled dynasties would stoop to that.

Many of the aristocrats owed their titles to some great betrayal. They earned large estates and rank from the Habsburg rulers by making common cause against the common people and the few aristocrats of exalted blood who stood behind the masses. When the Hungarian people rose against their Habsburg oppressors in 1848, only a few magnates joined their hosts. Most of the aristocrats rallied to the House of Austria. Hungarian history tells us that some of the aristocracy showed the invading Russian forces the way into the plains across the Carpathian passes. These were known as *oroszvezetők,* Russian guides.

There were numerous admirable exceptions who were public spirited, patrons of the arts and literature. Some of the world's best music was brought into existence with the help of music-loving Hungarian magnates. One of the top aristocrats of Hungary, Count Mihály Károlyi, was the leader of the democratic opposition before and after the First World War. In this work he was inspired by his wife, née

Countess Catherine Andrássy, member of a family which claimed descent from one of the followers of Árpád the Conqueror.

It is the way of all flesh that social classes should come and go and it was true of the Hungarian aristocracy, but only to a limited extent. With the new age came new problems; fortunes lost at baccarat could not always be recouped. Some of the aristocrats had to stoop to accepting "front" positions as directors of the large banks. But, taken by and large, the Hungarian aristocracy was a hardy perennial.

It was followed in the social hierarchy by the so-called "gentry," a word of English origin, which has become acclimatized in Hungary. These were mostly members of the lower nobility and similar social classes, who filled the higher offices of State and county, as *főispán* and *alispán,* chief county stewart and assistant county stewart, and *szolgabiró,* servants' judge—the mighty district official. In many cases they could be recognized by the "y" at the end of their names, corresponding to the French *de* and the German *von.* Győry János, for instance, meant John from the town of Győr.

The system of transportation in Hungary was poor and therefore the power of the local officials was great. As members of the local bureaucracy the gentry wielded very great power. Nominally, they were public servants, in reality they were public masters. In their presence the poor peasant trembled. Neither the peasant nor the gentry was conscious of the fact that the gentry were able to live so well because of the peasant's tax money. This is what an investigator, Gyula Rubinek, said about the rural social system at the turn of the century: "The population of the great plains consists of government employees, rich peasants and agrarian proletariat. These three groups live in isolation, hating one another. The government employees consider the rural districts as colonies and their jobs as colonial service."

Not all officials were "enemies of the people." Some were public spirited, hard working, intelligent, with broad horizons and a deep interest in the welfare of the people under their rule. This was all the more admirable because the bureaucratic "climate" was so different. Sometimes they succeeded in their constructive work.

The professions, especially in more recent times, ranked high in the social scale. There was one fairly democratic feature of this undemocratic system. You could acquire a minor status by obtaining a doctor's title from a university. That is why so many people who wanted nothing to do with philosophy or law obtained the titles of Ph.D. and *Doctor Juris.* Then you became a *Doktor úr,* "Doctor Mr." You had a title and you had a status, too. If you went into banking and had more money than a dozen aristocrats put together, you still did not have status, and so rich bankers and industrialists were in the habit of buying titles such as "Government Councilor" or "Court Councilor," which entitled you to be called *Méltóságos úr,* High Honor Mr., or *Kegyelmes úr,* Excellency Mr. The secondary school teacher became a Teacher Mr.; the bank clerk, Director Mr.; the real director, General Director Mr.; and the reporter, Editor Mr.

The industrial worker represented the new era. He became a member of the Socialist Party, if he was conscious of his special status, and he called his fellow worker not Proletarian Mr. but *elvtárs.* It is an unusual word, literally translated "principle-companion," companions bound together by the common principles of socialism. The Socialists in those days were considered traitors by the ruling classes, a member of which called them *"hazátlan bitangok,"* scoundrels without a fatherland—in open parliament. The Socialists liked the designation so much that they appropriated it as a badge of honor, somewhat as the early Christians appropriated the cross.

And what about the peasants? The rich peasants—and their number was not large—were tolerated, while the poor peasants were the pariahs, outcasts. They could be knocked about, addressed by their first names and with the contemptuous "thou," *te.*

The peasant's status can, perhaps, be best illustrated by two personal experiences, such as anybody could have. It was a good many years after the First World War. Friends took me on a trip in their car on a summer afternoon. A hay wagon drew closer to us from the opposite direction. Evidently, the driver had dozed off in the hot sun, as the team of horses veered somewhat too close to us. Our driver sounded his horn and the man woke up with a start. We gave him a "dirty look," such as you would on an American highway to a careless driver. But this man's reaction was entirely unexpected. Instead of going on his way or reciprocating our annoyance, he opened his eyes in deep horror, suddenly swung away his body, and ducked with his head, as if he had expected the sting of a whip across his face. The same atavistic fear was shown when we pulled up at a farm house for a drink of water. In front of the house stood a small child who broke into a wild cry and fled, as if pursued by devils. That was the children's usual reaction to the stopping of our car; "gentlemen" evidently were associated with blows in their minds. That fear must have been inbred for many, many years.

The peasants liked to keep as far from the gentlemen as they could. But contact with a *nadrágos ember,* the man in trousers (the peasant in the fields wore flapping wide pants of white linen) was almost inevitable in the armed services, which many peasants abhorred. If accepted for infantry service, the peasant had to serve for three years. In most of the regiments, the language of command was German, which the Hungarian peasant did not understand. He therefore appeared as a dolt. As a common soldier he was often treated as a slave. He was subject to humiliating punishments, such as the *kikötés,* being tied to a tree while standing on his toes, and even whipping, though these were not legal penalties. But not many officers cared about such trifles in connection with the peasant. Many young Hungarians sneaked across the frontiers of their country for fear of being forced to serve *Ferenc Jóska,* Francis Joey—the Emperor-King.

Politically, the "lower breeds" were without the law. Hungary had a parliament and a constitutional document, the Golden Bull, which patriotic Hungarian historians like to compare with the Magna Charta, never failing to point out that it was only a few years younger than that famous British document. Hungary's pride in her parliament was demonstrated by the magnificent Gothic legislative building on the Danube Embankment. True, it served a purpose. It enabled the opposition to sound its grievances and there was always a handful of men who stood up for the oppressed. They could accomplish little against the steam-roller of the government, but the country heard their voice, and sometimes the government was shamed into action.

We have seen that a peasant country like Hungary had no peasant Party, except an embryonic one, before the First World War. In all Hungary, only 6.5 per cent of the population had voting rights in 1914, as against 28 per cent in neighboring Austria. Ninety-eight per cent of the industrial workers had no vote. When the Socialists called out the masses in a demonstration for suffrage before the war, the government called out the army and blood flowed in the streets of the capital. The rotten borough system flourished. In certain rural districts sometimes one hundred to two hundred voters elected a parliamentary deputy, against ten thousand in Budapest. The eighty thousand electors of Budapest elected nine deputies, whereas the ninety thousand electors of Transylvania elected seventy-four. Transylvania was, of course, a close corporation. The voting was very often rigged. The opposition candidate was prevented from speaking. Opposition voters could not get to the distant polls, while government voters were transported there

in style. Undesirable voters' names were left out of the election regis-
ters. The gendarmes surrounded the polling booths and the voting
was open. If all these measures had failed to achieve their aim, the
booths were destroyed by "irresponsible elements," who were never
found. This was the political and social system hundreds of thousands
of Hungarians left behind them.

In an Upper Hungarian county, the governmental candidate for
parliament ran into language trouble, according to a story often heard
in Hungary. He was a Hungarian and his constituents were Slovaks.
They did not understand Hungarian and he did not speak Slovak. It
was an embarrassing situation but he remembered that emigration
from that district was great and that many of the inhabitants were
ex-Americans. He addressed his constituents in a language he spoke
and they understood—English—and naturally was elected.

There are only two flaws in this story. If the constituents had been
Slovaks they would have never been constituents, and if the candidate
belonged to the government party he would have been elected even if
he had been deaf and dumb. And this leads us right into the heart of
the nationality problem before the First World War. It is of special
significance, since a large part of those who came from Hungary belonged to the nationalities.

Hungary was a multi-national State with a uni-national system of
government. She had a population of 18,265,000 in 1910, with the exception of Croatia, which had a special status. Hungarians formed only
a bare majority of the population, according to the official Hungarian
census which probably did not err in favor of the minorities. In order
to distinguish Hungarian citizens from the "racial" Hungarians, some
students described the latter as "Magyars" and the former as "Hungarians."

If we accept the official census, the "Magyars" formed about 54 per
cent of the total population, while the rest was composed of the
"minorities" or "nationalities." Largest of these groups was that of
the Rumanians, inhabitants of large parts of the eastern marches of
the Kingdom, called the Land Beyond the Woods, Transylvania, a
lovely but not too fertile country of hills and dales, meadows and
woods, a region of great contrasts where primitive cattle-raisers lived
next to highly civilized cities. This section was a veritable checker-
board of nationalities, the obvious reason being the rugged nature of
the terrain which offered sanctuary to persecuted minorities. Accord-

ing to the Hungarian census, which the Rumanians did not accept as accurate, the Rumanians formed 16 per cent of the total population of Hungary.

Next in size were the Slovak and German groups, each about ten per cent of the total population. The Slovaks lived in the Northwest and North-Central Highlands, the Carpathian ranges and their foot-hills, a lovely and picturesque country, scented with pine and fur, en-wrapped in the seeming peace of a backward region. The Slovaks were called *tótok*—plural of *tót*—of whom the Hungarian proverb said: *A tót nem ember,* the Slovak is not a man—possibly because the Hun-garians (that is to say, the Hungarian ruling class) oppressed the Slovaks.

Scattered in the mountains were lovely old towns inhabited by Hun-garians and Germans, known hereabouts as Saxons and Swabians. The architecture of these towns was mainly German; some of them looked like Saxon and Swabian towns in Germany. Germans lived also in Transylvania, inhabiting storybook towns, very clean, very quiet, with gabled houses, having the substantial air of the *Buerger.* Legend had it that the German-speaking people of Transylvania were descendants of children lured away from their homes by the Pied Piper of Hamelin who took them into Koppelberg and so through a subterranean pas-sage across half of Europe into that distant eastern land. History told another story, of power politics and divide and rule, of kings and emperors employing these Germans to further their political aims by weakening the local people and to serve as frontier guards for their royal or imperial interests.

Considerably further down the list of nationalities were the Ukrain-ians and Serbians, two Slavic peoples. The former inhabited the north-eastern hill country, adjacent to the great land settlement of the Ukrainians, with whom they would have formed one group if they had not been broken up by Hungarians, Austrians and Russians. Their region was very beautiful and very poor. They were the prole-tarians among the proletarians, ignorant—because nobody looked after their education.

The other end of the country, in part of the South, was inhabited by Serbians and kindred South Slavic groups. It was a rich farm country, part of the Middle Danubian black soil belt. Their settle-ments were adjacent to that of Serbia which they joined after the First World War.

A few data will help us grasp the meaning of minority status in

Hungary. United States Census figures of 1910 in regard to illiteracy provide enlightening information. They show that while illiteracy among the Hungarian immigrants amounted to 11.4 per cent of the total, it amounted to 22.1 per cent among the Slovaks, 34.7 among the Rumanians, 36.4 among the Croats, 41.8 among the Serbians and 51 per cent among the Ruthenians. Schools were inadequate in number and inacceptable to the minorities, since they endeavored to denationalize the nationalities, especially during the years preceding the First World War, when the authorities sought to improve the loyalty of the peripheral people with an eye on the possibility of military needs.

Although the minorities were close to having a majority—and may have had one if the figures had not been "doctored"—fully 94 per cent of the State officials and 92 per cent of the city officials were "Magyars." The minorities occupied subordinate positions in the bureaucracy. We have seen how the common people were treated at the polls if they were racial Hungarian peasants. The minorities were given even worse treatment. If nothing else worked, the government set up a candidate at the last minute—sometimes the morning of election day —with the same name as the nationality candidate. The voters were confused and their votes were split. The candidate of the government was declared elected. Altogether only two to three per cent of the nationality population were qualified voters.

No wonder that the proportion of most of the nationalities' emigrants was higher than their proportion in the total population. There were two exceptions: the Rumanians and the Serbians, the former because they were too poor and the latter because they were not. The Rumanian peasant lived below the "emigration level," on which the prospective expatriate has the means to leave his country. The Serbians, as we have just seen, lived on some of the best parts of the land. Just the same, the proportion of the Serbians in the total population and the proportion of their emigrants among all emigrants from Hungary were not very far apart—5.5 per cent in the former case and 5.4 per cent in the latter, according to official Hungarian 1911-1912 figures. On the other hand, almost twice as many Slovaks left Hungary as their proportion in the total. About 5 per cent of the Slovak population of Hungary was in America on the eve of the First World War.

X

RIDING THE HIGH TIDE

THE "OLD" IMMIGRATION into the United States gave way to the "new" in the early 'eighties. Western Europe provided 95 per cent of the immigrants before that dividing line. By 1907 Eastern and Southern Europe provided 81 per cent of the immigrants. In the United States the "open door policy" of immigration prevailed, but for a few restrictions designed to protect the immigrants themselves from exploiters and to protect the American community from undesirable elements.

It should be a simple matter to say how many Hungarian immigrants came to the United States, but it is not, for several reasons. One is national policy and the other is international politics. It was the national policy of Hungary not to consider emigration that was not strictly legal, which means that Hungarian pre-First World War emigration figures understate the case up to fifty per cent. The United States immigration figures should be far more reliable but even there there is a hitch. Between 1899 and 1904 the figures are shown for the entire Austro-Hungarian Monarchy, and not for Hungary alone, possibly because of diplomatic reasons. A third set of figures are those of the European ports of embarkation, but those, in several cases, lump all America-bound emigrants together.

It is fairly safe to say that between 1,600,000 and 1,700,000 came to the United States from pre-war Hungary, including not only the "Magyars" but the national minorities. They were Hungarian citizens when they left their country and they entered the United States as such. Here, however, many divorced themselves from their "official" native land and became Slovaks, Serbians, Croats, etc. This explains the discrepancy between the immigration figures and Americans of Hungarian origin.

Our estimate is based mostly upon the official American figures, even though in some measure they may contain underestimates. There must have been quite a few national minorities that stated as their nationalities the countries they preferred and not the official country of their origin. They said they were Rumanians or Serbians, instead of saying they were Hungarians of Rumanian or Serbian nationality. Most of the immigration inspectors may not have known the difference, especially since the majority of the immigrants came from obscure places that may not have appeared on the maps at all. For the five years during which American figures for Hungary are lacking we have taken the data of the European ports. Adding them to the United States Census figures we arrive at a grand total of immigrants from Hungary between 1871 and 1913 amounting to 1,893,647, after making the necessary allowances for duplications and emigrants bound for other ports.

The emigration from Hungary was slow in getting started. The need of the peasant was not less than at the tide time, but he was so poor that he could not think of paying his fare, and the climate for the mass population transfer had not yet been created. The United States had not yet become the highly mechanized industrial nation it was to become a short time later.

The United States immigration statistics begin with three lone Hungarian immigrants in 1871. Three years later the figure rose to 1,347, but dropped down again to three-figure numbers until 1880, when with 4,363 immigrants, the rush began. If we were to represent immigration to the United States with a graph, we would now be in the foothills rising gradually in the next two years, reaching 11,240 in 1883, then 14,798 in the following year. From this high plateau we would drop down into a valley, with 9,383 in 1885, the last year short of five figures before the war. The foothills continued, with occasional rapid ups and downs, fluctuating between 10,000 and 37,000 a year, until the last year of the nineteenth century. Then the figures shot upward precipitately, with 54,767 in 1900 and rising tremendously and irrepressibly. The peak was reached in 1907, an all-time Hungarian immigration peak, with 193,460, about one per cent of the total population in one single year—a tremendous loss of blood for the country.

This was the time when official and semi-official Hungary began to notice that something was going on. "It is a sad fact," the Hungarian Chamber of Industry lamented, "that the population of our country has been decreasing at an alarming rate during the last few years. . . . Because of this huge emigration not only are we unable to develop our industries but even our existing plants are faced with the possibility of having to shut down."

From that high peak the mountain dropped down to a high plateau

between 1908 and 1912—its height ranging from 76,928 to 122,944—and
then there was another rise to 117,580 in 1913—moderate, but still far
higher than the nineteenth century foothills.

Official Hungary still did not grasp the meaning of this phenomenon. "It is hard to understand," it complained, "why workers leave this
country, since here they live under good conditions." True, conditions
in Hungary did improve somewhat, partly because of the comparatively vast emigration, which reduced the labor supply and increased
wages. But once the avalanche got started, it was hard to contain it.
Official Hungary comforted itself: "The measure of emigration does
not depend on us, but on the power of attraction of American industry."

A comparison of immigration from Hungary with immigration
from other countries is instructive. Hungarian immigration figures
fluctuated more violently than the total, for one thing. During the
fifteen year period beginning with 1890 the ratio of Hungarian immigration to the total increased from five to about sixteen per cent. In
1907 the number of immigrants to the United States amounted to
1,285,439, of whom, as we have seen, 193,460 came from Hungary.

Once the apathy of the population was broken down, and emigration acquired a momentum, the peaks and plateaus were established
by economic conditions in the United States. The National Bureau for
Economic Research undertook in a study to compare immigration
with economic conditions, which found that the immigration of men
coincided with the ups and down of the production of iron, probably
the most reliable thermometer of the economic climate of the United
States. The peaks of Hungarian immigration into the United States,
1892, 1896, 1903 and 1907[44] coincided with upswings in American
economic life. The rapid descents of the economic life of the United
States were followed by rapid descents in immigration figures. It made
little difference that some of these years were comparatively prosperous
in Hungary.

If immigration depends so much upon economic conditions in the
United States, the distribution of age groups, sexes and occupations
are also largely predetermined. The earlier Hungarian immigrants
came to a country in which—from the point of view of their home
settings—they were pioneers. Even though the United States was far
above their own native land in civilization, to them the change meant
a new and hazardous life. Therefore, fully 87 per cent of the immigrants belonged in the age group of fourteen to forty-four, the sturdiest

and most venturesome. The young and old shied away from the un-known dangers of the New World. People under fourteen and over forty-four formed only 13 per cent of the total. The relative proportion of the age groups changed after 1910. Then the United States was no longer the forbidding land in which danger lurked around every cor-ner, even though poor people earned enough money to eat meat. More younger and older people ventured to come into the United States. The middle-age group was now only 76 per cent of the total.

In the proportion of the two sexes we can also follow a significant change. In the earlier days of Hungarian immigration, the United States was a "he-man" country. Many Hungarian immigrants con-sidered themselves transients, bent on making enough money to return home and buy that piece of land which had been the object of their dreams. In the years around the turn of the century more than seventy-three per cent of all Hungarian immigrants were male—three-quarters of the total, while the females represented only one-quarter. The situa-tion on the eve of the First World War was entirely different. Then the male immigrants formed only 56.7 per cent of the total, while the women represented 43.3 per cent. These are the official United States figures. The Hungarian official figures show a predominance of women: 53.6 per cent, against 46.4 per cent of men. These Hungarian figures are, obviously, not reliable. Clearly, more women were shown because they came as "legal" emigrants, whereas many of the males were "bootlegged" out of the country, so as not to be caught in the military net if they were of draft age, as many of them were.

The occupational statistics of the Hungarian immigrants are instruc-tive. In the period just preceding World War I, 67 per cent of the total were farmers, 12.5 per cent were unskilled workers of all kinds, 12.4 per cent were miners and factory hands, 5.5 per cent domestic servants, and the remainer belonged to "miscellaneous occupations." The size of the professional group was microscopic. At the turn of the century their number had amounted to less than a score in a year. It increased very slowly, amounting to one-half of one per cent just before World War I.

What was the economic status of the immigrants? If they had not been poor, they would not have left their country. But if they had been very poor, they could not have left. In later years Hungarian statistics contained information as to the amount of money the emi-grant had in his pockets when leaving via the officially accredited port of Fiume. These were the people who could afford the higher fares

the Hungarian government made them pay at that port, and therefore
it may be assumed they were better off than the "bootlegged" emigrants. Even so, the official figures showed that they possessed an average of twenty dollars. Of course, one cannot be quite sure about that
either. The peasant—emigrant or not—was suspicious of the government, with some reasons; he may not have told the whole truth.

Once the Hungarian immigrant left home he underwent a remarkable sea change. At home he had been a peasant, hopelessly in love
with the soil which refused to yield herself to him. He was a peasant
not merely as an occupation but also as a profession of faith. He was
a Catholic or Protestant, but in his heart of hearts he was a nature-
worshiper, faithful to only one soil, his own, that of his own village,
his own very limited horizon. But when he reached America he never
thought of going to work on a farm. He, the thoroughbred peasant,
turned his back on the soil and turned toward the mine and the blast
furnace. He did this possibly because he remained true to his own soil.
In the mine and in the shop he would make money quickly. According to our city standards of today, his wages were small, but looking
at them from his own point of view, they grow to gigantic proportions. Then he would return home with his vast treasure of hundreds,
perhaps even thousands of dollars, and there he would show his love for
the only soil he knew. Moreover, as Géza Hoffman has shown: "The
former peasant, who had never left his hamlet at home, would wander
tirelessly from city to city. Formerly tied down to the soil, he would
become a migratory factory worker. This would take place without
any transition. In America he would become his own antithesis." [45]

What did the ex-peasants find in the United States? A former resident of County Komárom wrote home: "Here a man is paid for his
labors, and I am certainly not sorry that I am here. I work from six
in the morning until seven at night and get $10-11 a week. Just now
it's hot. When it gets cooler I'll make more money, perhaps double,
and then I'll work only eleven hours. There are 10,000 workers in this
shop and my wife is working here too. She makes $9.50 a week. At
home I made that much money in a whole month and people thought
my job was very good. Here I am sewing dresses on a machine. In
America there is no difference between one man and another. If
you're a millionaire you are called a Mister just the same, and your
wife is Missis." [46] Here is another testimony, contained in an interview: "In Hungary I had a wife, two children, house, six acres of land,
two horses, a cow, two pigs and a few poultry. That was my fortune.

This same land that afforded existence to my father and grandfather could not support us any longer. Taxes and cost of living in the last few years have advanced so greatly that the expenses could not be covered from what a small farm can yield. Things became worse, an early spring storm killed my crops, and I had to buy bread for money. My horses were killed from disease. I had to sell my cow to buy winter clothes for the family. There was no money to work the land and without horses and work the land will not produce. I had to mortgage my home. . . . As a farm laborer in Hungary, one can earn only enough for bread and water. How is one to pay taxes and living expenses? There was but one hope, America . . . We will never go back to Hungary. It only deprived us of our home and land, while in America the soil covers our child. We have a home, money, and business, everything acquired in America. We lost everything in Hungary. We love Hungary as our native land, but never wish to live in it again."

The Hungarian immigrants settled in the neighborhood of mines and steel furnaces. They settled everywhere the industrial molochs needed unskilled workers, ready to perform the least desirable types of chores. The hardest industrial job was easy in comparison with peasants' work; the working day was short, not more than ten to twelve hours a day. Most of the Hungarians settled in four States: Ohio, New York, New Jersey and Pennsylvania. Large groups settled also in Illinois, Indiana and West Virginia. New York City became the "third largest 'Hungarian' city in the world," with a population of 76,575 in 1920. Relatively, Cleveland's population was larger— 42,134 in that year, while the Hungarian populations of Chicago and Detroit were fewer than twenty thousand each.

We can judge their success by the size of their remittances to the Old Country. At the height of the immigration they sent home sometimes as much as one hundred to two hundred million kronen a year. It is estimated that the highest annual remittance was a quarter of a billion kronen—the equivalent of $50,000,000. It is recorded that an illiterate immigrant from the village of Endrőd in County Békés sent home 2,770 kronen between 1904 and 1906. A Hungary-wide investigation at the turn of the century [47] brought to light the fact that in County Torontál, where the authorities co-operated closely with the investigators, the immigrants had sent home eight and a half million kronen. The proposed disposition of this sum was significant. Two million was to buy land, an equal amount for savings and kin, and the rest to pay off mortgages. Taking the country as a whole, most of the money was for land purchases, mortgage payments and savings. Clearly, many of them planned to return to Hungary.

The desire to return to the native land was probably much stronger than the ability to do so. How many of the immigrants did return is hard to say, since even though these figures were computed, they were not reliable. The figures show that one-fourth of the immigrants returned to Hungary in the fifteen years up to 1914. Most of these ex-Americans were racial Hungarians—Magyars—and not members of the minorities who could not consider Hungary their own, especially after they had seen America. Between 1908 and 1914 the number of Magyar re-emigrants from the United States to Hungary ranged between ten thousand and thirty thousand annually. The grand total of all returning Hungarians between 1908 and 1924 amounted to 149,-906. Among the Slovaks the ratio of re-emigration was higher than among the Magyars, probably because, as Pinter explains, they were more typically birds of passage. The *drótostot* of my childhood may have been a typical example. The ratio of the re-emigrants to total immigrants in the other nationality groups from Hungary was much lower.

Many of these ex-peasants dreamed of their native land; they would go home, their pockets lined with money, and would "show them." Some went a long step further, and dreamed of a new and better Hungary. That is why so many of them gave such a warm welcome to one of the leaders of the Hungarian democratic opposition, Count Mihály Károlyi when he and some of his followers visited the United States shortly before World War I.

The Hungarians, always a musical race, often expressed their nostalgia in songs. In the coal patches of Pennsylvania the Hungarian immigrant sang:

> *Könnyeinket szénpor issza,*
> *Kacagásunk füstbe fúl,*
> *Kis falunkba vágyunk vissza*
> *Ahol minden fűszál értett magyarul.*

> (The coal powder absorbs our tears,
> Our laughter is drowned in smoke,
> We yearn to return to our little village
> Where every blade of grass understood Hungarian.)

Others were more defiant:

> Ha majd üt az óra,
> Akkor virradóra
> Felkapsz csodaszárnyon
> Repülő hajóra,
> Haza mégy és nem türsz
> Semmi cudarságot,
> Teremtesz magadnak
> Uj Magyarországot.

> (When the clock strikes
> And the dawn breaks
> You take to magic wings
> On flying boats
> Home you return and won't put up
> With any base deals.
> You will create for youself
> A new Hungary.)

Some did return home. Sometimes they bought a house and land but sometimes land was not available, because the region was entailed. Land prices rose very high as a result of the greater demand and speculators took advantage of the windfall. Equipment was expensive and very often the new owner lacked the "know-how" of management. The authorities may not have been helpful, the banks may have charged high interest on loans or attempted to squeeze out the ex-American. Some sold their lands and returned to the United States, never to try again. Others lost their money and reverted to their former status as landlack peasants, rebellious at first, remembering that in America "The President is Mister and I am Mister, too," and then no longer rebellious.

Others never returned to their homeland. The children were American-born and they did not even think of leaving the land of their birth. American habits became ingrained in the immigrants. They acquired American citizenship and gradually lost touch with their native country. They entered the vast American stream of life.

Emigrants were mainly peasants, therefore insignificant. Did they come or did they go? What difference did it make? But large masses of insignificant people added up to a large number of potential soldiers and large sums of taxes. Without soldiers there was no authority and

without taxes the soldiers could not be armed. Bayonets were needed
to sustain the prevailing way of life.

One day, the ruling class awoke to the reality of the situation, and
could not believe its eyes. To many of its members the poor peasant
was not a human being, and not even a beast of burden. The poor
peasant was merely vegetable. Imagine a vegetable pulling itself up
by its roots and simply walking away!

The Hungarian countryside became depopulated. Entire villages
were emptied, inhabited only by the very young and very old, who
were awaiting the steamship fare from America. People in Budapest
began to talk about "race suicide." What was going to happen to the
Hungarian nation if all the working people were to leave the country?
So an investigation was started, with the proper "frame of reference,"
conducted by the right people. They found that emigration was the
work of propagandists and demagogues. Obviously, only people of
that type would have the heart to induce wretched peasants to leave a
country like Hungary which, as everybody knew, was the "bouquet on
the hat of God."

Throughout much of this period, the Hungarian government displayed much hesitation in dealing with this subject. It did not quite
want to come to grips with it. Behind this hesitation was the uncertainty of the ruling classes. They did not want to or could not pay a
living wage to many peasants. It might be a good idea to let them
leave the country, rather than let them rot at home. People who
would leave the earthly paradise known as Hungary were no good
anyway, some argued, so let them go. If they were retained at home
they would develop into troublemakers and, who knows, even Socialists? On the other hand, the latifundia needed a large "labor reser-
voir" to be able to dominate the labor market.

Yet, the remittances of the emigrants were a boon, which played a
highly important rôle in the nation's balance of payments. Without it,
the country would have been completely bankrupt. The authorities
decided to do the usual things. One was to take no notice of what
was going on. The official Hungarian Statistical Office, for instance,
did not publish the amount of the emigrants' remittances among its
national balance of payments items in the belief that if it omitted
those figures the peasants would not know how well the emigrants
were doing in the United States and would not want to leave their
native land. The assumption was, of course, that the peasants read the

official publications of the Statistical Office, containing pages after pages of figures.

What the peasants did was to read the scribble of *János sógor,* brother-in-law John, or *Miska bácsi,* Uncle Michael, and the money orders, which transmitted the most incendiary information.

Sometimes the government decided that emigration was a cancer and then decided to treat it with a skin salve. Such a treatment was the first immigration law, passed in 1881. The law provided that emigrants would be permitted to leave Hungary only on authorized shipping lines. For nearly a quarter of a century no line was authorized to accept Hungarian emigrants. No authorization, no emigration. The royal Hungarian transportation authorities in 1887 issued an order forbidding railway personnel to sell tickets to foreign destinations if illegal immigration was suspected. Since there were no passport requirements in those years, the ticket was bought by somebody else or the prospective emigrant sneaked across the frontier. In spite of these measures, emigration began to assume larger proportions and then the ubiquitous gendarmes "arrested and tortured emigrants, sometimes confiscating their property." [48]

When these measures failed to stop the flow the Hungarian government decided to control it. It passed a law in 1903, by which emigrant transportation companies had to provide themselves with licenses issued by the Ministry of the Interior. The licensee was enjoined from encouraging emigration by the spoken or written word, and in order to ensure compliance with this he had to deposit a guarantee of one hundred thousand kronen. His license could be forfeited if he failed to live up to the provisions of the law. Emigration was forbidden to those who lacked a certain sum, or obtained it partly or wholly from private individuals, colonization societies or foreign governments.

In the following year, 1904, the Hungarian government signed an agreement with the Cunard Line, having its headquarters in Liverpool, in accordance with which that line was to introduce fortnightly sailings from Fiume to New York under the name of the Cunard Hungarian American Line. That line received the monopoly on transporting Hungarian emigrants to America. In exchange for this privilege it undertook to abide by the Hungarian emigration laws, accepted only Hungarian official documents and placed its agents only at posts prescribed by the government in Budapest. Cunard conducted this business in conjunction with the Hungarian Tourist Travel Bureau and the "Adria" Hungarian Royal Maritime Navigation Company.

This arrangement did not work for two reasons: it was enough for prospective emigrants to know that their government approved Cunard to turn their back on it, and the other companies, left supposedly in the cold, decided to fight Cunard by cutting their rates to the very bone. Some of them offered steerage to emigrants to North American ports at the ridiculously low rate of 40 kronen ($8) in 1908 and 1909. Besides, Cunard could not take all the emigrants—only forty thousand a year—and had to turn over the rest to German, French, Belgian and Dutch lines. These legal emigrants were then shipped to North European ports where they sailed with the "illegals" who paid only one-fourth of the fare.[49] Not more than one-third and sometimes as little as one-fifth of the Hungarian emigration for America left via Fiume.

A new emigration law was passed in 1909, supplemented by a new steamship agreement the following year. The Hungarian government granted a concession to the North Atlantic Conference, which comprised also German, French, Dutch and Belgian lines. In 1911 it took over the offices of the "Adria" on the frontiers. The Hungarian emigration laws, generally, were liberalized. Normally, people could leave the country, unless they were of military age, in which case they had to deposit a bond they forfeited if they failed to return home to perform their military service. Persons against whom criminal information had been handed down, who were subject to jail or fine, were not permitted to emigrate. Men charged with crimes often eluded the Hungarian authorities and escaped to the United States. These cases usually aroused tremendous interest in Hungary, giving an entirely distorted opinion of emigrants. There was a time when many people in Budapest believed that embezzlers formed the highest percentage of emigrants bound for America, which was not true, of course. Persons not eligible for emigration were not to be encouraged to leave the country. Licensed inspectors were to supervise ports of emigration, shelters, boats and the treatment of passengers. The government earmarked a special fund for emigration control and the repatriation of indigents. The law was to be carried out by emigration commissioners. "With the aid of administrative and police measures," a new emigrant commissioner announced, "the emigrant problem may be solved."

We cannot close this chapter without saying a word about the ticket agents in Eastern Europe. America was so short of hands in those days that desperate measures were applied to induce Europe's poor people to come to the United States. Large industries scoured the

Old World in search of laborers; the mines were on the lookout for industrial "human fodder." Most persistent were the steamship companies in ferreting out prospective passengers, persuading them to come to the United States, return to their homeland, come back again and so forth.

It was easy to make the agents appear responsible for emigration. In reality, they were the products and not the causes of a mass movement. They could not induce people to come who lacked the means, the will or the ambition. Their influence may have been greater in the case of returning ex-Americans. Their activities were sufficiently widespread to call for various investigations. President Theodore Roosevelt set up a commission early in this century to investigate the practices of the ticket agents. The Commission was shown letters written to Hungarians by agents instructing them about ways and means of leaving the country without governmental consent, and indicating routes to be followed in order to avoid control stations. In Galicia alone—part of Austria—thousands of agents were reported to be active for only two of the leading steamship companies. An inspector of the Federal Bureau of Immigration, W. W. Husband, maintained that some fifty thousand emigrants left Hungary in 1913 in response to the propaganda of the ticket agents. In Russia, Austria-Hungary, and to a lesser extent in the Balkan States, he said, the business of conducting groups of illegal emigrants had reached "enormous proportions," and scores of thousands crossed the frontiers of their countries annually.

Unauthorized agents were convicted, imprisoned and fined, but their work was lucrative and business went on as usual. An irrepressible urge impelled the masses to try their luck in the New World.

XI

Öreg Amerikás

John Szabó is an *öreg amerikás,* "old American," washed ashore with the great tidal wave of immigration on the eve of World War I. His name in Hungary was *Szabó János,* John Tailor.

János was a strong, hard-working lad, and intelligent too, a farm hand on a *tanya,* farm, of Baranya County. While his intelligence was not in great demand, his strong hands were. No matter how hard he worked, however, he could never earn more than a bare living. He was like one of those acrobatic dancers who appear to be marching ahead while remaining always on the same spot.

Of course, his life was not entirely bare, because his was the sun that tanned his skin and the smell of the soil which he loved with a deep and abiding love. He loved the wheatfields but not in the romantic and conscious way of city people who foolishly rave about the red poppies and cornflowers which the born peasant, János, loathed with all his heart, because they destroyed the wheat. János loved the wheat fields with the affection that only a peasant can feel toward the soil, the object of the eternally unrequited love, the heartless mistress that always gives herself to the highest bidder and never to an honest János.

János never even dreamed of buying a piece of land, because he was a sensible lad and even his dreams were sensible. Only the rich had a right to have such dreams, because dreams about land belonged to people with money, and he never saw real money, only pennies, *kraj-cár.* That is why the peasants were so sad and gay; very, very sad and very, very gay. Sad because it was all so hopeless and gay because it was all so hopeless; sad because life preyed on their minds and gay because great sadness turns into wild gaiety. *Sose halunk meg!* We'll never die! The peasants were gay, at baptismal and wedding feasts, and at funeral feasts, since it was a happy occasion to be born and to get married, and it was the happiest occasion of all to bury somebody, because there was one mouth less to feed and, who knows, you were happier in heaven. At such feasts the peasants drank and ate, singing and dancing; they lost their heads completely.

János was poor but not unhappy. When you are very poor, you do not care. Those who care, have something to lose, and they can be really unhappy because they are afraid. But you are not afraid of falling out of the window if you are on the ground floor. But somewhere in the back of János' mind, "under the threshold of consciousness," as some city people would say, he carried some disturbing notions which did not crystallize into articulate thoughts. Even though they were·no more than nebulous thoughts, they were strong as devils, and their heavy pitchforks cut into his living flesh.

To go away—that was the song of the devils. But where? Here he was at home, had his friends, the larks and dogs, the healthy cackle of the geese and the familiar shape of the well. The smell of the earth was his friend, too, and so was the dung. Elsewhere in Hungary there would be another Baron, no better than his own—because he knew that they never came better—and there would also be the gendarmes —worse than the local variety, because they are always worse, with their own pitchforks—sharp bayonets. Elsewhere in Hungary he would be a foreigner, and his friends, the local geese and the local dung, would be far away.

Then the tornado struck that part of Baranya County, leaving a swath of destruction in its wake. Worse than the tornado, was a swarm of locusts, which transformed the countryside into a desert. Entire villages were abandoned as the peasants beat a path to the nearest port.

Ferenc Bácsi, Uncle Francis, reached West Virginia, and wrote to the home folks about his glorious life in the guts of the earth. His glory was so great that he would be able to buy all of the county and the Baron would doff his hat to him. Uncle Francis was alone, and besides he wanted to show off to somebody. Also he had a good heart. So he found the usurer who lent him money to pay for János' steerage fare. He had to pay only twenty per cent for that hundred dollars, and he would have fully two years to pay it back.

Szabó János took the boat at Fiume, and on board ship he became John Szabó. After his arrival in the New World, he went directly to *Ferenc Bácsi,* known to his neighbors as Frank. The magnificent mansion turned out to be a hovel in a dismal coal-patch of the Scott's Run section of the West Virginia coal fields. He paid twenty dollars for the hovel—an exorbitant rent for that place. But John did not see its dismal misery. It had an electric light bulb. This was miraculous America.

John, a passionate lover of the land, never for a moment thought of

settling on it. He became a miner, working underground for long
hours which did not appear too long to him. Hours are long under
the sun, where the slow motion of time can be gauged by the increasing
shadows of the hayricks. Hours are not long in the mines, where there
is no sun and the shadows are the work of the flickering wicks. Hours
are not long when they add coins to one's small treasure, and when
each coin means a piece of black soil, not in America, but back home
in Hungary, where the soil is the mistress, the cruel and beloved
wench.

John began to feel his power. After he had knocked off work on
Saturday evenings he felt like a giant. Those were his hours of glory
in Morgantown, the nearest city. Then he did his shopping for the
week. He entered the stores and pointed at the things he wanted to
buy. The storekeepers understood his mute language and they were
friendly. He could afford to buy the best of meat, his favorite dish,
ham. When he bought his first pair of shoes in America, he walked
home on clouds. At home he would never have had such shoes. "I
bet," he thought to himself, "the Baron never had shoes like these."
The Baron was his standard of values.

The ritual he relished above all was reaching into his pocket and
producing his purse—a bulky Hungarian one which was an orna-
mental and superstitious part of his Old World farm outfit. Then it
was really that he felt his power. He did not like a suit of clothes he
was looking over and turned it back to the storekeeper, who was better
dressed than the Baron and probably had more money. The man
appeared to be disappointed although he tried not to show it. John
hoped that he was disappointed, because that would have been a clear
sign of his own supreme power. Then he entered another store and
there he liked the suit. The storekeeper appeared to be greatly
pleased and expressed his pleasure with an extra smile and a warm
handshake.

Yes, John Szabó became an important person and real gentlemen
began to court his favor. These gentlemen were certainly better dressed
than any he had ever seen, with frank eyes and great big smiles, slap-
ping his back in sign of their approval of him until his back hurt.
They insisted on telling him that he was all right—two words which
he learned early and which he accepted as if Emperor Franz Joseph
had conferred the Franz Joseph Order on him. The gentlemen also
told him that he was the smartest young man it was their good luck
ever to have met. They lowered their voices to a confidential whisper

to show that not everybody could listen in on such an important conversation. A bright young man must think of his future, they assured
him frankly and confidentially. Certainly these gentlemen were his
friends. He never would have thought people like them would have
his interests so much at heart.

They spoke Hungarian and John thought that was wonderful. Occasionally, they used English words, which he did not understand.
Perhaps for that very reason it was those words that made him trust
these gentlemen even more.

In a burst of confidence, lowering his voice to the softest whisper,
one of them told him that it was not impossible for a bright young
man of his type to rise high in the world, very, very high, indeed. But
why should not one tell the truth boldly, without any fear. Yes, John
Szabó could become the owner of a coal mine such as the one in which
he was working. Did the Baron in Baranya County ever own a mine?
It would cost him no more than a hundred dollars to be the owner.
And the gentleman showed him a beautiful document such as not even
Emperor and King Franz Joseph would be able to produce. This
document was embossed and it was a share of stock. "One Hundred
Dollars" was written all over it, of that there could not be the least
doubt. The gentleman showed the signature, too, and of that there
could be no doubt either. It was a signature, all right. Then he
showed the stamp, and it appeared to be extremely important. A
document like that would be of no value without a stamp. John knew
about these things from Baranya County. There, too, the stamp was
highly important.

John finally admitted that he had no hundred dollars because he
was a new-comer in this country, and he was working hard and hoped
to have it one day. No need to wait that long, the gentleman encouraged him. John could surely spare ten dollars a month in preparing
his future life as a very rich man. In fifteen months, all told, he would
pay for his share. That would make one hundred and fifty dollars,
John remarked. With the help of an avalanche of English words, the
gentleman explained that the difference represented service charges, as
no interest was computed. John did not understand the technical terms
but being naturally cautious he told the gentleman he could not afford
to buy the mine.

This remark aroused the gentleman and he asked John pointedly
whether he considered himself a good citizen. His pleasant smile gone,
he hinted darkly that anarchists were unwelcome in the United States,

since they undermined organized society and did not believe in buying mine shares. Did John want to be involved with the court and the police?

"No," he answered frankly.

"Well, then," the gentleman glowered; but evidently he could keep no grudge. He invited John to have a glass of wine and there everything was cleared up. John told him that he had saved up seventy-five dollars. The gentleman accepted the money. He did not even insist on the rest of the payment. Producing the beautiful document with a flourish, he handed it to John. He congratulated his young friend on having become the owner of a mine and then without too much ado he bade him farewell. John soon learned that the mine was under water and that his savings were gone.

This was a bitter lesson which he shared with many others, Poles, Lithuanians, Serbians, Italians. For the first time in their lives they had money, money to spend and money to save. They had heard about the fabulous fortunes made by audacity—the boldness of the Rockefellers and Morgans. Under the hypnotic influence of a glib talker they turned the exception into the rule. They could become millionaires overnight. Had this not happened? They were also dazed by the prospect of an improved social status. They could become owners of the mines in which they worked. A shareholder is an owner, indeed, and the glib crook did not even tell a lie. He merely told one part of the truth.

John also had the good luck to be introduced to a legendary Hungarian "leader," a New York lawyer touring the Hungarian settlements, becoming acquainted with the new-comers. The immigrants burned incense at his feet. In a strange land he was the man that protected them from unnamed evils. To them his name spelled security. He was a benign gentleman, who spoke unctuously, praised his own honesty and dropped remarks all along the way that great Judge X was his best friend. He did not want his dear Hungarians to be taken in by crooks. They should not hesitate to write to him if they ever had a brush with the law. He could "fix" everything. Some actually wrote to him, and the great man was as good as his word. No, he had not forgotten John or Frank, he remembered them as if they had been his own brothers and, naturally, was ready to help them in their present plight. Enclosed with his letter he sent a power of attorney containing the terms of his fee. He was a great believer in justice and so he took the cases to courts, and litigation is expensive. For that he was not to blame. At any rate, his fee was never higher than twice the amount of another lawyer's fees. His fame grew in the American-Hungarian community, as a public-spirited citizen. He had a winter home in the most expensive section in New York—and strangely that, too, was credited to his integrity—and a summer home in Westchester. It was a great honor to be invited into that shrine of greatness.

The dreams of returning to Hungary as a landowner—his first dreams—receded into the mists of fantasy, now that John's savings were gone. It was *Kocsis Juliska,* Julia Kocsis, daughter of another miner, living in another dreary hovel, who happened to be the sympathetic soul whose presence he needed. Only the outside of the Kocsis place was dreary; inside it was warm with a hospitality which only a family with a marriageable daughter could show toward an eligible young man.

Like John, the Kocsis family were from Baranya County, but recently from the Old Country. Mother Kocsis never tired of repeating that in the entire county nobody could prepare a better *paprikás csirke* than her Juliska, but, obviously, this was only sales talk. Every Sunday John was invited to Juliska's house and every Sunday there was a delicious paprika chicken in the pot.

John was young and Juliska was even younger. They were not bound together by formal engagement, but it was understood that they would get married in a few years. He would save up a little money again, but not by becoming the owner of a mine. Of that sickness he was cured.

The West Virginia mine was a hard school. Never again was he swindled as badly as on that first occasion. But how was he to know that his childhood chum for whom he underwrote the expenses of the fare to America would skip out of sight for ever? He suffered an injury in the shafts and a lawyer took the case to court. He received the award but the lawyer received most of the compensation.

Whenever he thought of the lay-off he felt fear grip his innermost being. He never felt like that at home, because there he had nothing to lose. But here he might lose Juliska; he might lose those glorious visits to the Morgantown stores, when he was the King, with money in his pockets; he might lose his peace of mind, as he would no longer be required to descend into the guts of the earth, could no longer count the imaginary coins dropping into his imaginary treasure house as he worked in the darkness hour after hour.

John could not forget his pal, Laci Kerekes, as good as any, with worse luck than most, accursed with a greater sense of justice than most and unable to keep it to himself. Why did he have to shoot his mouth off about that short weight in the shaft? Suddenly Laci found that there was no work for him and it was no use trying to prove to the hiring bosses that he was as good a man as any, perhaps even better. They would not listen to him. If nobody listens to you, then you are good for nothing, no matter how good you are. Laci took to drinking and then he took to talking and he sounded like a drunk even when he was not drunk. In the lunatic asylum he kept on talking, telling everybody that he was as good as the best of them and that plenty of *dzabs,* jobs, awaited him, because the bosses like a good man, especially if he was as good as he, Laci, the best miner in the State.

John had work most of the time and, generally, he could keep on paying his weekly visits to town, spending his money sensibly, and occasionally showing Juliska the magnificence of a cheap restaurant.

Gradually, the former Hungarian farmhand became an American miner. He began to pick up enough English—or the language that passed for English in that neighborhood—not to be dependent upon the sign language on his weekly expeditions to town. He talked quite glibly about the coming *pedá,* payday which he sometimes also called *tájm,* time. One of his buddies was thinking of a *cséncs,* change to a *fektri,* factory job where he would join the *juni,* union. Another *damflo,* damned fellow was talking big about a *dzsamp,* jump to San Francisco. That *bodi,* body from *Makkishpot,* McKeesport said he was working on an *incsáj,* engine of the *fanesz,* furnace for *bigány,* pig iron. He mixed his Hungarian with English words, using English terms with Hungarian endings. When he wanted to change cars, he said: "*Cséncsolom a karét,*" and when he wanted to go upstairs he said: "*Muffolok aptiszba.*" He was understood and he understood others speaking the same language.

America entered the First World War, and the factories needed men. He was just short of military age and so he decided to leave the mines if he could get a satisfactory job in a shop. He did not want to get stuck underground, and he was certain he could learn a new skill. A northern chemical factory was looking for hands, and the pay was satisfactory. This might be something for him. He made up his mind to try his luck at the new job, which beckoned from New Jersey.

Jancsi married Juliska before moving North. The wedding was wonderful, with wine and Gypsy music. Mother Kocsis was so overwhelmed with happiness that she cried all day and nothing could stop her. There was a lot of singing about wheat fields and larks, and there were tears in soot-bitten eyes.

John went ahead to explore the situation. The chemical factory was in the midst of a Hungarian settlement which looked almost like a Hungarian town. It had an all-Hungarian street, in which an inscription read *Patika,* pharmacy. It had a grocery store in which real *paprika* and real *kandi cukor,* rock candy, and lots of other Hungarian delicacies were on display. "Little Hungary" of that New Jersey city also had a *kocsma* a Hungarian saloon, as near like the real thing as you could find anywhere on this side of the ocean.

The factory needed hands in a hurry. It was a pharmaceutical shop and it was John's job to pour a syrup into blue bottles marching in front of him on a conveyor. On the first day his back was almost broken, on the second day he felt shooting pains all over his body and at the beginning of the second week his work was routine. The job paid more than the mine. The windows of the plant were large and he could look at the smoke of the adjacent plants and at a patch of the sky. Juliska made the trip North a month later. They made their temporary home in a boarding house, *burdos ház.*

The work was monotonous, it is true, but it did not kill his soul. He had time to think and—miracle of miracles—to plan his future, looking forward to a better life. He began to develop an ambition. Every young man is expected to have that, but not if he came from a *tanya,* farm, in Baranya County, especially if that farm belonged to an entailed estate, which could not be sold and divided. John learned gradually to dare to raise his eyes toward the future. Ambition was an ingredient of the air he inhaled.

As he reached for the bottle, filling it with syrup, he was thinking rhythmically. He was trying to cut down on time. By doing the work this way, instead of that, he could reduce the time for a single operation by a split second. The rhythm evoked a song, and the song made him dance in his thoughts.

He was working and the thought gave him pleasure. He was making money—more than ever before—and that thought gave him pleasure. He was making money so that he could buy dresses for Juliska, silk dresses, and one of those songs he was humming was about silk dresses for one's lady love. For the composer of that music that was a dream, but for John it was not. He was making money, enough to save it. For what? For that farm in Baranya County? Now he was no longer sure of that, and Juliska was not sure either. She could have a silk dress and this was America. She was wearing a hat, and this was America. At home she went around barefoot, and that was Baranya County. At home people would have laughed if she had gone around in a hat, and that was Baranya County.

John kept on working and thinking. After every two minutes he thought for a second—he had made a penny, and that thought gave him pleasure. Every ten minutes—a nickel. What could he buy with that? Lots. Every twenty minutes—a dime. The silvery tone of the dime served as the musical accompaniment of the song. Every three hours and twenty minutes—a dollar, and that was a landmark, celebrated with a more protracted meditation on this theme. He was not particularly money-minded. But if you have been a farm hand in Baranya County a dollar is not merely a piece of money, it is also power, prestige, command over the universe, his own small universe, in the grocery store and in the dress store.

Then his thoughts strayed to Juliska whom he had begun to call Julia, thoughts such as young men have about their young wives. He was also thinking of their house, but his thoughts on that subject were misty. Was that house in New Jersey or in County Baranya? As time progressed, the picture gained in clarity. The house was in New Jersey, but it was not a real house. It was a dream house, all pink silk and fluffy dreams.

His daydreams began to take the shape of practical plans. People who spoke English—not the "mixed" type—could get better jobs. They would matriculate in a school where classes were offered in English for foreigners. Their teacher was a young girl, the missionary type, who would never give up a fight. John forced his recalcitrant Hungarian tongue to accept the alien speech. That poor tongue of his had to perform all kinds of acrobatics. He thought himself a parrot at first, imitating sounds that were not his own, but he soon overcame this difficulty. Julia also came to grips with the difficulties of the new tongue. The teacher told them she was proud of them. This may have been a simple expression of courtesy, but to John and Juliska it was a medal of honor, which they accepted with inexpressible pride. Now they began to speak English at home, and to enter into conversations with non-Hungarian neighbors.

Life settled down into a small-town, industrial-plant routine. The years went by and at last the war was over. The soldiers were coming home and John looked into an uncertain future. Would he be kicked out of his job? Again he felt the grip of that unnamed horror. War veterans had the first call on jobs. Who was he, anyway? An interloper, a miner from West Virginia—not even that, a farm hand from Hungary. He had no place in that New Jersey factory.

Should they go back to the Old Country, to hold their reunion with the native soil, to show off to the Baron, if he was still alive, to tell about the glories of America to their rural neighbors? They had saved up a few hundred dollars. They were less sure than ever that they wanted to go back. Let us wait, they said, for the news. What will life be like over there?

Life was not pleasant over there. Life is never pleasant in a defeated country, and Hungary had been defeated. Pre-war Hungary shrank to a fraction of her former size. That Baranya County farm—was it still in the Old Country? Yes, it was, but the new boundary ran not far from it. Complaints began to pour down upon the American-Hungarians. Their Old Country had been amputated. "Hurry up and do something about it."

Nobody could "do something about it." This was a sign of the new age. The former nationalities became mistresses in their own houses. Now the tables were turned. Now the Hungarians became a minority. The land was filled with the laments of the irredentists proclaiming to the world that never would the proud Magyars resign themselves to their fate.

Hungary was an overcrowded, unhappy, restless country. The flood tide of re-emigration did not materialize. "Stay where you are," the handful of ex-Americans back again in their native land advised the others. John and Julia agreed that they would stay. Perhaps they would have stayed anyway.

John could have gone on filling bottles until some veteran replaced him. The endless procession of bottles did not dull his senses. One day he took a critical look at the label and thought that it was not sufficiently distinctive or graphic. He made up his mind to do something about this. One of his friends was good at drawing. John explained the problem to him and the friend drew up a new label, which was a great improvement over the old one.

Back in Baranya County it would not have occurred to John to suggest any kind of improvement to the Baron, since it was not the business of farmhands to concern themselves with such matters. It was not the concern of the gentlemen either to concern themselves with innovations, since it seemed to be preordained that things should go on in the same way for ever and ever. Anybody wanting to change the pre-ordained way of things was, of course, a good-for-nothing Socialist and that was the most awful thing in the world.

This was New Jersey and not the County of Baranya, and John need not hesitate to have a talk with the boss about that label. He made up his mind he would have that talk and making up his mind was a measure of his new status as an American. He got cold feet at the last moment. Then he summoned all his courage and went to the boss. The boss was quite friendly, listened attentively and asked John to leave the design with him. It was only then that John began to worry about what he had done. What had been the sense of his sticking out his neck? The boss may have been personally responsible for the old label and now he was offended. Had he been impertinent in taking up this matter?

A few days later John was invited into the office of the boss and was told that the labels would be changed. At the same time he was told that beginning next Monday he was to be in charge of a crew as a foreman, with a corresponding boost in wages.

That night John did not go home—he floated on clouds of pink satin, the color of the house of his daydreams. That night was not dark, unlike all other nights. The sun was still ablaze, his own personal sun, and he was navigating close to it on his own private cloud. From that dazzling height he looked down upon the midgets of the earth, flashing blissful smiles to them. His mind was pleasantly blank and he merely repeated to himself: *Szabó János, Szabó János,* as if he were talking to the poor farm lad on the *tanya* of Baranya County.

He could afford to buy his dream castle on his wages: seven hundred dollars down and the balance on first and second mortgage. The rate of interest was stiff, but he did not care, as long as the dream castle was theirs. The house was situated in a street which the local Hungarians called *alvég,* lower end, and other citizens named Gulyás Avenue.

It was a street of detached two-family houses, nearly all of which belonged to American-Hungarians. Down the entire length of the street two architectural styles alternated, Gothic and Byzantine. In front of each house, whether Gothic or Byzantine, there was a small plot of grass, and the houses were backed by small gardens, little more than backyards. Superficially, Gulyás Avenue looked no different from thousands of other streets in thousands of other American towns.

But in reality the difference was vast. The windowsills on Gulyás

Avenue were telltale windowsills. They were alive with what Hungarians consider Hungarian flowers, geraniums and magenta petunias. In the small gardens back of the Gothic and Byzantine houses were the "Hungarian trees," acacias.

The house consisted of a six-room and a four-room apartment. The Szabós occupied the larger one, and a young Hungarian couple was to rent the smaller flat. One of the first things John did after moving into the house was to go down into the cellar and then ascend to the first floor, counting all the steps. From the first floor he ascended to the second floor, again counting all the stairs. From there he mounted to the third floor, counting the stairs. He had covered four levels. There was also an attic in the house to which access was gained on a ladder-like stair, and that was the fifth level. He added up all the stairs, *his* stairs, and again he whispered to himself *Szabó János, Szabó János.*

Then it occurred to him to start a new game. He started counting the electric bulbs in the house. Time and again he was thrilled to find that he had overlooked some of the bulbs and then he would start counting them all over again. Then he added up the totals on all levels and again he whispered to himself: *Szabó János, Szabó János.* He was thinking of his childhood days on the farm.

In due time the furniture arrived from the New York department store. It was the type of furniture you could find in millions of American houses on hundreds of thousands of American streets, in thousands of American towns—good, solid, honest, unimaginative sofas, tables, lamps and rugs. Yet, when the Szabó house was furnished it did not look like millions of other houses on hundreds of thousands of other American streets. It had a touch of the Hungarian rural areas. Julia displayed her dowry of *Kalotaszegi,* embroideries, put up the fly-specked family pictures, a portrait of Lajos Kossuth with the Kossuth beard and hat and dress suit, and put up a painting of the Hungarian plains, all horizon and a lonely *gémeskút,* well, surrounded by cattle and cowboys. On top of drawers and cupboards she displayed all the knickknacks that were dear to her heart.

When the furniture was in place, John sank into his own capacious easy chair. How many times had he seen himself in that posture, and now here he was. It was unreal, as if he were looking at himself from the outside, as if he were a picture which he was studying. He held a newspaper, but was too excited to read it. Lolling in the chair, he experimented with the best illumination. Noticing that the Kossuth picture was askew, he straightened it, and was very proud of that operation. It was his picture and this was his house. *Szabó János, Szabó János.*

There was another curious thing about John's relation with the house. He was a former peasant, and now he had a small plot of soil of his own. You would have excepted him to start digging and planting, yet he never did. He was a foreman now in an American chemical factory and not a Hungarian peasant. On the other hand, Julia loved the smell of the soil, their own, the smell of the acacia trees and of the flowers. Every blade of grass of that plot was her personal friend. This was her own little realm and she transferred all the affection of which a peasant is capable to the house on Gulyás Avenue.

In that house Rosy, Tommy and Charley were born. They were an American family now. Providence had been good to them. The sky was serene over New Jersey towns in the late twenties and the chimneys of the countless plants puffed contentedly. The clerks in her bank had a friendly smile for Mrs. Szabó. Their savings account increased.

One day John had a great surprise for his wife, a shiny new car in front of the house. Part of the garden was transformed into a garage, but the acacia tree was not touched. The first Sunday after this event they drove toward the distant hills they could observe from their windows. As John drove into the distance, he was also driving into the past. Out of the past arose the mist which gradually assumed the shape of the Baron he had known in his youth. What had happened to that Baron? What would he say if he saw *Szabó János* in his shining new American car? Such cars were owned only by very rich people over there.

It was a carefree world, which seemed destined to endure for ever. It appeared to be the threshold of the American age and the Szabós were happy to belong to it. "Two cars in every garage," was the contemporary slogan. Security seemed to be within the reach of all the people who had no fear of work. The sky was constantly serene.

Out of that serene sky, without warning, came the rumble that heralded the end of the world Gulyás Avenue knew and liked. The end of the world of two cars in every garage, of one car in every garage, perhaps. An economic depression such as America, even the world, had never seen shook the foundations of the Szabós' universe. The nocturnal skies turned weird with the blueness of the sky, untarnished by the glow of furnaces. Work was doled out in small rations at the plant. John's wage cut had to be taken cheerfully. It was far more than the nothing that stared into millions of vacant eyes.

Then came the New Deal, which brought John Szabó within nodding distance of politics. In the past he had followed the crowd by becoming politically excited at election time. But now, politics ceased to be a seasonal pastime and became part of life. Having faced the abyss, he no longer considered social security a remote problem. It was his security—his old-age pension, his unemployment insurance. The popular slogans of the day penetrated into Gulyás Avenue. He heard about "rugged individualism" and the "American system." They sounded all right and they were all right. He himself was a product of the American system: hard work, hard life, but good life, a chance for hard-working people. And the children . . . Many other doors will be open to them. Doors . . . Factory doors, too? In times of depression? Here was the rub.

Labor unions? He had a prejudice against them. Maybe it was a Hungarian prejudice associated with the gendarmes. The gendarmes were against the labor unions, he had been against the gendarmes and so he should be in favor of the unions. Gendarmes or no gendarmes, the unions were associated in his mind with opposition to authority, rebellion. He was a law-abiding citizen, a believer in free competition and rugged individualism. Everybody for himself, and may the best man win. But did the best man win? There was Ferenc and so many others. There was the blue sky over the Jersey town, unpolluted by factory soot—the blessed, life-giving grime. And there were the vacant faces, eyes of despair; and the children playing in the streets, happy children, fed by the schools. Happy children, not knowing, nor would they have cared if they had known, that it was the food of charity.

"My friends . . ." the voice came across space. The President of the United States spoke. "My friends . . ." John had almost forgotten the name of Emperor Franz Joseph, the ruler of his childhood. "My subjects . . ." that ruler used to say, but John had never heard him. And now the President of the United States said: "My friend. . . ." It was addressed to him, and he felt the proximity of the President, the man who stood between him and privation, his real, personal friend.

Public-spirited citizens should take an interest in the facts of their country. Politics was the link between private and public fate. The Congressman of his district embodied that link. At the St. Stephen's Day picnic of his church the Congressman appeared in the flesh. He was late and he was in a hurry, because he had to help a poor widow. He went the rounds, cordially shook all the hands extended to him, looked deeply into the peoples' eyes and exuded that warmth of genuine human fellowship which only the best of actors can exude. Carried away, some people poured out their hearts to him, while he listened sympathetically and told them without a moment's hesitation and employing always the same labor-saving phrase that he "would see to it" in Washington. What he would see to he did not say, and that was the last people heard of him until the next election when he appealed to their votes and got them, because electors usually act on the belief that words are better than deeds.

People talked a lot about "isms" in those days, not so much on Gulyás Avenue as in big cities like New York, where people knew more about these things. But word about the "isms" reached also the Gothic and Byzantine two-family houses of Little Hungary. Bolshevism—that was something awful and John detested it thoroughly. Fascism—that was another one of those foreign-sounding words which many people mouthed without knowing anything about. Mussolini— the man who made trains run on time. Did it make too much difference? At any rate, there he was. Hitler—leader of the revolt against the peace settlement, the man with the funny moustache and shrieking voice. It took some time before city people discovered the real nature of Hitlerism and then Gulyás Avenue followed suit. Socialism—there were a few old-line Socialists on the Avenue, remnants of a fighting past. Now they were living on their memories, leaderless, addicted to words.

The old-time Socialists of Gulyás Avenue detested the semi-"ism" represented by Hungary's regent, Nicholas Horthy. "White Terror," they said, "the man responsible for the White Terror." But that detestation was not shared by many other residents of the Avenue. They had never seen him. Many had left the country long before Horthy reached the Royal Palace atop Castle Hill. They liked Horthy, whom they identified with Hungary. Horthy, the aloof ex-Admiral, who had expatriated himself from rural Hungary to maritime Austria. Horthy who spoke Hungarian with a foreign accent. He was their Horthy. Why?

Perhaps because oppressed peasants have a father complex. Strangely, that complex is often fixed on their oppressor. A powerful man, gigantic, tremendously aloof appears in a godlike rôle. God also oppresses the poor and yet they worship him. The more He oppresses them the more they cringe at His feet. They need him.

Or perhaps because Gulyás Avenue found it easier to visualize Hungary in one person. Horthy was not merely a person, but a symbol. And why should they venerate the country that had cast them out? Because it was the motherland. But if the mother is cruel, casting out honesty and hard work? Both God and man will forgive the children of such godless parents for turning their backs on her. Yes, but you can't do that with the mother country. The mother country is sacred, because it is a country, and a nation is sacred under our dispensation. The nation is not subject to human laws, nor to human ethics. In the veneration accorded to Admiral Horthy by the residents of the Avenue nationalism celebrated its supreme triumph.

At home these very people would have worshiped the country only if they had been able to go to school for several years, so that "education" could exert its effect. Not many had gone to school and on the *tanya* the nation is the detested gendarme and the equally detested petty public official, the notary, and the tax collector. At home they would not have paid homage to the State. In America it was different. Loyalty to the United States, naturally, but one could not be really loyal to the country of one's adoption without, at the same time, being loyal to the mother country. It was America that, indirectly, aroused their affection for the home country.

Gulyás Avenue was in America. Probably most of its residents were American citizens, and genuinely proud of that fact. It meant many good things to live in America and to be an American citizen. They were not conscious that even in the heart of the United States they were really on the outside. They associated with their own kind. A "real American" to them was a person of English-speaking parentage: English, Scotch, Irish. That world might be opened to their children, but not to them. In America one had to belong to a nation. With only one foot were they in America, and they had to put that other foot somewhere. So they put it in Hungary.

The Szabós were baptized Catholics, the religion of the majority in Hungary. There however, John could attend church only on rare occasions. In America the church became a part of his way of life. He liked to see the sun's rays refracted into the colors of the rainbow on the inlaid windows of the modest Hungarian church of the Jersey town. As the sun's shafts sought out the statue of a saint, his eyes followed it caressingly. A deep peace descended upon him, he felt secure, warmed by the fellowship of God and man. He relished the familiar chants, the full-throated sound of the organ. He enjoyed the words ground out by the priest without paying too much attention to their meaning. Hungarian words, melodious to his ears, now consciously so, the tongue that fitted into the church because.it was the tongue of his childhood days. Sitting by his side were his children, American-born, English-speaking. He wanted the Hungarian words associated with the words of Christ to percolate deep into those childish hearts so that the priest's sermon should not be alien to his children. So that he should not be an alien to them. The Hungarian language of the Hungarian church should be the link.

On August twentieth, St. Stephen's Day, the picnic on the banks of the river was an annual event in the Szabós' lives. There was fun there, jollity, a little bit forced, perhaps, but spontaneous before the end of the day. It was good for the children to blend into the Hungarian crowd, so that they should not acquire the uppishness of the indigenous people. These picnics were good, too, because by meeting the congregation John could measure his standing in the community. The smiles were warm, and comments upon the quality of the wieners friendly. It was good to be respected. Good to have children and good to have them see that their parents were respected.

Far and wide in the community Julia Szabó was noted for her *húsleves,* meat soup, *túros csusza,* cheese noodles, not to mention her real forte, *paprikás csirke.* Guests said after a meal offered by her that they would like to "lick their ten fingers," the greatest compliment to a cook in Hungarian. The former best cook of Baranya had never lost that magic touch. Cooking was an art, and was the only subject on which she could wax really eloquent.

Once a year she threw a big party, *lakoma,* to which the Szabós invited fully two scores of guests. For weeks in advance Julia would plan the minutiae of the meal. Days before that historic event the house would be fragrant with the scent of baking. She acquitted herself of that gigantic task all alone, as it was a point of honor never to accept any outside help.

A stage star on her opening night could not have been more excited than Julia on the great day of the party. She never got used to the culinary first nights, no matter how many of them she had. The guests lent themselves readily to the rôle of the enchanted audience. At psychological moments, now the one and then the other broke into enraptured cries: "Julia, darling, how did you do this? And, for heaven's sake, how did you do that? Could you, please, give me your recipe for this?" Very well did they know that she no more would part with her secrets than the medieval alchemist would yield his formula for the transmutation of base metal into gold.

Julia was a fanatic for cleanliness, a trait she shared with other women of her stock. On the Hungarian farms and in the villages, the peasants may have been very poor but they were also very clean. It was their pride that no amount of adversity would make them lower their standards. Always there was a *tiszta szoba,* clean room, a sanctuary not to be spoiled, a show place and a room to entertain honored guests. Cleanliness was an escape from the oppression of misery. You had your pride.

With time, Julia had become a stately matron. Her three children and the household absorbed all her days. She liked to leave important decisions to her husband, though she had a mind of her own. Barely literate, she had good common sense—horse sense; she was able to size up people with a shrewd glance. She could read their eyes and the inflections of their voices. John had every reason to be content with life.

The Szabós would probably have had only one child, if they had lived in Hungary. In their section of the Old Country they had the system known as *egyke,* one little one, since the people there felt they could afford to have only one child—if any at all.

In America they could have more children. Rosy was the first-born, a pink-skinned little angel. Julia thanked heaven for its gift, even though she admitted that it would have been more regular to have a boy as the first born. Tom was next—a perfect team, boy and girl. Then came Charley. It would have been ideal if the fourth child should have been a girl, but instead of a child, the depression came, and Charley remained the youngest.

The children gave the parents' life a different meaning. John had always been conscientious in his work—that was his nature. He had to give the best that was in him. But now he felt he would have to improve even his very best, for the sake of his children, so that they should see no want, should be proud of him, and he of them.

Years went by, and little Rose grew up to be a long-limbed, slender girl, with eyes of cornflower blue, and hair of tow. Her record at school was indifferent but, of course, the parents agreed that was understandable since that child was only a girl. The little girl became a big girl before the parents realized how such things happened. Her lips were dainty and her complexion could not be better. One day Julia discovered the trace of lipstick on those delicate lips and the girl confessed that she had wiped off the incriminating evidence on her way home from school. That night Julia slept little. This was one of those crucial meetings with "life." To her rouge and lipstick were still abominations which only "painted women" used in Baranya County. This was America, of course, and a different age. But countries and ages make no difference to a mother terribly afraid for her child. This was a tremendous problem and the following day it was discussed fully by Julia and John. He pretended to be unconcerned, playing the part of the modern parent. Julia pretended to resign herself to inexorable fate, but she never forgot.

The mother's perceptive eyes noticed one day that Rosy had something on her mind; it took some coaxing before she unburdened herself. That night there was a dance at school and Stevey was to call for her. Was it possible that their daughter should go out with a man? Of course, Stevey was just a boy, a nice boy, so what was wrong with it? John and Julia had been living in America for a long time now, much longer than they had lived in Baranya County. Yet even the lessons of a quarter of a century could not root out certain habits.

By the time the youngsters got home from the dance, it was almost eleven. The parents heard them raiding the icebox and then sitting down to what was probably a hearty meal. Then there was silence. "You must do something about it," panic-stricken Julia whispered to John. What was he to do? The boy might be kissing Rosy at that moment. In the County of Baranya people kissed only after the marriage ceremony. Were they to force Stevey to marry Rosy? His heart was broken. It was several days before they recovered from the shock. This was the hardest stress of their process of Americanization. They had to learn by personal experience that their daughter could take care of herself.

"Little" Tom was a tall, handsome boy. Strange how these American children became so leggy, John meditated. At home the children were shorter. Sports, he thought, and good food. Tom had just entered high school, had fair academic grades and was far ahead of his class in sports. He was so versatile that the coach could not make up his mind for some time where to put him, and it was only after much thinking that he decided upon basketball. Working hard at the game,

Tom soon revealed remarkable gifts. He became the star of the team in a short time.

When the inter-city cup game took place, sports writers from far and wide were to cover the great event. Tom and his team were the challengers. Surpassing his best previous performance he ran away with the show in the most dazzling way.

The editor of the local paper, carried away by laudable municipal patriotism, emblazoned Tom's name all over the front page. In the center of the page he placed the picture of the hero, Tom. The Szabós were naturally in the seventh heaven. This was their son, bearing their name, a household word in town, his glory reflecting upon the family. *Szabó János, Szabó János.*

The page with Tommy's picture was framed and the young boy placed it over his bed. There was only one newspaper for him and that newspaper had only that one issue, and that issue only that one page, with the story of his victory. He became a school celebrity and his teachers overlooked the fact that his sport achievements far eclipsed his academic work.

It was shortly afterwards that Julia saw Tommy at the corner drugstore surrounded by a bevy of admirers. He pretended not to see her. The day was hot, but she shivered on her way home. Tom pretended not to hear when they spoke to him in Hungarian, found all kinds of excuses not to attend mass in the Hungarian church, found an entirely new set of friends, outside of Gulyás Avenue. Tommy had fame, and he was too young to know that it would not last. Next year another boy got the banner headline and the honored position on the front page of the paper for his portrait. Tom fought for recognition, thought everybody ungrateful to forget his triumph, became haggard and harassed. He would wear the scars of early fame all his life.

Charley, the "baby," was clannishly attached to his parents. He did not have to be coaxed to accompany them to the Hungarian church. He liked to play at home. His father arranged a small workshop for him in the cellar, since the boy was gadget-minded. He wanted to become an engineer and hearing his childish plans the father's chest would swell. This was Charley, his own Charley, who would become an engineer, a great engineer, perhaps, because nothing was impossible in America. His father was a factory foreman, and Charley would become an engineer and so the Szabós would make their way ahead in the great American world. *Szabó János, Szabó János.*

This is the true story of an American family of Hungarian origin in a New Jersey town, one of the hundreds of thousands of such families. The Szabós have entered the broad stream of American life, a stream as mighty as the Mississippi, rolling toward the fulfilment of its destiny in nature's own inscrutable ways.

XII

Strength in Unity

"There is evidence showing that back of the familial and communal solidarity of the European peasant is the fear of death and its attendants and preliminaries—hunger, cold, darkness, sickness, solitude and misery. The peasant is strangely indifferent to death, but he fears any irregular features—suddenness, inappropriateness. He wants to die decently, ceremonially and socially. Since a man's death is usually the most conspicuous incident in his life, attracting the universal attention and interest of the group, since it is the occasion of judgments and speculations on the status of the family—whether they are thereby impoverished, whether they are rich—death and burial are not the only occasions of the natural idealization of the dead, but a means of securing recognition. Immigrant families are notorious for lavish expenditures on funerals." [50]

At home the Hungarian peasant had no communal organization similar to the pre-revolutionary Russian *mir,* village community; or the *zadruga* of some South-Slav peasant communities, the house community of close relatives living co-operatively or inhabiting a hamlet built around a leader's house. If the Hungarians' forebears ever possessed any communal organizations, they must have been disrupted by the cataclysmic Tatar invasion or Turkish occupation, although the corresponding Slavic communal institutions had weathered these disasters. Hungary may have been inhabited by too many nationality splinter groups to create strong social organizations of this type. If the serf fell ill under the pre-revolutionary feudal system the landlord was expected to look after him. The serf was a useful piece of machinery that had to be mended when broken. If broken beyond repair, there were certain social obligations. A family lost caste if it allowed a kinsman to be buried in a potter's field. In more recent times, life insurance never became a national habit in Hungary. Sickness benefits, too, were largely unknown on the farm. To a certain extent, however, they became known among the industrial workers of the larger cities, particularly Budapest.

As for social organizations, the church was in the van. It united many of the villagers on Sundays, and satisfied their artistic and cultural needs with music, singing and the sermon. The *café* was not a village institution. It flourished in the towns, a jack-of-all-trades meeting place, combining the functions of the concert hall, club, reading room, bar and dairy-lunch, as well as the restaurant. In the village there might be a *kaszinó,* casino, reserved for the elite: doctor, teacher, lawyer, veterinarian, public officials, and the *dzsentry,* gentry, the better people. It was definitely not for the peasant.

The peasant had the tavern, *kocsma,* low-ceilinged, smoke-filled, reeking with alcohol and soot. Occasionally, a *malacbanda,* a couple of forlorn Gypsies, strayed into it and then the tavern was filled with laughter and loud, bold words. There the Hungarian peasant pursued his pastime of *politizálás,* talking politics. Almost always he was a 'Forty-eighter, opposed to the Habsburgs, a follower of Kossuth, and hardly ever a 'Sixty-sevener, so named after the year of the great Compromise with the ruling House. In the inebriated immunity of the tavern he would talk big, but he could do little at rigged-up elections. *"Ha a föld Isten kalapja . . ."* he sang. "If the earth is God's hat . . ." then Hungary was the bouquet of flowers on it. *Sirva vigad a magyar.* The Magyar has a good time crying—and so he drank his cheap *homoki,* sand-grown wine, which he called *karcos,* rasper, because it rasped his throat, and *rabvallató,* third degree, because it was so bad as to make the accused confess. But he loved it. Then there was the *disznótor,* autumnal slaughtering of the pigs, and the husking bees, adequate substitutes for café and casino. There local news was peddled and the countryside kept well informed without as much as looking at a newspaper. Of cultural organizations there were none. A library was unheard of in the village. Anybody wasting his time in one would have been ostracized.

The peasant came to the United States and was transplanted into an entirely different setting. America was a nation of "joiners." People were expected to join all kinds of organizations to meet like-minded people, establish contacts, or just to show that they were "regular fellows." Democracy operated through organizations, in lobbies and out of them. He went into the mine or the steel mill, the hazards of which were great. He was alone as yet, with no kin to help him in times of stress. The fraternal sick benefit and funeral organizations met his most urgent needs. They were the first organizations the Hungarian immigrant in America developed and he has remained true to them throughout. They became the very lifeblood of American-Hungarian life.

The first such organization among the Hungarians came into existence when the first wave of Kossuth's immigrant followers reached the United States. The Hungarian Sick Benefit Society of New York was nursed into life by Charles Kornis Tothvárady, the founder of the first Hungarian-language newspaper in this country, and was short-lived. There were not enough Hungarian immigrants in those days, contrary to Tothvárady's expectations.

Shortly after the Civil War Hungarian organizations with a little more staying power came into being. The first of these was the *Erster Ungarischer Kranken-Unterstuetzungsverein,* founded by Hungarian immigrants of Jewish faith. The official language of this First Hungarian Sickness Benefit Association was German. It was followed by the *New Yorki Magyar Nőegylet* (New York Hungarian Women's Association), which also transacted its business in German. Cleveland residents of northern Hungarian Jews founded the *Cleveland Magyar Betegsegélyző Egylet.* Its official language was German, too.

The New York Hungarians felt the need of a social organization and so the *New Yorki Magyar Egylet* (New York Hungarian Association) was founded. Its first president was the revolutionary hero, Colonel Miklós Perczel, and one of its leading spirits was Michael Heilprin.

The Association rented a couple of rickety rooms at 319 Bowery. It had an ambitious program, holding meetings three times a week, at which much music was played. Some years later, it branched out into a choral society, *New Yorki Magyar Dalkör* and into a Hungarian Sickness Benefit Society. The stated object of the Association was to foster the fraternal spirit among the members, awaken sympathy for Hungary, study American institutions and endeavor to popularize them in Hungary, and to stimulate the industrial, scientific and mercantile work of Hungarians here.

The Association struck a keynote which may be summed up in one word: Nationalism. Strong Hungarian national sentiment characterized the American-Hungarian organizations. Paradoxically, the nationalistic feeling increased, rather than declined, as a result of transplantation to the alien soil. The immigrant could not participate in American life and therefore he attempted to create a situation here in which he could participate. He wanted to improve the status of the Hungarians, so that his own status might be improved in American eyes. Home became a much sweeter place when it was no longer his. In America, the immigrant's eyes were opened to the real nature of nationalism. Also he was free to talk and act. He wanted to help in the struggle for self-determination at home. He also may have wanted to gain recognition at home preparatory to his return.

As the tidal wave of Hungarian immigration set in, the fraternal insurance companies came into existence. One of the first of these was a sickness benefit and funeral association named after Count Lajos Batthyány, martyred Premier of the abortive 1848 revolutionary government. The story of its origin casts a vivid light on conditions in American Hungary then.

In Cleveland, the largest inland "Hungarian" city of the United States, an unknown Hungarian lived in a boarding house, alone and friendless and there he died. The landlord was in a great hurry to rent the dead man's bed. He called the police to remove the body. The police came at a late hour and took the body away. Word spread among the Hungarians of the East Side and they made a search for the dead man, but could find nothing. This is precisely the sort of thing the peasant, Hungarian or not Hungarian, dreads. Little Hungary was aroused. Several Hungarians of Cleveland got together and founded the Association named, characteristically, after the executed Premier. Similar societies came into existence in other Hungarian settlements of the East, especially in Pennsylvania coal towns.

Another tragic occurrence is said to have been responsible for the foundation of the organization which was to be the largest, oldest and most important in the American-Hungarian community: *Verhovay Segély Egylet* (Verhovay Fraternal Insurance Association). This happened in a Pennsylvania coal town, witnessed by a young Hungarian, Mihály Pálinkás. It was raining hard. From one of the boarding houses of a miners' slum, a screeching voice pierced the dark night outside.

"I want a healthy roomer, who can pay his rent, not this sick one."

Pálinkás saw a man being dragged out into the rainy street. It was a Hungarian miner, coughing, his cheeks red with fever. He was afflicted with pulmonary tuberculosis. Young Pálinkás, the records tell us, was not content with letting well enough alone. He called a meeting of his friends on February 20, 1886, at which they decided to found a fraternal insurance association. The Association was named after Gyula Verhovay, a Hungarian member of parliament, noted for his opposition to the Jews and aristocrats. It is claimed that the founders were not familiar with Verhovay's anti-Semitic reputation. However, it is a matter of record that they had seriously considered naming their organization after Győző Istóczy, another M.P., even more rabidly anti-Semitic.

The Association started with a capital of $17.25, which twenty-eight founders collected among themselves. (The Verhovay legend speaks of "thirteen simple miners.") Most of the contributions were fifty cents, and the largest was Pálinkás' two dollars. He became the first president.

Verhovay was chartered as a sick-benefit and burial association. A year after its foundation it had seventy-seven members and assets amounting to $126.83. The abuses were so numerous at first that provision was made that members were entitled to sick benefit only three months after they had joined. Burial expenses were not to be paid if the insured had stated his age incorrectly. The management was haphazard and unbusinesslike. The books of the Association covering several of its early years are missing, and its chronicler [51] suggests that they were spirited away to cover up numerous irregularities. The number of members increased, as the number of Hungarians in America grew. The resources of the Association increased. Its existence could be insured only if its business was placed on an actuarial basis, and this was done.

The new-comers were not content with having merely a sickness benefit and funeral association. They wanted to get together, enjoy a fraternal glass of wine. *Aki nem koccint nem testvér,* says the Hungarian proverb. He who does not clink his glass is not a brother. Those who shunned a fraternal glass were excluded from the privilege of holding office.

As the organization grew, its business practices matured. Premiums were paid according to the age of the insured. Verhovay entered into a re-insurance agreement with one of America's largest insurance companies before World War I, and a significant arrangement it was. The post-World War I influenza epidemic mowed down five hundred Verhovay members and but for the re-insurance agreement the very existence of the association might have been jeopardized.

Verhovay has had its occasional reverses. But it has grown with a fair degree of consistency, becoming the largest of all American-Hungarian fraternal orders. The pennies of former landlack peasants have built this impressive edifice with no help from the "gentry." The main Hungarian settlements boast of impressive Verhovay buildings. Its total membership in 1944 amounted to 52,292—twice the membership of the next largest American-Hungarian fraternal order—and at the end of 1945 it had total assets of $7,408,000, and 364 lodges.

It is a great distinction among American-Hungarians to be an officer of Verhovay. The officers' slate includes, among others, the Supreme President, Supreme Secretary, Supreme Auditor and Supreme Treasurer. Besides insurance, the aims of the organization are, as stated by the new Constitution and By-Laws: ". . . to foster and advance the fraternal life of American Hungarians, and the continued use of the Hungarian language and culture."

A dark-haired youth, full of swinging eloquence, took the floor at a meeting of a small group of Hungarian Protestants in a Pittsburgh suburb on a mid-summer evening of 1896. He was a Reformed minister, Sándor Kalassay.

"It is not enough," he said, "to found a Reformed parish in the United States. Good deeds must be performed, helping the parish and other parishes to be established to clear the high hurdles of the beginning." Carried away by the cadences of his sentences and the rapt attention of his audience, he threw out the challenge to build a "strong bulwark of Hungarian hope, faith and love."

The Protestants formed about one-fourth of Hungary's population, yet gave Hungary some of her most notable children. Their fraternal organization, *Amerikai Magyar Református Egyesület* (Hungarian Reformed Federation of America) has grown up to be the second of the Big Four of fraternal bodies.

Kalassay recommended and it was accepted that the Federation should be formed as soon as it had five hundred members. It was more easily said than done. Months went by and the small group of stalwarts was nowhere near that figure. The final decision was to be made at a Cleveland meeting on February 15, 1897. The report of the temporary officers was highly discouraging. There were no more than 320 members, who had paid in a total of $272.15.

Kalassay inspired the conferees with confidence. The start was slow, he conceded, but what matter. Was not the start of Christianity slow, too? Once they got started, prospective members would have more confidence. Success would beget success. Under his influence it was decided at the Cleveland meeting that the Federation should be established.

The Federation shared the fate of many similar beginnings. Adversities beset it at every turn. The 1901 Cleveland General Assembly admitted: "Our Society has passed through many storms and difficulties."

This was the great age of the Robber Barons, and their success dazzled many. They had many imitators on much smaller scale, some of whom had jobs in the Federation. They were unmasked but the damage had been done. The Federation, like other American-Hungarian fraternal organizations, lacked a scientific, actuarial basis. But the Federation was learning rapidly and shortly thereafter introduced more businesslike methods. The period of its more rapid growth began.

Early this century one of those conflicts between the nation and King arose in Hungary. The ruler, Franz Joseph I, had appointed a government without parliamentary approval. The precipitating agent of the conflict was the language of command of the armed forces in Hungary. The Hungarian opposition wanted it to become all Hungarian, instead of predominantly German, as it was then. The King was now ruling *ex-lex,* outside of the law. The politically conscious Hungarians in the United States took a hand in this constitutional struggle. They were living in America, true, but most of them considered themselves transients. Physically American residents, spiritually they were Hungarians. Just the same, they had been influenced by the attitude of the politically awakened part of the American public. In Hungary they would not have thought of exerting pressure on the government. The political atmosphere of the country did not encourage such manifestations.

The Hungarian Reformed Federation lent its corporate prestige to the fight for Hungary's "independence." Fighting the "tyrant" there was another Kossuth—Ferenc, son of the great Lajos. To Hungarian immigrants in America, living in the shadow of that great historic visit to the United States, it seemed that they must rally to the Kossuth tradition. They sent a message to him, as a leader of the parliamentary opposition: "The Hungarian Reformed Federation of America sends its warm greetings to the leaders and rank and file fighting for the freedom of our mother country. We entreat God's blessing on their work."

The Federation went a long step further. The real 'Forty-eighters at home could not act freely. Hungarians in America therefore had to act as the spokesmen of their country, untrammeled by an oppressive government. Recalling the historic act of the great Kossuth, the Federation issued the bold password: "Away from Austria! Long live Independent Hungary!"

It exerted a more direct pressure on the *ex-lex* Hungarian government by refusing to transmit insurance money falling due in that country. The amounts were not large, but the gesture was significant, and it did not fail to make an impression. Eventually monarch and country made their peace, but it was an uneasy one. Ferenc Kossuth disappointed the followers of his father. A great man had a small son.

The life of the Federation, like everything else, was affected by the First World War. Something of its atmosphere, as felt by the members, was recaptured in the report to the General Assembly held at Buffalo in 1919: "Even though we were not enemy aliens, war conditions were not comforting. We had to be on our guard constantly. When the war was over, uncertainty was also over. Nevertheless, the most critical and hardest period of our Federation began just then. Spanish influenza removed many of our members. Special assessments had to be imposed."

At the Buffalo meeting the decision was taken, which the chronicler of the Federation described as "epochal," [52] that a Hungarian orphan asylum should be built in America. The idea had been broached before the war. "Then our people did not feel the urgency of founding an asylum and their contributions were scant. America was a transit station to many of them, and they were longing to return to their Hungarian homes." The war had changed all that. The influenza epidemic made many orphans and the Federation felt it had to assume responsibility for them. The Buffalo meeting decided that each member should be assessed five cents a month for the orphan asylum. Thus a beginning was made.

Quickly the plans ripened into action and three years after the end of the war, the Federation bought a thirty-five-room house in Ligonier, Pennsylvania, for $28,000. Normally the house accommodated fifty children, but in times of great stress it was to shelter 110 orphans. Two years later, the Federation bought the adjacent Melville farm for $25,000 and turned it into a home for old people. The entire place was called *Bethlen Otthon,* Bethlen Home, after Gábor Bethlen, Prince of

Transylvania, Moldavia and Wallachia, a champion of Protestantism in Eastern Europe during the great religious wars.

Another important decision was taken in 1939; the former orphanage was to be turned over to the old people and a new orphanage opened at Ligonier, nearer the schools. Accordingly, a house for twenty-five girls was bought and a house for twenty-five boys was built in town. The Ligonier Town Council objected to the move on the ground that it would entail additional tax burdens on the population. The case was taken to the courts, which decided in favor of the Home. The total population of the old folks' home was thirty, and the orphanage was to care for fifty children. The Bethlen Home is a pride of the Hungarian Reformed Federation of America and of many other American-Hungarians who see it as a token of what the common man can do, if he has the heart and will.

In the Golden Jubilee year of 1946 the membership of the Federation was in excess of twenty-six thousand, and its admitted assets amounted to $2,652,357. The number of its lodges was close to 235, distributed all over the main American-Hungarian settlements. Pennsylvania led with seventy-six lodges, followed by Ohio, thirty-eight; New Jersey, twenty-six; and West Virginia, seventeen.

In an eight-year war early in the eighteenth century the romantic Prince Ferenc Rákóczi II rose against the Habsburgs, but failed. "The Rakoczi March" in Berlioz' *Damnation of Faust* is known throughout the music-loving world. After this Prince the *Rákóczi Segélyző Egyesület* (Rakoczi Aid Association of Bridgeport) was named. It became the third largest Hungarian fraternal organization. The Rakoczi was the second oldest of the Big Four, founded in 1888. Its still, small voice was barely heard, as it entered American-Hungarian history with an initial capital of $7.50. The hard work of an entire decade produced only a modest $6,500.

"The reports of the organization sound like war bulletins," a chronicler remarked.[53] "War bulletins" they often were, indeed, not merely in the Rakoczi but in the other Hungarian fraternal organizations. "Fraternal" was often a misnomer. Internal struggles were bitter and protracted. Members who were not invested with an office were disappointed. *Rangkórság*, title malady, was an endemic disease in Hungary. A name without a handle to it was no name, and so it was in the numerous little Hungary settlements of the New World. "The city slicker" was also on hand. *Nadrágos ember* was the city fellow's name in Hungarian vernacular—man in trousers. Strange name, indeed, in the Western world, but not so strange on the sultry Magyar plains, where the peasants worked in long loose leggings. The city slicker became such a pest that one of the fraternal bodies provided in its statutes: "Priests, journalists, tradesmen entertaining business relations with the Association cannot be elected officials."

The Rakoczi outdistanced several rival organizations but it nearly foundered on the reefs of World War I. It had invested some of its money in Hungarian war bonds. Hungary lost the war, and the Rakoczi organization lost the money. Along with the other similar organizations, it suffered greatly because of the influenza epidemic which laid low more than a hundred of its members. It pulled through only after extra assessments had been levied. Prosperity generated prosperity and depression engendered depression. During the depression following 1929 a resolution was passed "allowing members who, for good reasons, could not pay their dues, to remain members in good standing, with regular benefits, providing that the lapsed dues be paid when they become able to do so, or in case of death, the amount owing would be deducted from the benefits due to the heirs." Early in 1946 the Association had 24,222 members in 144 lodges, and assets close to five million dollars.

Religion was no bar to membership in other fraternal bodies, but in them the three main creeds, Catholic, Protestant and Jewish, formed more or less self-contained units. The religions were better blended in Rakoczi. Nor did nationality make any difference. Its historian pointed out with praiseworthy pride that Slovak-speaking countrymen were among the first members of the Association.[54]

The American Sick Benefit and Life Insurance Association, founded in 1892, and known before 1936 as the Hungarian Aid Association of America became the fourth of the Big Four. Its popular name among the Hungarians is *Bridgeporti* (the Bridgeport Association), because of its headquarters. In 1945 it had 14,045 members and assets of $2,114,727.

The Hungarian immigrant Catholic majority noted the success of the Protestant minority fraternal organization with interest. That dynamic Hungarian leader of the *fin-de-siècle,* Tihamér Kohányi, publisher of the *Szabadság* newspaper, called a convention in 1897 to look into the possibility of a Hungarian Catholic federation. The convention considered the conditions auspicious and founded the organization: Virgin Mary, Patroness of Hungarians, Roman and Greek Catholic Federation.

The statutes provided that members had to confess once a year at least and partake of the Holy Communion on Easter. Their marriages must be sanctified by the Catholic Church. Children were exhorted to go to Hungarian parochial schools. It was specifically provided that they were not to go to Slavic schools. The Federation was to support Catholic national movements. Members were to live as good Catholics and worthy Hungarians.

Those were the days when Hungarian immigrants considered themselves transients in America. At home the Slovaks were subordinated to the Hungarians. In America, however, the Slovaks could fall back upon the assistance of other Slavs and their voice was strong.

The Federation ran into great difficulty. The Hungarian ecclesiastical authorities took little interest in it, as they took little interest in the Hungarian Catholics in America. It was their attitude that Hungarians had no business to go overseas. The American Catholic authorities also showed little sympathy for the Federation. They did not approve of its pugnacious attitude toward the American Slavs, who were stronger in number as well as influence.

Finally the Catholic Federation blended into the American-Hungarian Catholic Society. That Society never came anywhere near the Big Four, even though it had absorbed the St. László Society of Bridgeport.

The Hungarian fraternal orders had a hard struggle at first. They could not help noticing that some of the other nationalities had done much better, particularly the Germans and the Slavs, and began to realize that organizations were successful if they were really "organized" and not broken up into small fragments. They reached the conclusion that the fraternal societies must get together, mutually support one another, and derive benefit from their united strength. In 1892 the Federation of Hungarian Fraternal Societies (*Magyar Betegsegélyző Egyletek Szövetsége*) was founded in Bridgeport. It was an attempt to unite all American-Hungarian fraternal societies, pooling their resources, spreading their risks and increasing their credit.

A convention of the Federation was called at Philadelphia in due time. There some of the delegates contended that the Federation should be a "roof organization" of American-Hungarian life insurance companies, while others insisted that it should be turned into a free employment agency. Some delegates were interested only in cultural matters, and others were interested in immigrant settlement. A disappointed observer philosophized about the *Magyar átok*, Hungarian curse—dissension. He explained it on the ground that once the pressure of authority was released—as in the United States—the Hungarians flew off at all angles, underlined their individualities, gave free rein to their temperaments, and overlooked the real essence of democracy which was not "one for one" but "one for all and all for one." The discussion went on endlessly, and then it was decided that final arrangements should be made at another convention, in Cleveland, where again the old ideas were broached and new ideas added. Dissension was not the most fateful feature of the convention; that was the decision that *no* appropriation should be made to the three Hungarian newspapers which, according to a previous plan, were to become "the official organs" of the Federation, and each of which was to receive ten dollars a year.

No sooner were the delegates at home when the sapping operations of the disgruntled newspapers began. Each of them found some fault with the work of the Federation. As a result of this disruptive work, the Federation was split wide open. Now there were three federations instead of one: The Hungarian National Federation, The Hungarian Christian Workers' Federation and The Bridgeport Federation. The three federations working at cross-purposes mutually destroyed one another and in a few years nothing more was heard about them.

Small fraternal organizations began to mushroom all over the American-Hungarian landscape. They were highly nostalgic, judging by their names. They were called after Hungary's historic figures, such as the inevitable Kossuth and just as inevitable Petőfi, Count Széchenyi, called the Greatest Hungarian, János Hunyadi and Miklós Zrinyi, the two Turk-Beaters, then Ferenc Deák, whom his countrymen called the Fatherland's Sage. Even the Habsburgs appeared acceptable from a distance and some of them gave their names to American-Hungarian organizations. Most popular were the names of romantic Habsburg princes and princesses, such as Queen Elizabeth, loved even by those Hungarians who detested her husband, King Franz Joseph I. Very popular was also their only son, the late Crown Prince Rudolph who came to a tragic end in his Mayerling hunting lodge, on Vienna's outskirts. His wife, Stephanie, was also honored by lending her name to a fraternal society. Many of the societies were named after saints revered in Hungary, such as St. István (Stephen) who introduced Catholicism into the country, his son, St. Emeric, whose name America purportedly wears, then St. Joseph, Virgin Mary, St. Peter, St. Ladislaus, St. Anthony of Padua, St. George and St. Elizabeth. Protestant orders were given the names of the great leaders of the Reformation, such as Calvin, and leaders of the Reformation in Hungary, such as Bethlen. Some society names, listed by the historian [55] are: *Istenben Való Bizalom Alatt Álló Első Magyar Keresztény Betegsegélyző Egylet* (First Hungarian Christian Sick Benefit Society Trusting in God) and *Akroni Isten Áldd Meg a Magyart Betegsegélyző Egylet* (Akron God Bless the Hungarian Sick Benefit Society).

A Hungarian Robin Hood, who robbed the rich to help the poor, Sándor Rózsa, gave his name to a Hungarian organization founded in Racine, Wisconsin in 1914. The reasons are instructive: "It was unanimously decided by our members to secede from the Count Batthyány Society of Chicago and to found the 'Sándor Rózsa General Aid Association.' The Hungarians' faith in associations named after aristocrats has been shaken. The officers' rights in such associations are enormous and so are the members' obligations. That is why there was a real need for the 'Sándor Rózsa Association' where the officers will have the obligations and the members will have the rights."

Many of those who came from Hungary joined American national organizations. One of the larger, was the I.W.O., International Workers' Order, which in 1945 claimed an adult membership of 149,651, juvenile membership of 21,082, and social membership of 2,790. Its Hungarian branch, *Testvériség* (Fraternity) was patronized by Left-wing followers.

American-Hungarians of the Jewish faith founded so many fraternal orders that these were able to support a weekly newspaper of their own, *Egyleti Élet* (Association Life), founded in 1922. These organizations were usually given the names of historic Hungarian persons, such as Kossuth, or Joseph Kiss, a popular Hungarian poet of the Jewish faith, or Theodor Herzl, founder of modern Zionism, himself of Hungarian origin. Sometimes they were named after a Hungarian county or region.

When the Second World War broke out, the lives of many Hungarians—mostly Jews—were endangered in a Europe which was soon to belong to Hitler. The American Committee for Hungarian War Refugees was founded. An attempt was made to save the lives of a few thousand Hungarian Jewish children by making an appeal to

Congress to admit them into the United States under a special law. These pleas fell on deaf ears. In the subsequent reign of terror most of the children were slaughtered.

The Committee helped several Hungarian intellectuals whose lives were in particular danger because of the Nazis' anti-intellectual attitude. When the war was over, it formed an Emergency Division—Save the Children of Hungary—which sent food and clothing as well as financial help to Hungarian organizations catering to the children's needs.

The end of World War II found Hungary badly damaged. During the war much of the country had been turned into a battlefield, bitterly defended by the Nazis and their Hungarian satellites, fighting with their backs against the wall, hoping for a last-minute miracle to save them from the hangman's noose. The ravaged country looked to the American-Hungarians for help. The Washington relief agencies insisted that all factions of Americans of Hungarian origin in the United States should be represented in one fund-collecting agency. The American Hungarian Relief was founded, and received federal government approval to operate. It united several of the divergent political groups in Hungarian America. However, the disruptive forces were too strong and soon the Right wing shook off the Left wing. The work of the relief agency was greatly handicapped by the distrust between the two extremes.

On a smaller scale, the work of the United Hungarian Jews of America was far more effective. The Hungarian Jews had lost about half a million of their number during the war, killed in labor camps and gas-chambers. Some two hundred thousand survived, mostly because the Nazis and their Hungarian *nyilas,* satellites—Arrow Cross Fascist—lacked the time fully to carry out their murderous design. The United Hungarian Jews of America made an attempt to make life a little easier for many of the surviving Hungarian Jews.

The primary function of these associations has been to insure their members' lives, with the exception of the last-named World War II and post-war relief bodies. Sickness insurance did not flourish, because of the difficulties of operation. Many of the fraternal associations, however, have developed social programs. The members met to transact business and several developed real interest in their organization. Some discovered that they enjoyed having an audience for their views. Others found that their neighbors were congenial.

On Saturday, the American-Hungarian, *Amerikás,* made a pilgrimage to his association to pay his weekly dues. He might be in a position to pay larger instalments, but he preferred to visit the fraternal office once a week, for it gave him a chance to meet people. The official in charge was usually sympathetic and, if not too busy, ready to lend him a friendly ear. Then there was the great event of the year, the annual picnic, and the *Amerikás* looked forward to that with real pleasure. There was fun all day and topic for conversation all year. The annual ball, usually on New Year's Eve, saw hundreds, even thousands of members assembled under the same roof. The ex-peasant, a social "isolationist" by nature, discovered the pleasures of social life. If he had had no language difficulties, he might have preferred to associate more with "Americans," his neighbors of German, Austrian or Polish background. But he found America compartmentalized; he had no place in groups outside his own. At home he may never have had a group. In America he had to become a group-minded Hungarian. To be alone on the great Hungarian plains may have been part of his life, but to be alone in city slums would have been too much to bear.

American-Hungary made many attempts to create a congenial social and cultural life in its numerous settlements. One of the most serious was the *Magyar Társulat* (Hungarian Association) of which Dr. Árpád Gerster, greatly admired by his contemporaries, was the driving force.

The need for a Hungarian-language cultural association was great. Immigration was in full tide, and was not selective. Many were the failures, for whom America's dynamic life was too much. The M.T. soon found that it had also to go into charity.

The going was very hard, and the reasons for the hardship were analyzed in an outspoken article of the *Amerikai Nemzetőr* in 1887: "The Hungarian malady is ravaging. First, enthusiasm runs high, and eloquence runs wild. Then, nobody comes around when work is to be done. *Magyar Élet* is vegetating, *Magyar Dalárda* is on paper only, the free Hungarian-English evening school, opened by the city, had to be closed for lack of students, and the *Magyar Társulat* is unable to scare up a quorum for its directors' meeting, according to its President." *Magyar Társulat* was more tenacious than some of the others. It could not operate as a cultural association, so it continued as a travel bureau. It could not operate as a travel bureau, so it became an exchange office. It could not operate even as such, and finally had to close its doors.

But the need was there and bold "promoters" were always on hand to make a new start—and, often, very little else. *Magyar Müvelődési Szövetség* (Hungarian Cultural Federation) was formed and failed. *Magyar Nemzeti Szövetség* (Hungarian National Federation) was formed and failed. The ever-active Tihamér Kohányi refused to admit defeat. The trouble was, he argued, that the organizations were too small. In unity there was strength. Let there be strength by uniting all the small associations. This was done in the "Hungarian" city of the Middle West, Cleveland. The year was 1906. All Hungarian societies of a non-fraternal character were to be merged. The new Federation was to establish free Hungarian libraries, as well as shelters and hospitals for Hungarian immigrants. Since the number of castaways was increasing, a fund was to be set up for indigent Hungarians. The Federation was to cultivate the Hungarian language. It may have been a good program, but it did not get the organization very far. It began to crumble and soon little was heard about it.

As the tidal wave of Hungarian immigration struck America, new attempts were made to get the Hungarians together in cultural associations. A few of the more highly educated new-comers took matters in their own hands, and organized a *önképzőkör,* which they translated as Literary Society. The First Hungarian Literary Society in New York was destined to live a long life. Similar societies were set up in places such as Chicago, Cleveland, Bridgeport, Akron, Youngstown, Trenton, Passaic, and Perth Amboy.

Literally translated, *önképzőkör* means self-training center, in Hungary usually attached to a secondary school, where students made an attempt to teach themselves. The founders also followed the examples of the Chautauqua circuits and lyceum associations. This was the pioneer age of adult education in the United States through the lecture platform. The object of the First Hungarian Literary Society in New York was to arrange debates and lectures, to foster literature and social life among the members and to maintain a library. The Hungarian Cultural Association of Philadelphia set out to foster sympathy for Hungary, secure American interest for Hungary's future political independence, foster the Hungarian language and promote business contacts between the United States and Hungary. The founders' optimism about the future was reflected in these words of exhortation: "If our American Hungarian brethren heed our words, the Hungarians may become the leaders among America's nationalities."

The Detroit *Magyar Klub* (Hungarian Club) entertained and was entertained by some of the most famous visiting Hungarian artists and welcomed some of the best-known Hungarian statesmen. Chicago Hungarians took a bold initiative when they founded the *Egyetemi Kör* (University Association), for members with academic backgrounds. Equally ambitious were the attempts that gave life to the *Amerikai Magyar Diák Egylet* (American Hungarian Student Association) and the *Amerikai Magyar Mérnök és Épitész Egylet* (American Hungarian Engineer and Architect Association) which survived the First World War.

The life of these societies was ephemeral. Sometimes an ambitious program chairman arranged good lectures, debates and musicals, but interest languished. The struggle for life dulled receptivity for cultural matters. The intellectually curious new-comers drifted away from the Hungarian settlements. Card playing in many cases replaced cultural activities.

The end of the First World War saw the influx of a large number of college-bred Hungarians—physicians, scientists, and former lawyers. They struggled hard to keep their heads above water. They lacked introductions into American society. The Budapest café had taken care of their social needs, but there were no corresponding cafés in New York. Several of the intellectuals got together in the early twenties and founded *Ady Endre Társaság* (Ady Endre Society) named after Hungary's greatest twentieth century poet. The Ady Society served as a bridge between the Hungarian-born *intelligentzia* of New York and Budapest. It became a tradition for visiting Hungarian artists to appear on the platform of the Ady Society. New York intellectuals of Hungarian birth took a deep, but fleeting, interest in this organization. A few ardent officers carried on, but there was no new crew to continue the work.

The same fate befell the *Kultur Szövetség* (Cultural Federation) which rallied a band of gifted young artists. This organization had a stage of its own. It, too, went the way of similar attempts.

Other organizations came into existence in other places of the Hungarian diaspora. They corresponded to urgently felt needs of social life, and the variety of functions was great. In the Hungarian sections of Cleveland, for instance, the following were some of the organizations that had their day: Hungarian Merchants' and Artisans' Association, Club of County Gömör, The Democratic League of Cleveland, East Side Labor Home, West Side Hungarian Choral Society, First

Hungarian Spiritist Church, First Hungarian Club of Widows, and of Single Men and Women.

Disunity was not a specialty of American-Hungarians. It was typical of most diasporas in the United States, especially of nationality groups coming from the "autocratic belt" of Eastern Europe, where Hungarians, as well as other nationalities, were living under the oppressors' rule. The immigrants came into a country where there was no police registration, and no police to watch the citizens' (or residents') steps. Their first reaction was that of great relief. Their next reaction was the familiar attitude: "I am as good as you are." The president of any organization became familiar with this state of mind. It was impossible to enforce corporate discipline. Jealousy and rivalry did the rest.

Several attempts had been made to unite the Hungarians. There was one issue on which nearly all ex-Hungarians in the United States agreed after the first World War, and that was the question of Hungary's boundaries in the Trianon Peace Treaty. Even the least nationalistic Hungarians agreed that the frontiers were not just. Large bodies of Hungarians in the border regions were included in the neighboring States. Hungarian irredenta swept the entire country, assuming the proportions of an elemental force.

On New Year's Day 1929 a proclamation was issued to the "people of Magyar America" to send representatives to a grand assembly at Buffalo, to "establish the long-desired American Hungarian unity, express everlasting loyalty to America, and lay down the lines along which a just revision of the Treaty of Trianon can be rendered possible."

The grand assembly met at Buffalo on May 29, 1929, in an optimistic and solemn mood. Fraternal organizations, the churches and the press —the spokesmen of American-Hungarians—were well represented. It was decided to form an American Hungarian National Federation. The delegates' interest veered instantly to the Hungarian boundary problem. The attention of all America was to be called to it in the most spectacular way. Those were the days of the first trans-Atlantic flights. So it was decided to rally to the plan of spanning the United States and Hungary by the trans-Oceanic flight to be undertaken by George Endresz and Alexander Magyar in a plane characteristically called "Justice for Hungary."

The "Federation," launched with such enthusiasm, quickly followed the grand parade of wrecked unity ventures. One of the Hungarian editors wrote its obituary around the theme of *Magyar szalmaláng,* Hungarian straw-flames, flaring up dramatically, as straw on fire, and rapidly turning into ashes. Others meditated on the difficulties of reconciling political divergences, or blamed the failure on the fact that while everybody was perfectly willing to grace the platform and donate a speech, few were ready to work in obscurity and to contribute funds. The "leaders" had made their speeches, had received their share of publicity and now they wanted to rest on their laurels.

The Federation lapsed into oblivion and for years no similar attempt was made to hammer the Hungarians into one bloc. During the decade of great depression the Hungarian-born were too much concerned with their personal problems of livelihood.

In 1937 a World Hungarian Federation was formed in Budapest to unite all Hungarians, at home and abroad, on a common platform. The most important, perhaps the only, plan of that platform was irredenta, the recovery of the regions Hungary lost after the Great War. On February 24, 1939, Regent Nicholas Horthy signed the anti-Comintern Pact which was reputedly directed against communism, not the Soviets, but in reality was a camouflaged war alliance against Russia and, possibly, other nations. On March 15 of the same year, Germany and Italy awarded Hungary a part of dismembered Czechoslovakia. On November 20, 1940, Hungary became a full-fledged member of the Rome-Berlin Fascist Axis.

When World War II broke out, many American-Hungarians felt that they must speak out. Their country of birth lay along the Nazis' road of conquest. Geographical location and diplomatic commitments paralyzed the movements of the Hungarian government. Hitler was the leader of a global irredenta, the champion of the victims of the Versailles and Trianon treaties. Therefore, from the official Hungarian point of view he followed in Hungarian footsteps. Were not the Hungarians the first to launch a war against the peace settlement? True, they had not been able to achieve much but that was the fault of their weakness and not of their will. Now Germany came to the fore with the same program and her voice was heard around the globe. Could the Hungarian ruling classes betray their own past?

Naturally, the Hungarian ruling classes disliked Hitler. He was an upstart, an ex-lance-corporal and a former house painter. Such things were not forgiven in their exalted circle. But Hungarians were the slaves of their geographic location. Their next-door neighbor was

Austria and Austria was Hitler. Czechoslovakia was also Hitler. Hungary was robbed of the chance to act according to her own interests and will. That was the essence of the argument of some Americans of Hungarian origin. America was the home of the largest number of Hungarians outside of the home country. While the voice of Hungary was silenced by the force of circumstances it was the duty of Americans of Hungarian background to speak on behalf of their enslaved country.

The United States was not yet officially in the war when a new American Hungarian Federation was launched in order to give voice to what its leaders considered the real Hungary. On January 7, 1941, the Federation presented a memorandum to President Franklin D. Roosevelt. It was called by its sponsors: "The birth certificate of the new American Hungarian Federation." The Federation pledged the loyalty of American citizens of Hungarian birth to the United States, willing and anxious to fulfil their duties of citizenship in the world's greatest democracy. It recalled the services of Colonel Michael de Kovats in America's War of Independence. Then it stated that "American citizens of Hungarian origin learned with deep regret that the government of Hungary found it impossible to avoid signing a pact with the Axis powers." By doing so, the signers of the document claimed, the Hungarian government had lost its freedom of independent action. The Hungarian people were no longer free to express their will. "The pact is a direct threat to the ancient independence of Hungary, the country of our origin." The Executive Committee of the American Hungarian Federation, therefore, considered it its duty to lead a movement for the preservation of an independent Hungary and for the freedom of its people.

The Federation spoke again a few days before Pearl Harbor. It declared that while it would not accept a Hitler-dominated world, neither would it accept a world of the nineteen twenties "in which the seeds of Hitlerism could be planted," a reference to the post-First World War peace settlement in which Hungary had lost the largest part of her territory. Then the Federation claimed that it would feel at liberty to continue its peaceful struggle for Hungary's "one-thousand-year-old rights" and proposed the fullest autonomy, political and economic equality to all Slovak, Ruthenian and Rumanian nationalities within the boundaries of ancient Hungary. This was an assumption that Hungary, then an ally of Hitler, would have her "ancient boundaries" restored to her. Furthermore, the Federation went on record in favor of a Danubian Confederation, in which Hungarians, Austrians, Slovaks, Bulgarians, Serbians, Rumanians, Croatians, Slovenians, Moravians, Bohemians, and, eventually, Poles would be united for the common good with a view to protect themselves against "either German or Russian aggression."

One of the leading statesmen of Hungary, Tibor von Eckhardt, was then a new-comer in the United States. As a young man he had been the leader of the *Ébredő Magyarok,* (Awakening Hungarians), the prototype of subsequent Fascist movements in Europe. Gradually, he moved away from his extreme stand and headed the *Kisgazdapárt* (Small Landholders' Party). His policy seemed to favor the landlack peasantry, *nincstelenek,* those without nothing, and to oppose the Germans and the Nazis. In foreign relations his policy had long been pro-West, and strongly anti-Communist. There were several suppositions about the object of his American visit. It was said that he had come here as a representative of Regent Horthy, who thus hoped to have both irons in the fire. Officially, he was an ally of the Axis, while unofficially he was a friend of the anti-Axis Western forces. It was also assumed that Eckhardt's object was to prepare an operational basis against the Germans in the United States.

The Federation gave its support to Mr. Eckhardt, but he was given the cold shoulder by Americans of Hungarian-Jewish descent who remembered his early activities only too well. Perhaps more important was the opposition of certain Allied governments to Mr. Eckhardt, the strongest from the Czechoslovak government-in-exile which did not want Hungary to be recognized as a semi-belligerent and thus reap the harvest of victory after the expected Allied triumph.

The Federation committed a grave error in representing itself as having the backing of the American State Department as well as the Department of Justice. That was by no means the case and both departments strongly repudiated the Federation's attempts to appear as the officially approved spokesman of the Americans of Hungarian origin. This was a great blow. Mr. Eckhardt gradually faded out of the picture, while, evidently, maintaining many important Washington contacts.

Other organizations, too, endeavored to rally American-Hungarians for a public demonstration of their unswerving loyalty to their country. They would also help to reach the ears of the Hungarians in their enslaved country. One was a Left-wing organization, Hungarian American Council for Democracy, under the honorary chairmanship of Count Mihály Károlyi, Hungary's post-First World War President, and the chairmanship of Béla Lugosi, the film actor. The policy of the council paralleled that of the Hungarian Council in England, headed directly by Count Károlyi. The Hungarian American Council for Democracy succeeded in enlisting the active help of a considerable number of ardent workers not only in New York, but in other main Hungarian settlements, especially in Illinois, Ohio and California.

Another World War II organization was The New York Council of Hungarian Americans for Victory under the chairmanship of Professor Louis Toth, an internationally recognized authority on accounting. The Victory Council went into several important phases of civilian defense, such as war bond drives, blood donations for the armed forces, Red Cross work, aid to war refugees and the Allied nations' relief fund drives.

One of Hungary's noted criminologists and sociologists, Professor Rusztem Vámbéry was the founder of the Movement for a New Democratic Hungary (*Uj Demokratikus Magyarországért Inditott Mozgalom*). It was a movement of Hungarian citizens living in the United States and it may have been an attempt to create an official representation for "muzzled Hungary," a representation in exile. It failed to achieve that object, but it helped in the war effort by preparing useful memoranda for government agencies and publishing an informative periodical *Harc* (*Fight*) founded by a liberal old-time fighting Hungarian newspaperman, László Fényes, who carried on the battle until his death.

Imre Déri, a well-known journalist, writing in the September 29, 1927, issue of *Az Ember,* militant liberal Hungarian-language weekly published in New York, summed up the story of the organizations of American-Hungarians, as he saw it, in these words:

"The Hungarian American, as an organic body, has never existed. Since immigration began, there have been small and large Hungarian organizations, but they have never had a unified life. One group of immigrants shared no common interests with another group. The Mid-Western miner had no common interest with the New York lawyer . . . the two of them occupying different cultural levels. . . . American Hungarian life has thus grown up around the Hungarian drugstore, the Hungarian butcher shop, the Hungarian sacristy, the Hungarian bank and the Hungarian saloon. . . ."

This is, no doubt, an overpessimistic appraisal. The Hungarian fraternal organizations have filled a need and, incidentally, they have helped create an embryonic social unity. In the long run, of course, it is the fate of all diasporas to be dispersed. It is the fate of these organizations to try, and to fail. Before they fail, they often help accomplish an aim. Exceptions are the life insurance societies which help relieve the great insecurity which is the fate of man.

XIII

RELIGION IN LITTLE HUNGARY

DURING THE TIDAL wave period of immigration, before the First World War, the Church was one of the main buttresses of the Hungarian State, and in return the State supported the Church. "The peasant fears the gendarme, but he fears God even more," was a predicate of the governmental policy. God was represented as a super-gendarme, who saw to it that disobedience to authority was punished by eternal torment in a jail filled with brimstone and fire.

The State was a stern institution, the expression of the voice of authority. The Church, too, was stern, closely allied as it was with the State. It was represented as God's dispensation that land should belong to the few, and that the poor should be always among us. That was the way the true Christian could practice charity, in theory, at least. Besides, the poor would have their compensations for earthly woes in celestial bliss.

There were ministers of the Gospel who entertained different ideas of their mission. They took pity on the downtrodden masses and their hearts went out to them. One of them achieved great fame in Hungary, János Hock, called the "golden-mouthed," because of his dazzling eloquence. He visited the United States after the First World War.

The new Hungarian in America wanted to be attached to his church. Cast into a new environment, a new world, he felt out of his element. He wanted to feel the warmth of familiar sounds and scenes. The awful struggle of adjustment turned the thoughts even of the godless toward a saving grace. All week long the new American worked in mine and mill, endless hours, heartless and brutal hours, but Sunday was his day at home, when he was a free man, and at the church where God understood his language, which men did not understand. The church was to be a link with his children to whom he clung with all his might. He shepherded them into the House of God where they heard the Hungarian tongue, the language of God as the parents understood it. The church was an instrument in keeping his children from becoming strangers in the parental house.

The attitude of the pre-First World War Hungarian governments toward the Hungarian-language churches in the United States reflected the official attitude toward the American immigrants. In the official view, there were two classes of the people: good and bad. The good immigrants were expected to sweat in America, amass a fortune, then return home with their money, and settle down to an obedient and God-fearing life. It was not in the Hungarian government's interest to encourage these good immigrants to make their permanent homes in the United States. Providing them with good churchmen would have amounted to encouraging them to regard America's soil as no less sacred than Hungary's. The bad Hungarians were the trouble-makers and lawless elements. A troublemaker was any one with a mind of his own, and the lawless were those who had escaped the heavy hand of justice. There were not too many of the latter, but people who did not dig into immigration statistics were apt to generalize from spectacular incidents. The bad people did not deserve and were not expected to want servants of God in their midst.

A diplomatic problem complicated the case of the Hungarian church-men in America. Hungary, being a part of the Austro-Hungarian Monarchy, had a joint diplomatic service with Austria, and "joint" meant predominantly Austrian. Hungarians in America were the concern of Austro-Hungarian diplomacy which being mostly Austrian neither cared nor knew too much about Hungarian immigrants. Many American ecclesiastical authorities assumed that Hungarians were Slavs, since they came from a predominantly Slavic part of Europe. The number of Slavs in the United States far exceeded that of the Hungarians. Because of that and also because they were better known to the church authorities, the Slavs had churches of their own.

We have seen that the Slavic group of the Slovaks were Hungary's underdogs. In America, being more numerous and having influential friends among other Slavic groups, they appeared to be more important in matters of church organization. It happened often that American church authorities assigned Hungarian communicants to Slovak churches, unaware that they could not have committed a graver error. The Hungarian immigrant came to America, the land of freedom, only to be shackled to the despised Slovak and, abomination of abomi-nations, shackled to him in church, which he wanted to be his own, for himself and for his children. The early church history of the Hungarian immigrant in the United States is a record of his constant battle against the Slavs.

Hungarian immigrants in Cleveland took matters in hand. In the late eighties they decided to build a Catholic church of their own. However, their good will was far more potent than their means. Thereupon they turned to the local religious authorities who promptly recommended that the Hungarians should get together with the Cleveland Slovaks. That was precisely what the Hungarians did not want, but it was one thing not to want something and another thing to carry their own plan into effect. No matter how much the Hungarian immigrants wanted to have their own church, they could not raise sufficient funds. They had to get together with the Slovaks, if they wanted to have a church of some kind, and that was what they eventually did.

In due time the church was completed and—a great victory for the Hungarians—was named after St. Ladislaus, an erstwhile King of Hungary. But the Slovak members were more numerous than the Hungarian and so, in accordance with the principle of numerical superiority, the American church authorities assigned a Slovak priest to the new house of worship. The priest, known to Hungarian-American church history as Pan Marton, may have been an excellent priest but he was not a good diplomat. It came to pass some time later that the Hungarians of the church wanted to have their tricolor flag of red, white and green, consecrated in the church. Pan Marton was ready to perform the ceremony and he delivered his sermon in—Slovak.

This was entirely too much for the harassed Hungarians who approached the Papal Prelate in Washington with the request that he send an official letter to the Hungarian Primate entreating him to dispatch a Hungarian priest to the Cleveland Hungarian Catholics. This the prelate did, writing to the Hungarian Primate in the city of Esztergom in compliance with the ardent desire of the good people, requesting him to send a priest, according to the specifications of Cleveland's "forsaken Huns, (yclept *Hungariano*.)"

The request of the "Huns" was heeded and Hungary's Primate issued a call for applicants, one of whom impressed him greatly, we are told, mostly because Károly Boehm did not raise the question of compensation. Father Boehm was then a priest in the women's penitentiary at Mária Nosztra. From there he left for Cleveland in the winter of 1892. Upon arrival in the United States, he had the usual troubles with the Slovaks. Thereupon he conceived the idea of building an "all-Hungarian" church. It was not easy to raise the money from poor miners and factory hands of a country where money raising for such purposes was little known, but he was a man of unusual

energy and he did raise the money eventually. Even so it took fully
three years to build the church and when it was completed the Catholic
Hungarians in the United States had their first church.

A priest of evangelical zeal, Father Boehm undertook more than
merely looking after his own flock. He saw to what extent the spiritual
needs of the immigrants were neglected and undertook to fill the gap.
In his missionary work he covered a vast region, all the way from the
Great Lakes to the Atlantic. All who were familiar with his indefatigable industry admired him greatly.

The fight against Pan-Slavism in the church continued for many
years. Sometimes it burst into the open, as at McKeesport, Pennsylvania, where the Hungarians were bent on breaking Slavic influence
through their own church work. There, too, they wanted to build a
church of their own and enlisted the services of a fighting priest, Kálmán Kováts, who was also a newspaper crusader as the editor of the
weekly paper *Star of the Hungarians.* Subsequently, Catholic churches
were built in scores of other Hungarian diaspora centers, such as
Bridgeport, Toledo, South Bend.

We obtain a glimpse into the connection of the Hungarian government with the immigrant Hungarians' churches through the findings
of an investigation of the United States Senate during the First World
War.[56] "The Hungarian government," the Senate document says,
"maintained its hold on both the Catholic and Protestant Hungarian
churches in this country through salaries that were granted to the
priests and ministers."

The investigation brought out the fact that the Hungarian government employed the priests and ministers to promote certain financial
interests of the Hungarian Postal Savings Bank: "In July 1911, Baron
Kornfeld, sub-manager of the General Credit Bank of Budapest, came
to New York to establish in this country an organization known as
Transatlantic Trust Company. The T.T.C. upon investigation made
during the war, turned out to be the agent for the United States of the
Hungarian Postal Savings Bank. Its ostensible purpose was 'to further
and protect the interests of the Hungarians in this country.' As a matter of fact, its purpose was to monopolize, in the interests of the Hungarian government, the business of collecting and forwarding to the
home country the earnings of the Hungarian immigrants in this country . . ."

Then the Senate document continues:

"The priests and ministers became agents for the Transatlantic Trust

Company which, in the words of one of the witnesses, 'used them as drummers and paid them a commission to get immigrant savings to export.' This money, after its return to the home country, was used by the returned immigrants to purchase land. The effect was to increase enormously the price of farm land in Hungary. 'Land which sold, twenty-five or thirty years ago, for $50 an acre, is selling or was selling just before the war, for $500 an acre.' In this way emigration has become for Hungary, as it has for Italy, a national speculation.

"The control which the Hungarian government exercised directly over its churches, by the payment of salaries to priests and ministers, was exercised indirectly over the Hungarian press through the medium of advertising for which they were indebted to the Transatlantic Trust Company. . . ."

It would be rash to condemn the priests and ministers. They were evidently confronted with a *fait accompli;* they had to make their living and, in many cases, the return trip was barred. Futhermore, these business connections were probably represented to them as patriotic acts. Later we shall see some of the other facts the Senate investigation brought out in regard to some prominent members of the Hungarian Protestant clergy in this country.

Hungary was a predominantly Catholic country. But about one-fourth of her population before the First World War—at the high tide of immigration to America—belonged to Protestant creeds, Lutherans and Calvinists. The Hungarian Protestants played a rôle in the history of Hungary which was entirely out of proportion to their numerical strength. They have given the country some of its ablest statesmen, as well as writers and other creative artists. The most important statesmen of pre-war Hungary, members of the Count Tisza family, were Protestants. After the First World War, Admiral Nicholas Horthy, the Regent-Governor during the entire inter-bellum era, was born a Protestant. After the Second World War, an ex-Protestant clergyman, Zoltán Tildy, was elected President of Republican Hungary.

The Hungarian Protestants in the United States also had their early struggles against the Slavs, based on their fear of being swamped by the Slavic masses and thereby being denationalized. The First Hungarian and Slovak Evangelical and Reformed Church in the United States did not last very long.

Protestant Hungarian immigrants turned to their other American coreligionists. The Reformed Church in the United States was the first to lend a helping hand to the struggling Hungarians. One of its able ministers, Andrew Moody, a Scotsman, knew the Hungarians and had lived among them for years. He helped the Hungarian Protestants obtain competent ministers from the Old Country. The Presbyterian Church as well began to take an interest in the Hungarian ministers, with the best motives which were completely misunderstood; it was thought the Presbyterians were contesting the ground gained by the Reformed Church. A feud ensued which ran the regular course of such things, as trifling imaginary wrongs were magnified into major problems which, in turn, were transmuted into grievances, while personal rivalries were rationalized into religious controversies.

The controversy reached the point early this century where it had to stop. Those were the years of "flaming patriotism" among the Hungarians here. The Habsburgs at home appeared to be weakening and the hope was entertained that the Hungarians' national grievances would be redressed. Zoltán Kuthy was the main proponent of the idea of an all-Hungarian Protestant church in America as an integral part of the Protestant churches of Hungary. At the general assembly in Johnstown, Pennsylvania, the Hungarian churches were to break with their American parent bodies and join the Hungarian parent organizations. Largely as a result of Kuthy's work the project was whipped through in record time, but the unseemly haste created a strong reaction. An internal feud broke out among the churches that had joined the parent body and those that had not. The feud was extremely bitter as feuds among brothers usually are and by the time it blew over the original issues may have been forgotten but not the wounds inflicted on one another.

The connection of Zoltán Kuthy with the Transatlantic Trust Company was also brought out at the Senate investigation in Washington, to which reference has already been made. The Senate document states: "So close was the relation between the Transatlantic Trust Company and the subsidized Hungarian churches that on October 27, 1914, the following circular was sent out to the Hungarian churches of the Eastern diocese to be read to their congregations:

"Beloved Brother Co-Religionists:

"Your superior Church Authority, the Dean of your Diocese, sends you a message. He sends you the message that our sweet Hungarian fatherland is in danger. All her arm-bearing sons have enrolled under the flag, and even if one thousand deaths await them, they take their healthy lives with determined readiness into the fire of battle with this exclamation: 'We will either triumph or we will die for the Fatherland!' But, out in the battle, only men fall. They left at home wives and children; and old people must live, and, they, perhaps, are starving; because the breadwinner has gone to heroic battle—for all of us! Brothers! Sorrow and poverty are at home. Children's lips are asking bread from sad mothers. It is not true that you who are at home and can give enough bread to your children are happy in the thought. Oh, do you hear across the sea, no matter how great the ocean is, that many hundred thousands of Hungarians are exclaiming to you: 'Help us, you who are in America!' Brothers! Those who have at home parents, children, brothers, or relatives in this famine, do not forget them. . . . And he who sends money home shall send it through the Transatlantic Trust Company (207 Second Avenue, New York), the money-sending blanks of which, after this service, will be distributed at the church door, and which money institution is in every respect reliable and which is *officially recommended* also for the support of the churches by the *Most Reverend and Right Honorable President of the Conventus*. Brothers! Hear my words and then *act!* Send money home through the Transatlantic Trust Company to members of your family in Hungary, to your relatives, and every cent and every dollar of yours will be blessed!

"All of you are greeted with love by

Dr. Zoltán Kuthy
The Dean of the American Eastern
Reformed Diocese."

During the war the "joined" churches—those that had joined the Hungarian parent bodies—were taken over by the Alien Property Custodian. After the war, they were absorbed by the American Reformed Church, in accordance with the so-called Tiffin Agreement.

The largest of the Protestant churches of Hungarian-born Americans after the war was the Reformed Church in the United States, consisting of the Eastern, Central and Western Districts. Most prominent in the Eastern District was the Rev. Géza Takaró, a liberal and dynamic minister, recognized not merely in the Hungarian but in the American Protestant community as a leader of Americans of Hungarian descent. He was the motivating force behind many public-spirited progressive actions, and during the Second World War he came as close to being recognized as the undisputed leader of progressive Americans of Hungarian background as was possible for that community. Nation-wide attention was attracted to his initiative during the Second World War in attaching the Star of David to the garments of the members of his congregation in New York at a special service, at the time when that star was used to designate the Jews of Hungary as marked persons.

The Hungarian churches affiliated with the Presbyterian Church in the United States, built up numerous churches in the industrial and mining regions of the East. The Rev. László Harsányi, minister of the New York church, gained great reputation among Americans of Hungarian descent because of his public-spirited work.

The Independent American Hungarian Church comprised several parishes over much of the Hungarian regions of the United States. The Protestant Episcopalian Church also had Hungarian-language parishes and so had the Southern Presbyterian Church. The Independent Hungarian churches must also be mentioned.[57]

Small congregations were maintained by the Hungarian Baptists, Methodists, Seventh Day Adventists and Unitarians. The last are apt to call theirs the "Hungarian creed" because in the early days of its agitated existence, the Unitarians gathered strength in the sheltered hills of Transylvania, which was later reunited with Hungary. Transylvania was, indeed, after Poland, the homeland of the Unitarian creed.

A word must be said about the minister's mission in the Hungarian colony, and it applies, in many cases, not only to the Protestant denominations. The pastor's function in the immigrant colony is even more important than among the native-born, since the immigrant, when he first comes here, is cast into a great void. Then the frailty of man is revealed and even the strong tremble, seeking admission into God's presence.

The best among the Hungarian-born pastors in America are inspired leaders. They are personal friends of their parishioners and especially of those who stand in need of help. They visit the sick and the aged, bringing them solace that only fullness of the heart can give. They find the right words to heal smarting wounds and sit at the bedside of the dying. They do not talk down to their congregation from their lofty pulpits, but raise them to their own level, and give them the spiritual nourishment that only men of heart can give. The ministers at their best are social leaders who cultivate interdependence, co-operation and the cult of ethical values.

The following letter, written by one of his parishioners tells the story of what one Hungarian minister has done for his congregation: [58] "His first task was to build a new church, dedicated in the fall of 1924. Within a year it was paid for, a rare occurrence in the history of Hungarian churches in the United States.

"This event inaugurated a new era in the religious life of the American-Hungarians in that section of the Eastern Ohio coal and steel country. His Sunday school classes have always been attended by a large number of children. The Bible class of his church is famed in the district. Its Ladies' Society is reputed for being always first in charitable and welfare work. Its girls' choirs and clubs are providing fine music for the services and wholesome association for the younger set. Its religious and social work is many-sided, comparing favorably with the work of congregations in the larger Hungarian colonies of the United States.

"While American to the core, the minister keeps alive the Hungarians' best cultural traditions, thus enriching this great land of intellectual, political and religious freedom."

The enlightened Hungarian pastor knows there is a natural tendency among the immigrants to congregate in colonies and a similar trend among the native-born to avoid the "foreigner," and therefore makes a special effort to bring the native-born and the Hungarian-born under the same roof. His own home may be turned into a social center in which the two groups find a common ground, or he may arrange for inter-cultural church services in which the native-born and Hungarian-born participate. He may arrange Hungarian exhibitions, dances and other cultural activities at which the "old stock" and "new stock" become acquainted. A Mid-Western minister scored success by arranging harvest festivals at which non-Hungarians were introduced to the artistic gifts of their Hungarian neighbors.[59] When calamity strikes the old country, as it often does, or when war comes to the new, the church becomes a community center in new ways. Then the church premises become beehives of public-spirited people working for a new cause.

It would be too much to expect all ministers to be of this high caliber. The nationality pastor often knows that he wages a losing battle. The language of his sermons has no roots in American soil, while his own roots are in the Hungarian language. It is vital for him to keep alive the Hungarian traditions and Hungarian language in the United States. Up to a certain point that is a laudable undertaking, since it helps prevent the separation of fathers and sons. But there is a limit, which can be easily overlooked, when the cult of the Hungarian language becomes the principal cult of the church. In a Hungarian West Virginia colony I saw a Hungarian pastor sweat blood over the attempt to make immigrant miners' American-born children learn the Hungarian text of the then popular song: "Gloomy Sunday." You might have thought that the minister's own salvation depended upon his pupils' memorizing the depressing words of that dismal song, and it probably did. He may have wanted to be sure that a large enough supply of Hungarian-speaking parishioners would be available for his old age.

For the same reason, the pastor of any nationality may become the spokesman of Old World jingoism. His great fear is that his parishioners—above all, their children—may be sucked into American life. If that actually happens he is bound to lose his own livelihood. He will pay the expected lip service to the United States, but it will sound hollow. In his heart he says: "Hungary, my country, right or wrong." It makes little difference to him whether or not the Hungarian government is democratic. Admiral Horthy's cabinets between the two wars were certainly not that. Yet some pastors professing loyalty to American democracy were also devoted to Hungarian autocracy. By attacking the Horthy regime they were afraid they might cut the ground from under their feet. They might alienate their parishioners' sympathies not only from one man and one regime, but from what that man and that regime stood for—the minister's livelihood, Hungary.

It also happened sometimes that pastors of not too great intellectual attainments obtained parishes in immigrant colonies. At one time it was not unusual in certain parts of Europe to have difficult pastors "exiled" to America by their church authorities. One of these ministers received a questionnaire from his superiors, asking him, among other things, about the social activities of his church, and he replied indignantly: "I have nothing to do with socialism."

More and more the Hungarian-language churches in this country will feel the necessity of supplementing their actual church services with social services, to insure the sympathetic interest of the younger generations brought up in the American way. How long the foreign-language churches can function under the system of restrictive immigration is a question which only time can answer.

The path of the Hungarian-born Greek Catholics, known also as

Uniates, was beset with difficulties in the United States. Before the
First World War most of the Greek Catholics came from what was
then Hungary, while the rest came from that part of northeastern
Austria known as Galicia.

The Greek Catholics recognize the Supreme Pontificate of the Pope
but they have their own Eastern rites. As soon as they were ready to
support a church of their own in this country, they petitioned the
Holy See to send them priests, since their rite was little known in the
United States and priests of their denomination were not available
here. They did not realize what complications they faced.

In due time, the priests arrived, a group of bearded men, several
with their families. These were some of the features in which the
Greek Catholics differed from the Roman Catholics: they could wear
beards and up to a certain ecclesiastical level they could marry. But
the American Roman Catholic authorities did not know that, when
these events occurred toward the end of the last century. They had
never seen bearded priests with families. They thought that this was
a group of heretics who should be placed under the ban. Rejected
brusquely by the American Catholic hierarchy, one of the bearded
priests of Hungarian origin, Elek Toth, impetuously turned to the
Greek Orthodox religion, which was not and is not in communion
with Rome and does not recognize the Pope as the head of the Church.
He was then placed under the nominal universal—oecumenical—head
of that church in Constantinople, capital of the Ottoman Empire.
This universal head, the patriarch, was supposed to be the direct suc-
cessor of the oecumenical head of the Eastern Church flourishing
in Constantinople until the coming of the Turks in the mid-fifteenth
century. With the arrival of the Turks, the Eastern Church was broken
up, its most important segment becoming the Oriental Orthodox
Church in Russia, headed at first by a Patriarch and, later, by the Holy
Synod, which was hand in glove with the government of the Russian
Czars.

This is necessary for an understanding of the complications that
followed. The step of Elek Toth in joining the Eastern Church was
not merely an ecclesiastical matter,—it appeared to be also a significant
political step, since it was at that time Russia was trying hardest to
fight her way to southern warm waters. In that attempt she was employing a veritable armory of devices, one of which was the Eastern
Orthodox Church. Russia represented herself as the keeper of the
Third Rome, and the protector of all Eastern Orthodox communicants.

Most of those outside of Russia were situated in the Balkans and adjacent regions, including eastern and northern Hungary. Toth's conversion therefore appeared to promote Russian aims and he was duly denounced as a traitor to the Hungarian cause. The Czar's government appears to have scored a point.

The majority of Hungarian Greek Catholics, however, did not follow Toth's example. They sent an urgent petition to Rome with the request to send them a bishop of their own kind. Their call was heeded but not in the way they wanted. And here again politics entered the religious scene.

This happened on the eve of the Great War which was to see the Austro-Hungarian Monarchy and Russia at daggers drawn. In preparing for the showdown, the Habsburgs needed to insure the loyalty of the doubtful borderland nationalities, one of which, the Ukrainian, had a very large number of Greek Catholics. Because the Habsburgs were influential at the Vatican, the Greek Catholic Bishop sent to America was not a Hungarian, as expected, but a Ukrainian. The Hungarians needed no such sop—they were considered reliable. A religious issue thus had become a political one. The Vatican at the same time wanted to pacify the American Roman Catholic hierarchy which could not conceive of priests being married.

The new Bishop dispatched by the Vatican was Stephen Ortinszky Soter, a Galician, and a protégé of the Cardinal of Lemberg, the largest Galician city. Formerly he had belonged to the Basilican Order. He brought with him a Papal Bull, *Ea Sempre,* which provided, among other things, that the Greek Catholic clergy in America could be stripped of its right to marriage. He was to publish the Papal Bull at an auspicious moment. The Hungarian Greek Catholics were aroused against the Galician bishop and somehow they got wind of the Papal Bull, which they did not like. The weight of authority was on the side of the Bishop, while the weight of the masses was on the side of the clergy. A protracted tug-of-war ensued and finally a compromise was reached. The Bishop gave his pledge to keep aloof from politics and not to publish the Papal Bull, in exchange for which the Hungarian communicants in this country accepted his rule.

When the Czars were gone after the war, the Greek Orthodox Church in Russia went into eclipse as a political force, and Greek Orthodox Hungarians were no longer a political football. They received a bishop of their own.

It is a curious coincidence that Hungary gave three of the greatest rabbis of modern times to the United States, representing the three great trends of religious thought. Rabbi Philip Klein became a leader of ultra-conservative Jewry in the United States. Rabbi Alexander Kohut became the leader of the conservative reformers. Rabbi Stephen S. Wise became known as the leader of the reformers and of Jewry throughout the world.

Rabbi Philip Klein was born on the morrow of the defeat of the Hungarian liberal cause espoused by Kossuth, and after rabbinical work in Hungary and elsewhere in Europe he came to the United States in 1890 where he became the American leader of the ultra-conservative *Agudath Israel,* and honorary president of the Union of Orthodox Rabbis of the United States and Canada. He died in New York in 1926.

Sándor Kohut, known to the Jews of the world as Alexander Kohut, was born in the Hungarian town of Félegyháza in 1842 and was called to a New York congregation in 1885. It is said that his coming sharpened the differences between the radicals and conservatives which precipitated the calling of the Pittsburgh conference in the year of his arrival here. At that conference the reform group of rabbis declared their independence from tradition. Kohut was the author of the monumental Talmudic dictionary, *Aruch Hashalem,* in nine volumes, in which he presented the etymology of Talmudic words and cleared Talmudic passages of later accretions. He was professor of Talmudic methodology at the Jewish Theological Seminary of America until his death in New York in 1894. His wife, Rebekah Kohut, born in Kassa, Hungary, became well known in the United States because of her welfare work, particularly in the field of employment. George Alexander Kohut, her step-son, and son of Alexander Kohut, made a name for himself as a teacher and rabbi.

The great Jewish leader of the first half of the twentieth century was Stephen Samuel Wise. He was born in Budapest in 1874, of many generations of rabbis running back to the seventeenth century. His mother was Sabin de Fischer Farkasházy, a member of the Hungarian nobility. It is interesting to reflect that his father, Aaron Wise, was for a time identified with the ultra-orthodox religious movement in Hungary. The father of Aaron was himself a chief rabbi, Joseph Hirsch Weiss, the original name of the family in Hungary. Before the family settled in Hungary, it lived in Moravia and its name was Weissfeld.

Stephen was brought to the United States from Hungary when a small child. After his education in New York, he headed the Madison Avenue synagogue in the last decade of the nineteenth century. He married Louise Mayer Waterman, his companion and inspiration. During the next six years Stephen S. Wise served as the rabbi of Beth Israel Synagogue in Portland, Oregon, and even at that time he revealed remarkable gifts as a leader. He founded the Oregon State Conference of Charities and Correction, becoming its first vice president, and founded the first section of the Federation of American Zionists. He also became Commissioner of Child Labor in the State of Oregon.

In 1906 an event occurred which was to leave its mark upon his future work and the history of the American Jews. In that year he was called to New York with a view to his occupying the pulpit of Temple Emanuel, the most influential synagogue in the country. He had a talk with the president of the congregation, Louis Marshall, a noted Jewish leader of his day. It was Marshall's contention that on controversial issues the pulpit should be under the control of the board of trustees of the synagogue. Rabbi Wise rejected this proposal even though he knew that in doing so he was losing the most desirable synagogue pulpit in America. Next year he founded the Free Synagogue and there announced two unbreakable principles: the rabbi was under the control only of his own conscience, and there were no reserved pews.

Rabbi Wise was a reform Rabbi. Emphasis was shifted to the living language of the worshipers—to English—instead of Hebrew. The faithful uncovered themselves in the reform synagogues. Rabbi Wise revealed an oratorical ability that had no parallel, and his admirers did not overstate their case when they called him the greatest orator of America. His impressive presence, rich voice and a full heart that spoke to the heart turned his sermons into great events. His pathos fitted in perfectly with his personality and yet was not out of place in an age which seemed to stress the matter of fact even in spiritual matters. He had the gift of persuasively presenting Jewish problems to Gentile audiences and thus became a link between Judaism and the Gentile world.

Even before this, he founded the Zionist Organization of America. It is of interest to note in this connection that the greatest Zionist leaders of the world, with few exceptions, have been Hungarians. The founder of the Zionist movement, Theodor Herzl, was a Hungarian.

So was the greatest writer of the Zionist movement, Max Nordau, and so was the greatest orator and one of the greatest organizers of the movement, Stephen S. Wise. And yet the Hungarian Jews were the most anti-Zionist Jews on the surface of the globe until the Second World War. Then the majority changed their minds.

Rabbi Wise founded the American Jewish Congress to represent the Jews of America and help them solve their special Jewish problems. He was the president of the delegation of the American Jewish Congress at the Peace Conference in Paris in 1919. He founded the World Jewish Congress to co-ordinate Jewish self-defense activities against discrimination and persecution throughout the world. He founded and became the President of the Jewish Institute of Religion, which was to train rabbis who were to be also social leaders in their communities.

Rabbi Wise played an important part in arousing world public opinion to the dangers of Hitlerism and was influential in promoting the idea of a boycott against the Nazi Third Reich. After World War II the organizations he founded were largely instrumental in collecting material on the guilt of Nazi war leaders supplied to the international tribunal at Nuremberg.

His two children have distinguished themselves in American life: James Waterman Wise as an author, and Justine Wise Polier as a judge and social worker.

As a national religious community the Jews of Hungary did not play an important part in the United States. Most of Hungarian immigration before the First World War was non-Jewish. If the Jewish immigrants joined any group, most likely it was a neighborhood synagogue without any special nationality affiliation. They did have a few smaller synagogues of their own, mostly Orthodox, in which they readily mixed with other European strains. There was therefore no modern Hungarian synagogue in America when, on the eve of the Second World War, conditions in Hungary forced many Jews to seek safety in this country. It was then that a former rabbi of Nagyvarad, George Lányi, founded a Hungarian congregation *Uj Fény,* in which the more progressive religious traditions of Hungarian Jewry were to be perpetuated.

XIV

Print in the Native Tongue

Opinions regarding the use of the foreign-language press in the United States are divided. It dulls the edge of Americanization, some observers believe; the immigrant would more easily become acquainted with American ways if he had nothing to read but the vernacular press. The foreign-language press perpetuates the nationality "ghetto," which in turn disturbs the unity of American life.

The other side maintains the diametrically opposite conviction that the foreign-language press performs an important mission. Most of the immigrants from the non-English-speaking countries are ignorant of the language of the United States and would be virtually deprived of the freedom of the press without their own, which can be a beneficial and potent instrument for acquainting the "greenhorns" with the American way of life. It is a commonplace that only a well-informed citizenry can inspire well-informed national policies or is in a position correctly to evaluate the qualifications of candidates for public trust. Without the foreign-language press, a large number of immigrants would lack the necessary information for good citizenship. Even after immigrants have mastered the English language they may still want detailed news about the home country, native literary trends, or institutional and church life.

The press in the United States attracted the very people who at home had read few papers, either through lack of opportunity or a distaste for the stereotyped journals of an oppressive regime. They found themselves in a land where newspaper reading was a habit. Working time here was shorter and even the comparatively poor people could afford to spend a couple of pennies for their favorite daily. Moreover, usually the immigrant now lived in the city, where life throbbed with excitement—sports, the latest news about that dream car, a fire, a sale, a hold-up, a show, a murder, a dance. In America the immigrant could improve his lot, but in order to do so he had to be informed.

The interesting fact has been noted about the foreign-language press that, with the exception of the Left wing, it is extremely nationalistic in home country affairs. "National consciousness is inevitably accentuated by immigration. Loneliness and unfamiliar environment turn the wanderer's thoughts and affections back upon his native land. The strangeness of the new surroundings emphasizes this kinship with those he has left." [60]

"The nationalistic tendencies of the immigrants find their natural expression and strongest stimulus in the national societies, the church, and the foreign-language press—the institutions most closely connected with the preservation of the racial languages. In these the immigrant feels the home ties most strongly; they keep him in touch with the political struggle at home and even give him opportunities to take part in it. Both consciously and unconsciously they might be expected to center the immigrants' interests and activities in Europe and so keep him apart from American life." [61]

These remarks apply to many Hungarian-language newspapers in the United States. The average paper is inclined to accentuate Hungarian nationalism for the identical reasons that the churches of the Hungarian-born accentuate it. The clever newspaper identifies itself with the homeland, burning incense to it, representing it as the beloved parent. The immigrant, saturated with these ideas, will overlook the reasons that made him turn his back upon the dearly beloved homeland—a homeland so devoted to its more highly privileged children that it had little more than the bread of exile to offer the underprivileged.

Then, too, as we have already seen in another connection, the immigrant, even though his one vote counts as much as the vote of the native-born, feels that he is in a world apart, a kind of purgatory, and that not he but his children will be privileged to enter the kingdom of American heaven. Knowing this—often inarticulately—he will compensate by working up a pride in his home country which at home he never had. It is a curious case of delayed loyalty.

As in so many other things, the name of Lajos Kossuth is associated with the beginnings of the Hungarian-language press in the United States. *The Hungarian Exiles Journal* (*Magyar Száműzöttek Lapja*) of Charles Kornis Tothvárady, is the first Hungarian-language newspaper on record. It attempted to be the spokesman of Kossuth's followers, but there were never too many of them, and they were scattered all over the country, so that this paper never had more than 118 subscribers—not enough to make a paper prosperous even in those leisurely days.

The Hungarians in America had another newspaper before the tidal wave period of Hungarian immigration struck these shores beginning with the eighties. A couple of literary people, Dr. Wilmos Loew, about whom more will be said, and Árkád Mogyorossy, sought to convince the public that a Hungarian-language newspaper was a public need. In 1879 they established *Magyar Amerika* (*Hungarian America*) "devoted to the cultural interests of Hungary and America." It is interesting today to read a part of its program, revealing the contemporary mentality: "*Magyar Amerika* wants a mighty, thriving, happy Hungary. It wants universal well-being for all Hungarians wherever they may dwell. It wants to help raise Hungary's beautiful literature to the high place it deserves, wants to acquaint broad segments of American life with our fatherland, our national habits of thought, culture, spiritual and material resources, thus counteracting the nefarious work of our malicious neighbors. We also want to depict our new country to our readers, providing them with a truthful picture. . . ." Obviously, the accent was on Hungary and the United States was merely a transit station. The two editors expressed their pet ideas in two issues of the paper and then it went out of existence.

The first Hungarian-language newspaper with greater staying power was *Amerikai Nemzetőr* (*American National Guard*) first published on February 1, 1884. It described itself as a "journal devoted to the cultural interests of Hungary and America," and later as a newspaper "devoted to the interests of over 600,000 Hungarians in the United States." In those days there were no more than about fifty thousand Hungarians in the United States. The following reasons were given by the editors for the existence of the paper: "The Hungarians in America have no contact with one another. Our business and other interests have dispersed us all over the continent. . . . It is imperative that the Hungarians living in this country should have a newspaper to manifest their manly courage in defending the interests of their native country abroad." Obviously, here, too, the accent was on the Hungarian native land. "We may have lost our Hungarian citizenship," the editors remarked, "but no law can deprive us of our right to be devoted to our own fatherland."

Guiding spirit of the paper was Gusztáv Sz. Erdélyi, the Nestor of

Hungarian journalists, a born reporter and a devotee of printer's ink. He had a thorough knowledge of Hungarian immigrant mentality. He knew it was not sufficient to defend Hungary in the abstract. The fatherland must be defended against a real enemy and no more ideal foe could be found than the Slav. Erdélyi carried on a crusade against the Slovaks, who were oppressed in Hungary, and were free in the United States, where they outnumbered the Hungarians.

The time became ripe for a "big-time" Hungarian press when the great wave of immigration struck the United States. Erdélyi was not the right man to get it started. He was too emotional and temperamental, too subjective and inconsistent. His fighting spirit did not always show up well in print. Occasionally, his paper sounded like a querulous provincial sheet.

Erdélyi's modest fame was in decline when there came to America the Hungarian immigrant who gave American Hungary her first full-fledged newspaper, Tihamér Kohányi. We are told that his early life was "full of student stunts, political fireworks, primadonna-chasing and duels." [62] In 1891 a fellow immigrant lent him a few hundred dollars to launch a newspaper, which he named Szabadság (Liberty). It celebrated the fiftieth anniversary of its foundation in 1941, the oldest and one of the most important Hungarian newspapers.

Six years later Kohányi merged a galaxy of small papers, one of which was significantly called The Star of Hungary (Magyarok Csillaga), the others being Magyar Farmer, Esti Ujság, Amerikai Magyar Hirlap, Magyar Hiradó. He was a man of great energy, a good organizer and very vain. He expected unstinted admiration and received it. He wanted to become the Hungarian leader in the United States and came closer to it than most. His leadership was recognized in Hungary as well, so that when he paid a visit to his home country in 1901 he received a hearty welcome. It must have been the source of great satisfaction to the ex-scapegrace. The President of the United States, William Howard Taft, paid him high tribute at the twentieth anniversary celebration of Szabadság. One of Hungary's noted writers, Géza Gárdonyi, wrote to him: "Your paper has become a beacon light flashing to our dispersed brothers. Through your paper the Old Country and the New World are shaking hands every day."

A pessimistic view of the Hungarian-language press and its readers was given by one in the field just before World War I: "The editors of *Szabadság* have a curious theory which shocked me a great deal when I first joined the paper, but which I found later was working smoothly enough. It is usually summed up in the motto, 'Anything is good enough for the buddy'—buddy being the universally used term for the Hungarian immigrant worker. The word, adopted originally by the Pennsylvania and West Virginia coal miners, has been assimilated into the American Magyar idiom and is now spelled 'bodi.' ... The average Magyar reader has no sense whatever for news value; in the outlying districts he gets Monday's *Szabadság* on Wednesday, then saves it for Sunday, when the whole week's editions are carefully perused from beginning to end. The 'buddy' calls any item found in a newspaper a *hirdetés,* meaning advertisement; the editorials, the news and feature stories, are all 'advertisements.' This does not imply —what is often the truth—that these items have been paid for; advertisement in the American Magyar idiom simply means reading matter. The big display ads of patent-medicine druggists are perused just as religiously as the front-page war stories. In fact, they are liked better, because they are printed in bigger type and are more closely related to everyday life. And, indeed, while the editorial and news columns in most Magyar papers are written with an almost incredible carelessness, these 'real' advertisements often display much ingenuity and skill—in a way, they are the most 'American' items in the whole paper. . . .

"In the case of the Hungarian-American newspapers within the range of my personal observation, the leading consideration, as far as details of editorial routine are concerned, was simply to get the paper out with as little effort as possible. Viewpoints of editorial and even business policy were frequently overshadowed by the editors' unwillingness to exert themselves, by their determination to 'take it easy.' In other words, a more or less unconscious editorial sabotage was being practiced. The explanation lies in the conditions of the trade and the type of men engaged in editing Hungarian-American newspapers. The men working on the editorial staffs of the *Szabadság* and *Népszava* were not, for the most part, professional journalists at all—that is, they were not journalists in the old country. . . . They resign themselves to a hand-to-mouth existence, and simply cease to care. . . . To work for the *Népszava* and *Szabadság* means not only getting into a rut, but being bottled up in a cul-de-sac.

"In regard to the smaller 'one-man' weeklies, the situation is not much better. For the publisher-owner-editor the chance of 'making good' has hardly anything to do with the journalistic-literary quality of his sheet. As a rule, he has no local competitor, and his sources of revenue lie mostly in the way of the petty graft of parish-politics and fraternal society intrigue.

"I do not hesitate to say that in the instances within my range of observation the influence exerted by the *Szabadság* and *Népszava* on the social life among Hungarian-Americans has been almost without exception an evil one. This is to be accounted for, not by any particular personal wickedness on the part of publishers, but by the isolation of the Hungarian-American settlements and by the fact that Hungarian-American newspaper power constitutes a monopoly compared to which the condition of the American press seems democratic."[63]

When World War I broke out the Hungarian press was rent by a conflict of loyalties. Many, perhaps most, of the immigrants of those days considered themselves transients. They wanted to return to a prosperous Hungary after the war.

"In trying to write what would please their readers, and at the same time avoid offending the United States government, the editors often had to steer a tortuous course, making sudden shifts and tacks."[64]

The vicissitudes of the editors are well exemplified by the following excerpts:[65]

What the Editor Wrote about Hungary

Central Powers Period

"If German militarism were destroyed today, it should be resurrected tomorrow that it might save civilization." (January 16, 1917)

Period of Wavering

"The American Hungarians singing the ever-stirring American national hymn, the 'Star Spangled Banner,' with a sigh in their hearts for the country of a thousand years, will say inwardly, 'God save the Hungarians.'" (April 6, 1917)

American Period

"For several centuries the Austrian double-eagle has dug his talons deeply into the entrails of the Hungarian national body. . . . Every Hungarian is fully aware of the fact that neither Germany nor Austria was ever a well-wisher of Hungary . . ." (October 9, 1918)

What the Editor Wrote about America

Central Powers Period

"Yes, we are loyal to our country and to the flag. We are ever ready to sacrifice our lives in defense of our rights . . . but we would not be worthy of our citizenship if we would for political reasons hide under the mantle of hypocrisy and do homage against our own conscience to the Chief Executive of this nation." (February 24, 1917)

Period of Wavering

"For a long time we did not know why Lord Northcliffe transferred the capital of his Kingdom of hatred and instigation from London to the United States. Now we know why: It is to work against the foreign press in this country and against peace. The sad thing is that some day the war will end and then the German-Americans as well as the other foreigners will be nice men again, for they will be greatly needed. But destroyed cities can be rebuilt; destroyed love, never." (August 22, 1917)

American Period

"Registration is over. The Austro-Hungarians, too, have registered, not merely because it was made their duty by law, but because they realized that if they help their adopted country—the United States—they also serve the land of their birth. We have explained a hundred times . . . that in this great war America is also fighting Hungary's war for independence." (September 14, 1918)

The growth of the Hungarian press reflects the growth of Hungarian immigration and the increase of literacy among the immigrants. In 1884 the Hungarians in America had only one newspaper. In that same year the number of German-language newspapers in the United States was 621.

For the next six years the entire Hungarian-language press in the United States consisted of a single newspaper. The following year, however, the number increased suddenly to four. In 1892 it dropped to three and remained on that level for the next seven years. In 1898 the number of Hungarian-language newspapers rose to five, staying at five for four years. It fluctuated between five and twelve until 1913, when the number increased to fifteen. Although immigration was cut off by war, the number of the Hungarian-language newspapers increased. They reached twenty-seven in 1918 and have remained at about that number since then. The Hungarian press grew because America was no longer a transit station. More newspapers had been launched, of course, than survived. Between 1884 and 1920 the number started was sixty-seven, most of which, however, ceased publication. The mortality rate in the foreign-language press is high and this ratio of births over deaths was not at all abnormal.

The largest Hungarian-language daily in the East and one of the most important papers in the Hungarian colony was launched in 1899 by Géza D. Berkó, *Amerikai Magyar Népszava* (*American Hungarian People's Voice*). Unlike *Szabadság,* which began as a weekly, *Népszava* started its career as a daily. This may explain why each claims to be the oldest Hungarian-language daily paper in the United States. Berkó was an able newspaperman and gave his readers what they wanted; he made no attempt to educate his reader to want more refined fare.

The Left-wing press was represented by *Előre,* which was transformed into *Uj Előre* and, after a period of hibernation, emerged as *Magyar Jövő* (*Hungarian Daily Journal*), describing itself as "A Democratic, Anti-Fascist Daily," and claiming forty-five years of previous existence in 1946. Most of the time it was rather combatively anti-capital and sentimentally fond of the Soviet system. It was one of the few newspapers that did not attempt to pursue a nationalist Hungarian policy in the United States and never waged a war against Czech, Slovak or any other Slav. *Előre* was the publication of the American Hungarian Socialist Federation and *Népakarat* belonged to the American Hungarian Socialist Labor Federation.

The Second World War found the Hungarian-language press of the United States in a position that was not basically different from its position during the First World War. In the First World War Hungary, as part of the Austro-Hungarian Monarchy, was on the side of Germany. In the Second World War, too, Hungary was lined up with Germany, as one of the satellite States. Shortly after Pearl Harbor, the Hungarian government declared war on the United States.

There was one difference, however. The Second Reich of Kaiser Wilhelm's Germany may have had some extenuating circumstances in the eyes of those who tried to find them. Its crimes did not in any way compare with the hideous deeds of the German Third Reich of the Nazis which would have been inconceivable in the darkest ages even of the most backward countries. There was a degree of American sentiment for the Germans in the First World War, while there was no open public sentiment for the Nazis, with the possible exception of the inevitable lunatic fringe. We have seen that attachment to the *anyaföld*—motherland—had been stressed by numerous Hungarian-language newspapers in this country. Hungary, in their eyes, could do no wrong. Therefore, they had to explain away her relation to the Germans. Two explanations seemed possible: Hungary had acted under duress, and was impotent to act against the German juggernaut; Hungary was not an ally of the Germans, except in name; in reality, she was rooting for the Allies' victory.

Some of these papers developed the technique of an editorial double-talk, paying tribute to the American soldier in one sentence (many readers' sons were in the United States armed forces) and casting doubt upon the justice of the cause of the United Nations, suggesting directly or indirectly that the other side must not be ignored. Such editorials would make no sense to the uninitiated outsider, but evidently did make some sense to some readers, who were made to believe that for obvious reasons the writer could not express himself freely. The impression was conveyed that the reader should look for hidden meanings.

When Hungary entered the war on the side of the Axis, some of these publications were extremely bold in their attacks against this country, "even to inciting their readers to return 'home' and take up arms against the United States." [66] Another newspaper asked: "How has the World War begun? America, still a neutral country, was beginning to give aid to Hitler's enemies." Attacks were concentrated on two members of the United Nations—Czecho-Slovakia and the Soviet Union, the former because the Czechs had always been the pet foes of Admiral Horthy's Hungary. The Soviets were attacked during the war—and not merely afterwards—as the enemies of civilization.

The extent to which some Hungarian newspapers were permeated with an anachronistic old Hungarian spirit was amusingly illustrated by one of them which described American soldiers of Hungarian origin not as Corporal Michael Ban, for instance, but as "Vitéz Michael Ban, corporal." *Vitéz* was the designation of the Horthy regime for its special favorites who had distinguished themselves on the field of battle. It means "stalwart."

These papers, however, formed only a minority. The best representatives of the Hungarian press stood loyally by the United States, categorically denounced the double game of the Horthy regime, and indulged in no double talk.

The principal Hungarian settlements are the main Hungarian-language newspaper publishing centers. New York, Cleveland, Detroit, Pittsburgh, Chicago, and other cities in Ohio and New Jersey have their Hungarian newspapers. Altogether about forty Hungarian-language newspapers are published in the United States. Three of these are dailies, most of the others are weeklies, and a few are fraternity publications with a limited circulation. Most of them describe themselves as "Independent" or "Non-party," while a few call themselves "Democratic," "Catholic" or "Religious." There is a lone "Republican" paper. There is even, at the time of writing (1947) a monarchist monthly publication, promoting the candidacy of Otto von Habsburg to the "Hungarian throne."

The combined circulation of the papers giving out that information amounts to about a quarter of a million. These figures are mostly "publishers' statements," and do not in the least appear to be understatements. The decline of the foreign-language press can be clearly traced by following the circulation figures given in the years 1942 to 1947.[67] The daily *Szabadság* reported in 1942 a circulation of 40,612 (Post Office statement) and in 1947, 22,709 (sworn statement), a reduction of almost one-half in five years. The corresponding figures for the *Népszava* were 27,984 and 25,045.

One of the most vigorous Hungarian weeklies, *Az Ember, (The Man)* has a unique history in Hungarian journalism. It was founded in Budapest on the morrow of the First World War, under the editorship of Ferenc Göndör. He supported the Hungarian Republic under Count Mihály Károlyi, but did not support the short-lived Hungarian Communist regime after the First World War. From Budapest the weekly was transferred to Vienna where it fought Hungarian reaction. Göndör became one of the most hated men in the Hungary of Regent Nicholas Horthy. While many of the former political exiles were gradually forgiven and some of them returned to their native country, Göndör moved his weekly from Vienna to New York, where it was established in 1926. It became known as a vigorous fighter for liberal causes and, subsequently, a great admirer of the policy of President Franklin D. Roosevelt. The paper made many friends as well as foes.

Other weeklies, too, took a vigorous hand in fighting for liberal causes and popularizing Americanism among the new-comers. Among the dailies, *Szabadság* took an effective stand for liberal democracy.

The readers of the Hungarian-language press in our day have few pretensions to literary interests. Most of them speak an American Hungarian jargon and subtleties would be lost on many of them. They are interested in the story, and not in the style. An idea of the nature of this press may be gained by an analysis of an issue selected at random in the post-Second World War era. There was no design in selecting that particular issue and this newspaper was selected only because it claims the highest circulation among the dailies.[68] The issue contained six standard-size pages, and of these about one and a half pages were devoted to ads. The first page contained half a dozen news items, divided between the world, America and Hungary. The items were highly condensed—as they must be by the very nature of most foreign-language papers. A strong criticism of the Soviets was contained in a signed editorial, which, evidently, the paper wanted to feature. Most items on the second page were devoted to fraternal, charitable and church organizations, and other features of Hungarian-American life. It also contained news dispatches from New Jersey and Detroit where the paper probably had its largest body of readers. Sprinkled over that page, too, were some items of world events and domestic affairs. The third page contained a collection of national and international items, an instalment of a novel, and a featured report about the expected arrival of American food shipments in Hungary. Ads on this and on the preceding page were of resorts, movies, Hungarian restaurants, employment and money remittances to Hungary. The fourth was the editorial page, the center of which was occupied by a United Feature Syndicate cartoon showing a world politician modeling "that promised brave world" out of common clay entitled "old mistakes." There was a second editorial criticism of the Soviet Union apropos a speech by Britain's Secretary of State for Foreign Affairs, and the other editorial discussed current Hungarian problems. The same page contained two feature articles: one from Budapest, describing how the women of that city were turning rags into costumes, and the other an account of the trip of an editor of the paper to a Maryland farm owned by a Hungarian, full of bucolic scenes, written, obviously, for ex-farmers. The fifth page contained a medley of such news as a folksy honeymoon trip and military discharge, a golden wedding story from Buffalo and a Tarzan strip. Finally, the last page contained a foreign and a domestic item, while the rest was devoted to ads—physicians advertising as specialists for sex diseases (one of them specifying that he charged only two dollars for an examination).

The Hungarian-language press—like the other foreign-language presses—is facing the problem of survival. The older generation's ranks are thinning, and there is very little replacement. The second generation turns to the English-language press. In order to prolong its few remaining days in the sun, some of the foreign-language papers add English sections. There again the difficulties are great. An English-writing staff must be acquired. Once part of the paper is published in English, the standards of comparison become more exacting.

In the special case of the Hungarians, the larger part of the post-war immigrants were intellectuals who either knew English or set out to master it. They were quick to see that in America one should live as an American and that the American press is one of the best keys to American life. Among these Hungarian-born there developed a cult for *The New York Times,* their secular Bible. There they found stories about their own country and other regions in which they retained an interest. More and more the younger generation introduced into the homes of the foreign-born the habit of reading English-language papers. The decline of the circulation of the Hungarian-language press was a clear indication of its impending doom.

Part 5

A HUNGARIAN INTERMEZZO

XV

THE BIRTH OF AN INDUSTRY

THE FIRST WORLD WAR cut deeply into human destinies, but the life of individuals and institutions went on. The boats disgorged their human cargoes and all along the Ohio the sky began to glow with the light of countless plants. Bright patches of light were dropped along the Eastern Coast, the Great Lakes, the Erie Canal, the Hudson, the Delaware, Susquehanna and countless other American rivers. The American Century was in the making—the century of organization and concentrated industrial power, the century of mass production and mass consumption. Consumption by people who had previously never consumed such quantities and qualities. The shops and mines devoured the steerage, and disgorged purchasing power, ambitions and bold dreams. Most of those dreams were buried with the dreamers, but sometimes they came true.

What makes dreams come true? A bold dreamer must dream it, ready to risk all, to lose all or to win all. The dream must be contemporary, fitting into the age and place. To such dreams the moving picture industry owes its existence. And two of the pioneer dreamers were Hungarian immigrants, Adolph Zukor and William Fox.

"Bread and circuses," the Roman masses shouted. Throughout history bread and circus were companions. Bread the Hungarian plains produced in abundance and the circus became an important Hungarian product. Perhaps the mating of East and West in the Mid-Danube basin had fertilized the national genius. From France Gallic wit irradiated this part of the Danube, while from the opposite direction the brooding Russian Slav made his influence felt. From the South came the radiation of the Latin and from the Near-West came the Teutonic influence.

In years to come the Hungarian theater was to dazzle a large part of the world. In the fourth quarter of the last century a Hungarian expatriate, Bolossy Kiralfy, created vast "spectacles" in the circus and on the vaudeville stage. He was considered a pioneer by his age. Not many years later came Max Reinhardt, born on Hungarian soil, even though he considered himself an Austrian. His meteoric rise was unique in stage history. Adolph Zukor did not know anything about these men in his Hungarian youth and he probably was not conscious that Hungary's intellectual location may have had some connection with his future fate.

His birthplace, Ricse, will not be found on most maps. The year in which he was born, 1873, was auspicious for that small village. We may be sure that there was little organized entertainment in that place. Naturally, there was no theater and as to music, the inhabitants provided it with their lungs. Husking bees and wedding feasts were the occasions which the younger people anticipated. At the burial feasts the older people had a good cry and a good time. Adolph Zukor was orphaned in his childhood, brought up by an uncle, animated by the best intentions to help his nephew become a man. The boy felt the loss of the parents deeply. Or perhaps he merely wanted to get away from the confining influence of the Magyar town. People of that type are urged onward by an inner driving force. He made up his mind to go to the United States and was only fifteen when he reached New York.

He shared the fate of the masses who went from ship to shop. His hours were long, the pay small and an error at the sewing machine might cost a week's pay. There was only so much a young man could take of that. Zukor paid his apprentice fee and then struck out for himself. What could he lose, except time, and he was too young to worry about that. Business acumen was the quality he possessed. As American standards of life rose, he realized that he could reap a rich harvest by going into the upholstery trade. With higher standards came softer chairs.

With higher standards also came more and more customers for fur, an index of the rising national prosperity. If young Zukor had been sentimental, he would have developed an attachment to upholstery and might have worked in that trade all his life. But he was not so involved and so he crossed the lines into the fur trade, which seemed to him the trade of the future. You could make a lot of money on furs those days; later you could make large fortunes. Fate willed that young Zukor should not tarry in that trade too long. A debt of three thousand dollars had been coming to him from a friend who had thought he could turn the money to good account by buying a penny arcade of peepshows. That was entertainment which masses throughout the world, whether in Rome or New York, seemed to crave. The friend was not doing too well and Zukor was not in the habit of letting three thousand dollars go overboard. So he decided to look into his friend's peepshow business.

In the early nineties, the fertile brain of Thomas Alva Edison hit upon an exciting idea—a photograph with a fast-moving shutter that took a large number of pictures in a very short time. Usually, the pictures revealed men of heroic stature flexing their huge muscles. This thing, the kinetoscope, began its promising career on April 14, 1894.

Two years passed, and an improvement called the vitascope came into being. It was a screen projector devised by Thomas Armat, which freed Edison's peepshow from the confining box, projecting it on a screen. This marvel was first revealed to the public in the "Music Hall" of Koster and Bial. The vitascope fare was provided by dramatic incidents, such as a fire engine in a fire-alarm death ride, a policeman chasing a luckless tramp, or a snowstorm weirdly scouring deserted streets.

An Edison cameraman, Edwin S. Porter, conceived the next idea, a bold one indeed. The cinema, "moving picture," should tell a connected story—a plot—instead of merely depicting an incident. *The Great Train Robbery* was a classic of that era. Itinerant showmen displayed films on portable projectors. Custard pies flew back and forth between Mack Sennett and Ford Sterling. Bobby Herron dashed into disaster in pursuit of the voluptuously swaying grass skirt of Mae Marsh. The first theater devoted exclusively to the showing of "movies" was opened in a Pittsburgh storeroom. The price of admission to the fifteen minute show was a nickel, hence the name "nickelodeon."

The penny arcade which Adolph Zukor inspected was situated in the great New York amusement belt of Fourteenth Street and Union Square, and one of its alluring items was a nickelodeon. The sweaty crowd might not have impressed a less perceptive person, but to Adolph Zukor they were mankind in search of satisfying a great human need

—entertainment. If he had stopped at this philosophical observation nothing would have happened, but he did not stop there.

This type of entertainment was then a "penny-ante business." Why? These arcades, Zukor meditated, could be turned into far more profitable ventures if they were taken more seriously. He was business-minded by training and thought in terms of investments. His friend had lost the three thousand dollars because he had been penny-minded. Zukor got together with several friends and they raised a capital of $76,000 with a big ho-heave-ho. This was big business.

"I was not merely stepping down," he observed, "but also stepping out of respectable society." The fur trade was a respectable occupation; the penny-arcade was not. Having come from Hungary, he must have been very conscious of social values—or perhaps just sub-conscious of them. If his former set would not stoop to the entertainment business, he would lift its level to theirs—or even higher.

The nickelodeon, which was the best part of the arcade, did not appeal to the so-called better crowd. It was a pastime for children and adults with immature minds, they said. And so, indeed, were the early thrillers, such as *The Outlaw and the Child, True Love Never Dies, The First False Step* and *Mary's Strategem*. A blunt director put it all into one telling sentence: "People want action, never mind the acting." Films were boosted as having a strong moral tone. Crime, of course, never paid in the end, but it was lots of fun while it lasted. In refined homes brows may have been raised, but the films flourished just the same. Soon nickelodeons covered the Eastern cities, parading under the de-luxe names of Bijoux, White Way and Lyric.

Zukor happened to see a color film made by Pathé, the French producing firm, in 1907. It lasted fully forty minutes, much longer than the average film. It was hand-colored, not very skillfully. The subject was a biblical scene, not well presented and wholly uninspired. The film must have been boring, according to the standards of today. But Zukor was interested in it and, even more, he was interested in the audience. People in the audience, used to the films' pie fare, were deeply moved and some of the spectators, thinking momentarily that they were in a church, fell on their knees.

Adolph Zukor was not thinking in terms of man's eternal groping for self-expression and the projection of himself on the screen in the form of a heroic substitute. He merely saw that there was a tremendous future in pictures. What the masses needed was mass entertainment. The legitimate stage was not that by its very nature. It reached a limited number of people and production costs were high. But the costly hero could be multiplied many times on the screen, so that the share of each exhibitor was small. There was no telling how far this "toy" could go.

In those days, moving picture producers—curiously—were not primarily interested in the films. Mainly, they were interested in selling projection instruments. In later years the plight of the broadcasting companies was to be somewhat similar at first. They were interested in selling receiving sets. The producers could not sell projection instruments to the distributors unless the latter had something to project. Therefore, the producers had to provide the films, but merely as byproducts. Whether the films were good made little difference to some producers, who thought that films were a passing fad and were bent merely on making hay while the sun shone.

Moving picture production was then in the hands of a "trust," the Motion Picture Patents Company. The early twentieth century, when Zukor went into the films, was the age of bigness in the United States. Since trusts dominated many important industries, it was natural that a trust should dominate the cinema. The film trust was described as an "airtight monopoly." It followed the line of least resistance. As long as the public appeared to be content with its products, what was the sense in changing them? And the public would remain content with what it had as long as it was prevented from comparing it with something better. That "something better" was therefore to be kept from the public. If Zukor tried to improve the quality of the movies he would run into the hostility of the trust. An insignificant little man in appearance, he was indomitable in action. The trust had money, and money could be fought only with more money. That he did not have, but he was going to get it. Another cinema pioneer, Marcus Loew, could be persuaded into following the Zukor line. The two launched their project.

The American trust limited production to two-reel films. In Europe there was no movie trust, and there they were experimenting with multi-reel pictures of some artistic merit. The best European film, in Zukor's opinion, was *Queen Elizabeth,* produced in Paris by Lou Mercanton. The title rôle was played by Sarah Bernhardt, and Lou Telegen played Essex. Zukor decided to buy the American rights of the film which cost the then fabulous sum of $18,000.

The hold of the trust was so great that even foreign films could be exhibited only with its approval. Zukor, therefore, had to apply for a license issued by the Motion Picture Patents Company. It is recorded that he had to cool his heels for three hours before he was admitted into the presence of the monopoly moguls. The scene behind doors has not been recorded, but the little man must have advanced some telling arguments to induce the Patents magnates to grant a license.

It was one thing to have one multi-reel picture but it was something else to have such films accepted by the public as its regular fare. It was then that Al Lichtman entered the picture in a major rôle. Al was also of Hungarian descent and although young he had had an adventurous life. Stage-struck, he had started his career as a theater "water boy," peddling trays of water to audiences at Tony Pastor's Theatre in Fourteenth Street, New York. From the auditorium he found his way to the stage, but was unable to conclude a pact with success. An unemployed actor was not even as good as an employed "water boy," so in order to have something to do and to get his three meals a day he joined the army. Now a poster about *Queen Elizabeth* was shown on the boards of the Old Revere House in North Clark Street, Chicago, announcing that that stupendous film was available to a young man of ambition to sell to out-of-town distributors. Al's military service at an end, he went on the road selling the picture and, to use a modern cinema term, he was a "sensation." He returned with $80,000 worth of contracts in his bulging pockets.

The première of the film took place in the Lyceum Theatre in New York. All those who had an interest in this experiment seemed to agree in advance to accept its success or failure as a test. The public, brought up on the pie-flinging two-reeler, might not like a four-reeler dramatic subject. But the public loved it. "This is it!" Zukor commented. His mind was made up. The public did want good actors playing in good dramas. The moving picture industry could be turned into an adult entertainment and Adolph Zukor's prestige would be enhanced.

The movie trust had evidently been represented at the opening. Here was a challenge to its conservative policy. It launched a campaign against the innovation. "Feature craze" was the derogatory name the rivals concocted. The public would not stand for the eyestrain required by a multi-reel film. It could not sit through a film lasting a full hour. Just in case it could, the trust saw to it that it would not have a chance. It refused to issue licenses to Zukor and obtained injunctions against him on some trumped-up reason or no reason at all. The trust thought that it could give the "works" to a meek little fellow like Zukor. Even his own associates misunderstood him; they called him "creepy." But that was only a superficial impression. If he had had punch only, they might have floored him, but he had craft also, and plenty of it.

He could not get features from the trust and it would not license his foreign importations. There was only one thing to do: go into production himself, in collaboration with a small group of friends who trusted the little man with the big ambition. His first selection was a hardy perennial of the stage, *Prisoner of Zenda,* the first American-made full-length feature film. The ice was broken. The paternity of the modern film industry is interesting. Adolph Zukor, the pioneer adventurer, had been a furrier. Carl Laemmle, who introduced the modern star system into the films, had been a clothing dealer. Another product of Hungary, William Fox, produced the first "super-film" in a field which he helped to turn into a "super-industry," and he had been a commission merchant.

The trust and the independents could not thrive on the same grass and so the independents trekked westward. On the outskirts of the southern California deserts, in the very heart of nowhere, they founded Hollywood. It was a remarkable place for original locations of all kinds. Within the radius of a few miles the producers had real deserts, real snow-capped peaks and real ocean surf. Pursuing the independents, the trust also moved westward. True to its loyalties, it kept on turning out "shorts."

Zukor's example fired the imagination of several other producers. The adult fare of the movies now included such films as *Cardinal Wolsey* by James Young, and *The Birth of a Nation,* by D. W. Griffith, America's first "super-feature." As an independent, Zukor was beating the trust hands down. His Famous Players' Film Company grew into the Famous Players-Laski Corporation and it prospered as California flowers do under spring rains. The best-known players of those days were signed up by Zukor: John Barrymore, John Mason, Mrs. Fiske, to mention just a few.[69] Zukor's next venture was the Paramount Pictures, which became one of America's largest motion picture companies. One technical improvement after another was achieved. Years later, sound, elusive for years, became a triumphant reality. Then came technicolor.

The film industry had been raised to an extremely high level of technical proficiency. It was a blend of several old arts—a new art. It could afford to employ the best in everything—best writers, best players, best designers, best musicians and best directors. The arts in the past catered to the mature-minded, and their number was always limited. This was an art that catered to hundreds of millions. Hollywood became a by-word in Africa and Asia. The names of American film stars were no less well known in Warsaw, Poland, than they were in Detroit, Michigan. What Hollywood represented as the American way of life became the American way of life in the eyes of hundreds of millions from Murmansk to Capetown. Here was an unheard-of chance to reach those millions who could not be reached by the traditional arts. Here was the great opportunity to acquaint the people of one part of the world with the people of another part, to inculcate forward-looking, progressive, bold ideas into mankind—the vastest educational project in history.

Some of the pictures Hollywood produced were art and a few of them were more than that—they were inspired art at its very best. The movie industry projected some peaks on the world screen—but most of its products were lowland. Who was to blame for this: Adolph Zukor and the other movie pioneers?

The answer can only be guessed. Zukor staked only a few thousand dollars when he staged his "revolution." Today a single film may cost millions and such ventures normally do not breed revolutionaries. Play safe, go slow, are the slogans of caution. It is hard to find a common denominator for the professor of the Sorbonne and the water boy of Baghdad. It is hard to find a common ground even in the United States. It requires time for the masses of the people to take to superior entertainment. Why take risks? Adolph Zukor made his contribution to the films in his day. Have all the film magnates made theirs?

Zukor became a famous American institution, but the graves of his parents exercised a strong magnetic force. His visits to Ricse brought the magic touch of Hollywood to Zukor's native village and made some of its fondest wishes come true.

Another film pioneer was William Fox, born in the Hungarian village of Tolcsva (which he misspelled "Tulchva"). The year of his birth was 1879, and he was only a few months old when he was brought to the United States. As a youth he began his career as a commission merchant and, like Zukor, he was fascinated by the potentialities of the movies. He did not share the view of those who regarded the film as a passing fad. He believed firmly that it had a tremendous future and in that belief he was ready to stake all his fortune, $1,600, on the success of the industry.

Fox had two principles in his years of *Sturm und Drang,* as he saw it in retrospect: "For more than thirty years I avoided carrying a watch. I never wanted to know what time it was. My day ended when my work was completed." And the other principle: "All these years I craved something more than just eating, sleeping, working, but I had missed it. And now the thing that attracted me to this picture business was that I was able to give pleasure to some one else. I was rather inspired. I had the feeling that I was doing just a little bit more than making money." [70]

He acquired fifteen show "Palaces" in Brooklyn. He organized the Box Office Attractions Film Rental Company to buy and lease films. When he found that the material was inferior, he went into production himself. Whatever he touched, promptly turned to gold. He wanted money, no doubt, but he insisted in later years that money was the means merely, and not the end. He had a sense of fulfilling a mission, while he was making money. His Fox Film Corporation made money. His first major production, *Life's Shop Window,* made money. A group that invested $400,000 in his enterprise saw the market value of its original investment increase twenty-five times in fourteen years. The market value of the securities of the Fox companies amounted to the fabulous sum of $300,000,000 in about a decade. The gods were jealous of lucky people in classical times, and William Fox found out the banks perform the rôle of jealous gods in modern times. The record announced blandly in 1930: "William Fox sold his interests in the Fox Film Theaters."

The story of that sale was told by Upton Sinclair in a thick book of more than three hundred closely printed pages. It was a sad story of jealousy and greed converging upon a man who had tried to get away from the hungry pack. He could not. He was set upon and despoiled of the fruits of his labors. Upton Sinclair was not aroused because a super-millionaire became a mere multi-millionaire (when the expedition against William Fox was over, he was still in possession of twenty million dollars), but he was irked by the brazen indecency of a campaign of spoliation. This was a story of *You Can't Win,* but not the kind Hollywood likes to show. It was an illustration of the fact that you can't win even if you are a multi-millionaire, if you fall prey to the greedy pack. Sinclair used the fate of William Fox as the background for his thesis that the film industry was potentially the greatest educational force in the world. It could become a force to unite the people of the globe, bringing them closer together in pursuit of a common aim. Having that cosmic force it must not be allowed to be exploited by greedy people for private profit. It must be run for the public benefit, intellectually as well as financially, filling not only the purses of the few but the minds of many.

William Fox helped the moving picture industry reach more people. Perhaps his intentions of improving the quality of the films were greater than his achievements. But he did have a strong sense of responsibility. Had he been allowed to continue his work he might have been better able to live up to those lofty principles.

These two Hungarian-born pioneers of the film industry set the pace. We shall see that the Hungarian-born in the American film industry were destined to play important rôles later on as well.

Part 6

A NEW WAVE

XVI

An End and a Beginning

An age was dying; was a new era being born? The moribund age held out a bold promise and a hope for a sane world in which nations would not exterminate one another for the sake of a better world. Horizons had been extended to include not merely the globe but the entire universe. Man dared to think in terms of himself, and not in terms of old myths. It appeared conceivable that words of promise could be translated into action. All men should have an equal start in life.

Today we know that the First World War was not a cataclysmic line of division. It was merely a landmark on the long road mankind travels. At one point there was a fork in that road; one road continued precipitately upward, the other dropped steeply. Technical progress continued on the rising road and social progress on the other.

Some prophets proclaimed the impending doom of man. His progress passed through cycles in the same way seasons of the year followed one another. Summer is followed by autumn and winter drives out the fall. Could we expect the leaves of elms to sprout under the December snow? Could we expect the sun to rise at midnight in the Arctic at Christmas time? Others tried to explain the disaster by pointing out that this was the age of the masses, untrained in self-government, unschooled in restraint. It would take generations before the masters learned how to conduct themselves. Meanwhile we would experience the explosion of a democracy of intolerance and ignorance. Adding up the ignorance of millions did not make for a perfect system. Democracy was not free from the taint of bigotry. The rule of the masses was not necessarily superior to the rule of the few if the masses represented mass crudity. Still others maintained that our troubles followed a historic pattern, that mankind was ready to shed the skin of one type of civilization. The nation was the skin to shed, as the institutions of feudalism had been shed. The institution of nationalism had caked into an almost indestructible mold, and rivers of blood would be spent before it yielded to a more inclusive political organism. In the meantime, we would pass through a Time of Troubles. That, eventually, might be followed by a united world.

The great change that came over mankind was most apparent in Europe. How else could one explain the fact that so many millions were ready to turn their backs on their native lands, testing their strength in a new and alien world. On the eve of the First World War, the number of alien admissions to the United States in a single year amounted to a million and a quarter, nearly all from Europe. Clearly, the cradle of Western civilization was too crowded; there must be something basically wrong with a continent that had to eject such vast masses of people every year.

The rush of immigrants was broken by the First World War. Millions of potential immigrants found their new homes in graves on the battlefields scattered all over the continent. What would happen after the termination of the war? An impoverished Europe could support its teeming millions even less well than in the supposed golden age of pre-war times. Would Europe's tens of millions force the gates open and overcoming all obstacles press their way into the United States?

Immigration was resumed two years after the end of the war on a large scale. In that year the number of aliens admitted was 430,000, and in the following year it was nearly double—805,228. If immigration was unchecked, would America be flooded by the surplus of Europe? The United States had been the only country of vast vacancies to welcome countless millions in the past. Canada, while hospitable, had never encouraged large-scale immigration. The large new continent of Australia had welcomed only immigrants from the British Isles. South America had only recently emerged from economic colonialism, even though more or less politically independent.

After the war, the United States passed through a brief period of depression which, however, from the European point of view, looked very much like prosperity. The United States still appeared to be the continent of the future and perhaps even more so than before. A debtor country in pre-war times, she was now a creditor nation. All the rest of the world was indebted to her. In the rear rank as an industrial nation in the past, she was now far in the van. The gap be-

tween American and European standards widened further. Parts of
Europe were physically devastated, northern France and Poland, for
instance. Psychologically all Europe was demolished. For centuries
the Queen of the continents, now she was about to become their servant. Europe seemed to be a small extension of the vast Eurasian continent, overcrowded not merely by people but by hatreds. Europe was a
nervous wreck, the great casualty of the war. The power of attraction
of the United States became irresistible. Past history provided few
parallels for such disparity of standards. Perhaps there was a parallel,
the more historical-minded wondered, long ago when Rome stood in
the center of the world. Then, too, there had been a rich people surrounded by a hungry universe. The hungry world finally converged
upon the rich and the days of Rome were numbered.

Some such thought may have been in the minds of the American
lawgivers, when Congress passed the Emergency Quota Act in 1921.
It was a revolutionary break with America's past as the land of free
immigration, which would have revolutionary consequences for Europe
and, perhaps, for the rest of the world. The Emergency Quota Act
limited immigration in any year to three per cent of the number of
each nationality in the United States, according to the 1910 Census.
Under this act only 5,747 persons of Hungarian birth could be admitted into the United States in any one year, a tremendous drop from
the pre-war annual average. The act, which applied to all countries
with the exception of those in the Western hemisphere, was to be in
effect for one year, but it was re-enacted again with some changes for
a period of two years.

In 1924 a new act was passed, establishing a quota of two per cent
of the number of any nationality residing here in 1890, with certain
exceptions. It provided that the two per cent quota should remain
in force until 1927, when it should be replaced by what was called the
quota of National Origins. Government experts were to find out what
was the real composition of the American people in 1920 and immigration quotas were to be apportioned among the nationalities admis-
sible under the quota. Total immigration from all countries under the
quota was limited to 150,000 a year. The new scheme entered into full
force in 1929.[71]

Hungary's annual quota under the new law was 869. For the sake
of comparison, let us mention the fact that the quota of the United
Kingdom was 65,721, while that of Germany was 27,370. Here was the
expression of that basic change in American immigration policy. The

new policy had the twofold aim of restricting, and selecting, the number of immigrants admitted into this country. The selection was made on the basis of their national origins and not on individual capacities. The existing "racial structure" of the United States was to be stabilized by restricting quota immigration to the racial composition of the country. While the lawmakers did not say so, the laws hit hardest those regions of Europe which before the war provided the largest portion of new-comers—Southern and Eastern Europe. Again, the legislators did not say so, but the facts did state that the law was directed against Catholics and Jews, Italians and Eastern Europeans. Western Europe was to produce the largest contingent of immigrants. Altogether, the total number of immigrants was to be reduced fully 85 per cent from the pre-war high.

In the early post-war years a great fear haunted a seemingly influential section of fair-haired, blue-eyed American public opinion—the fear of radicalism. Russia had gone Communist, a Soviet Republic had been set up in Hungary and radicalism had penetrated as far as Munich where another Soviet Republic had been set up, and the Rhineland where the Left wing had attempted a coup. The red flag had been hoisted over Italy's factory districts. Two American-Italian anarchists, Sacco and Vanzetti, were railroaded into death because they resembled the devil in his radical disguise. Bolsheviks and radicals, generally, were the enemies of man, and many of them had swarthy skins and dark hair.

American labor also had a hand in the selective immigration act. Unlike European labor in those days, American labor was not "ideological," but pragmatical. It was concerned merely with wages in the United States and believed that large-scale immigration would increase the supply of labor and thereby reduce its price, wages. It was not concerned about Europe's millions whose lifeline would thus be severed.

Other countries followed suit and one gate after another was slammed in the face of prospective immigrants from Europe. The millions who could turn to America before the war were shut up now in a jammed continent, with all their poverty, hatred and hopelessness. In due time Italy's dictator, Benito Mussolini, began to rave about the need of his people to find a place in the sun. The keynote had been struck and a bevy of dictators arose to rant about *Lebensraum,* living space. Shell-shocked Europe now also had claustrophobia.

In the first post-war decade, 1921 to 1930, according to the U.S. Immigration and Nationalization Service reports, 4,107,209 aliens were admitted into the United States. In the second decade, with the quota laws in full effect, the number dropped precipitately to 528,431, and in the period of 1941 to 1944 it went down to 132,833.

The war over, a minor wave of immigration began to beat against American shores, depositing here an average of six thousand Hungarian newcomers in each of four years, within the existing United States laws. Then the full force of restrictions began to make its impact felt.

The figures for 1929 and 1930 are especially instructive. Non-quota immigrants from Hungary account for the increase from 857 in 1928 to 1,045 and 1,265. Again these figures show that the expulsive power of the country of emigration is less potent than the power of attraction of the land of immigration. Hungarian economic conditions in those years were not worse than in previous ones. On the contrary, with many of the war scars healed, the economic trend was toward improvement, especially with the aid of foreign capital. But the United States had just reached the peak of frenzied "prosperity."

The rapid decline of Hungarian immigration to the 1934 low of 284 is also significant. American consular officials abroad had instructions to keep down admissions. The cataclysmic depression in the United States served as a deterrent to immigration anyway. The labor market was cluttered by more than ten million unemployed.

When the Second World War came to Europe, admissions to America increased greatly: 1,348 from Hungary in 1939, 1,902 in 1940. Wisely, our government decided to save people from the Gestapo hangmen, when the Nazis were poised to overrun all Europe. Unfortunately, not enough of them were saved.

The figures on emigration tell a dramatic story of immigrant fate. There was 1921, with its very high figure of emigrants (12,153 to Hungary alone), the accumulation of several war years. People who had been prevented by the war from returning home, those who had left their families in the Old Country, or people who had accumulated capital to satisfy that great urge to buy a piece of land, now decided to trek eastward.

However, the tide of emigration slowed down rapidly. Foreign countries had fallen heir to many Hungarian immigrant homes. Life in Hungary was not enticing; it never is in a defeated country. Just the same, emigration was in excess of immigration in the years of the great depression, 1932 and 1933, and up to the last moment some Hungarians kept on returning to their country, even though the war was on. Most of them were "Aryans" who did not mind Hitler and possibly wanted to occupy their privileged places in the "New Order" of a racially "purified" Old New World.

The United States and Hungary were enemies during the Second World War and yet the figures show that Hungarian immigrants kept on coming into this country, even though their number declined to the mere trickle of 54 in 1945. These were Hungarian-born from Allied and neutral countries.

The nature of Hungarian immigration to the United States changed completely in the inter-war period. We have seen that the large majority of Hungarian immigrants before the First World War came from the rural districts, ex-peasants, who entered the grand army of unskilled labor in the United States. Under the operation of the postwar quota laws, the ratio of peasants in the small Hungarian quota was insignificant. The majority of the new immigrants were professionals—lawyers, physicians, scientists, engineers, artists and, generally, white collar workers. This was a change significant enough to enlist our interest.

More Hungarian peasants would have come, no doubt, if it had been possible under the quota laws, and if steamship fares had not risen. Kinsmen in America could have defrayed the fares and sometimes did, but in many cases the war had severed connections. But there were more important reasons than these for the peasants to stay at home. A "climate" was created by the authorities which did not encourage the peasant even to think of leaving his country. It was considered "unpatriotic." Human cannon-fodder must be stockpiled, not merely inanimate war material. The climate was that of an impending war and the entire national economy of several European countries was placed in the service of the coming conflict. The ramparts had to be manned. That was also the policy of the leaders of Europe's New Order of perennial warfare, Mussolini and Hitler, who turned human stockpiling into a system. Not content with having a large surplus population on hand, they designed plans to increase that surplus through the speed-up production of babies. An overcrowded human market would generate the explosive forces that would help blow the old order sky-high.

Then, too, Hungary, along with other parts of the Danube valley, was becoming industrialized, slowly, but surely. According to American standards the industries were small and wages low, but according to regional standards the change was notable. If the Hungarian peasant could not work in Pittsburgh, he would make his way to the Csepel plant in Budapest.

Before the First World War—as we have seen—the peasant was scorned in Hungary. The passage of time brought about changes. An agrarian party came into existence, and the peasant was now courted. At long last, something like agrarian minimum wage laws were enacted. The wages were small and the landlord found means to evade his obligations, but the peasant felt he had some protection. Everywhere else in the Danube valley the large estates were broken up and distributed among the small peasants. In Hungary the land-reform was less than half-hearted, affected only a small fraction of the total. The beneficiaries were a privileged class of farmers groomed to become the praetorian guard of an extremely conservative regime. While reform did not relieve the pressure for land, some peasants may have thought that it was only a beginning.

Above all, the anti-Jewish policy of the post-war Hungarian regime held out much promise to the tillers of the soil.

After the First World War Hungary had a short-lived democratic republic under Count Mihály Károlyi, followed by an even shorter-lived Soviet Republic in which an ex-prisoner of war in Russia, Béla Kun, played the leading rôle. The latter was an extremely amateurish affair, carried on by people untrained in government, acting upon dramatic impulses and imitations of Russian precedents which most of them did not even understand. Quite a number of Hungarians of Jewish origin were involved. In that part of the world, so near the great Pale of Jewish settlement, the anti-Semitic belt of Europe, the Jew was the underdog, and had to make common cause with underdog organizations which usually were the Marxist parties. It was particularly unfortunate that some of the Jewish leaders in the extremist ranks lacked all balance. In power they lost their heads and often lived up to the caricature anti-Semites flaunt. Reaction came in the form of the White Terror and not only radical Jews but Jews as such had to suffer. Long before Hitler, Hungary was the first country in Europe to erect concentration camps for "undesirables." A large number of Jews were killed in cold blood. Laws were passed to oust Jews from the government, the army and universities.

Hungarian reaction was unlike Hitlerism in the eyes of which there was no redeeming feature for any Jew. The New Order of Hungary made a distinction between two types of Jews, "good" and "bad." The good Jew was ready to go along with the reaction even if it was at the expense of the downtrodden little Jew. The good Jew was ready to help along Hungarian reaction by putting it in touch with foreign capital or placing domestic capital at its disposal.

Hungarian reaction might not have made even this distinction if it had not been that the ruling Hungarians in the past had always looked down upon such occupations as industry and banking. Hungarian Jews therefore were forced by circumstances to occupy those positions. Reaction tolerated them because nobody else could take their places for the time being. But it trained a new guard to take over and when the final preparations were made the distinction between "good" and "bad" Jew was erased. On the eve of the Second World War, the Hungarian anti-racial laws entered into full force.

Anti-Semitism in Hungary—elsewhere, too—developed into far more than a movement directed against one group of the population. It turned out to be a magic key. The miserable peasant was now allowed to dream about the untold wealth he was going to inherit on this earth just as soon as the pariah Jew had been despoiled. Extreme reaction which struck the country in the wake of Hitlerism was little more than a criminal plot to rob the Jews. That was its "ideological" content.

Most of the intellectuals who left Hungary for the United States were born Jews. This statement requires a double qualification, however, before we can go on.

In the second part of the nineteenth century, Hungary was considered a paradise for the Jews in that part of the world. After the compromise with Austria in 1867 the country entered an era of economic ascent. It needed bankers, tradesmen, organizers, but the native ruling class was not well adapted to the task. From all over the North and East Jews came across the mountains into the Danubian Promised Land. While Jews were massacred in Russia and Rumania, the Jews of Hungary lived in comparative peace. Many became tremendously attached to their country, and married into the highest aristocracy and came to occupy highly important positions in the judiciary, academic world, trade, industry, banking and even in the government. There was no country in the world in which the Jews were assimilated as thoroughly as in Hungary. They were assimilated not merely in thought but in appearance. When the "Miss Nationality" idea struck

Europe later on, "Miss Hungary" was a Hungarian Jewess, more often than not.

The assimilation of the *tonangeber,* key-noter, Hungarian Jew produced interesting results. The founder of modern Zionism was a Hungarian Jew, Dr. Theodor Herzl, which should have been an additional reason why Hungarian Jews should take to it, a world-shaking idea of one of their own. Far from that, Hungarian Jews were among the very few who rejected Zionism completely. They were Hungarians, patriotic Hungarians, and would have nothing to do with a Jewish homeland. The assimilation of many of them went so far that they embraced the dominant religion of Hungary, Catholicism. Comparatively few became Protestants. The "Catholic Jews" of Hungary were at first less subject to discrimination than others. But as anti-Semitism in Central Europe got the upper hand, the official church attachment of the convert made little difference.

Another qualification must also be made. Great, creative Hungarians of whatever faith, had long been in the habit of finding their careers outside their native land. It is curious that a small country like Hungary should have produced so many remarkable people in so many fields. Any objective test will show that their ratio in that part of the world is very high. The explanation may be the Magyar melting pot, which for many years attracted nationalities from all over the Danubian world. Or maybe the impact of the East and West is responsible for this amazing fertility. But, in most cases, Hungarian genius came to fruition outside of the country. Hungary's great scientists, artists, writers became great in foreign countries. The caste policy of the ruling classes may be to blame, or, possibly, the fact that a peasant country had no need for the products of these great men. The exodus of special types of talent from Hungary, therefore, is not only a post-war development. In the post-war period this exodus made history for the United States, as the story of the Hungarian immigrant contribution to the atomic bomb will show.

The difference between the pre- and post-war emigration from Hungary can be discerned in the pages of *Who's Who in America* and *American Men of Science.* János Kovács, steel hand in Bethlehem, Pennsylvania, was as essential for America's greatness as world-famed Professor XY, the atomic scientist, but it is Professor XY whose name is noted in *Who's Who.*

It is customary to speak of immigrants who came to the United States pursued by Hitler's hordes as refugees. The law of the United

States makes no such distinction. They were either immigrants or visitors for a temporary stay. A few could change their status into that of immigrants during the war, when emigration from Hungary was closed and the quota was not filled. In the chapters that follow we shall deal with all immigration from Hungary after the First World War. Before doing so however let us see how the Hungarian has taken his place in the great American melting pot a hundred years after the first Hungarian immigrants began to arrive here following the failure of Hungary's War of Independence in 1848.

In 1940, Hungarian was spoken in the United States by 453,000 persons, about one-half born in America and the other half abroad. Some of the third-generation Americans spoke Hungarian—13,800.

More than four-fifths—82 per cent—of the people of Hungarian descent lived in six great industrial States of the East and Middle West —New York, Pennsylvania, Ohio, New Jersey, Illinois and Michigan. The largest concentration, 75,254, lived in New York State, the second largest, 49,185, in Ohio, while Pennsylvania and New Jersey ran third and fourth with 36,045 and 33,816 each. Illinois and Michigan ran neck and neck with about 21,000 each, Connecticut followed with nearly 10,000, Indiana with 7,733, Wisconsin with 6,500, then Missouri, 3,481, and West Virginia, 3,221. California was the only western State with a fair-sized population of Hungarian origin, 8,041, and not all of them connected with the movies. That population was growing rapidly. Sunny Florida attracted 1,444 for more or less permanent residence. Each of the other States had fewer than a thousand people with Hungarian background. North Carolina, which calls itself the "most native-born," Utah and Arkansas, had fewer than a hundred each, while Nevada brought up the rear with forty-two, probably prospective divorcees. The great farming States, such as Kansas and the Dakotas, had very small Hungarian populations. The Hungarian peasant did not come here to become a farmer.

Most of the Hungarian-born prefer the cities, where they are not cast adrift in uncharted waters of an alien tongue, where they can find Hungarian-language churches and secular institutions, and where Hungarian stores cater to their tastes. There Hungarian travel agencies and banks are close at hand to help them with their problems. There they have a Hungarian-born physician and the *szülésznő*, midwife, whom many of them regard as as good as the doctor, only less expensive, and the Hungarian funeral "parlor" where a Hungarian prayer will bid them the last farewell. Before that happens, there is the Hungarian restaurant, serving native dishes, including *gulyás*, although in a strongly Americanized edition, to be eaten with the *hosszú lépés*, long step, light wine with soda water, a Gypsy band or a band calling itself Gypsy and such records as *"Király Ernő mulat,"* "Ernő Király Having a Good Time," so named after an idol of yesteryear. A Hungarian movie may be near by, showing the faded native films. The photography may not be first rate and the story far from brilliant, but the words are Hungarian and evoke nostalgic memories.

While the Hungarian immigrant tends to be clannish, he does not carry it to such extremes as do some others. For instance, a study of a New York Little Italy between the Bowery, Mulberry Street, Canal and East Houston Streets [72] showed that Italians of the same province at home stick not merely to the same neighborhood, but also to the same blocks. Immigrants from the Basilicata, for example, did not mix with immigrants from Naples. Clannishness went so far that among the *Sicilianos* themselves, immigrants from Palermo did not like to mix with their fellow Sicilians from Messina or Girgenti. The Hungarians of New York cluster around Seventy-ninth Street, from Lexington to First Avenue, in the Yorkville section, rubbing elbows—but doing little else—with the Austrians, Czechs and the Germans, a few blocks further up. Curiously, they thus recreate the conditions under which they lived in the Austro-Hungarian Monarchy at home.

Melting pot efficiency is frequently measured by inter-marriages. Marriages with outsiders were rarer in America's Hungarian settlements before the First World War. An interesting study of this problem is provided by the *Golden Book of Hungarians in America*, published by the Cleveland Hungarian-language daily *Szabadság*, dealing mostly with old-time immigrants. The large majority of persons included in the book married Hungarians. More than that, in many cases the boy from County X married a girl from County X. Naturally, one must allow for the fact that these people were presumably readers of a Hungarian-language daily and therefore perhaps more attached to their Hungarian locale than others.

The following information refers to more recent times, comparing conditions in 1941 with those prevailing in 1928.[73] In 1928 fully three-fourths—75.5 per cent—of the Hungarian-born grooms married Hungarian-born brides in America. In 1941 this type of marriage increased to 81 per cent. On the other hand, the corresponding percentages of Hungarian brides marrying Hungarian grooms were 75.5 in 1928 and

68 in 1941. A comparison of these figures with percentages for Italians and English may prove interesting, since they contrast opposites. In both key years, fully 90 per cent of the Italian brides were married to Italian grooms. On the other hand, the corresponding figures for the English were 63.8 in 1928 and 44.5 in 1941.

The conditions prevailing among native-born American brides and grooms of Hungarian-born or mixed parentage were entirely different. In 1928 41.8 per cent of these grooms married brides of Hungarian stock, while in 1941 the rate was down to 23.1 per cent. In the same years, 30.6 and 25.3 per cent of such brides married grooms of Hungarian stock. Again it is interesting to see that the corresponding figures for the British were 21 and 19.5 per cent, and for the Italians 87 and 85 per cent; and that a larger percentage of Hungarian stock marry non-Hungarian stock than is true among Scandinavians. The particular significance of this lies in the fact that our present immigration laws assign a very small quota to the Hungarians and a high quota to the Scandinavians presumably on the principle that the former are hard, while the latter are easy, to assimilate—an assumption belied by these facts. The rate of assimilation is thus seen to increase rapidly in the second generation. In the case of the Hungarians, the rate is much higher than the corresponding rate among the Italians, while not as high as that among the English.

Everyday experience shows that religious differences account for considerable variations so far as intermarriages are concerned. Hungarian Catholics are inclined to marry Hungarians. Otherwise, they are inclined to marry Slavs—particularly Poles—Austrians and, in rarer instances, Bavarian Germans—all mostly Catholics. They do not often marry Italians. Second-generation Hungarian Protestants more frequently marry "old stock" Americans. Hungarian Jews, too, often marry out of the Hungarian colony.

Marriage chances of Hungarian-born girls in this country are slighter than those of the older stock, especially in the eastern cities. There the advice should be: "Go West, young woman!" or at least: "Keep out of the Northeast, if you can." Hungarian immigrants, like other foreign-born, marry later than the native stock, as a rule. In the past the Hungarian immigrant family was larger than at present.

What does the "average" American think about the Hungarian immigrant in this country? What does the Hungarian immigrant think of the American? The racial attitudes of 1,725 native-born

Americans of different strains, mostly "Nordic," toward other nationalities in the United States were analyzed by Professor Emory S.
Bogardus, who went about his task by asking the tested persons about
their attitude toward marrying members of those other nationalities.
After that, he tested their reactions to the mere presence of these
nationalities in the United States. Then he arranged the nationalities
in a descending order of favorable reactions to the idea of close kinship by marriage with members of the group, with this result: [74]

English, native white Americans, Canadians, Scotch, Scotch-Irish,
French, Welsh, Germans, French-Canadians, Swedes, Dutch, Nor-
wegians, Danes, Spaniards, Finns, Russians, Italians, Portuguese, Poles,
Hungarians, Rumanians, Armenians, Czechoslovaks, Indians, German-
Jews, Bulgarians, Russian-Jews, Greeks, Syrians, Serbo-Croats, Mexi-
cans, Japanese, Filipinos, Negroes, Turks, Chinese, Mulattoes, Koreans,
Hindus. The Hungarians rank about halfway down the line. This is,
therefore, the attitude to which they react.

The Hungarian approaches the United States with certain precon-
ceived notions. Before the First World War America was the "land of
unlimited opportunities." Translated into the language of the Hungarian peasant, this meant that he could afford to eat meat every day
and, on top of that, save enough money in a few years to enable him
to buy a piece of land at home. Otherwise, America did not rate as
high as England and France in the scale of Hungarian values. The
country was young and the Hungarian was tradition-bound.

After the First World War a change in the attitude of the Hungarian toward America was brought about by the change in the
status of the United States. Before the war America was visualized
as a rough frontier territory where ethical standards were low. After
the war, America was considered a mature country, the country no
longer of the future, but of the present, a country that was the greatest
success of the age, the heir to the world empire of the British.

Having arrived in this country, the immigrant faced a different
reality. He succeeded and then America was a great country; he
failed, and America was a disappointment. As we are wont to say
these days, he "rationalized" his own failure.

A sharp distinction must be made between the reaction of the "average man" and the intellectual. There were certain factors however
which affected both groups. First, there was the language difficulty.
A person, no matter how mature, who is unable to speak the language
of his neighbors will act like a child. This is what Martin Gumpert,

an immigrant himself, called the "sudden degeneration of adult dignity into infantile helplessness." Second, there was an awful loneliness. People were afraid of him; he was so hard up that he might want to borrow money from them. His hands were empty, he had nothing to offer. He was like a person afflicted with pestilence. It was about immigrants that Marcus E. Ravage wrote in *An American in the Making:* "Cut adrift suddenly from their ancient moorings, they were floundering in a sort of moral void. Good manners and good conduct, reverence and religion had all gone by the board, and the reason was that these things were not American." Third, there were all the prejudices heaped upon the "foreigner," the person different from us. With this went ridicule, accentuated by derisive calls from street boys. The more recent their own origin the more ridiculers felt the necessity of demonstrating their superiority. Released from past restraints, they were uninhibited and they mistook the free expression of bad manners for the free expression of their inner selves.

"For every person who comes unscathed through poverty," wrote Hungarian-born Rebekah Kohut in *My Portion,* "there are a dozen others upon whom it places its mark, whose spirit it crushes, and whose outlook it warps, leaving them twisted, unhappy, embittered creatures." Louis Adamic wrote in *Two-Way Passage:* "From the beginning up to the present, immigration from Europe to North America has been an escape from the undesirable to the promising." And Henry Pratt Fairchild wrote: "For the bulk of the ordinary immigrants the economic and other advantages are offset by terrible hardships and losses."

The Hungarian ex-peasant had escaped an oppressive minority status in his own country. He had been under the heels of the *gendarme* and *szolgabíró,* the district potentate. He was considered inferior. In the United States he had no fear of the police and had nothing to do with the authorities. His children got a good education, and they were not inoculated with the poison of self-abasement and humility. On the contrary, the American school taught them to be self-confident and to consider themselves as good as anybody else. "Every native-born American can become President of the United States."

Beyond that . . . well, beyond that there was his own world. As a greenhorn he was considered legitimate prey for everybody. He was kicked around until he was bruised all over. Physically, he was in the United States, but spiritually he was not. He was living in the Hungarian colony. That was largely his own choice. Behind the walls of that ghetto he felt somewhat more secure. People understood his language, and did not deride his exotic ways; he did not have to wonder whether his Anglo-Saxon neighbor considered him one cut above or below the Turk. He had his living and his family. Whatever the conditions here, they were much better than they had been at "home." Occasionally, he obtained a glimpse of America beyond his ghetto wall. He saw it mostly in the movies and, less often, in the popular press. People drank a lot in that other America and they killed one another frequently. He did not know whether he wanted to scale the walls of his isolation.

Sometimes he had a head-on collision with that mysterious life beyond the walls. One occurred during the Second World War, in a Connecticut suburb. A native-born American sailor of Hungarian descent, Andreas Kovács, was shot and killed by a drunken "socialite" with an Anglo-Saxon name. The prosecutor dropped the charge. The Hungarian-language press registered the case, along with the English-language papers. A Left-wing paper suggested that a fund should be collected to buy justice at the bar. Nothing of the kind happened, but the case left a bitter taste in many mouths. It did give the impression—rightly or wrongly—that a foreign-sounding name reduced the value of one's life.

How do Hungarians fit into the American social structure? It is known that like-mindedness is one of society's strongest cohesive forces. It is at the bottom of every group, beginning with the family all the way up to the nation. In social groupings like-mindedness plays an even more important rôle, since there the association is not accidental. This is a more important problem for the intellectual than for others who, often ignorant of English, prefer the protection of their native settlement. The intellectual speaks English. He left his country for a reason and does not want to move into it again on American soil, unless he is to make his living among his former countrymen.

The country from which the immigrant came had not only a political and economic, but a social class system. The dukes and princes mattered little, but it did make a difference to many people whether they were found acceptable in this or that club. Their social status often depended upon such associations. In America, what did the immigrant find?

First, he found a color line. He was not personally affected by it, since his skin was white. If he made his home in certain parts of the country, he was forced to adopt it himself. He thought a lot about it and in many cases this was what he thought: "I belong to a minority because of my religion or my accent. A minority status is not a pleasant one. But luckily for me there is a more obvious minority here than that I belong to, since its status is shown on its skin. As long as antagonism is concentrated on the Negro target, I have a measure of protection." Or he may have thought something like this: "The way the Negroes are treated is awful. Even today there are lynchings in the South. They are a minority and I belong to a minority. If it can happen to them today, it may happen to me tomorrow."

Then, the immigrant found a religious line. In America the Church and State were separated, unlike many parts of Europe, including Hungary. Yet the fact was that in Hungary—a Catholic country— some of the highest positions of the State were occupied by Protestants. The highest government office, Premiership, was occupied more than once by Protestants. In the United States there was no written law barring non-Protestants from the presidency, but everybody knows what happened to the Catholic Alfred E. Smith when he made his bid for the presidency as the candidate of the Democratic Party. When William Jennings Bryan recommended that Justice Louis D. Brandeis of the Supreme Court of the United States should be nominated presidential candidate of the Democratic Party, his recommendation was received with a reverberating silence because the Justice was a Jew.

The immigrant was bound to notice that there was also an accent line. A person speaking with an accent was, obviously, a foreigner and no matter how badly he wanted to become an American, he felt the presence of an invisible dividing line. In government positions an accent was a great handicap, barring the usual exceptions due either to extraordinary gifts or to a more than usually effective power of push. Then there was a "racial line" although it was never called that. We have seen that our immigration laws of today are racial laws. In certain fields of employment these racial laws were closely observed. The federal government did its best not to indulge in such practices, but other employers did not—in industry, banking, education, and certain professions. This was a complete reversal of historic precedents. In many European countries it was the authorities who discriminated against the minorities. The perceptive immigrant noticed other things, too, such as the large number of Mayflower Descendants and Sons and Daughters of the American Revolution. Attachment to historical memories is not undesirable but to turn such an attachment into a dividing line between fellow countrymen is reprehensible. However, he could not help feeling that the popularity of such associations carried the seeds of their own destruction; judging by the number of *Mayflower* descendants, pretty soon it might be a mark of distinction not to be one.

Then he noticed America's *Almanac de Gotha,* the distressingly selective *Social Register* and discovered the basis of its selectivity. He came across beaches that were barred to common clay, because they belonged to clubs. He came across luncheon "clubs," which, he found, were that merely because some people did not like to be near other, unselected people. He found that simple commercial restaurants called themselves clubs—though they admitted everybody ready to pay their prices—just to be able to charge extra for snob appeal. Some of this "exclusiveness" was childish, but some of it was not. Some of it was simply an attempt to stake out better claims to the country on the basis of earlier arrival. That, surely, was not in any book about democracy. But those who practised this type of discrimination compensated for it by their eloquence on the advantages of democracy.

There was great advantage for the immigrant in being assimilated to the American "higher orders." One way—and a perfectly legitimate way—was to marry into an American family. Then one reached the real America which an immigrant could penetrate only via the movies. Others sought to compensate for real or imagined defects by joining churches they associated with the American ruling classes—sometimes the Episcopalian, hallmark of the elite. The next step in assuming protective coloring was to move into a fashionable residential section, preferably in a suburb. A "good address" atoned for many sins. But it was bad tactics to move in by groups since then the "natives" would move out.

In order to compensate for supposed defects of origin, a remarkably large number of immigrants from Hungary blossomed forth with a prefix of nobility, corresponding to the French *de,* or to make it somewhat more authentic, with *von,* since Germany is closer to Hungary. I know of a case—and it may not be unique—where a Hungarian immigrant certainly not of exalted rank at home did not discourage a whispering campaign to the effect that he was a "Prince" by birth. The origin of this title may have been the prevailing opinion that he was a "prince of a man." The fact that he blushingly refused to use the title was ascribed to his native modesty. At one time there were quite a few Hungarian "Barons" in America who, evidently, received their titles in this country.

Bedecked with the protective coloring of his new environment, the immigrant was now ready to face American life. His children, invested with a new habitat, new religion, and new name would be well able to complain about the influx of inferior, foreigners and drop modest hints about their Norman ancestry. People doing this kind of thing usually rationalized their actions by saying that they had no right to let their children start the race of life with a handicap.

Many of the intellectuals found the odds too heavy, and settled down to money-making at which some of them did remarkably well. Others were lost to their vocations and sometimes to life. Some developed split personalities. The great highway of American life is strewn with broken careers of intellectuals from abroad. Those who died were more fortunate than those who lingered on, their minds clouded, casualties of a great disappointment.

Let us see now a discriminating presentation of the problems of a foreign-born intellectual and a criticism of his criticism by a Hungarian-born American intellectual: ". . . I am sure that I could be really useful to this country, produce some really important cultural values. But my incipient enthusiasm for American cultural development never has any chance to mature, because I realize at every moment that American society does not feel any need of my or any other 'foreigner's' co-operation, is in general perfectly satisfied with itself, and perfectly able to manage its own future in accordance with its own desires, to create all the values it wants without having any 'imported' values thrust upon it. In analyzing the evolution of my attitudes toward this country, it seems to me that much of my growing criticism and dissatisfaction with American conditions has been due to the gradual realization of this self-complacency of American society. . . . No European society I know acts as if it possessed and knew everything worth while and had nothing to learn, whereas this is precisely the way American society acts toward a foreigner as soon as he ceases to play the rôle of a passing 'curiosity' and wants to take an active part in American life. I do not think that most Americans realize how revolting to a more or less educated immigrant is their naive attitude of superiority, their astonishing self-satisfaction, their inability and unwillingness to look on anything foreign as worth being understood and assimilated. . . .

"In the same line, and perhaps even more revolting for the reflecting foreigner who comes with the idea of working and settling in this country, is the current tendency of American society to interpret the relation between the immigrant and America as that of one-sided benefit and one-sided obligation." [75]

To which the other Hungarian-born American intellectual critic answered:

"It is true that European intellectuals are invariably dissatisfied with American life, and much of the bitterness with which they criticize American conditions is doubtless justified. But in the interest of fair play the question: 'What's the matter with intellectual America?' ought to be supplemented with this other one: 'What's the matter with the European intellectual in America?'

"First among the sources of discontent with which the European intellectual confronts American life is the lowering of his status. An attempt to fix his own place on the social ladder will lead him to the realization that he was better off in aristocratic Europe than in demo-cratic America. For in Europe he belonged—if he achieved any recog-nition at all—to the upper middle class. Even a moderate degree of literary or artistic eminence secured him admission to the most inter-esting quarter of a society where money, however important, was never the sole criterion of gentility. . . . In all European capitals there are certain centers of social intercourse where members of the three aris-tocracies of birth, riches and intellect meet in a congenial atmosphere and on a basis of full equality. . . .

"Probably he made much less money in dollars and cents, even at the old rate of exchange; but his smaller income insured to him a higher place in the social hierarchy and a much greater amount of comfort. . . . Europe was different. The things he craves for, books, engravings, theatre and concert tickets, good clothes, good home-furnishings, were comparatively much cheaper there. Above all, travel was much cheaper. . . .

"I believe that the European intellectual not only exercises a right, but discharges a very substantial duty by applying his native standards to a fearless examination of American culture. He may be prone to exaggerate the value of his contribution, and to expect special regard and compensation from a public none too appreciative of intellectual achievement at best. . . . But this tendency is merely a counterpart of the no less unreasonable assumption of the native American that for-eigners owe a special debt of gratitude to this country for opportunities accorded, as if Americans admitted foreigners and provided them with jobs because they love them, and not because they need them. . . ." [76]

All of which leads up to the summation of the case by a great justice of the United States: "Democracy rejected the proposal of the super-man who should rise through sacrifice of the many. It insists that the full development of each individual is not only a right but a duty of society; and that our best hope for civilization lies not in uniformity but in wide differentiation.

"The movements of the last century have proved that whole peoples have individuality no less marked than that of a single person; that the individuality of a people is irrepressible and that the misnamed inter-nationalism which seeks the obliteration of nationalities or peoples is unattainable. The new nationalism proclaims that each race and people, like each individual, has a right and duty to develop, and that only through such differentiated development will high civilization be attained. Not until these principles of nationalism, like those of democracy, are generally accepted, will liberty be fully attained, and minorities be secure in their rights." [77]

Bearing these words in mind in relation to those who have come from Hungary and every other country, the United States can develop all those matchless opportunities which only a land of many lands, and a nation of many nations is in a position to acquire.

XVII

LIFE IS SCIENCE

CONTEMPORARY HUNGARY HAS produced some of the great scientists of the age and the United States has absorbed many of them. Yet Hungary is an agricultural country. The hands of peasants are gnarled and unsuited to precision instruments. Hands and minds are linked and the Hungarian peasant did not develop a gadget-mind. Maybe he rationalized—to employ a fashionable word—his poverty into the conviction that what was old was good, what was good was cheap. The iron plow was cheap, the complex machine was not.

The Hungarian social system was not favorable to science. Industry was considered defiling for a long time; hence the handmaiden of industry, science, was not in great favor. The life of the Hungarian ruling classes was temperamental and in many cases superficial, in other words, rhapsodic. Brilliant flashes of wit were greatly appreciated in the social centers of the Hungarian cities, the cafés. In modern science inspiration is really perspiration, methodical and plodding work.

The United States, on the other hand, was born into the machine age of our common Western civilization. Its birth certificate was written during the Industrial Revolution. America's English heritage accentuated the trend. The immense industrial raw materials of this nation made industrialization inevitable. The character of a nation is impregnated with the memories of its period of infancy. The effect of industrialization is cumulative. The more machines were created, the more machines were needed. Success and fame beckoned to the bold adventurers of industry. The United States attracted the greatest industrial minds of the age to a phenomenal degree. It is true that the French Huguenots fructified the industrial soil of a good many nations, including that of America, after the Revocation of the Edict of Nantes in the late seventeenth century, but it was a tiny movement in comparison with the revolution the United States exerted on scientific talent in the twentieth century.

Its attraction became irresistible as the Nazi shadow began to lengthen in Europe. The demented Hitlerites evidently did believe that what they called "Aryan blood" had a magic quality. They never lived to see the day they could rue their criminal insanity, since they were not the type of people to rue anything. But the time did come when everybody could see, if such evidence was needed in the saner parts of the world, that human genius has nothing to do with blond hair and blue eyes.

Among the scientists attracted to the United States just prior to the Second World War, Hungarians played a part out of all proportion to the size of their country. We shall see that they played a remarkable rôle in the unleashing of the most formidable energy man has found so far—the atom. Energies accumulated in the native country were ejected from it into countries that appreciated the importance of this remarkable flowering of human gifts.

In the life stories of several of the great scientists there is a pattern. They were born in Hungary and had their technical education there. Hungarian technical education was good. In many cases they could not find the right occupation and were forced to leave their native country. The number of these scientists was very large under the inter-bellum Horthy regime, which was anti-intellectual and anti-Jewish. A large number of these scientists were what the Nazis called "racial Jews." From Hungary they went westward, but usually did not stop in Austria. That country, too, was corroded by intolerance in the later post-war period. They went to the West, to England or, closer to home, Switzerland. Many had gone to pre-Hitler, Weimar Germany, which was extremely hospitable to scientific gifts. Many of the latter stayed in the Reich until Hitler took power, then they dispersed, many of them coming to America.

Before they came, the tidal wave period of immigration had deposited several remarkable inventors on America's shores. A curious paradox should be noted in this connection. These Hungarians had come from a country in which the ox-team was the popular method of transportation. In this country, however, several of them worked on what was then the most modern method of transportation—the motor car.

Ford was the great pioneer of the motor car age and attracted some Hungarians of that earlier generation. Jozsef Galamb is credited with having helped to perfect the original Ford model. Another Hungarian-born Ford engineer, Charles Balough, later produced industrial motors that achieved a world-wide vogue. At one time, the factories of the Soviet Union, reputedly, used his motors for some of their cars. Another noted motor engineer was István Fekete.

One of the famous industrial "firsts" was the work of a Hungarian-American, Tivadar Puskás, who was the pioneer of wire-transmitted entertainment, the ancestor of the radio. *Telefón hirmondó,* telephone messenger, was introduced in Budapest toward the end of the last century, and transmitted news and music to its subscribers. It picked up the music in the Budapest Royal Opera House or in a concert hall and piped it into the homes of subscribers who listened through earphones. This was one of Budapest's first "firsts." (It may be of interest to note that the suspension bridge and subway were other firsts of Budapest. The Chain Bridge—*Lánchid*—of Budapest was the first major suspension bridge in the world and created a world-wide sensation at the time it was built in the middle of the last century. The other famous first was the Budapest subway built under Andrássy ut, the Fifth Avenue of the Hungarian capital, toward the end of the last century. Born as an infant prodigy, it has remained that ever since, running over the same route, never growing up.)

Tivadar Puskás became one of the original collaborators of Edison, who appraised him highly. Eventually, he became director of the Edison World Exhibition and general manager for Edison's business interests abroad. Béla Alexay, of the General Electric Research Department, improved the electric bulb and helped reduce its price.

The scientist does not seek the clamor of the market place. His thinking must be highly concentrated and he avoids diversions that might deflect his attention from the object of his pursuit. He works in a field which yields its secrets only to experts. It is impossible for the outsider to evaluate the real achievements of the scientist, so an account of the record of Hungarian-born scientists in the United States can never be complete. It is not complete even in specialized reference works, as I have had occasion to note. Therefore, only the more obvious records can be presented here. But there is another difficulty in writing about any prominent person from the area in which Hungary is situated, as an example will perhaps make clear.

Among American scientists of Hungarian origin, one of the most obvious names is that of Béla Schick. Among the dozen most famous Americans of Hungarian birth his name is mentioned with the note "Hungarian." He has a world-wide reputation not only in the medical world but among laymen. There cannot be many people who have not heard of the Schick Test for determining susceptibility to diphtheria which he discovered in 1913. Dr. Schick's first name is Béla, and that, with its accent, is as Hungarian as the *puszta*. He was born in Hungary, Boglár, on the most Hungarian of all lakes, Balaton. More than that, his parents were Hungarians. What other criterion does one need to determine the nationality of a person? But Dr. Schick does not consider himself a person of Hungarian origin, in spite of the fact that he was born in Hungary of Hungarian parents and has a Hungarian first name. His parents, residents of Austria, were vacationing on Lake Balaton, not far from the Austrian frontier, when it became obvious that the mother could not return home for the confinement. Schick had his education in the Austrian city of Graz, began practice in Vienna and was professor of pediatrics in the Austrian capital. He regards German as his native tongue.

There can be no doubt about the Hungarian background of Theodor von Kármán. I well remember his paternal home in Budapest. His father, Maurice von Kármán, was my professor on the law faculty of the Royal Hungarian University of Budapest before the First World War. That, however, would hardly qualify Maurice von Kármán for the Hall of Fame. Contritely, I must admit now—since nothing can happen to me at this late date—that I did not attend too many of Professor Kármán's lectures on ethics. Not that he was not good; on the contrary, he must have been very good. But besides having a full program at the university, I also had a full-time job in a lawyer's office, where my hours were very long. It was customary for law students to hold down jobs and see the university only around examination time.

However, I did have occasion to visit the Kármán home in the Hungarian capital. University students in Hungary had to have an *index,* a black book containing their lecture records. The professor had to sign his name at the beginning and the end of the semester, thus validating it for the student. The professors signed the *index* in class, as a rule, but when a student failed to attend classes, he visited the professor in his home and tried to persuade him to validate his half-year. That was a long time ago and yet I recall every incident vividly. The street was in Buda, on the right bank of the Danube, and the house was in a garden. After entering, I had to pass through countless rooms, the walls of which were stacked high with books. The place looked far more like a library than a villa in Buda. Finally I reached the room in which Professor Kármán was poring over a book. There was no need to explain the reason of my trip. He held out his arm, took the *index,* signed it automatically, while continuing to read the book. I was tremendously impressed by the performance.

In this setting Theodor grew up. In the paternal house and outside of it, in Hungary philosophy ranked high in the scale of scholarly values, since it stood closest to theology, considered the queen of sciences. It required courage to tear oneself away from that mental discipline, especially in Hungary where industrial life was not yet well developed. Theodor Kármán was bold enough to take no interest in the royal line of academic disciplines, and to take a great interest in mechanical engineering, which was far from having the social prestige of philosophy and theology.

Theodor von Kármán matriculated at the Royal Hungarian Technical University at the turn of the century. While the record of his academic work is not available, the results show it very clearly. He was a very young man when his own alma mater gave him an appointment as an instructor and one of Hungary's largest industrial establishments, the Ganz Machine Manufacturing Company, employed him as a research engineer. Such an early start in Hungary usually evoked the classical comment: *Sic itur ad astra.* Thus the stars may be reached.

After that, Kármán's early career showed the typical pattern of the gifted industrial scientist. Hungary was moving too slowly toward industrialization and so gifted youth went west to Germany, then in her industrial prime, forging ahead of Great Britain, birthplace of the first Industrial Revolution. Young Kármán took advanced work at the University of Goettingen and received his doctor's degree there in 1908. A light as brilliant as his could not be kept under a bushel and his new alma mater asked him to stay, as a *Privatdozent,* assistant professor. That position he held until 1912, when he was appointed professor and, at the same time, received an appointment as the director of the Aeronautical Institute at Aachen. That was the pioneering age of airplanes, and Kármán was one of the earliest pioneers.

When the First World War broke out, Kármán returned to his native Hungary. That Danubian region was not highly air-conscious then, but young Kármán was, and he became head of the research department of the Austro-Hungarian Aviation Corps. Austro-Hungarian "brass hats" were more impermeable than the Western European kind and Kármán was too young a man to command the attention he deserved. Had they listened to him, the Austro-Hungarian

Monarchy might have been able to steal a march upon many other countries. He held his position until the end of the war.

Hungary was deeply steeped in agrarian reaction and Kármán returned to Aachen to resume his pre-war work. This was the Germany of the Weimar Republic, hospitable to foreign scholars and especially to Theodor von Kármán. The type of work he performed was not unnoticed in the United States, which always had a place for an original scientist. The first step was a trip to America to lecture at research institutions and universities under the auspices of the Guggenheim Foundation for the Promotion of Aeronautics. His work aroused so much attention that he had to undertake a trip around the world, lecturing at the universities of China, Japan, the Soviets, Britain, France, Belgium and India. In 1928 he became research associate at the California Institute of Technology, shuttling between Aachen and Pasadena. Subsequently, he became director of the Daniel Guggenheim Graduate School of Aeronautics at the California Institute of Technology, and in 1930 he settled in Pasadena, while continuing to be adviser to the Tsung Hua University, and visiting professor of the C.B.R. Foundation in Belgium.

Prophets may go unrecognized in their native lands, and that goes for Kármán, too, but the rule evidently does not hold good for adopted countries, for America lavished her most coveted awards upon this Hungarian-born scholar. Kármán became a major general of the United States Army—a distinction no other contemporary Hungarian-born citizen of America shared—and as such visited his native country after the Second World War.

Top scientists paid tribute to Kármán for his discovery and presentation of new conceptions of phenomena that had remained unexplained, for reducing to clear terms material which had been confused and apprehended only in part, for discovering the essential physical elements of complicated engineering problems, so that rational and simple approximate solutions could be obtained.[78] He had more than sixty important publications to his credit at the time of his sixtieth birthday. They included papers on applied mathematics, physics, strength of materials, stress analysis, theory of elasticity and vibrations, on the mechanics of compressible and viscous fluids, turbulence, aerodynamics of aircraft, hydrodynamics of planing surfaces, and heat transfer. The "Karman Theory" of turbulence is said to be known the world over. Together with a collaborator Kármán wrote a two-volume book on general aerodynamic theory and a standard work on mathematical method in engineering. Those best qualified to evaluate a record of this nature agree that Professor Theodor von Kármán deserved well of the United States and the United States deserved well of history for the peerless opportunities it gave him.

Few of the numerous Hungarian-born men of science have received higher praise than the mathematician, John Von Neumann, described as "the greatest mathematician of the age," "greatest genius," and "one of the great creative thinkers of the age." His early life followed the pattern, already described, of a young man with far more ability than his cramped country could accommodate. He was only twenty-four when appointed *Privatdozent* of mathematics at Berlin University. At the age of twenty-seven he was already visiting professor of mathematical physics at Princeton University and a year later full professor—not an ordinary accomplishment. In 1933 he was appointed professor at the Institute for Advanced Study at Princeton.

Professor Neumann's broad interests cover the theory of sets, mathematical logics, quantum mechanics, the theory of Hilbert space, the theory of groups and measure, and fluid mechanics. He was only twenty-five when he wrote a highly technical paper on the theory of games, *Zur Theorie der Gesellschaftsspiele*. Some years later, in collaboration with Dr. Oscar Morgenstern, he wrote a volume of some six hundred pages on the *Theory of Games and Economic Behavior,* which critics described as tremendous, which *The New York Times* discussed on the first page of its main news section [79] and of which one learned reviewer wrote: "The techniques applied by the authors are of sufficient generality to be valid in political science, sociology and even military strategy." The authors showed that the "typical problems of economic behavior are strictly identical with the mathematical notions of suitable games of strategy." During World War II Professor Neumann was mainly concerned with projects of fluid mechanics and the theory of explosives. He was credited with highly important contributions in the field of atomic energy.

In another field of science, Franz Alexander, psychiatrist and psychologist, gained a large measure of public recognition. Like Kármán, he was brought up in a scholar's home. We young collegiate students adored his father, Professor Bernhard Alexander of the University of Budapest. Franz Alexander, the offspring of a humanist, nibbled at pathology, bacteriology, hygiene, neurology and physiology, a modern Dr. Faust. During the First World War he was in charge of an

Austro-Hungarian bacteriological field laboratory and malaria prophy-
laxis station on the Italian front.

He was one of the young Hungarians fascinated by the teachings of
Sigmund Freud. Vienna, the Mecca of psychoanalysis, is only a short
jump from Budapest and young Hungarian scholars flocked to that
hallowed sanctuary. Franz Alexander was especially interested in the
connection of mental and brain processes. He reached the conviction
that many hitherto closed doors would be opened by psychology, and
turned to the analytic process. As a psychiatrist and psychoanalyst he
worked hard in Berlin, then very hospitable to gifted foreign scholars.
So notable was Alexander's work that in 1921 he received the Freud
Award of the International Psychoanalytic Association for the best research work in the field, *Castration Complex and Character*.

Probing into the dark caverns of the human soul, he made important
discoveries. One was the indivisibility of the human psyche. While
man's physical and mental ailments must be studied in detail, his real
nature will escape understanding unless it is considered as a whole, *in
toto*. Since man is a highly integrated creature, even a seemingly small
physical lesion may have far-reaching effects on his psychology. Before
an attempt can be made to understand the individual, the interrelations
must be bared. Dealing with the problem of the unity of personality,
Franz Alexander gave a series of lectures at the Berlin Institute for Psychoanalysis, later collected in a volume under the promising title, *Psychoanalysis of the Total Personality* (*Psychoanalyse der Gesamtper-
soenlichkeit*).

Another fruitful line of exploration led Dr. Alexander to Cesare
Lombroso's *l'uomo delinquente,* delinquent man. In the case of criminality certain problems can be studied in the raw. The criminal is
usually an uninhibited person with inadequate conceptions of social
patterns. Uninhibited deeds of men without social conventions permit
the observer to draw significant conclusions about more conventional
persons, who are deterred from unrestrained actions by their fear of
adverse social reaction. In a much-discussed book Dr. Alexander explored the relation of the criminal and his judges: *Der Verbrecher und
seine Richter*.

American men of science had their eyes on Alexander. In 1930 he
was invited to the University of Chicago as a visiting professor for that
year and was prevailed upon to stay. The following year the Judge
Baker Foundation at Boston invited him to undertake a research project in criminal psychology and his book, *Roots of Crime,* was the

result. One more year saw him director of the Chicago Institute of Psychoanalysis, devoted to research and training workers in that field, and said to be the only institution of the kind in those days to maintain an out-patient clinic. If the influence of a scholar may be gauged by the frequency of references to his works in scientific publications, Dr. Alexander stands far in the van. Particularly, he came to be recognized as an authority in the study of psychogenic factors as causes of such maladies as asthma, ulcer and endocrinous disturbances.

Alexander early reached the conclusion that the individual's ailments could be probed only in relation to the entire "indivisible" person. Subsequently, he was driven to the conclusion that the totality of men, society, was also indivisible. This turned out to be a fruitful thought in suggesting that the individual is heir to the afflictions to which all humanity is heir. The nervous condition of the individual no less than his physical condition is the result of his social heredity and social environment. Therefore, the creative physician—and every genuine physician is creative—must understand his age.

Our Age of Unreason, published in 1942, was one of Alexander's much-discussed books. In his own words, it was an attempt to apply the principles of modern dynamic psychology to group phenomena and particularly to current events. He turned a critical searchlight on political thought and the emotional structures of different types of cultures, including the democratic and totalitarian. Incidentally, it turned out to be the psychoanalysis of the American scene. Our age of unreason is not merely our age, but all ages. That many human actions are irrational is a commonplace, but it is by no means a commonplace that the gap between rational thinking and irrational action is broadening. No previous age had come anywhere near ours in precise thinking. A millionth part of an inch may make all the difference in the world in today's scientific experiments. The true scientist of our age takes nothing for granted, accepts no ready-made promises and seeks to leave no loopholes. And yet in this very age of scientific precision, Dr. Alexander finds, we are acting far more irrationally than our unscientific ancestors. We seem to be acquainted with many of the significant answers reached by the scientific method, and yet our actions are as crude as the stone weapon of the caveman. We have scientific minds and unscientific temperaments. While Alexander does not presume to prescribe the remedy for the social malady of our age, he does say that it is a type of disease for which a high degree of specialization is needed.

The diagnosis must be made by a psychiatrist of society, the prescription written by a prophet, administered to the patient by a saint.

American psychoanalysis has profited greatly from the work of other Hungarian-born specialists in the field. Géza Roheim is an oft-quoted authority. In trying to understand the human soul he found himself inquiring into the workings of the mind of man unspoiled by social conventions. He was particularly attracted to the study of Australian primitives. He probed into their myths and rituals, into Australian totemism, the mythology and religion of the moon. He turned his attention to the secrets of animism, magic and the significance of the divine King. If man was to be understood, his origins must be understood and an attempt must be made to solve the riddle of human origins.

The disciple of the master, Freud, Sándor Rado was for years editor of the periodical devoted to a study of the application of psychoanalysis to the humanities. It attempted to explain social processes both statically and dynamically in terms of Freudian disciplines, and treated the problems of society as the composite of the problems of the individual and the problems of the individual as related to those of society.

Other notable Hungarian-born workers in the same field were Terez Benedek, Sándor Loránd and Béla Mittelmann, authors of numerous works on a large number of special and general problems in the study of the human soul.

Psychoanalysis made a bid to take exclusive control of the field of mental and nervous disorders. Just the same, psychiatry continued to hold its own, greatly influenced, no doubt, by the analytic method. Among the Hungarian-born psychiatrists scientific literature, particularly in pre-Hitler Europe, paid close attention to the study of Árpád Pauncz on the Lear complex, which he described as the opposite of the Oedipus complex, the victims of which fall in love with parents of the opposite sex; the daughter afflicted with the Electra complex is in love with her father, while in the Lear complex it is the father who falls in love with his daughter. Pauncz followed the history of this aberration through clinical cases and historic precedents recorded in literature.

The great minds, whom Central European reaction cast off, eventually found their way into the Western world where they helped the decent world cast off Central European reaction. This is the story of the atomic scientists and of the new age they inaugurated.

The application of atomic energy to explosives was introduced into the United States by Hungarian-born scientists, as the official record of atomic energy for military purposes clearly shows. Hungarian-born Dr. Leo Szilárd, one of the veteran atomic scientists, was the first to think of the application of the atom to bombs. "At that time [in January 1939] American-born nuclear physicists were so unaccustomed to the idea of using their science for military purposes that they hardly realized what needed to be done," observed Professor Henry D. Smyth, official chronicler of the atomic bomb.

Dr. Szilárd was one of the young scientists whom post-First World War Hungarian reactionary thought could dispense with. He went to Germany under the Weimar Republic and did some highly important research work in physics at the leading scientific institutes. Hitler came, and he went. Oxford was the first stop. Brilliant young scientists had their eyes on the United States and the United States was scouring the globe for brilliant young scientists. Dr. Szilárd reached Columbia University and there engaged in research work dealing with uranium.

It was a "small group of foreign-born physicists, centering on L. Szilárd," as the official report states,[80] "and including E. Wigner, E. Teller, V. F. Weisskopf and E. Fermi," who conceived the idea of getting government support for atomic energy work and of restricting publication, so that discoveries here should not fall into enemy hands. Three of these atomic scientists were Hungarian-born: Eugene P. Wigner, professor of physics at Princeton University, later head of the theoretical physics work of the Metallurgical Laboratory at Chicago, Professor E. Teller, of the University of Chicago, and, of course, Dr. Szilárd himself.

The early experiments entailed not only tremendous mental work but enormous mental strain. There had been atomic research, but this was different. How could the power of the atom be drawn upon to destroy the Axis?

Something of the emotional experience of those days was conveyed in a report by Dr. Szilárd: "On March 3, 1939, Dr. W. Zinn and I, working on the seventh floor of the Pupin Building at Columbia University, completed a simple experiment to which we had been looking forward rather eagerly. Everything was ready, and all we had to do was to lean back, turn a switch, and watch the screen of a television tube. If flashes of light appeared on the screen, it would mean that neutrons were emitted in the fission of uranium, and that in turn would mean that the liberation of atomic energy was possible in our lifetime. We turned the switch, we saw the flashes, we watched them for about ten minutes—and then we switched everything off and went home. That night I knew that the world was headed for sorrow." [81]

The insistence of Szilárd and his small group of scientists on stopping publication of atom research data must have appeared outlandish to native-born American scientists. Szilárd knew that two German scientists, Hann and Strassman, had discovered an important atomic reaction but he had reason to believe that the German group was contending with raw materials and other problems. They must not be helped by learning about the progress American scientists were making. It was uphill work to convince the scientific world in America that secrecy could not be avoided. Finally, the formation of a censorship committee to control publication of all American scientific journals was proposed at the April 1940 meeting of the Division of Physical Sciences of the National Research Council. Publication of data about uranium fission must be controlled. A censorship committee was set up eventually and one of its sub-committees dealt specifically with uranium fission. Professor Wigner, one of the Hungarian-born atomic scientists, was asked to serve on this sub-committee.

Even before that, work on the problem was "slanted" to the military needs. "From March 1939 until October of the same year," Szilárd related, "work in the field of atomic energy was carried on by a handful of men who lacked many of the things they needed and most of all official recognition. From October 1939 to the end of 1944 we still lacked many things, but we suffered from too much official recognition. Our increasing anxiety about what the Germans might be doing made our slow speed all the more intolerable."

In March 1939 the Columbia University nuclear physicists established contact with the United States Navy Department which registered "interest" and asked to be "kept informed." Such requests were, of course, official routine.

This was not enough for Szilárd and Wigner. The official route was roundabout and full of detours. The Germans were sitting on top of the world and one day might drop an atomic bomb on our civilization. A short cut must be found into the White House. They conferred with Professor Albert Einstein at Princeton. He in turn knew Alexander Sachs, a New York economist, who had the ear of President Roosevelt. Einstein gave a letter to Sachs who handed it to Roosevelt. The President was impressed and appointed an Advisory Committee on Uranium which met in October 1939, and included the three Hungarian-born scientists, Sachs and two other scientists. Szilárd wanted to induce the government to buy graphite and uranium oxide for the experiments. The President could not be on hand for every small step, and so progress was far from swift. In February 1940 the first funds were transferred from the army and navy for the purchase of materials for the experiments. The amount thus appropriated was the munificent sum of $6,000—which started the chain reaction that shook the world.

Two significant facts were now in the possession of Szilárd, Wigner and their associates. One was that Germany's most important scientific organization, the Kaiser Wilhelm Institute in Berlin, had been set aside for uranium research. The other was the discovery that uranium fission of the needed type occurred only in the so-called U-235 isotope.

Mid-summer 1940 arrived. The Germans had overrun Europe. How long could Britain hold out? Quick action was needed. So the scientists decided to ask for a larger appropriation. This time they asked for $140,000.

Time was getting short; England was fighting with her back against the sea, and America's conflict with Japan became more serious. The National Defense Research Committee was formed. At the same time a few thousand dollars were set aside for new activities at Columbia. "The scale of expenditure is at least a rough index of activity," Professor Smyth observed. "It is therefore interesting to compare this figure for atomic development with those in other branches of war research. By Nov. 1941 the total budget approved for the Radiation Laboratory at the Massachusetts Institute of Technology was several million dollars."

The most essential work was concentrated by June 1940 in the hands of Fermi and Szilárd at Columbia University. Wigner, meanwhile, was working on the problem of poisons released by radioactive fission. The possibility was then seriously considered that the Germans might make surprise use of radioactive poison. Defensive measures were planned.

By the end of 1941, there was an important change "in the wake of a visit," Dr. Szilárd explained, "which Dr. Oliphant of Birmingham, England, paid to this country. . . . He attended one of the meetings of the Uranium Committee as a guest and was not very much impressed by the organization and official guidance of our work. Disregarding international etiquette, he told any one who was willing to listen what he thought of us. Considerations other than military secrecy prevent me from repeating the exact expressions he used. But he got results."

Work had progressed so far that little doubt could be entertained that it was possible to produce atomic bombs and that they would have enormous destructive power. The official mind, which recognizes only results, was inclined to be impressed, too. It was decided that work should be expanded and an organization called Metallurgical Laboratory set up in connection with the University of Chicago. Atomic projects had the most innocent names. The three Hungarian-born pioneers of the atomic bomb did much of their work at this laboratory.

"After the reorganization of our work," Dr. Szilárd continues, "we were happy for a while. Sometime during 1942 the army was brought into the picture, but the officers who were attached to us realized that they did not know what it was all about and did not make it difficult for us.

"Toward the end of 1942 and during the first-half of 1943 all sorts of troubles developed, not all of them originating with the army. At that time it became evident to most of us that unless our organization could be changed quickly we would have no bombs ready by the spring of 1944, when we expected the invasion of Europe to begin. . . . During 1943 and 1944 our greatest worry was the possibility that Germany would perfect an atomic bomb before the invasion of Europe. I myself was firmly convinced that the Germans were ahead of us in this work. Today I know that I was wrong and that when the war ended the Germans had not reached the point from which we started when our work began in earnest."

Many thousands were now engaged on the projects. The Hungarian-language press of America reported that an eighteen-year-old scientist, John George Kemeny was working in the ranks of the junior staff. A new laboratory was established in the spring of 1943 at Los Alamos, New Mexico, under J. R. Oppenheimer, and it was there that the final touches were made on operable atomic bombs.

"In 1945," Szilárd continues his story, "we ceased worrying about what the Germans might do to us, and we began to worry what the government of the United States might do to other countries. . . . There were those among us who thought that we should not set a precedent of using atomic energy for the purposes of destruction. About sixty of us at Chicago took the view that Japan was essentially defeated and that it would be wrong to attack its cities with atomic bombs as if atomic bombs were simply another military weapon."

The atomic bombs exploded over Hiroshima and Nagasaki. The Axis had been beaten. The scientists were almost too late for the Second

World War. Were they just in time for the third one? Precisely that question was worrying them. If the atom were allowed to go its own destructive way, not for very long would there be an atomic problem in the world. An Atomic Development Authority must be set up, Dr. Teller argued.[82] Special agents should check up on the atomic work of each country. Each country should be permitted to send to any country as many agents as it pleased. "These agents would be nominated by the country they represent and approved by the Atomic Development Authority. . . . These agents should have the right freely to inquire into any activity which may seem to them directed against their own country, or against world peace.

"It should be considered the duty of every citizen of every country to give full information to these agents of the Atomic Development Authority. International law—superior to any national legislation—should protect men who have given such information. . . .

"The agents of the Atomic Development Authority would be in a position to start breaking down the barriers which now separate nation from nation. They should not, in their usual function, be considered as policemen. They should work for world unity and they must try to remove reasons for friction—both material and spiritual."

Dr. Szilárd went straight to the heart of the problem. He considered the possibility of atomic rivalry between America and the Soviets. "If these two countries . . . accumulate large stockpiles of atomic bombs, war is likely to break out, even though neither country has wanted to go to war."[83] Wars were waged not merely by men, but also by arms. Nations could no more refrain from employing their atomic bombs than children could refrain from shooting off their firecrackers. The destructive power of man would equal his creative power, demonstrated in harnessing the atomic energy. The superman had reached the tallest peak and there he met his alter ego, the cave man.

"If the United States and Russia were to agree to an arrangement ruling out both stockpiles and manufacture of atomic bombs," Dr. Szilárd said, "it appears very likely that such an arrangement would be acceptable to all major powers of the world and could be extended to them. . . .

"The arrangement itself should provide for rights of inspection to be exercised by an international agency attached to the United Nations organization. . . ."

The atomic scientist who was, probably, the spiritual father of the atomic bomb, deeply felt his responsibility for letting loose a spirit that

mankind might not be able to control unless prompt measures were
taken. Measures of supervision, Dr. Szilárd saw, would be palliatives
—not solutions. "Clearly," he continued, "the crucial point in this
transition will be reached when a world government will in fact operate
in an area of security of police functions. . . . If we wish to avert an
arms race, we will have to give up our own atomic bombs and scrap
our own manufacturing facilities before we can have a fool-proof peace
system. We shall have to take risks, and we shall have to derive courage to take risks from the conviction that we are on our way toward
the solution of the problem of permanent peace."

The atomic bomb put the scientist on the map. The famed ivory
tower was gone, perhaps for ever.

In the field of science it is not noses that count. But, looking through
recognized reference books about scientists in the United States, one
finds some revealing statistics. Inquiring into the nationalities of American scientists, one finds that among the foreign-born the Germans are
in the van. That is easily understandable, since Germany was one of
the most highly industrialized countries in the world and the most
highly industrialized one on the European Continent. Next come the
Russians and that is more difficult to understand. Russia was a typical
agrarian country and it was only years after she had become the Union
of Soviet Socialist Republics that she went into industrialization on a
truly large scale. Evidently, much scientific talent had been expelled
from pre-revolutionary Russia to find its level in the United States.

Getting down to the smaller nations we come across a remarkable
phenomenon. Hungary ranks with Austria, Sweden and Switzerland
as having made the largest contributions to American science. The
curious fact is that Hungary's background is different from that of the
other countries. They are highly industrialized nations, whereas Hungary is even today in the earlier stages of industrialization. Here again
we come across the phenomenon of expulsion and compensation. A
large amount of scientific talent was accumulated in Hungary and was
necessarily expelled into countries offering opportunities to these gifted
individuals. Thanks to Hitler, a large part of Europe was denuded of
some of its most talented scientists, and it was not an accident that the
United States was the first country to develop the atom bomb.

Among the Hungarian-born scientists in the United States there is
a veritable *embarras de richesses,* so that it is possible only to pick out

a few names at random, referring the reader to the accepted reference books.

A nationally recognized authority on animal diseases, Adolph Eichhorn, held the position of director of Animal Disease Station of the Bureau of Animal Industry in the United States Department of Agriculture and wrote about experiments in vaccination against anthrax, the contagious abortion of cattle, Malta fever and its control in goats. Also in the Department of Agriculture, Stephen Brunauer investigated soils and fertilizers, wrote studies on the action of bodies in holding and condensing gases and vapors, known as adsorption. During the Second World War he became a consultant of the National Defense Research Committee and branched off into work in explosives.

Budapest-born Peter Carl Goldmark was described [84] as the author of the "most notable television demonstration of the year. . . . For an hour, an ingenious new receiving set was tuned in on a filmed fashion-show and football game. . . . The broadcast was over ultra-high frequency, radar wave lengths. The reception, as vivid as a Van Gogh painting, made black and white television look antiquated. Boasted the Columbia Broadcasting System: 'The insurmountable obstacles' have been hurdled; in a year, if demand is great enough, color television can be in the United States home."

G. Galambos of Harvard, together with D. R. Griffin, studied the problems of certain sounds. For instance they found that the bat finds its way in the dark by emitting a note of high pitch which is reflected by such objects as a wall—something like radar, with sound as the disturbance to be reflected instead of the radio wave.

Gabor Kron performed important work in synchronizing sound with pictures in Hollywood and spent years as a consulting engineer with General Electric as an industrial troubleshooter who, according to the communication of an enthusiastic friend of his, "has done more than anybody else to solve seemingly insoluble problems more quickly and precisely than anybody else."

As an anthropologist, George Herzog went to Liberia with a University of Chicago expedition in 1930. He wrote, with a collaborator, on the proverbs and maxims of primitive Liberian tribes, and about music in the Caroline Islands, and compiled a bibliography of folk music in the United States and the West Indies. Subsequently, he became associated with Columbia University.

As a physiologist, in his younger days, Theodore Koppanyi had the reputation of an "infant prodigy" for his work in transplanting the eyes of animals. He was then working at the University of Vienna. Still young, he came to the United States and gradually veered toward pharmacology. His works cover such subjects as the barbiturates, the effects of poisons, the antagonism of drugs and modern problems of biology and the "conquest of life."

George Polya, mathematician, studied the theory of functions, numbers, probability and location of roots. Tibor Rado, another mathematician, wrote on the problem of plateaus, conformal mapping, area of surfaces, partial differential equations. Gabor Szego, also a mathematician, made his name first in Germany before he came to the United States to devote his attention to orthogonal polynomials and other mathematical problems.

American science gave high citations to the bacteriologist, Jules Freund, for his work on T.B. serums and to Paul Kaufman for his work on the immunization against pneumococcus bacteria.

Max Thorek became known as a surgeon throughout a large part of the world; he was made a knight of the Legion of Honor of France, knight of the Order of the Crown of Italy, commander of the order of St. Alexander, Bulgaria, and received the Medal of Honor of Venezuela, and the Aztec Eagle of the Mexican government. He wrote three volumes on modern surgical technics, considered a standard work. His autobiography, *A Surgeon's World,* has received much favorable notice.

Maria Telkes, physical chemist, connected with Westinghouse and the Massachusetts Institute of Technology, worked mainly on the utilization of solar energy and thermo-electricity. Clara Torda saw a lot of Europe in Italy and England before coming to the United States where she turned her main attention to the mechanism of neuromuscular transmission, adrenals, and Vitamin C. Camille Kereszturi did pioneering work in pediatrics. Max Goldzieher wrote authoritative volumes on endocrinology; Stephen Rosenak worked on cancer research. Frederick S. Reiss had his globe-trotting beginnings at Basel, Vienna, Budapest, Geneva, London and Paris, lectured on dermatology and syphlogy at the Dung Dai Medical College of Shanghai for over a decade, and until 1941 was head of the department of dermatology at the National Medical College in Shanghai. He wrote extensively and became an authority on leprosy. Erwin Raisz became associated with the Institute of Geographical Exploration of Harvard University. László Károly Ernő Zechmeister had his scientific start in organic chemistry in Zurich, Berlin, Copenhagen, and Pécs, Hungary. In 1940 he became professor of organic chemistry at the California Institute of Technology, Pasadena. He wrote about the principles and practice of chromatography and a textbook of organic chemistry.

With the coming of the Second World War an additional group of Hungarian scientists came to the United States, and in a short time established reputations for themselves: Andras Angyal, psychiatrist; Tibor Benedek, dermatologist; Oscar Benesi, anatomist; Paul Erdos, mathematician; Imre Horner, physiological chemist; Balint Orban, oral histologist; George Polya, mathematician; Joseph Stasney, pathologist; and Edward Teller, whose name has already been mentioned.[85]

Naturally, a large number of scientists from Hungary are not to be found in reference books. It is in the very nature of the true scientist that he works in obscurity for many years, and it is not easy to ferret him out of his hiding place. Thus it could happen that the atomic scientists, who became world famous because of their spectacular work, had not hitherto been mentioned in scientific publications. Only the publicity attending the "A bomb" made their names known to the layman.

XVIII

LITERATI AND ILLUMINATI

THE PUSH AND pull effect of economic forces largely regulated the heavings of Hungarian immigration into the United States during the tidal wave period of the global *Voelkerwanderung* before the First World War. Economic conditions pushed the migrants out of their country and pulled them into America, but these forces did not operate fully in the case of the literati.

In the latter part of the nineteenth century, America's energies were absorbed by the claims of the frontier. It was the economic frontier which attracted hosts of immigrants to this country. Nobody could foresee the coming of the American Century, and no poets heralded it. America's attention was absorbed in production, exploiting the vast resources of the country. How vast these really were nobody could foresee. Think boldly, act boldly and live boldly, was the motto of men of action and the economic frontier offered the highest rewards to audacity. Occasionally the cry of a St. John issued from the intellectual desert of the Gilded Age—a Walt Whitman. Scattered beacons of individual genius suggested the possibilities of the intellectual frontier—a Mark Twain.

Contemporaries wanted to hear no criticism of the advancing factory age. God was kind to those who were good to Him, rewarding them with earthly riches. Gold was the hallmark of real value, and worship of gold was not worship of the golden calf. It took a world war and a world depression to make the nation accept the seers' self-examination when they tore deeply into conventions and exposed the sham of gentility. Few literatures dared to face reality as boldly. But the age of Theodore Dreiser and Sinclair Lewis was yet to come.

At the other end of the bridge to the Old World, for our purposes, was Hungary. She was engaged in shaking off the shackles of scholasticism and academic pedantism. She also had a frontier in the fourth quarter of the last century. The frontier was small and its exploiters were not bold enough. Otherwise, those Hungarian hosts would not have crossed the ocean. The economic frontier did not absorb very much of Hungary's intellectual energies. Best remembered by the world is the fabulous Mór Jókai, of the one hundred and one novels many of which read like fables of the one thousand and one nights, a prodigious storyteller of Hungary's past and present, of the age of romanticism and unreality. A painter of word tableaus of idyllic life was Kálmán Mikszáth, also serving a romantic public that considered it poor manners to come to grips with the real. The age of truth was to dawn only later.

The peasants came from Hungary, but very few city dwellers. The writers stayed at home, attached to the language that was their livelihood and frequently their very lives. What could they have done in the United States? They would have been sentenced to the mines or the blast furnace, and their poetic imagination would have been stultified in the absence of the red poppy and the cornflower, the *puszta* and the *Alföld,* steppes and plains. The offspring of the new-comers could have responded to the challenge of the new land. There was plenty to write about—the grit and smoke, the misery and privation of the coal and steel towns, the glorious feeling of stuffed stomachs, the marvel of not having to scrape and bow to the authorities. An American literature could have been created in Little Hungary, as a Hungarian-language press was created in this country. But that did not happen. Literature was a step-child of American civilization in those days and little was left of the national energies for poetic daydreams which increased neither coal nor steel production, or so at least the world believed.

There were exceptions, naturally, as we have already seen in the case of the remarkable Heilprin family. There was also an occasional autobiography, such as *My Portion,* by Rebekah Kohut, wife of a great Hungarian-Jewish leader in America, in which she described the hard struggles demanded by an exacting country, offering high rewards but only for the greatest effort.

One who tried but did not always succeed was William Noah Loew, a Hungarian writer in the United States at the turn of the century. He came from a line of intellectual aristocrats and became a worshiper of the Word at an early age. A poet in phraseology but not in evocative flights of fancy, he became the vicar of the poets as the interpreter of their works. Hungarian to the core—sometimes defiantly so—he developed into a missionary of the Magyar verse. Loew could not have given his best if he had not believed with all his heart in the excellence of his literary heroes. Because he believed he placed some of Hungary's poets on the level of Baudelaire and Verlaine. He held that mid-century Hungary had an Olympian peer of Goethe himself in the greatest of the great of the *Alföld,* the poet Sándor Petőfi, lost in the Hungarian War of Independence. Loew translated many of his poems into English. He also translated the epic poems of János Arany, author of *Toldi* and *Toldi's Eve,* the fable of a legendary hero set in the Hungarian countryside where every single blade of grass emitted the aroma of the plains. He translated *The Tragedy of Man,* by Imre Madách, which he considered equal to Goethe's immortal *Faust,* a drama of human frustration and hope.

In Hungary Andor Garvai had been one of the fighting Left, a Socialist, receiving no support from the ruling powers, although he did know a moderate measure of success with some of his plays. He craved the free air of the West and came to the United States. The material benefits of life were lost on him, and he did not find here what he had been looking for. Word reached him after the First World War of the triumph of his ideals, as he thought. The Left was in power at Budapest, the age of the common man was at hand. He arrived just in time to witness the bungling finale of Hungary's cari-cature of a collective regime. What he saw under the rule of Budapest Communism disheartened him sadly. He returned to the United States, rent by doubt about his gifts, as failures were compounded. Again and again he tried to obtain a hearing on the American stage, receiving much encouragement from those who had little to say about a dramatist's fate and seldom able to pierce the secretarial line of de-fense of the truly mighty. The despair in his face disqualified him for success anyway, as he found out that most people want to help only those who need no help. It was as a common laborer that his frus-trated life ended. He was not the only "failure" among the literati.

An infant prodigy in letters when he came here before the First World War, Eugene Szekeres Bagger gave much promise. During the war he had a fruitful career as a journalist. After the war, he began to make his mark as a writer. The book that first called attention to him was a series of studies in continental reality, the stories of some of the post-war great or near-great people of Europe, *Eminent Euro-peans.* It was written with a sharp pen and many embellishments in an obvious attempt to imitate the ways of Lytton Strachey, famed author of *Eminent Victorians.* The book was a success and no less a success was *Francis Joseph, Emperor of Austria, King of Hungary,* the life story of the Habsburg monarch who ascended his throne in the stagecoach era and left it in the age of the airplane. It was a dazzling performance especially for one to whom English was an acquired tongue. Bagger himself passed judgment on the book in a later and much mellower mood, when he described it as too "brilliant." Occasional magazine articles interrupted a philosopher's meditation which lasted for several years. Hitler forced Bagger out of his contemplative life overseas, and during the Second World War he published what he called an "impersonal autobiography," *For the Heathen Are Wrong*. This was a different Bagger, seeking the meaning of his life, critical of his past, searching for the sense of life in religion, detached from the jousting market place and attached to values which are not of the fleeting moment.

The gap which exists between American and Hungarian literatures called for a builder of bridges. Joseph Reményi, a college professor, set himself the task of acquainting Hungarians with American authors and Americans with Hungarian authors. Every Hungarian child knew, of course, about James Fenimore Cooper and Mark Twain, but that usually exhausted the knowledge of the Hungarian general public. In his *American Decameron*, Reményi endeavored to acquaint the Hungarian public with such American authors as Sherwood Anderson, Ernest Hemingway and William Faulkner. At the same time he made an attempt to introduce America's scholars to some of Hungary's most influential writers, especially Endre Ady who is considered Hungary's greatest twentieth century poet. Reményi was one of the few latter-day authors who tried to create a Hungarian-American literature. During the First World War he published a collection of stories dealing with the life of the Hungarian immigrant in America. He wrote very long novels revealing his gift for telling description and characterization, in the epic style, with great wealth of detail. His *Emberek ne Sirjatok* (*Thou Shalt not Cry*) was published in four volumes and *Elni Kell* (*You Must Live*) in two.

Hungary made her contributions to American letters through the children of immigrants. Few of them achieved the success and fame of Edna Ferber, the daughter of a Hungarian immigrant. She herself was native-born, a child of Kalamazoo, Michigan. Edna Ferber's story is largely the story of best-seller novels, such as *So Big, Show Boat* and *Cimarron,* and of stage hits, mostly in co-operation with that other famous hit-smith, George S. Kaufman, such as *The Royal Family, Dinner at Eight,* and *Stage Door.*

Ralph Borsodi made his reputation in an entirely different field. In Hungarian his name means "from Borsod County," but he was born in New York City. There may have been an atavistic urge in him, the city-born economist, to return to nature. "Back to nature" movements are not new to modern man. Rousseau and Tolstoi, for instance, advocated a personal return to nature but no basic changes in their environment. It was different with Ralph Borsodi. The United States he knew was that of the post-First World War years, the America of super-billion dollar corporations, of endless rows of factory chimneys, an America in which even agriculture took pride in calling itself an industry, in which the Indiana corn fields and Kansas wheat fields were open air factories and the farmer a gadget-minded factory hand. Ralph Borsodi pointed out that it cost far more to distribute goods than to produce them and called this *The Age of Distribution.* Like rashes, factories covered the erstwhile beauties of nature, polluting streams, poisoning vegetation, turning a thing of beauty into *This Ugly Civilization.* It marred not merely the landscape but also man's soul and mind. A slave of the machine, he came to depend upon canned food and canned music. His versatility, formerly the pride of man, was now completely stunted. Civilization would be extinguished unless quick remedy was applied: *Flight from the City.* Not content with merely preaching return to nature, Borsodi founded the School of Living, the Independence Foundation, the Bayard Lane Association and the Van Houten Fields Association.

The School of Living at Suffern, New York, attracted wide attention. Its purposes were, in the words of its author, to associate a selected group of artists, craftsmen and teachers in a demonstration of the contribution which decentralized, self-sufficient living in the country may make to redress the economic and psychological insecurities of our industrialized civilization; to study and develop the possibilities of the home and homestead as a productive and creative institution; to furnish to men and women the opportunity to follow a carefully developed plan of learning and experiences in living securely, comfortably and richly and in leading others to live equally well.

The First World War, as we have already seen, was followed by an exodus of intellectuals from Hungary. Most of them were scientists and artists. Very few were writers for the obvious reason that language is a tool which one acquires at birth and very seldom later. English has only a minimum of grammar, as everybody knows, but prospective writers found out to their grief that it is a hard language to learn because it consists mostly of idioms and not the simple juxtaposition of words, as do most other tongues. Chinese ideographs, as contrasted with the Latin alphabet, offer the best parallel between English and other languages.

Hungarian literati did come to the United States in the early post-First World War years but not in large numbers. One was Oscar Jászi. In pre-war Hungary he had tried to raise alarm over the problem of national minorities which did not exist at all to the average Hungarian. Hungary was Hungarian and that was all; the Magyar closed his eyes to the fact that the highlands all around Hungary were inhabited by several nationalities, spilling into the plains. The then Hungarian governments, too, sought to "settle" the nationality problem by pretending that it did not exist. Jászi knew that such "solutions" could only be temporary and that Hungary's future could not be assured unless she reached agreements with her minorities which almost formed a majority. He contended most emphatically that as a uni-national State Hungary was an absurdity and that she must be transformed into a multi-national country. Not far distant from Hungary's western marches he saw a successful solution of this problem. Switzerland was inhabited by four different nationalities speaking as many languages, drawing from four different traditions, German, French, Italian and Romansch, often antagonistic to one another. In spite of this, Switzerland was prosperous and the very image of peace. Instead of fighting each other, the four nationalities were engaged in amicable competition. Here was a ready-made example for Hungary and, possibly, some of her neighbors. The idea of "Eastern Switzerland" was born.

Each "canton" of Eastern Switzerland would be delimited along ethnic frontiers and would possess a large measure of self-government. An ideal blend would result by combining the constructive qualities of these peoples who in the past had defeated their own aims by working at cross purposes. Before the war, the Austro-Hungarian Monarchy was a political monstrosity, since it took no account of the most dynamic force of the age, nationalism, while at the same time it was an economic necessity because it united a variety of interdependent regions producing most of the essentials of economic life. Oscar Jászi followed in the traditions of Lajos Kossuth, who, in later life, saw the solution of the Southeastern European problem in the formation of a Danubian federation of friendly States, dependent upon their own strength rather than serving as cat's-paws for foreign interests.

Under the First Hungarian Republic, headed by Count Károlyi, Oscar Jászi served as Minister of Nationalities. Hungary had been defeated and the remedies that might have helped when the minorities were begging for concessions were of no use whatever now that they held the whip hand, and not even Jászi's earnest endeavors could turn the scales. He personally had numerous friends among the nationalities, but Hungary's friends were few. The former servants in mistress Hungary's mansion now had become mistresses themselves.

Jászi went into exile after the downfall of the Hungarian democratic Republic and, preceded by high reputation in scholarly circles, eventually reached the United States. Here he accepted a position on the faculty of Oberlin College in 1925, became professor of political science, and taught there for fully seventeen years, his fame reaching into many corners of the United States. He wrote a standard book, *The Dissolution of the Habsburg Monarchy* and made many notable contributions to books and scholarly periodicals. After the Second World War he saw his ideas about Hungary's future vindicated, as it became crystal clear that the region of the mighty Danube was a unit.

It was three years after the end of the First World War that the writer of this book came to the United States. I had been a prisoner of war in Siberia during the war, having served in the armed forces of Austria-Hungary and been taken prisoner by the Russians in the summer of 1916, during the crucial Brusilov offensive on the Eastern front. My first contributions to the American press appeared a few months after my arrival in the United States, in publications as diverse as *The New York Tribune,* conservative, and *The Nation*. At a party given by Willy Pogány I met Beauvaix Fox, then editor of the drama section of the *"Trib,"* and he asked me, rather absently, whether I would care to write a story about the Hungarian theater for his section? Would I, indeed? Then began a long collaboration which was transferred to other sections of the *Tribune,* then to *The New York Herald Tribune,* when it came into existence.

The contact with *The Nation* was established also in those early days. I was sitting on a bench at Bowling Green, near the southernmost tip of Manhattan, looking hungrily at the busy life all around when my eyes fell on the name of Anatole France, on the cover of *The Nation*. A few months before, I had passed through Paris on my way to America and during the few hours I spent in that city of light I thought constantly of the fact that I was breathing the same air as Anatole France, my idol among the French writers. Here I was in a strange country, but there was Anatole France, my best friend (whom I had never seen). I must buy that paper, but it cost fifteen cents. That was a fortune, of course, for a new-comer and I must have fingered a dime and a nickel thin before I could make up my mind to part with them. It turned out that Anatole France's name appeared attached to a manifesto, along with other names. The wide-awake editors of *The Nation* picked it out and put it on the cover. I liked the magazine and it became my ambition to write an article for it. Soon enough that ambition was realized.

The Hungarian immigrant intellectual's Bible is and has for a long time been *The New York Times*. Naturally, I wanted to contribute to it. That ambition was realized, too, and the beginning was quite auspicious. The magazine section of the *Times* published a series of articles I wrote about *L'Aiglon,* the son of Napoleon the Great, based on material found in the secret Habsburg archives of Vienna.

At the end of the first decade of my stay in America I began writing books. I was spending a fortnight in upstate New York, and there was little to do there. My mother, who was with me, had always urged me to jot down my experiences in the Russian prison camps during the First World War, and I began a couple of days after our arrival. I wrote the manuscript in Hungarian and it literally poured out of me. At the end of the fortnight, I had the manuscript of a book.

Then I returned to New York, still broiling under its cruel midsummer sun. What was I to do with a Hungarian manuscript? America had no Hungarian-language publishers and I had written too critically about the ruling Hungarian Horthy regime for it to be published in its territory. I liked the manuscript and so I decided to translate it into English myself. *Cattle Car Express* was the title. It was a fictionized account of my experiences in Russian captivity. Not everybody understood the title, I am afraid. A railway organization wrote in for a free copy for their archives of technical books on railroading problems. The critics liked the book very much. The London *Times Literary Supplement* predicted hopefully that it "will live in literature," and *The New York Herald Tribune Books* critic detected "Tolstoian depth" in it and expressed the hope that its author would keep on producing books of this quality. But its author did not produce any more books of fiction.

My first non-fiction book was *Hitler,* published in 1932, the year before the *Fuehrer* was invested with the Chancellor's powers in the same Wilhelmstrasse which was to see his end twelve years later. That book earned me one of the greatest honors I have ever received, a place on the list of those whom the Gestapo was to take into custody after the invasion of Britain by the Germans. This list was found in Germany by the Allied armies. *The Cauldron Boils,* my next book, should have placed me on the list of true prophets because I forecast in it that the Second World War would break out in the Polish Corridor. The book deals with the minority problems of pre-Second World War Poland. It was followed by *The New Deal in Europe,* not a felicitous title, devoted to a discussion of the various "isms" then doing their worst to discredit humanism, the only acceptable member of the clan. *Millions of Dictators* deals with the average man in the key countries and shows him as having a say in his fate even though ruled by dictators.

When the Second World War broke out my book *The Danube* was published. My next book was *Turkey,* followed by *Dakar: Outpost of Two Hemispheres* and *Siberia.* Then came a high school textbook, *America's Role in World Affairs.* Books of this nature seldom net either fame or fortune, yet the very thought that I wrote that book makes me happy. It is my contribution to a better understanding of the world scene by America's youth.

In all these books I tried to show that every part of the world is one with every other part and that we *are* our brothers' keepers or we are nothing at all. I endeavored to put complicated problems in simple language so that they might be understood by lay leaders. That is, of course, a major sin in the eyes of those for whom a book has profundity only if it is unbearably dull. Translating from the French, German and Hungarian languages into English, lecturing, and writing a film scenario kept me busy, aside from my books. I began teaching at universities in the middle thirties and have been teaching ever since.

Few Hungarian-born Americans published books in those days. One was Charlotte Lederer, a grandmother in her middle sixties, and mother of Anna Rosenberg, one of America's leading women in labor questions, about whom more will be said. Mrs. Lederer achieved success with her book *The Eagle's Nest: A Prince's Flight for Freedom.* A versatile artist, she illustrated her own books and also wrote in collaboration with others.

Hungarian-born Louis Rittenberg became a notable figure in the

English-speaking Jewish literary life. He served, in turn, as editor of
the *American Hebrew, Universal Jewish Encyclopaedia* and *Liberal
Judaism*. He was also the translator of numerous Hungarian books
and plays, including those by Ferenc Molnár. Among translators from
Hungarian into English, Beatrice Tolnay and George Halász became
best known.

The halcyon days of the post-First World War period were soon
over, the days when war broke out only sporadically and could be confined to certain regions by diplomatic ingenuity. The League of
Nations, once the hope of man, was moribund and the dictators,
Adolph Hitler and Benito Mussolini, were on the rampage. Nazi
youth chanted jubilantly: "Today Germany is ours and tomorrow ours
will be the entire world." The so-called "have-not" nations declared
war on the "have" nations. In reality, it was criminality that declared
war on decency. Czechoslovakia was raped and Hitler invaded Poland. As the brown tide advanced in the wake of French defeat, several Hungarian writers found themselves tossed on the shores of
foreign countries, and some of them came to the United States.

Best known was Ferenc Molnár, the most successful practitioner of
the sophisticated, worldly wise comedy. He wrote indulgent, polite
plays on manners and human frailties, about polished gentlemen acting as lovesick cave men, about perfumed cave women—the battle of
the sexes. This was not the social criticism of an Ibsen or the social
satire of Shaw. But it was first-class theater, which many attempted to
copy without the happy Midas touch of Molnár. World-wide reputation preceded him to the United States.

This country saw his first international success, which he wrote as
a very young man, several years before the First World War—*The
Devil*. Particularly, this country knew his *Liliom*, a tender tale of
crime and punishment, the story of a Budapest thug who wanted to
do a good deed for his child in the great beyond and, true to type, stole
a star. That play was performed in countless variations on the stage,
the screen and the music hall. America was far ahead of the author's
own Budapest in appreciation of *Liliom*, in spite of the fact that a
happy ending was then a convention. Unhappy endings were compounded in this play, in which the unhappy ex-bouncer lost not
merely his life but his chance of redemption in the other world.

Molnár seemed to have a magic touch as success followed success, with the presentation of *The Guardsman, The Swan, The Wolf,* and *The Play's the Thing.*

He followed the Central European tradition in being many-sided. Several of his novels were translated into English, such as *The Prisoners, Eva and the Derelict Boat* and, above all, *The Boys of Paul Street,* the story of a gang of boys that made many eyes grow misty all over the world. That book was a bravura performance for a man of Molnár's special gifts; in it he painted a world entirely different from his universe of well-dressed society wolves. Molnár also developed a genre of sketches of humorous conversation which convulsed pre-war Hungary with laughter.

The world was threatened with a global conflict when Molnár came to the United States. Here he found an audience that wanted both escape and social significance in books and plays. He tried to impart that significance to his works but his public agreed that he was at his best as a dissecter of social customs and an entertainer for entertainment's sake. Trying to live a retired life in New York, he was discovered by the tradesmen of social gossip. Even by them he was treated with the respect he deserved as a benefactor of mankind, a man who made millions laugh.

Another notable literary figure who came from Hungary was René Fülöp-Miller. After a journalistic career in Berlin, Paris and Vienna he settled down to write a large number of noted books, such as *The Mind and Face of Bolshevism, Lenin and Gandhi, Rasputin the Holy Devil, The Power and Secret of the Jesuits, Leaders, Dreamers and Rebels,* the last an account of the great mass movements of history and the wish-dreams that inspired them. Among his many other books, he wrote about the American and Russian stage.

Another Hungarian author with an international reputation who came to the United States in the "time of troubles" of Second World War days was Ferenc Körmendi. He sprang to fame when he was awarded the International Novel Prize in 1932. Among his books, *Escape to Life* became best known. A prolific author, he wrote about life in Budapest and elsewhere with a picturesque pen and a sharp eye for revealing detail. Particularly, he revealed remarkable gifts in dissecting social shortcomings without losing hope. While his descriptions of life are true, he leaves the impression that man is not doomed to stumble toward his fall in ignorance of his own ulterior motives and in desperation over the ultimate success of his strivings.

Another of those who came from Hungary was Edward J. Byng.

Before the First World War he had received part of his early education
in England, a precocious youth with a great aptitude for languages.
It was he who first introduced the Boy Scout movement into Hungary
and, incidentally, became an all-round amateur sportsman. His globe-
trotting career continued during the First World War when he was
assigned to the Ottoman Empire as a liaison officer of Austria-Hungary
with a roving commission in some of the Arabic regions of that realm.
There the foundation of his knowledge of the Arabic world was laid,
and there he acquired his knowledge of Turkish. After that war he became a correspondent for the United Press, one of the large newspaper
syndicates of the United States, and subsequently European syndicate
editor of the feature service of the U.P., in which capacity he became
acquainted with some of the world's leading makers of history, such as
the Soviet's Lenin and republican Turkey's founder and first President,
Mustapha Kemal. Later, coming to the United States, Byng wrote a
Five Year Peace Plan and a history of the Arabs. He was consulted
by newspapers as an authority on Near Eastern affairs.

Another Hungarian-born author in the United States much quoted
in connection with Oriental questions was Felix Valyi, who wrote
about the political and spiritual revolution in Islam.

The dream of many Hungaran writers is to come to the United
States and make a name here. As a land of "unlimited possibilities" this
nation is thought to have an insatiable appetite for the products of
"genius." It does not take long for young hopefuls to realize that long
lines of publishers do not await every arriving boat from Europe,
greedily tearing writers from one another's arms and signing them up
for fabulous sums. On the contrary, it is soon found that America is
near the saturation point for literature and arts, and that success
beckons only to a few. That discovery broke the heart of many. But
there were others who were ready to take the odds. The case of Stefan
Lorant is instructive since it shows that the field is wide open if the
new-comer finds the things America does want and it also shows how
adaptable Hungarian new-comers can be.

Stefan Lorant was a very young man between the two World Wars
when he brought into being some of the most popular magazines in
England. He then came to the United States where he must have
been told that the saturation point had been reached. But he was not
ready to abandon the fight. In his attempt to make his name in this
country he turned to logical thinking. The best things are the ones

the public wants. What does the American public want in the publishing field? It wants different things at different times, of course,
but one of those things—at the top of the list—is the desire to come
closer to its historic figures of whom Abraham Lincoln is probably the
most beloved, because the most human and the most American. The
American public, Lorant found, also likes pictures. Why not combine
the two? The pictures would have to be presented in the grand manner, so that the book containing them should become a cherished family
possession, perhaps even a family heirloom. Lorant dug deep into
Lincoln photographic lore and brought forth a book which the American reading public took to its heart. He was ascribed as the "outstanding authority on Lincoln photographs." His next move was to delve
into America's earliest history and bring to light picture material which
until then had been scattered all over creation. That also was successfully published in the grand manner. So a man of Hungarian birth
found one of the most effective means to cater to the historic-minded
American family.

Another Hungarian-born American became a leading authority on
the pre-Columbian art and civilization of this hemisphere. The two
volume *Medieval American Art* by Pál Kelemen was a pioneering
venture. In this study Kelemen covered the Maya, Aztec and Inca arts
from our own Southwest to northern Chile, approaching his subject
from the point of view of art history, combining it with the study of
archeology, anthropology and ethnology. He wrote *Battlefield of the
Gods,* devoted to Yucatan and Aztec history, art and exploration. In
writing about these supposedly recondite subjects he declared war on
what he called "de-humanizing the humanities"; art historians, he
thought, tended to alienate public interest by writing in endless
meandering sentences, in a style that hobbles along on the stilts of foot-
notes, Latin and other foreign quotations.

Another Hungarian-born newcomer found himself acclaimed as a
prophet in the United States. Emery Reves tasted the bittersweet fruits
of knowledge at several European universities, in Germany, France and
Switzerland. He was successful in Europe as the head of a concern
that published the important journalistic works of leading statesmen.
Turning to writing himself, he wrote about one of Weimar Germany's
most notable figures, Walter Rathenau, a capitalist-Socialist statesman-
financier, who was assassinated by German reaction at the very time
he was engaged in the work of building a bridge between his native
Germany and the rest of the world after the First World War.

Shortly after his arrival in the United States Emery Reves wrote his book *A Democratic Manifesto* which critics called the credo of a citizen of the world. Next he wrote *Anatomy of Peace* which enjoyed a vogue few books of that type have seen. Reves analyzed the various "isms," the importance of religion for the contemporary world, and the hold of nationalism. He found that the mold into which the world had been cast was breaking apart. Nationalism received the worship of hundreds of millions and yet modern civilization had turned it into an anachronism, as outmoded as the plumed knight of the Middle Ages. The solution was a World Union. The book appeared at a psychologic moment when the war was won and peace appeared to be lost. The United Nations was in operation but doing not much better than the decrepit League. Followers of the World Union could assure themselves wistfully that all would be well if the people of the world would co-operate, as no doubt it would be indeed. But what force is going to weld mankind into one? Had followers of this movement been told that great ideas required a tremendous amount of preliminary spadework some of them might have lost interest in this dazzling City of God beckoning to them from the mountaintops. Had they been told that before a Universal Republic could be established their own country would have to abandon its policy of trade and immigration restrictions several of them might have made wry faces.

One of the younger generation who reached these shores during the Second World War gained instant acclaim with his book *A Thousand Shall Fall*. Hans Habe wrote several novels in German, which were translated into English. In *Sixteen Days* he fictionized the story of the terrible days that led up to the great betrayal known as the Munich Agreement. *A Thousand Shall Fall* gave the reader an insight into the forces working behind the sudden collapse of France in the face of the Nazi onslaught. Habe's next book was *Kathrine,* the story of a two-faced woman. As a captain in the United States Army, he played a leading rôle in setting up a German-language press in the American zone of the Reich. His father, Imre Békessy, wrote a book about Barabbas, the biblical prisoner released by Pilate instead of Jesus.

A Hungarian-born author in the United States who achieved great success with his writings was John Pen. When twelve, he began writing verse and we are told that he was first published at the age of fifteen, and that before reaching fame he wrote stories under several pseudonyms for the movies, one of which received an Academy award. Attention was called to him with the publication of his novel *You*

Can't Do That to Svoboda which the more discriminating critics praised highly, but he made his name with his novel *Temptation,* which is the best description of the life of the poverty-stricken masses of the Hungarian village and city the writer of this book has ever read. Anyone who wants to know why Hungarian peasants, so passionately attached to their native soil, tore up their roots and faced the uncertainties of a new world, should read this book of John Pen.

A Hungarian man of letters with a great European reputation was called *Ignotus,* a nom de plume. In Hungary he was a founder of the literary magazine *Nyugat* (*West*), the program of which was implied in its title. It was to be a bridge between Hungary and France, and countries farther west. He had already reached an advanced age when he came to the United States during the Second World War. In this country he received a literary award from the American Academy of Arts and Letters. He wrote virile articles for the Cleveland liberal daily, *Szabadság,* and redefined the essence of democracy in a stimulating paper he read at a series of lectures at the New School for Social Research in New York.

International law found an industrious worker in Ferenc Deák, author and co-author of numerous important works in the field, including one about Turkey and the Straits question. Albert Halasi, the economist, made his name in Weimar Germany's labor movement and in the United States wrote about such problems as money, gold and tariffs, mostly for the American labor conference on international affairs. A highly gifted member of a gifted family, Baroness Antonia Hatvany-Deutsch, devoted her attention to such matters as the United States Senate and the World Court, the question of security and war, in collaboration with Frances Kellor, one of America's notable workers in that field.

Charles de Tolnay became recognized the world over as an authority on certain works of Michelangelo, particularly the murals on the Sistine Chapel ceiling in Rome, and the paintings of Pieter Brueghel the Elder, Hieronymus Bosch, the Dutch painter, Huybrecht and Jan van Eyck, Flemish painters and founders of the Flemish school of painting; and the history of the technique of old master drawings.

Paul Henry Lang of Columbia University wrote his monumental *Music in the Western World,* the history of music from the Greeks to the present, as set against the social life of the succeeding ages of the Western world.

László Farago followed a Hungarian tradition in writing about countries of the Middle East and Africa. Some of the best-known explorers of that part of the world were Hungarians. Farago wrote about Arabia and Palestine, strategic locations in the Middle East and therefore important in Great Power politics. He also wrote about Abyssinia at the time of Mussolini's African adventure. Farago then turned to a study of the Axis grand strategy and of Germany's psychological warfare. In these fields he served as a pioneer. During the Second World War the United States turned his specialized gifts to good account in our psychological warfare against the Axis Powers.

Distant countries were the subjects of a young writer of much promise, Edgar Laytha. He wrote about Japan with an eye for the picturesque and revealing incident, then about gold prospecting in the far northern regions of Canada. In the early days of the Second World War he studied Australia as a base of Pacific military strategy. He lost his life in the Pacific later on, as a member of the armed forces of the United States.

A perceptive world traveler before coming to the United States, Tibor Köves wrote of his peripatetic experiences with the detachment of a philosopher and the revealing pen of a journalist. He also wrote of Nazi Germany's would-be Talleyrand, the over-smart Franz von Papen, who reached very high and landed very low.

Among members of the younger Hungarian-born generation of Americans George Bernard de Huszár wrote about the social psychology of democracy, and edited college textbooks dealing with persistent international issues and new perspectives of peace. Nicholas Doman wrote about the coming age of world control in terms of a hoped-for transition to organized world society.

The best-selling novel *Paris Underground* had a Hungarian-born co-author, Oscar Ray, who also wrote the story of a young Alsatian impressed into the German army during the Second World War. Nándor Fodor wrote many tracts in the field of psychic phenomena, and an encyclopaedia of physic science. Marcel William Fodor wrote about plot and counter-plot in Central Europe under Hitler's regime and sought to interpret the march of events in Europe under the Nazis' disastrous New Order in a book entitled *The Revolution is On*. He also made his name as a foreign correspondent of leading American newspapers. Another noted American correspondent of Hungarian origin, Fred Tyrnauer, represented one of the important newspaper syndicates of the United States in Vienna for many years. László Fodor edited and illustrated numerous popular travel books. Emery Balint, a novelist with a Left-wing orientation, was highly praised by numerous critics for his book *Alpha.* Victor Kelemen wrote stage plays and did a notable translation of Heinrich Heine's *Deutschland,* at the very time during the Second World War, when readers needed to be reminded of those traits which the great German poet perceived. Among members of the large American publishing houses, Ben Huebsch, of Viking Press, had a Hungarian background.

We have seen that Hollywood was partly the creation of Hungarian immigrants. Since those early days, the Hungarian-born have played an important part in the colony, although there was much exaggeration in the rumor that the cinema world of our Pacific West Coast was all Hungarian. That over-statement was exemplified by the sign in all movie studios—a sign everybody quoted and nobody saw: "In this studio it is not enough to be a Hungarian."

Here again we have excellent illustrations of the remarkable adaptability of gifted Hungarians. The Hungarian Jew, Árpád Steiner, became identified with the typical Englishman and was beloved throughout the world under his stage name: Leslie Howard. Judging by his productions few people would believe that the work of the director Michael Curtiz, was not that of a typical Yankee, familiar with all the nooks and corners of American folklore. Yet his name in Hungary was Kertész Mihály and he directed typically American pictures with a Hungarian accent which was an unmitigated delight to hard-working stagehands. His *Yankee Doodle Dandy* was a truly "all-American" picture. In 1943 he received the coveted "Oscar"—the award of the Motion Picture Academy for direction. He had had a perambulating career in Weimar Germany, Norway, France and Sweden.

George Dewey Cukor became another headlined director of the movies. He began his career as an assistant stage manager in New York, starring such players as Ethel Barrymore, Jeanne Eagels and Laurette Taylor. He became director for Metro-Goldwyn-Mayer in 1933 and directed *Dinner at Eight, David Copperfield,* and *Romeo and Juliet,* among others. Joseph Pasternak, born in Hungary, began his career as a motion picture producer for Universal Pictures in Europe; then, transferring his activities to Hollywood, he produced a large number of popular pictures in which he nearly always managed to introduce a little Hungarian touch. One of the greatest names in the cinematic world was that of the Korda family. Sir Alexander Korda, an English subject, became a pioneer in the cinema as an art—not merely a craft. Some of the classics of the film world were created by him and his two brothers, Vince and Zoltan. They shared their time between England and America—hence their names are not out of place here.

The number of movie actors and actresses of Hungarian background is large. One of them was Vilma Banky, a great name in "silent days." She shared some of the cinematic fame with Maria Korda, one of the most fetching Helens of Troy the stage or screen has ever seen. Paul Lukas, a Hungarian-born player, received the Academy Award for his work in *Watch on the Rhine*. Before he came to America, he had been one of Hungary's best known actors, creator of the title role of Molnár's *Liliom*. Cornel Wilde, a young actor, forged to the front with many famous creations, such as the leading rôle in *A Song to Remember*.

The story of Szőke Szakáll is unique. His stage name is Hungarian for "Blond Beard," for his beard was blond when he began his stage career in Budapest. He achieved great success in three languages and two worlds; first in Hungary, then after the First World War, in Germany where he became a star in short order, until Hitler came and Szőke Szakáll went. He crossed the ocean to the United States and made a name here, too, with his fascinating ways and irrepressible Hungarian accent. Only a few of the other Hungarian film players may be named here: Ilona Massey, Stephan Békássy, Victor Varconi, and Béla Lugosi who was best known to the film-going public as impersonator of the cruel Dracula.

The light "continental" touch distinguished the numerous scenario writers of Hungarian origin. Ingenious, flexible, tongue-in-cheek writers found the Hollywood atmosphere congenial. Many more tried than succeeded. American-born and Hungarian-sired Mark Hellinger, was one of the highly successful fraternity. He reached Hollywood via a popular newspaper columnist career, and besides writing films, also produced several.

One of the earlier Hungarian-born scenario-writers was Ernest Vajda. In his younger days as dramatist in Budapest he found the gates of Olympus closed to a playwright with a Hungarian name. The public seemed to favor only shows with the Anglo-Saxon stamp, and so he adopted the name of Sidney Garrick, under which name he rode to victory. In Hollywood he became the most popular writer of his day.

The Hollywood fame of Melchior Lengyel was preceded by his stage fame as the author of the play, *Typhoon,* a success around the globe, which depicted the mysterious Japanese abroad, working themselves into a sweat for the benefit of their native land. He also became widely known as an author of scenarios, one of his greatest successes having been *Ninotchka,* a satire on life in the Soviet Union.

At one time there was a saying among scenario-writers that not only was it not enough to be a Hungarian, but that one had to be called László before success would smile. László Fodor saw international stage success before being drafted for Hollywood. László Vadnay informed the chroniclers of his career that he had 176 one-acters and 15 full-length plays to his credit. László Görög was claimed by Hollywood after a newspaper career. László Bús-Fekete's name was also given credit for film best sellers. Then there was Miklós László (this time László is family name) who had won recognition on the Hungarian stage, including a play in the National Theatre of Budapest, the dream of every playwright. He was at his best with tender, sentimental stories such as the film, *Shop Around the Corner* and the stage play, *St. Lazare's Pharmacy.*

But there were also Lily Hatvany-Deutsch, another member of the gifted clan which we have already encountered, Ferenc Partos, Endre Bohem, Francis Edward Faragoh, who had his beginnings as a modernist in drama and managing director of the highly modern Playwrights' Theatre in New York, Géza Herceg, co-author of the international hit, *Wonder Bar.* Miklós Rózsa received considerable recognition as a winner of the Motion Picture Academy "Oscar," award.

The American film would not have become what it is without its Hungarian high priests. Naturally, it has not lived up to expectations. How much the screen can achieve has been demonstrated only in a few instances, but it is no less true that the American film, as a whole, has captured not merely this country but most of the world. If it is deficient it may be so because its public is too vast to be artistically discriminating. Obviously, it should not merely follow the public taste but set the pace in refining it. That is, however, only a promise of the future.

XIX

Melodies and Colors

"The Hungarian is happy when crying." "*Sirva vigad a magyar.*"
He has good reason for tears; Tatar and Turk devastated his land, and
worse than Tatar and Turk was his own *földesúr,* the landed master,
the lord, blood of his own blood, his ruthless oppressor.

That is why the Hungarian folksong is sad. For years Hungary's
two great twentieth century composers, Béla Bartók and Zoltán Kodály,
visited the Hungarian villages, collecting folksongs. They let the peasants sob their plaints into the recording machine, the sob of the fright-
ened child, the outcry of the grown-up trapped by fate.

Sometimes, but not often, the song is gay, almost wildly gay. It is
gay because the peasant wants to forget, and because the lark in the
fields is gay, and so is the sun, the swish of the scythe and the home-
coming from the backbreaking fields.

Ki a legény a csárdában? Who is the cock of the walk? The one
who knows how to crow best—the best singer, the best fighter. The
best singer may be the saddest singer. There is plenty of song in the
Hungarian *kocsma,* tavern, plenty of song and plenty of fight, and
much of the song is sorrowful, and so is the fight. Everybody wants to
be the cock of the walk, it is human nature, and that nature bursts
into the open in the *kocsma* where a man becomes a man as he forgets
his sad life.

There was plenty of music in the cities, too—in Budapest, for instance, even though taxi-drivers seldom took the liberty of breaking
into song, as one-day visitors into Hungary liked to claim. There was
song in the open air restaurants on the hills of Buda overlooking the
Danube, and it was natural that there should be because nature inspired
the art of man who built the bridges across the Danube and designed
it and nature could not be more beautiful than when combined with
the magnificent palaces on the embankments. There was music on
the Hill of Roses, *Rózsadomb,* sloping toward the Danube, overlook-

274

ing Margareten Island with its rose gardens and ancient oaks, with its beautiful women.

There was music also in the Detroit restaurant which we visited not long ago. An American restaurant, in an American street in the heart of one of the most American cities producing the most American of all American machines. Yet the tables were covered with chintz, as they are in Hungary, and on each table was a candle and the guests sat at the table with a Hungarian abandon, just as if they had been in the Hungary of yore. There was music and it was called Gypsy music. Maybe it was—it does not matter. What did matter was a young woman, because she forgot that the restaurant was full of people; or perhaps she did not forget it. She began pianissimo and then above the hubbub and the instruments her rich, full voice could be heard triumphantly improvising a concert for us. That was typically Hungarian and yet it happened in a typically American city.

Hungary sent only a few musicians of note to the United States before the First World War, but some of them became very famous. America did not attract as many musicians for she was then so much absorbed in the music of the dynamo that she had little time for the music of the concert hall. In those days, most of the aspiring Hungarian musicians sought to make their careers in the then musical centers, Vienna, Paris and Milan.

Several came to the United States as guests. One was the Court violinist of Queen Victoria of England, Edward Reményi, a noted artist of the *fin-de-siècle,* one of whose accompanists had been a person no less noted than Johannes Brahms. It is said that many of Brahms' famous Hungarian dances and rhapsodies were inspired by his association with the great Hungarian virtuoso of the violin. Reményi came to the United States on a concert tour. He died in the United States, at San Francisco, just before the close of the century.

One of America's contributors to serious music in pre-World War I days was an American-born composer, son of a Hungarian-born composer. Musical literature and the opera stage remember the father very well, Karl Goldmark, one of the noted composers of the last century. The musical world would be much poorer if the fate Karl Goldmark once faced had actually befallen him. He was to be shot as a "spy" after the defeat of the Hungarian War of Independence and it was the providential last-minute arrival of a friend that saved his life. He composed the opera *Queen of Sheba,* a repertory piece in many lands. His son, Rubin Goldmark composed sonatas, tone poems, overtures, symphonic poems and songs in this country, and when he died in 1936 though he was little known by the general public he was well remembered by the musical elite.

Hungary was the birthplace of the man called the "master of the masters," and the "greatest teacher," Leopold Auer, whose teaching genius turned out such world-famed virtuosos as Jascha Heifetz, Mischa Elman and Efrem Zimbalist. Auer himself started on his musical career as a violinist; he studied at the Budapest Conservatory of Music and then moved on to Vienna. From there he was invited to the Conservatory of Music at St. Petersburg, Russia, where he was a professor for many years. Then he became the director of the Russian Imperial Music Society symphony concerts. Since he was a Jew, the anti-Semitic aspect of the moribund Russian imperial regime did not appeal to him. Finally, past seventy, he came to the United States in 1918, preceded by a world-wide reputation as a great teacher. At that age he became the master of the masters of the contemporary world. He died at eighty-five in 1930, his loss felt by the entire musical world.

An American of Hungarian birth, Anton Seidl, reached the peak of a musical career as conductor of a great American orchestra. Seidl was born in Pest—not yet Budapest. In his early youth he assisted Richard Wagner in the preparation of the score of the *Ring*. He left Germany for the United States, succeeding Leopold Damrosch as conductor of German opera at the Metropolitan Opera House of New York, and Theodore Thomas as conductor of the New York Philharmonic Society. He was especially noted for his conducting of Wagnerian operas and for presenting the American première of Anton Dvořák's *New World Symphony* in 1893.

Among American-Hungarian composers of the pre-war generation few had a richer vein of melody than Lajos Serly, composer of Hungarian songs in the folkways. His creative vein was rich, but his mellow creations did not harmonize with the raucous staccato of the punching machine.

After the First World War, the United States took the leadership in the musical world. Europe was impoverished, America was rich; while artists are expected to live for their art, they must also eat. The more they came here, the keener became the competition and the greater the challenge to succeed. Between the two wars, some of Hungary's best musicians came to the United States. Béla Bartók was acclaimed as Hungary's great composer of the century and one of the great composers of the age.

At the turn of the century he created a furor with his *Kossuth Symphony,* a product of "flaming youth." His *Rhapsody No. 1 for Orchestra* was already the work of a seasoned artist. The music of his ballet, *The Miraculous Mandarin,* on the other hand, was described as "indecently modern" and "decadent." Bartók fell under the spell of Richard Strauss' *Also Sprach Zarathustra,* a magnificent example of the new romantic school, which Bartók considered of dashing audacity.

Some of Bartók's music was used on the stage, such as *Prince Bluebeard's Castle,* a one-act opera, and the mime-ballet, *The Wooden Prince,* both of which suffered from the opera composers' bane, inferior libretti. Some of his other works were: *Hungarian Folk Songs, Two Portraits, Music for Strings, Percussion and Celesta,* and a *Dance Suite.*

Bartók and Kodály had long suspected that Hungarian folk music was richer than even the experts thought, and as a result of their indefatigable efforts they struck gold. A frail man, Bartók wandered from village to village, spending endless days in peasant huts, coaxing hundreds of scores out of the peasants. In the course of his work he discovered that national boundary lines were not frontiers of creative veins. Recording Hungarian folk tunes, he ran into Slavic ones. Pursuing those strains, he encountered Romanian strains. He was now ranging far afield, seeking the elusive sources of Eastern European tunes. He found that many of those contained Anatolian undertones, so he went there and continued his researches among the Turkish peasants. He collected some six thousand folksongs of Hungarian, Slovak and Transylvanian origin, hundreds of South Slav, Moldavian, Turkish and Algerian tunes.

Under the influence of this pioneering work he wrote his *Székely Ballads,* so named after a group of Hungarians—called Székelys—inhabiting the eastern marches of Transylvania, and numerous other compositions. In his work he had found an ancient scale of Magyar folk music, which he began to use, bringing new and unexpected harmonies to life. This, in turn, led to his adoption of the twelve-tone scale, capable of new harmonic combinations.

Bartók came to live in the United States in 1940. Very sick, he still had a lot to say. He knew he was a doomed man and worked against time to get on paper at least a part of what was in him. His was the awful tragedy of the artist who could not demean himself to become also a salesman, cultivating useful friendships, particularly of public-spirited old ladies who usually had their own scales of values of greatness. Working in his very modest New York flat, he "made a living," as he said with a wan smile, adding wistfully how wonderful it would be if his collections of Rumanian and Anatolian tunes—the work of many years—could be published for the benefit of the entire musical community, and how marvelous it would be if once—only once—a radio network invited him to play the piano. But all efforts to have those exotic tunes published were futile and nobody invited him to play over the radio until he was dead. Then he was played over and over again, extolled as one of the great. At the age of sixty-four he died in New York in 1945. "Bartók was many things," a critic wrote, "an intellectual and a seeker of passionate convictions and feelings, a scientist and folklorist, a fanatic and mystic, a friend of all and none." More famous dead than alive, he had now many friends.

One of the great composers of "Vienna" music also came to the United States during the time of troubles preceding the outbreak of the Second World War. He was Imre Kálmán, a Hungarian, like Franz Lehár, the most famous of the composers of Viennese music. Millions were familiar with the melodies of *Countess Maritza* and *Sari,* though they might not know the name of the composer. Some years after his arrival in America, Kálmán appeared on the New York stage with a new operetta, *Marinka,* the romantic story of Crown Prince Rudolph of Austria and Hungary and his inamorata, Baroness Marie Vetsera, the lovers whose dead bodies were found in Rudolph's hunting lodge in the Vienna Woods. Another man from Hungary, Karl Farkas, was the author of the libretto.

A Hungarian became one of the most successful composers of popular operetta music in the United States: Sigmund Romberg. Just to enumerate his principal compositions is to name some of the most famous musical hits—the *Student Prince, Maytime, Blossomtime, Desert Song, New Moon, Nina Rosa, East Wind* and *May Wine.* The remarkable adaptability of the Hungarian to the American scene is uncommonly well illustrated in the case of Romberg.

Albert Szirmai (Sirmay), from Hungary, has also enriched America's musical life. Dr. Sirmay arranged the music of the *Songs of the Rivers of America,* edited by Carl Carmer, and a collection of more than a hundred songs from Gilbert and Sullivan operettas. Among the more notable compositions of his own was *Mézeskalács* (*Gingerbread*), the book by the Hungarian poet Tamás Emőd.

A younger composer and conductor, Zoltán Fekete, discovered a veritable treasure trove in Handel's thirty-two oratorios, forty-six operas and many other immortal works which had been lying waste. He extracted the most appealing parts which he presented to the public in the form of symphonic suites under the titles of *Joshua, Samson, Saul, The Triumph of Truth,* and *Lamentation.*

Another Hungarian-born musician of the younger generation was Tibor Serly, pupil of the Hungarian Big Three, Bartók, Zoltán Kodály and Jenő Hubay. Besides being a violinist and conductor, Serly was a composer of symphonies, a ballet for orchestra, suites, chamber music and orchestral music.

One of the Hungarian tragedies in America was that of Paul Abraham, a highly successful operetta composer in Europe, whose tunes at one time were on everyone's lips. His mind clouded, he became one of the most tragic casualties of American-Hungarian life.

It would be out of the question to enumerate all the noted singers Hungary has given to the United States, so that again selections must be made at random.

One of the most promising Hungarian-born opera singers was Lajos Rózsa, the object of an anti-Semitic demonstration in the Budapest Opera House after the First World War. He came to the United States and appeared on the Metropolitan Opera stage with success. In the pink of condition, he appeared to be on the threshold of a great future when he met an untimely death. His son, Miklós, carried on the family's musical tradition as a successful film music composer.

Tragedy haunted another Budapest Royal Opera House singer, Maria Samson. Comely, artistic, with a beautiful voice, she was the perfect Madame Butterfly. She, too, came to the United States because of the post-First World War anti-Semitic trend in Hungary. In this country she won high praise, but no high operatic career. She learned that luck and connections were no less important than natural gifts in making one's way in that overcrowded world. Disappointed in her expectations to reach a major operatic stage, she wound up as a teacher of singing on the West Coast. There she committed suicide, one of the casualties of the highly competitive artists' life.

The rest of the story is much happier. One of America's recognized Wagnerian singers was Hungarian-born Friedrich Schorr, baritone, pupil of famed Adolph Robinson of Vienna. His operatic career began in the Austrian city of Graz. The New York Metropolitan Opera

House first saw him in 1924 and he was going strong in Wagnerian and other rôles two decades later.

The Hungarian-born contralto, Margarete Matzenauer, was another "name" in America's operatic history. Her operatic debut was made at Strasbourg at the turn of the century. From there she was invited to the Wagner Festivals at Bayreuth, then to the Covent Garden of London, to the Teatro Colono of Buenos Aires, recognized as the most important South American stage. She reached the Metropolitan in 1911 of which she remained a member for a score of years.

Americans of Hungarian birth have grown specially attached to Anne Roselle (Gyenge Anna), who had her first American debut as Nedda in *Pagliacci* in Birmingham, Alabama, and sang in the operas both of the Old and the New World.

Alexander Svéd made his Hungarian Royal Opera debut in *Il Trovatore* in 1927, sang in State operas in Vienna, Berlin and Munich, at Covent Garden, the Paris Opéra Comique, the Teatro della Scala of Milan, at the Teatro Reale of Rome, in the festivals of Firenze, Salzburg and Bayreuth, at Buenos Aires and Rio de Janeiro, at the Chicago Civic Opera, winding up at the Metropolitan of New York, with a repertory of thirty-four rôles, singing in Italian, German, French and Hungarian.

A remarkable operatic success story is that of the tenor Miklos Gafni. While attending medical college in 1942 at the University of Debrecen, Gafni was taken by the Hungarian Nazis to slave labor camps in his own country and Upper Silesia. It was while in the Silesian camp, working in the coal mines, that he first discovered he had a singing voice. Three fellow inmates, former vocal teachers, heard him and volunteered to give him lessons at night after working hours. His coaches were subsequently killed, but before they went to the gas chambers they had taught him the fundamentals of singing. Liberated by the Russians, he went to Budapest, where he made a sensation when in October 1945 he made his first appearance at the Hungarian State Opera in the leading tenor rôles of *Traviata* and *Tosca*. He also gave concerts in Budapest, and then in 1946 went to Italy, where he studied with Mario Terni in Milan and Ricardo Stracciari in Rome.[86]

He was twenty-three when he gave his first concert in New York early in 1947. "Coming unheralded to the United States five weeks ago," *The New York Times* music critic wrote the following morning, "Mr. Gafni needed but his first hearing here to establish himself as a vocalist of exceptional gifts. . . . As remarkable for volume as for quality, the voice compared favorably with the greatest of the day." One critic went so far as to hail Miklos Gafni as the "Hungarian Caruso."

Another Hungarian-born singer to earn high praise was the contralto, Enid Szánthó. She had her musical education at the Royal Academy of Budapest, her debut at the Vienna Opera in 1928, and her American debut with the New York Philharmonic in 1936. She appeared at the Bayreuth Wagner Festivals, Covent Garden, the City Center and Metropolitan Opera of New York. Marta Eggerth, operetta and screen actress, wife of the opera singer Jan Kiepura, came to the United States with a Europe-wide fame.

American concert audiences became well acquainted with Catherine Reiner and Margit Bokor, the latter an artist of the Hungarian genre. Hungarians were well represented at the Metropolitan 1946-1947 season: Ella Flesch, soprano, Leslie Chabay, tenor, Alexander Svéd, baritone, Lorenzo Alvary and Dezső Ernster, bassos. Announced for the next season was Michael Szekely, basso.

Several Hungarian-born conductors have become household words in the United States. The success story of Eugene Ormándy should be compulsory reading for gifted children to show that child prodigies may make good. He was a pupil of the Hungarian Big Three, Bartók, Hubay and Kodály. As a child prodigy he received the Hungarian State Diploma for violin playing and the medal of the Bruckner Society. At the age of seventeen he was appointed professor of the State Conservatory of Budapest, which was no mean achievement in such a highly musical city. He sailed to America with the opera singer, Rózsa, whose name has been mentioned, and had to bide his time before recognition beckoned. It was as a concert master in the Capitol Theater of New York, under the energetic management of the legendary Roxy, that he began his career. Roxy believed that it was not only possible but profitable to give first-class music to the masses. After the usual peregrinations as a guest conductor, Ormándy was invited to head the Minneapolis Symphony Orchestra which became one of the best in the country. From that post he became in 1936 the coconductor of the Philadelphia Symphony Orchestra, a position of international prominence.

Budapest-born George Széll could also tell a success story. His musical career began at the age of eleven, and at eighteen he was already assistant conductor of the Royal Opera of Berlin. He was subsequently appointed conductor at Strasbourg, then at Dusseldorf, became principal conductor of the Berlin State Opera and professor of the *Hochschule fuer Music* in Berlin. From that post he was called to the Prague Opera as director, and became professor of the Prague Academy of Music. On the eve of the Second World War, he was conductor of the Scottish Orchestra at Glasgow and of the Reseidenti Orkest, den Haag, Holland. The war brought him to the United States as a conductor at the Metropolitan. He also composed symphonies, overtures and chamber music.

Fritz Reiner, another noted Hungarian-born American conductor, made his debut in the Landestheater of Laibach in Austria at the age of twenty-two. For a time he conducted at the Dresden Opera in Germany and the Peoples' Opera of Budapest. Among the first post-war arrivals in the United States, he became the conductor of the Cincinnati Symphony Orchestra; later, of the Pittsburgh Symphony Orchestra, head of the orchestra department and teacher of conducting at the Curtis Institute of Music.

Among the first American conductors to offer classical music to the "unseen audience" of the radio, Ernő Rapée performed pioneer work. He also gave classical music to the millions who made the acquaintance of New York via the sumptuous movie palaces, the Capitol, Roxy's and Radio City Music Hall. He died in 1945.

George Sebastian had his debut at a very early age in Berlin and was for years conductor of the Moscow Radio before he made his radio debut as a conductor in the United States. László Halász became a pioneer of good music for the "little man" in New York at the municipally sponsored City Center. Sándor Harmati won a 1922 Pulitzer Prize of music for a symphonic poem and served as a conductor. He met an untimely death. Joseph Honti made a name for himself in the world of radio music. Anton Dorati conducted ballet music before he took over the Dallas Symphony Orchestra.

The *embarras de richesses* of the Hungarian-born in America is nowhere more evident than in the field of solo music. Although Tin Pan Alley made such a din that it was feared the sounds of serious music would be drowned, that tragedy never came to pass. With the best opera house, the best symphony orchestras and the best artists, the United States became the musical center of the world. Moreover the organization of musical life was casual, often incidental to what Thorstein Veblen might have called the "conspicuous consumption" of art, manipulated by society women of great means who not infrequently subordinated artistic ideals to purely personal tastes for picturesque personalities, and the publicity-seeking, ego-centric artist had a far better chance of success than the more introspective, modest and purely artistic person.

Among the first musicians to come to the United States was the violinist and concert master, Lajos Bleuer, later to become director of the Detroit Philharmonic, which was to develop into a first-class national institution. Also among the "pioneers" was Dezső Antalffy-Zsiros, an organ virtuoso, former professor of organ at the Budapest Academy of Music and erstwhile assistant conductor at the Cologne Opera House. In the United States, which he first visited in the early post-World War I years, he played the organ at concerts, over the radio, in music halls and was for a time a member of the faculty of the Eastman School of Music. He also composed a stirring oratorio, entitled *Voice of the Millions,* the eight-voiced *Hungarian Rhapsody* for men's chorus, a *Hungarian Suite for Orchestra,* and a light opera, *Faschingabenteuer.* He died in the spring of 1945.

Among the "frontiersmen" of music in those days was another former professor of the Budapest Academy, Béla Várkonyi, a fellow prisoner of war with me in a Siberian camp during the First World War. Even there he never compromised with the quality of music and he certainly helped us to carry our crosses. His piano sounded in the drabness of prison life like the "music of the spheres." It was he who made us devotees of the classics. In the United States he turned mostly to teaching.

László Kun had also been a professor of the Budapest Academy, a composer and a virtuoso of the cymbal, *cimbalom,* without which a real Hungarian orchestra is unthinkable. Károly Horváth was another noted cymbal-player.

The "musicians' musician" was the name given to the violin virtuoso, Joseph Szigeti, whose name has been bracketed with those of Heifetz and Yehudi Menuhin. His master was the great Hubay and he had his debut at the hypercritical Royal Academy of Music of Budapest. His American debut was with the Philadelphia Symphony Orchestra in 1925. For several years he was the head of the master class of the Geneva *Conservatoire* in Switzerland. A globe-trotting artist, like most of the great ones, he was liked in Hong Kong no less than in Melbourne, in New Zealand no less than in South America. During the years of uneasy peace he had his home—an artist's home, which he seldom saw

—on the French Riviera and came to the United States annually. Each year New York heard him in Carnegie Hall. When darkness closed down upon the Old World he came to the United States and made his home on the Pacific Coast.

Many are the younger Hungarian-born artists who have made their names in the United States. Ernő Balog, piano virtuoso, received a special accolade when he gave a "command performance" at the White House in the days of President Franklin D. Roosevelt. Other pianists were Andor Földes, who crossed and recrossed the Continent many times with his writer wife, who described their amusing and touching experiences in a book of recollections, *Two on the Continent,* György Sándor, Miklos Schwalb, Tibor Kozma (also a conductor), Árpád Sandor, Otto Herz and Sári Biró.

Among those who scored with their violins only a few can be mentioned: Alexander Harsányi and Erwin Nyiregyházi; Edward Kilényi, also a composer; the erstwhile child prodigy, Duci Kerékjártó, a concert and screen artist; Edith Loránd, who had a great name in Weimar Germany, and was preceded here by the fame of her records of spirited Hungarian music.

Among the youngest: Frigyes Balázs, who won the Reményi Prize for music at a very early age, worked as concert master of the Budapest Symphony Orchestra, made a tour of Europe, came to the United States, where he served in the army both as a technical sergeant and as a well-known virtuoso at service shows; also Gábor Bánát and Louis Simon.

Among the cellists, Gábor Rejtő was a pupil of Pablo Casals, a member of the Lener and Gordon String Quartets and of the Alma Trio. Other Hungarian-born artists to make their names as cellists were János Scholz and Otto Déri.

String quartets from Hungary all but "cornered" that field. Best known were the Roth Quartet, headed by Feri Roth; the Budapest String Quartet; and the Lener Quartets. Zoltán Kűrthy, a member of the Hans Lange Quartet, made his name as a viola player and a composer.

The Hungarian countryside is colorful and so is much Hungarian painting, as colorful as Hungarian embroidery, Hungarian song, and Hungarian history. Hungarian painting is a projection of the Hungarian personality of the artists, especially colorful because it was not subjected to the standardizing influence of industrial life.

Painters from Hungary made their pilgrimages to France, above all to Paris, which made and starved her artists, where they could measure their strength against a long line of rivals. They visited Paris also because they wanted to capture the moods of the Sacré Coeur on the Montmartre, the changing face of Nôtre Dame. They made pilgrimages to Avignon to watch the march of shadows on the massive walls, to the Riviera and to St. Tropez in the Pays des Maures where they sought to capture the colors of the dwarfed bushes of the *maquis*. For a long time few came to the United States, since they thought, rightly or wrongly, that America was not interested in the artist's work. After the First World War they began to come, as many of them sensed that Europe was dead, and the dead cannot be captured by the artist's colors. They came also because America was beginning to turn attention to the arts.

Among the first was Henry Major, Hungary's foremost caricaturist. In the United States Major combined caricature with painting. He fell under the influence of El Greco and Daumier who saw man's inner being reflected in his face, and that was, mostly, no pretty picture. It is an exacting task to see man as he is and Major must have felt the need of looking at nature as well. He painted Cape Cod, the dunes, the sea, the swamps with their green weeds, and everything that nature created on the tip of that tongue of land.

In the hectic morning-after of the First World War, Zoltán Sepeshy came to the United States and began a greenhorn's hectic life. As a house painter and a painter of billboards he could make little use of the artistic gifts he later displayed. As a window-trimmer for a drugstore chain, he had a trifle more chance to create "art." This period was followed by a spell as layout man for advertising firms and a draftsman for architects. He painted pictures in his free time, and one depicted prancing horses under a shady elm which made such a strong appeal to his barber that he bought it for twenty dollars and thus became Sepeshy's first Maecenas. Encouraged by this success, he began to exhibit pictures at State Fairs at which, in his biographer's words, "he shared blue ribbons with livestock."

Such experiences either make or break a young immigrant. Sepeshy was one of those whom adversity steeled. A friend with great confidence in his talents helped him, suggested that he look at New Mexico scenery, and presented him with a railway ticket. Sepeshy immersed himself in New Mexico and then settled down to transfer his vivid impressions to canvas. They blazed with the radiance of the sun-drenched Southwest. Sepeshy took them to Detroit, his home, and the murky city liked their radiance. The artist was now commissioned to paint murals for one of America's largest motor car plants, and appointed to a post with the Society of Arts and Crafts. This was the turning point of his life. Evidently, he would not be starved by lack of understanding.

In 1933 Sepeshy made his New York debut in a one-man show under the sponsorship of Dr. W. R. Valentiner, head of the Detroit Institute of Art, and in the same year became associated with the Cranbook Academy of Art, at Bloomfield Hills, Michigan, a score of miles outside Detroit, as director of the Department of Painting. Many of America's leading museums acquired Sepeshy pictures. His painting was described as having the "clarity and precision of etching, with the added veracity of coloring which the black and white medium can only suggest. . . . He can represent such refinements of line as rain drops, the twine of fishing nets, single hairs and the down on the back of a woman's neck, the gradations of fibrous matter in the cross-section of a blasted tree-trunk."

A far more controversial Hungarian-born artist was László Moholy-Nagy. A rebel against conventional art in Weimar Germany, he held that things of beauty could be turned out by mass-production machines. He preached the new art of *Sachlichkeit,* functionalism, in lectures and a book entitled *The New Vision.* He was a teacher at the *Bauhaus* of Dessau, holy shrine of the artistic iconoclasts. Among the subjects he taught were "texture" and "construction." A versatile man always looking for new means of self-expression, he turned typographer and type-setter. He printed everything in lower case on the ground that capital letters were wasted time and effort. Perhaps he also knew that conventional patterns seldom attracted attention.

Just one jump ahead of the Nazis, he left the Reich for England, and from there he came to the United States, where he first went into industrial designing. He designed, among other things, a curtain of air jets from the ceiling to keep out drafts, wrap-around tables to reduce the effort needed to reach for food and a machine "for emotional discharge" to make people laugh and newspapers write about. Moholy-Nagy also attracted attention with what he called "space modulators," which he could have called something else without doing injustice to the idea. These modulators were abstract, painted sculptures, identified by numbers and letters—unsigned—in the spirit of our age. Non-objective was the description of much of what Moholy-Nagy was now doing—a long step from the *Bauhaus*—combining utility and emotion in a higher synthesis. The "shapeless shape" of harmony, simplicity and contrast were ingredients of this art. The description is nebulous but, then, so is life which art seeks to capture. Moholy-Nagy died at a comparatively young age.

Two of the most successful Hungarian painters were Arthur Halmi and Lajos Mark, endowed with great facility, reveling in colors. There was a time when it was almost as much of a social obligation to be painted by Halmi or Mark as to be included in the *Social Register*. Undoubtedly highly gifted, some of the best creative efforts of these two painters went into flattering portraits. Luckily, they found time also for a different kind of art.

Ferenc Erdély had a distinguished career in Europe, where he made his mark in Holland and France and saw the Spanish Civil War. His colleagues were lavish with their praise of his bold personality and the audacious strokes of his water colors and oil paintings.

Willy Pogány had a thorough European grounding in art at Budapest, Munich and Paris, winning medals there and elsewhere. He described himself as "illustrator of more than 150 books, stage decorator and costume designer, mural painter and art director of motion pictures." Also, he became widely known as illustrator of children's books, such as Stevenson's *Home Book of Verse for Children, Tales from the Arabian Nights, Bible Stories,* and *Gulliver's Travels.*

The painting team of Andrew Károly and Lajos Szántó did its most notable work on large murals, the best known of which is the "freedom of speech" mural at Poughkeepsie, New York, depicting the history of the American press. Both of them do etchings and Szántó has painted numerous portraits. Lajos Jámbor is also a muralist, with works in several cities of the United States, particularly Philadelphia and Atlantic City, in auditoriums and churches. Frank Imrey considers his principal works the mural in Convention Hall, Atlantic City, the cyclorama "Little America" in Syracuse, New York and murals for the United States War Department.

Lipot Gedő reached the United States as one of the well-known "reporter-illustrators" of Hungary. In this country he worked as an author and illustrator, recognized by the confraternity as a gifted painter. The picture of a Negro, "Old Tom," became the best-known painting of the Cleveland artist, Sándor Vágó. Sándor Leidenfrost and Aurel Raskó are noted painters in the American-Hungarian community. Lily Füredi had one of her paintings, "The New York Subway" hung in the White House in Washington.

The Hungarian-born have also made their name in the art of etching. "Fatherless," by Stephen Csoka, was one of the prize winners in the 1947 national print competition conducted by the Associated American Artists. The etchings of Ralph Fabri were often described as "brilliant" and "outstanding."

As illustrators the Hungarian-born American artists have few peers. It was with a firmly established reputation in France that Marcel Vertès came to the United States. Here he showed again that illustration is an art and can be made into a great art. Frederic and Anthony Várady, George and Helen Rátkai also made their fame as illustrators. American-born Stevan Dohanos made his name as an illustrator and painter. He is of Hungarian origin. Among the illustrators and writers of children's books Maud and Miska Petersham are best known. A generation of children has grown up on their numerous books, of which some of the best known are *Miki and Mari,* and *Stories from the Old Testament.* Emery Göndör and Mariska Karasz are also illustrators of children's books. Anna Lesznai became known among Hungarians as a painter and a poet. The late Leo Kober had a name on the old *New York World* as a newspaper illustrator. Margit Varga made a name for herself as an art editor.

The cartoon is today a special field of art. In the world of political cartoons the famous team of "Derso and Kelen"—Alois Derso (Alajos Dezső) and Imre Kelen—established a world-wide reputation. In the old League of Nations days at Geneva it was a common saying that it could not be an international gathering if Derso and Kelen were not present. "The League of Nations consists of the Assembly, the Council, the Secretariat and Derso and Kelen." When the funeral services over the League had been read, Derso and Kelen attended the baptism of the United Nations in the United States. Mrs. George S. Szekely, who signed herself as "Kay Kato" was also a cartoonist. Among the later arrivals, Oscar Berger's name became a trade-mark.

Among the sculptors, Alexander Finta had a name before he came to the United States. He created monuments to war heroes in Yugoslavia and Czechoslovakia, a sixteen-piece group in the Cathedral Dom Pedro, Brazil, and a twelve-foot granite monument "Strength" in Rio de Janeiro. Among his numerous other works are a bronze portrait relief of Michael de Kovats, whose name we have encountered, exhibited in the museum of the New York Historical Society, a marble

portrait of St. Stephen, King of Hungary, for the Catholic Church of
St. Stephen, New York, a portrait of the late Cardinal Patrick Joseph
Hayes, temporarily exhibited at the Metropolitan Museum of Art, New
York. Erwin Körmendi also made a name for himself as a sculptor.
Frank Nagy began his American career, after the usual vicissitudes, as
an architect. From architecture he turned toward sculpture and dis-
played great strength in its varied fields, especially portraiture. Julio
Kilényi was active as a sculptor in Argentina before the First World
War. He came to the United States during that war, and here he
turned to medallions and plaques many of which are on permanent
exhibition in museums in New York, Cleveland, Boston and other
cities, at the Smithsonian Institution in Washingon, in the British
Museum and elsewhere in England.

In photography the Hungarian-born also had few peers. Martin
Munkácsi scored great success by taking his models out of the studio
into the open air, in the sunshine, photographing them in motion. He
was hailed as an innovator and the creator of "open air" photography.
"Mad photographer" was the name given to Robert Capa, since he
feared no danger in "shooting" battle scenes. "If Capa is not there,
it cannot be a war," it was said. Fascinated by danger, he began his
work as a very young man in China at the time of the China Incident.
He followed danger to Spain when the Civil War broke out and did
his work on the Loyalist side. There a tragic accident deprived him
of his young wife. When the Second World War broke out, Capa
was wherever there was danger, ashore with the G.I.'s in Africa, in
Normandy and elsewhere. Andre Kertész came to America with a
reputation made in France. His artistic interest turned toward in-
teriors, that of André de Dienes toward models, while "Ylla," a young
woman, specialized in photographing cats, dogs and other animals.
Among the earlier Hungarian-born photographers in this country
Nickolas Muray and Arthur Muray were "commercials," as were
Gábor Eder and Zoltán Farkas. Nicholas Haz, a distinguished practitioner of the older school, used the camera for psychological studies.
Gabriel D. Hacket came to America during the Second World War.
He witnessed our "Vichy gamble," while we maintained diplomatic
representation in a German-controlled France, and preserved a valuable
record of that distressing chapter of French history. In the United
States he turned to portrait photography, though retaining his interest
in reportage. Another photo reporter, Lucien Aigner, formerly corre-

spondent of a chain of Budapest popular dailies, the so-called *Est* papers, became interested in education as a photographic study.

Finally, a word about the theater. For long it has been one of Hungary's most favored arts. Shortly after the First World War there was a time when the New York stage was practically swamped by Hungarian plays—almost a score in one single season. That was the time when almost any play by a Hungarian writer had a more than fair chance of being performed. Then came a strong reaction when Hungarian nationality was a detriment.

Curiously, Hungary has not given many stars to the American stage, no doubt due to language difficulties. Several of the screen players we have mentioned in another chapter have known success on the Broadway stage, most particularly Paul Lukas. Lili Darvas, wife of Ferenc Molnár, and a Max Reinhardt star, was one of the few Hungarian-born players to appear on the New York stage. A noted Hungarian actress, Juliska Keleti, came to the United States shortly after the First World War.

We cannot leave the world of the players without mentioning the Dolly Sisters, who held theatergoers breathless in their day. They were a team of dancing twins, managed by a fabulously energetic mother who knew how to get the most out of her daughters. Rozsika and Jancsika. The name of the family had been Deutsch. "The Dolly Sisters" became an international trade-mark. In the days when the Palace Theatre of New York was to vaudeville what the Metropolitan was to opera, the sisters had an entire evening's program built around them. In Europe of the twenties their name was a household word. Supposedly sophisticated Paris lay at the feet of what the French called *Les Dolli Sistair*. They suffered an automobile accident and plastic surgery tried to redeem whatever could be saved. However, the average expectation of life of a dancing team is not very long and gradually they saw themselves replaced. One of the twins committed suicide.

To come now to stage directors, Max Reinhardt was born on the border line of Hungary, not far from Austria. It was his habit to answer inquiries by saying that he had been born near Vienna, thereby creating the impression that he was Austrian-born, and as it was his wish to be taken for an Austrian, the chronicler must defer. He did belong first to the German-speaking world before he belonged to the entire world of the stage. It was in German-speaking countries that he first revolutionized the stage by introducing mass scenes and the open air stage and by attempting to break down the wall dividing the player from his audience.

Among American theatrical producers of Hungarian origin the names of Martin Beck and Al Wood stand out. The memory of the former is preserved in one of the large theaters of New York. He had his finger in many theatrical pies, including vaudeville. Besides what he called a *Fingerspitzengefuehl,* horse sense, for the stage, he was a very well read, even learned, man who could quote entire pages of German and English classics in the original.

His closest assistant was Charles Feleky, who deserves special notice because he devoted much of his time to building up a unique library of *Hungariana,* English-language books about Hungary, by Hungarians or authors of Hungarian origin, as well as rare documents by great Hungarians such as Lajos Kossuth. Between the two World Wars the Hungarian government used the Feleky library as the nucleus of its information service in the United States. During the Second World War the library was closed and then placed in Columbia University.

One of the theater's "star gazers" was Al Wood, the man with the lucky eye for new talent. He produced numerous plays, discovered many famous actors, among whom John Barrymore was to achieve the greatest fame.

Among the Hungarian-born producers of more recent times Mrs. Yolanda Mero Irion began her career as a piano virtuoso and only later turned to the production of plays. She became the "spark plug" of the New Opera Company which gave the New York public revivals of some of the world's most famous operettas, such as Johann Strauss' immortal *Fledermaus,* produced under the name of *Rosamund* and Franz Lehár's *Merry Widow.* Among theatrical agents of Hungarian origin Edmond Pauker became the best known in his field.

Summing up, it may be said without any exaggeration that had it not been for the contributions of the Hungarian-born in these many fields, the artistic life of the United States would have been less colorful. While these contributions were fitted into the American scheme and followed American taste, the special flavor of the Hungarian background lingers on.

XX

ABOUT LEADERS OF MEN AND OTHER PIONEERS

AT HOME IN Hungary the Hungarian is addicted to political discussion, *politizálás*. Before the First World War he could get excited about Lajos Kossuth, the great mid-century leader of independence, whom he called *Kossuth apánk,* our father Kossuth, and spoke of himself as a *negyvennyolcas,* a 'Forty-eighter, an adherent of the liberal ideals of the national uprising of 'Forty-eight. Not too many of the peasants, but many members of the *uri osztály,* class of the gentlemen, boasted of being *hatvanhetes,* 'Sixty-seveners, so called after the year 'Sixty-seven, when the *Ausgleich,* Compromise, was concluded between the Vienna Court and the Hungarians, a compromise which, nominally at least, created the dual monarchy of Austria-Hungary.

Sometimes voices were raised and tempers flared between the adherents of the two political ideals. Hungary had a parliament, reputed to be one of the oldest in the world. It was not a parliament in the modern English sense, but it was an exciting place just the same, where political passions often boiled over. To find a debate covering the entire front page of a newspaper was no rare occurrence in Hungary. Those dispatches were eagerly read and commented on.

In spite of this, Hungarian political life was mostly sterile, since the common man was represented only if a deputy, a member of the higher classes, developed an interest in him. Bills became laws in behind-the-scenes discussions long before they reached the floor of parliament where the big show was performed for the public. Most Hungarians who came to the United States had little schooling in the essence of parliamentary democracy. This may account for the fact that Hungarian immigrants have not contributed many notable statesmen to the United States, but some of the few they gave to America have written important chapters of history.

It was a Hungarian-born immigrant, Victor Berger, who became the first Socialist Congressman of the United States. When I had occasion to visit him in Washington shortly after the First World War,

I found him highly conscious of his origin in Hungary. He spoke a strongly accented English, and some Hungarian. His native language appears to have been German—not unusual in certain cities of Hungary of the last century. Berger was a youth of eighteen when he came to the United States and made his home in the part of the Middle West where Central European 'Forty-eighters had introduced ideas of European socialism. In Milwaukee he became editor of the Socialist daily *Vorwaerts,* a post he held for half a dozen years. German-speaking immigrants were then mostly the pioneers of socialism. From that German-language paper Berger went as editor to the English-language *Social Democratic Herald.*

In those days a Social Democrat was supposed to be an awful person whose burning ambition was to see the world go up in flames. Voting was secret, of course, particularly if one voted Republican or Democratic: socialist voters often had vigilant eyes resting on their backs. Apparently unmindful of social ostracism, the Socialists went their own way, and Berger forged ahead in their ranks. One day he found himself in the influential position of the editor of the Milwaukee daily newspaper, *Leader.* He was one of the first to help organize the Socialists in this country under the leadership of that famous ex-grocery clerk, ex-locomotive fireman, Eugene V. Debs, five times candidate of the Socialists for President of the United States. With the picturesque, heart-warming Debs, the Socialists became an important third party in the country, arousing the fear in some breasts that one day it might become the second, nay, first party of the land.

On the wave of that pre-war popularity, Berger was elected to the United States House of Representatives in 1911, the first Socialist in Congress. Being a Socialist, he was also a pacifist and therefore opposed to America's entrance into the war. On that ground he was indicted for giving aid and comfort to the enemy in time of war and sentenced to twenty years in prison. That sentence was passed not so much on the pacifist as on the Socialist dissident, in the reaction to the wave of idealism that had animated a large part of the population during the war. Nevertheless, Berger was re-elected to Congress in 1918, then again in 1919, but Congress did not seat him on the ground of disloyalty. He was out on bail, while his conviction was carried up the judicial ladder to the Supreme Court which reversed his sentence in 1921. He was re-elected two years later and served in the House of Representatives until death overtook him in 1929.

David E. Lilienthal reached one of the most important public positions in the United States. The rôle of Hungarian scientists in devising the atom bomb has been noted. It was probably pure coincidence that Lilienthal, the son of Hungarian immigrants, should have become the supreme authority on atomic energy in the United States. Before reaching that position he achieved nation-wide fame in another important governmental field.

He was born in Morton, Illinois, the son of Leo Lilienthal and Minna Rosenak. This is what he wrote me in response to my question about his ancestry: "Both my father and mother were born in Hungary. My father was born in the village of Ipoly-Pásztó which is about forty miles air-line from Budapest in northern Hungary near the present border of Czechoslovakia. As a youth he lived in Budapest and Pressburg, now the Czechoslovakian Bratislava. My mother was born in Smolenc, a village near Trnava, which is now part of Czechoslovakia and which was then part of Hungary."

David E. Lilienthal had his education in the Middle West and at Harvard, then went into law practice at Chicago. His law partner was Donald R. Richberg, a member of President Roosevelt's original Brain Trust who called the President's attention to Lilienthal as a man distinguished by great idealism and practical sense, well versed in the problem of public utilities, and a good administrator. When the great White House dream of the Tennessee Valley Authority was about to be realized, President Roosevelt appointed Lilienthal as its director and a few years later, in 1941, appointed him its chairman. Lilienthal wrote the story of what happened in the Tennessee valley as a result of the great hydro-electric project in the book *Democracy on the March,* published in 1945. He spoke as a frontiersman of America, a pioneer not working with a spade but with huge generators. His work and his book were remarkable demonstrations of America's ability to create people in her own image: the son of immigrants native to the Danube valley helping to realize the great dream of America, the dream of pioneers, and thus becoming the apostle of an idea which, translated into action, could immeasurably improve the masses' lot.

Then came the atomic age. The civilian commission dealing with atomic energy would have tremendous power in its hands. Who would be nominated chairman of the commission? President Harry S. Truman sent the name of David Eli Lilienthal to the Senate of the United States for confirmation as chairman of the United States Atomic Energy Commission. After some hectic opposition by self-seeking politicians, Lilienthal was confirmed by the Senate as chairman of the commission. That Hungarian immigrant boy certainly came near the stars.

Other children of the Danube gave their best to the American community and the American community gave its best to them. We have already come across the name of a gifted mother, Charlotte Lederer, author and illustrator. Her famous daughter was Mrs. Anna M. Rosenberg, conciliator in industrial disputes, member of numerous high government commissions, recipient of the highest distinctions in the keeping of this country. She received the Medal of Freedom on the recommendation of General Dwight D. Eisenhower, in October 1945, for her services in the European theater of war, and in May 1947 she received the Medal of Merit from the hands of Secretary of War Robert P. Patterson with a citation of her merits which concluded with the following words: "Only a person of Mrs. Rosenberg's vision, courage, administrative ability, qualities of leadership and untiring and unstinting devotion to her country could have carried on so many jobs so successfully and made such an outstanding civilian contribution to the war effort of the United States." [87]

International reputation was the reward of another woman of Hungarian origin, Henrietta Szold, known the world over as the "First Lady" of Zionism. Her father was Benjamin Szold, a Hungarian conservative rabbi, who was among the first Hungarian immigrants to the United States. He settled in Baltimore and there performed most of his work: the compilation of a prayer book, and help for Jewish refugees from Russia.

Henrietta Szold was born in Baltimore in 1860 and there she participated in social work at an early age. The economic liberation of the American Negro was especially close to her heart, but she also helped her father care for Jewish refugees from Russia, after Czar Alexander III had selected the Russian Jews as the scapegoats of his inefficient regime. As a young woman Henrietta taught in a fashionable school during the day and in a school for immigrants in the evening. She accepted a position on the staff of the Jewish Publishing Society of America in 1892, which she held well into the First World War. A hard worker, she translated, indexed and proof-read scores of volumes. She became a "Zionist" at a time when that term was not even known, a believer in the proposition that the Jew should have a homeland. She paid her first visit to the Holy Land in 1909 and wrote back to America: "If not Zionism, then nothing. I am more than ever convinced that our salvation lies that way." During the First World

War she worked for relief for Palestine, and in 1919 she returned there, her second home. From that time on until her death after the Second World War her name and Zionism was synonymous.

She founded the organization of Jewish women in the United States devoted chiefly to the maintenance of schools and hospitals in Palestine, *Hadassah,* myrtle, the name of the Esther of the Bible. Henrietta Szold and Hadassah became one. Many times she crossed the seas to further the cause of the Hadassah in the United States. In 1927 she became the first woman to serve on the Zionist Executive and for months at a stretch she carried the responsibility of its work on her frail shoulders. Three years later she was elected a member of the National Council of the Jews in Palestine, *Vaad Leumi,* in charge of the social service department. She was the honorary president of the Hadassah. In 1933 she laid the foundation of the Rothschild-Hadassah University Hospital in Jerusalem, by far the best-equipped hospital in that part of the world today. When the Nazis took over in Germany she became the leader of the Palestinian Jewish organization working to save the lives of Jewish children in Germany, the so-called Youth Aliyah. More than eight thousand children were brought to Palestine and new life under her auspices. Grateful youth founded a settlement in 1935, named *Kfar Szold,* in southern Palestine. In 1942 she joined the praesidium of the Palestinian Jewish organization devoted to the foster-ing of unity between Jews and Arabs, *Ihud.* Past eighty, she lived to see victory after the Second World War, and her memory is enshrined in millions of hearts.[88]

Her kinsman, Robert Szold, also a Zionist leader, was elected chair-man of the Zionist organization of America, and in 1931 became vice chairman of the Council of the Jewish Agency, world-wide representa-tion of Jewry for building a Jewish homeland on a sound economic basis.

Rosika Bédi-Schwimmer became the center of a *cause célèbre.* Be-fore that, however, she had a highly active life. At the age of twenty, she helped organize the Hungarian feminist movement in the Austro-Hungarian Monarchy of Franz Joseph. That required vision and audacity, since even suffrage for men was largely a dream in the Hun-garian part of the dual realm. In working for that cause, Rosika Bédi-Schwimmer made contacts with leaders of the feminist movements in the Western world. She began to take part, in 1904, in the work of international congresses for equal rights for women, and became widely known for her dynamic presence and great energy.

When the First World War broke out, she was attending sessions of the Women's Suffrage World Union in London. She considered it the duty of women to work for peace and promptly set out to arouse interest in that cause. In Europe she frequently conferred with crowned heads and in America she was called to the White House, conferring with President Woodrow Wilson and his political adviser, Colonel E. M. House. In January she helped Jane Addams, American social settlement worker, peace advocate and later Nobel Prize winner, found the Women's Peace Party. Rosika Schwimmer was introduced to Henry Ford, the automobile manufacturer, who then had the reputation of being a friend of peace and a liberal, and who had but recently introduced a profit-sharing plan in the Ford Motor Company.

Ford discussed the prevailing conditions with Mme. Schwimmer and reached the conclusion that a spectacular gesture could greatly further the cause of peace. A conference of the friends of peace should be called, of the people themselves, men and women, whose blood was being shed. The governments would have to heed the voice of the masses. It was decided that these ardent friends of peace should call a peace conference in the capital of a neutral Scandinavian country, Christiana, as it was then called, the capital of Norway. "Henry Ford offered every cent of his then fortune of 150 million dollars," Mme. Schwimmer stated. This was in 1915. To give the conference a build-up and attract world-wide attention, it was decided to charter a "Peace Ship," a modern version of Noah's Ark weathering the deluge of the world disaster, and to that ship the olive branch of peace was to be brought at the end of the proposed conference.

The mission failed, as it was bound to do, and Henry Ford turned away from liberalism. After more travels in the cause of peace, Mme. Schwimmer returned to Hungary. There at the end of the war the government of Count Károlyi appointed her Minister to Switzerland. Women diplomats were little known in those days, the little Alpine country was highly conservative, and the appointment was severely criticized.

When liberalism failed in Hungary, Mme. Schwimmer went abroad and reached the United States a few years after the First World War. In the application for American citizenship the question is asked if the applicant is willing to bear arms in the defense of the United States. Mme. Schwimmer felt she was bound by her pacifist convictions to answer no. The case was taken all the way to the Supreme Court of the United States which considered it on theoretical rather than prac-

tical grounds. The applicant was a woman and, as her defense pointed
out, past military age, anyway. The court decided that a condition of
citizenship was willingness to bear arms for the defense of the country,
irrespective of sex and age. On these grounds the application for
citizenship was rejected and thus she became the most famous "woman
without a country" in the United States. This test case was subsequently applied to other cases of a similar nature. Just the same, her
numerous admirers intervened to have her granted the award of the
International Committee for World Peace a few years later. During
the Second World War she elaborated a peace plan which, naturally,
shared the fate of other plans for peace. Before that she turned her
undoubted gifts to the writing of a book of Hungarian tales, entitled
Tisza Tales, named after the most Hungarian of the rivers in the
Danube basin.

Not many Americans of Hungarian descent have reached high
political positions in the United States. One reason for this phenomenon has already been mentioned—the rank and file of Hungarian
immigrants received little practical political training at home. There
is another reason, which has been noted in this book from time to
time. The Hungarians are too individualistic to form united and
strong political organizations. They like to pull in all directions, convinced that each of the participants knows the best way to success.
Also, "political arithmetic" seldom works in the Hungarians' favor,
since they are scattered over large regions of the United States, nor is
their number in this country as large as that of some other nationalities.

Occasionally a picturesque figure arises in the political field, not
necessarily on a high level, and therefore the story of a commissioner of
the Ellis Island immigrant station, Marcus Brown, is told here, as related to me by Géza Herceg, the newspaperman and scenario writer,
who was present at the incident. The story throws a revealing light on
the character of President Theodore Roosevelt. It happened in 1910.
After leaving the White House, "Teddy" led a big-game hunting expedition to Africa in 1909 and 1910. The record says that when he returned to Europe "he was highly honored." Indeed, the eyes of the
world were on him and if ever there was a man of the hour, that man
was he. On his way north he was the guest of the major nations. A
"Roosevelt frenzy" swept that part of the world.

Among the rulers who invited him to be their guest was Emperor-
King Franz Joseph of the Austro-Hungarian Monarchy, head of Eu-

rope's oldest major dynasty, and as haughty a monarch as haughty can be. The reception was to take place at a Vienna railway station, and the honor committee was headed by the old monarch himself, an unusual gesture under the Habsburgs' rigid Spanish rules. Such receptions were normally accorded only to high dignitaries of equal rank and Teddy was now a private citizen. Glittering in their colorful uniforms, bedecked with medals, stood the entourage of the Emperor and King. The traditional purple carpet had been rolled out to connect the railway carriage door with the Imperial Waiting Room, complete with potted palms. Facing the imperial reception committee, the assemblage of the common people stood behind a line of police.

Slowly the special train ground to a halt, at the exact place where the purple carpet indicated the presence of the exalted personages. Now all eyes were on the door through which the great Teddy was to emerge. In accordance with international etiquette, the military band struck up the anthem of the United States, followed by the Habsburg anthem. The Emperor-King stood at rigid attention, and the ex-President emerged from the car, formidable jaw and all. He promptly sized up the situation, the magnificent reception committee on one side and the mob of commoners on the other side. Among the latter he spotted his old crony from New York, Marcus Brown, who had introduced him to the culinary delights of the city's "Gulyás Avenue." The ex-President's face showed real delight at seeing a New York friend so far from home, and forgetting about Emperor, King, Habsburgs, etiquette, glittering entourage, he yelled to Marcus Brown:

"Hey, Marcus, I want to see you. Look me up at Hotel X." Then Theodore Roosevelt turned the remnants of his attention to His Majesty Franz Joseph, Emperor of Austria, King of Hungary, King of Bohemia, King of Jerusalem, etc. etc. etc.

On being introduced, in a group, to the then Mayor of New York, Fiorello H. LaGuardia, he greeted us in Hungarian. The record shows that after his father's death in the United States, his mother took her family to Hungary, where she lies in a Budapest cemetery. Early in this century, LaGuardia was attached to the American consulate in Budapest, and subsequently became a consular agent at Fiume, then in Hungary. His sister continued to live in Hungary and was married to a Hungarian. Considering all these links with Hungary, the story got around in New York that the Mayor might be at least partly of Hungarian origin. Naturally, this was too juicy a piece to miss and so I wrote to him, pointing out that while only cities vied for the honor of claiming the great Homer as their own, evidently several countries did the same for Fiorello H. LaGuardia. The following lines were received in answer: "I am sorry I cannot qualify. I do not know how the story got about that any part of my family came from Hungary. None of them did. It so happened that my sister married a Hungarian, and that is about as near as we come to it."

Americans of Hungarian origin have become judges, commissioners, city councilors and perhaps also mayors of smaller towns in the United States. One of them, Hugo E. Rogers, was elected Borough President of Manhattan in 1945.

Hungarians have distinguished themselves in numerous other fields which can be mentioned here briefly—in industry, banking, art galleries, insurance, publishing, and other occupations.

Among the manufacturers of Hungarian origin, the name of Charles Louis Fleischmann is very well known. He was born in 1834 near the Hungarian capital, and became the best-known yeast manufacturer of the United States before his death in 1897. John Polachek was a leader of the bronze industry. The late Gabriel Wells became an international figure in the field of rare books and manuscripts before he died at the age of eighty-five in 1947. He sold some of the most important manuscripts and books now in American public and private collections, including about thirty copies of the First Folio of Shakespeare's plays. Zoltan Haraszti became known as an expert librarian in rare books, and Augusta Markowitz, a New York librarian, made her reputation by building up the largest collection of Hungariana in the "Empire City." Bela Szekula became one of the largest stamp dealers of the world, often referred to as the "stamp czar." Jacob L. Freeman made a name for himself in the clothing industry, and was known for his liberal labor policy, and for sending promising young men through college at his expense. Alfred Vámos became a leader in the shoe industry; the Haydu brothers in the manufacture of precision parts for the vacuum tube industry. Hungarian-born in this country distinguished themselves in fields as far apart as custom jewelry, screen color photography, the manufacture of "mouton fur," new types of fountain pens. Among the art dealers Joseph Brunner, E. and A. Silbermann, and George Binet distinguished themselves. In the field of banking, Andrew L. Gomori; in the field of insurance, Frederick Mezei established names for themselves. In the field of industrial arts Adolph Finali was successful, while George Pal was credited with the creation of film "puppetoons," film puppets. George Vajna was one of the leading booksellers of Budapest, also a publisher in the Hungarian capital. He came to the United States shortly before the Second World War and specialized in importing books from England. Later he branched out into the publishing field. Americans of Hungarian origin came to play an important rôle in the export-import business. One of the best known maîtres d'hôtels of the United States, the famous "Theodore of the Ritz" in New York was the Hungarian-born Theodore Szarvas.

Traveling in the United States, one comes across unexpectedly interesting careers of Hungarian-born Americans or Americans of Hungarian origin. It was, for instance, rather surprising to find an ex-Hungarian as the editor of the English-language newspaper of Fontana in California—Cornelius de Bakcsy. He appeared to be the dynamo of numerous social activities of that city of citrous fruits and blast furnaces in the enchanting southern California country. A man with a Hungarian name, Fred C. Halmos, was the commander of the Veterans of the A.E.F. in Siberia, in Los Angeles, and vice-chairman of the Fourth Area War Council of the American Legion, Department of California. During the Second World War the owners of the Pacific Screw Products, Inc., employing some four thousand workers in California were James W. and Stephen A. Campos, or to give them their Hungarian names: *Kampos János* and *Kampos István,* ex-peasants from Veszprém County, Hungary, and graduates of Pit College, former coal miners. An ex-Hungarian in a West Coast city turned out to be the largest junk dealer of the town and, in spite of his Hungarian origin, not ashamed to call himself a junk dealer. His air-conditioned house was certainly far better than anything a top Hungarian aristocrat would consider adequate.

It was a constant delight to meet American college professors of Hungarian background, instructing in all fields of studies. Occasionally, one came across an ex-Hungarian in a place where one would least expect him, such as a Hungarian Baptist minister in an upstate New York Indian reservation, celebrating Thanksgiving Day with his Indian charges. That was certainly an excellent example of forgiveness and brotherly love on the part of the Indians.

XXI

The Drums and an Epilogue

We are now approaching the end of our story. It was a Hungarian who said when the skies of the Allies appeared to be darkest: "The United States cannot lose this war. The Hungarians are on the opposite side."

Distrust of the Germans is in Hungarian bones, as is to be expected. The German, mostly in the form of the German-speaking Austrian Habsburgs, represented oppression and a strongly anti-Hungarian attitude. One of the most popular proverbs of the Hungarians exhorts them: *Ne higyj magyar a németnek*. Trust not the German. Another popular proverb runs: *Huncut a német*. Crafty is the German.

There was no need to set up detention camps in this country for disloyal Hungarians, nor was it necessary to strip naturalized Hungarian-born citizens of their nationality; they were not even treated as enemy aliens. How many Americans of Hungarian descent participated and suffered casualties in World War II? I addressed this question to the departments of our armed services in Washington, and the following answer, received from Major General Edward F. Witsell, Adjutant General in the War Department, was typical: "I am not unmindful of the desirability of cooperating with you. However, the War Department has never classified individuals in the military service according to their ancestry; nor has it prepared casualty lists, broken down accordingly."

One cannot but agree that Americans called upon to give their lives for their country should be known only as Americans, and not according to any other classification of nationality. All we can do is to mention a few American servicemen of Hungarian descent and to point out that no greater merit is claimed for them than for members of any other nationality.

The highest military rank among Hungarian-Americans during the Second World War was reached by Theodor von Kármán, with the rank of a Major General, who was called upon to do special work for the Army Air Force. Colonel Martin Himmler, a newspaper publisher, was entrusted with numerous missions in Central and Eastern Europe, which continued for at least two years after the war. Francis Kalnay, who had compiled and edited a handbook for new Americans, occupied a responsible position in the Office of Strategic Services, dubbed the "cloak and dagger outfit," because of the secrecy surrounding it. The nation at arms called upon countless civilians of Hungarian descent to help in the common effort. The writer of this book lectured in United States army camps, helped to prepare a plan for the postwar treatment of Germany and served on the Writers' War Board.

Picking out a few names from the Hungarian-language press merely gives a taste of the nature of the contributions of the service men. It would disrupt the framework of this book to attempt to record too large a number of individual cases.

There was, for instance, the case of Colonel A. L. Johnson, a professional officer, whose name certainly did not indicate his Hungarian origin. Yet he was born in Budapest. Before the First World War he was commissioned a lieutenant in the cavalry—this may have been a Hungarian touch. He served in the First World War, and in the Second as a special service officer in Australia before retiring in 1944. He died in 1947.

Captain Julius J. Toth, of Columbus, Ohio, received his citation for his work on Leyte island in the face of heavy Japanese fire. A parachute officer, in complete disregard of his own safety he crawled to a point where he could overlook enemy positions and, where, incidentally he could not be completely concealed from the foe. He directed American artillery fire with his portable radio from that exposed position and largely as a result of his work the Japanese were dislodged from their advanced posts.

Ferenc Gyoevoei, of Whitesville, West Virginia, fought at Luzon at the beginning of the war, when the Japanese overran it. He was with the Twenty-sixth Mounted Regiment. The regimental flag was in danger of capture, according to the citation. That, of course, was inconceivable and so Gyoevoei got hold of the flag. The enemy pursued his group and it was herded into Bataan, which turned out to be a trap. He thereupon turned over the flag to a trusted Filipino woman who sewed it into a pillow case. The young soldier was captured with the rest of his unit and remained in war prison throughout the hostilities. After liberation, he rejoined his regiment and attended the solemn ceremony when the flag was restored.

A sad fate befell another young soldier with a Hungarian background: First Lieutenant K. Keszthelyi, who received the posthumous award of the Distinguished Service Cross. His story is best told through extracts from the citation in General Orders No. 207, in August 1945, by command of General McNarney's headquarters of the Mediterranean Theatre of Operations.

"Award of Distinguished Service Cross (Posthumous).

"Tibor K. Keszthelyi, 01704213, First Lt. Army of the US, for extraordinary heroism in action against the enemy from 7 Oct. to 12 Dec. 1944. With full knowledge of the extreme hazards involved, First Lt. Keszthelyi volunteered for an intelligence mission into the heart of enemy occupied Czechoslovakia. As an officer in charge of a sub-detachment of liaison and intelligence team which operated for many weeks in close association with resistance forces, First Lt. Keszthelyi had as specific missions the establishment of contacts in the Czechoslovak underground and the infiltration into Hungary of civilian agents. Within a few days after his arrival in Slovakia, he successfully concluded arrangements with the underground for entrance of two men into Hungary and personally conducted them over the border. One of the two men dispatched later accomplished a vital intelligence mission in Budapest. During the ensuing weeks First Lt. Keszthelyi carried on with great skill and intrepidity his duties as a liaison agent with the Czechoslovak underground, obtaining in the process much valuable information on such matters as the disposition and strength of enemy forces, early notice of enemy troop movements by rail, detailed report on industrial production and significant information on the state of German morale. He rendered important aid in the rescue and evacuation of a large number of Allied fliers. When the food supply of the group became critical, First Lt. Keszthelyi was particularly active in the leadership of foraging parties whose activities were extremely hazardous by reason of the constant presence of enemy patrols. On 12 Dec. 1944, while First Lt. Keszthelyi and an enlisted man were visiting a village in an attempt to obtain horses for transportation of seriously ill members of their group, they were captured by a German patrol and subsequently executed. First Lt. Keszthelyi's activities until his capture contributed intelligence of distinct value to the war effort. His heroism and selfless performance of duty reflect the highest traditions of the armed services. By command of General McNarney, M. White, Major General, GSC, Acting Chief of Staff."

The Americans mentioned in this book have come from a country which nature endowed with many gifts. Yet that country remained poor so far as the masses of the people were concerned, thus demonstrating that wealth is not merely—not even primarily—what nature provides but what the hands and brains of man can produce.

The many highly creative immigrants of Hungarian descent found in this country the opportunities needed for the flowering of their special gifts. No other country has been as hospitable to the immigrant as the United States. It is probably human nature to make the most of all possible advantages, including the order of arrival. The earliest arrivals consider themselves entitled to better places, as if the entire nation were a vast queue in which the latest comer is forced to take the last place. Many of the more recent arrivals do not think this is part of the democratic way which would be to accord everybody an equal chance irrespective of the date of arrival. Yet there seems to be a strong trend toward the formation of privileged groups. The stratification of society is growing apace. That may not be obvious to the native-born American, but it is very obvious to ex-immigrants who know social stratification when they see it.

There should be no foreigners in this country—except people who want to retain their foreign nationalities. Irrespective of accent, American citizens should be considered American citizens, not members of an inferior breed or—at best—curiosities. America will continue to be great so long as she continues to provide the most favorable conditions for the mating of opportunities and human gifts. That combination must not be tampered with on pain of losing the greatest advantage that has helped to make ours a great country.

REFERENCES

1. Snorri Sturluson, *Heimskringla, or Lives of the Norse Kings.* Edited with notes by Erling Monsen and translated into English with the assistance of A. A. Smith. Cambridge: W. Heffer and Sons, Ltd., 1932.
2. Eugene Pivány, *Hungarian-American Historical Connections:* From Pre-Columbian Times to the End of the American Civil War. Budapest, 1927. "A treatise read /in part/ on the occasion of assuming his seat as a foreign member of the Hungarian Academy of Sciences by Eugene Pivány, Budapest, October 4, 1926."
3. *Antiquitates Americanae.* Edidit Societas Regia Antiquariorum Septentrionalium Studio et Opera Caroli Christiani Rafn. Hafniae, 1837. Folio XLII. (In Icelandic, Danish and Latin.) Quoted by Pivány, *op. cit.*
4. Pivány, *op. cit.*
5. Pivány, *op. cit.*
6. Pivány, *op. cit.*
7. Pivány, *op. cit.*
8. Aladár Póka-Pivny, "A Hungarian under Washington," *The Hungarian Quarterly,* 1939.
9. *Ibid.*
10. *Ibid.*
11. Data collected by the late Charles Feleky of New York and reproduced by Pivány, *op. cit.*
12. *California: a Guide to the Golden State.* American Guide Series. Sponsored by Mabel R. Gillis, California State Librarian. Books, Inc. Distributed by Hastings House, N. Y.
13. Thomas A. Bailey, *A Diplomatic History of the American People.* New York: F. S. Crofts & Co., Second Edition, 1942.
14. Chauncey M. Depew at Cooper Union memorial services, April 4, 1894.
15. At Concord, May 11, 1852.
16. Bailey, *op. cit.*
17. Bailey, *op. cit.*
18. Bailey, *op. cit.*
19. Fornet László, *Fornet Kornél 1848-Az Honvédörnagy Amerikai Ezredes Élete,* Adatok az Amerikai Magyar Emigráció Életéhez. Budapest: 1946.

20. Kende Géza, *Magyarok Amerikában—Az Amerikai Magyarság Története*, Két kötetben. Cleveland: A. Szabadság Kiadása, 1927.
21. Xántus János, *Utazás Kalifornia Déli Résziben*. Pest: Lauffer & Stolp, 1860. Prepost István, *Xántus János Levelei Északamerikából*. Pest: Lauffer & Stolp, 1858.
22. Bailey, *op. cit.*
23. Kende, *op. cit.* quoting *Osaka Mainichi Chinbun*.
24. Gustav Pollak, *Michael Heilprin and His Sons*. New York: Dodd, Mead & Company, 1912.
25. Pivány, *op. cit.*
26. Edmund Vasváry, *Lincoln's Hungarian Heroes:* The Participation of the Hungarians in the Civil War, 1861-1865. Washington: The Hungarian Reformed Federation of America.
27. *Ibid.*
28. *Ibid.*
29. *Ibid.*
30. Harry Jerome (of the staff of National Bureau of Economic Research), *Migration and Business Cycles*. New York: National Bureau of Economic Research, Inc., 1926.
31. Franz Oppenheimer, *Das Bevoelkerungsgesetz des T. R. Malthus und der Neueren Nationaloekonomie*. Berlin und Bern: Akademierverlag der Sozialwissenschaften, 1901.
32. *Ibid.*
33. Harold Underwood Faulkner, *American Political and Social History*. New York: F. S. Crofts & Co., Fourth Edition, 1945.
34. A. S. Pinter, *"Az Északamerikába Irányuló Magyar Kivándorlás Története 1900-tól Napjainkig" (A Kivándorlás Okai és Következményei Szociális, Politikai és Gazdasági Szempontból)*. Budapest. In manuscript.
35. *Ibid.*
36. *Ibid.*
37. *Jövendő*, January 4, 1906. Quoted by Géza Schütz, *La Situation Matérielle des Classes Laborieuses en Hongrie avant la Guerre* (1890-1913) Menton: Imprimerie Mentonnaise, 1930.
38. E. R. Krejcsi, *"Gesetzentwurf ueber die Regelung der Rechtserhaltung zwischen den Arbeitgebern und landwirtschaftlichen Arbeitern,"* *Archiv fuer soziale Gesetzgebung und Statistik*. 12 Band, 1938.
39. L. Zs. Szeberényi, *"A Parasztok Helyzete Magyarországon, Békéscsaba, 1907,"* quoted by Schütz, *op. cit.*
40. Pinter, *op. cit.*
41. Pinter, *op. cit.*
42. Samuel Gompers, *Labor in Europe and America*. New York: Harper & Brothers, 1910 (letter from Budapest, dated August 15, 1909).

43. *"Essais de Statistique Comparée du Surpeuplement des Habitations de Paris."* *Comptes-Rendus du Congrès,* Budapest, 1896. Quoted by Schütz, *op. cit.*

44. Quoted by Pinter, *op. cit.*

45. Géza Hoffman, *"Akkulturation unter den Magyaren in Amerika,"* *Zeitschrift für Sozialwissenschaft,* 1913.

46. Pal Farkas, *Az Amerikai Kivándorlás.* Budapest: Singer & Wolfner, 1907.

47. *Ibid.*

48. Gy. K. Szentiványi, *Egyén és Társadalom.* Budapest, 1892.

49. Pinter, *op. cit.*

50. Robert E. Park and Herbert A. Miller, *Old World Traits Transplanted.* New York: Harper & Brothers, 1921.

51. *"Verhovayak Lapja,"* *Journal of the Verhovay Aid Association,* Szerkeszti Daragó József, February 21, 1946.

52. Alexander Kalassay, "The Hungarian Reformed Federation of America, 1896-1923." In manuscript. Placed at the author's disposal through the kindness of Rev. Edmund Vasváry.

53. Kende, *op. cit.*

54. László Lakatos, editor, Rákoczi Aid Association, *Golden Jubilee Book.*

55. Kende, *op. cit.*

56. Sixty-sixth Congress. First Session. Senate Document No. VI. II. Quoted by Robert Park, *The Immigrant Press and its Control.* New York: Harper & Brothers, 1922.

57. Kende, *op. cit.*

58. Private letter from a member of the congregation of Dr. Arthur Várady, minister at Crescent-Martins Ferry, Ohio.

59. The Rev. Lajos Bálint, at Milwaukee and later at New Brunswick, N. J.

60. Park, *op. cit.*

61. Park, *op. cit.*

62. *"Az Amerikai Magyarság Évkönyve,"* *Hungarians in America.* Cleveland, *Szabadság.*

63. Eugene S. Bagger, "The Immigrant Press in America," in manuscript, quoted by Park, *op. cit.*

64. Park, *op. cit.*

65. Park, *op. cit.*

66. *The New York Times,* July 1, 1947, letter by Ferenc Göndör, editor of *Az Ember,* dated June 23, 1947.

67. N. W. Ayer & Sons, *Directory,* Philadelphia: N. W. Ayer & Sons, 1942, 1944, 1946 and 1947 editions.

68. *Amerikai Magyar Népszava,* June 6, 1946.

69. Terry Ramsay, *A Million and One Nights:* A History of the Motion Picture. In two volumes. New York: Simon and Schuster, 1926.

70. Upton Sinclair, *Upton Sinclair Presents William Fox.* Los Angeles (West Branch), published by the author, 1933.

71. Faulkner, *op. cit.*

72. Robert E. Park and Herbert A. Miller, *op. cit.*

73. Metropolitan Life Insurance Company, *Statistical Bulletin,* Vol. 27. No. 5, May 1946.

74. Emory S. Bogardus, *Immigration and Race Attitudes.* New York: D. C. Heath & Co., 1928. Quoted by Donald Young, *American Minority Peoples:* A Study in Racial and Cultural Conflicts in the United States. New York: Harper and Brothers, 1932.

75. Autobiography of an Intellectual, in manuscript, quoted by Park and Miller, *op. cit.*

76. Statement by Eugene S. Bagger (Magyar intellectual) "made at our request," Park and Miller, *op. cit.*

77. Louis D. Brandeis of the Supreme Court of the United States in an address at Carnegie Hall on January 24, 1916. Quoted by Park and Miller, *op. cit.*

78. *Theodor von Karman's Anniversary Volume,* published by friends of Theodor von Karman on his sixtieth birthday, May 11, 1941. "The scientific papers in this volume are contributions of a small number of close friends, who are outstanding workers in the field of applied mechanics." (Clark B. Millikan)

79. "Mathematical Theory of Poker as Applied to Business Problems," by Will Lissner. *The New York Times,* March 10, 1946.

80. Henry DeWolf Smyth, consultant, Manhattan District U. S. Engineers, written at the request of Maj. Gen. L. R. Groves, U.S.A. *Atomic Energy for Military Purposes:* The Official Report on the Development of the Atomic Bomb under the Auspices of the United States Government, 1940-1945. Princeton: Princeton University Press, 1945.

81. *The Nation's* eightieth anniversary dinner on December 3, 1945. *The Nation,* December 22, 1945.

82. E. Teller, "A Suggested Amendment to the Acheson Report," *Bulletin of the Atomic Scientists,* Vol. 1, No. 12, June 1, 1946.

83. Dexter Masters and Katharine Way, editors, *One World or None.* New York: Whittlesey House, McGraw-Hill Book Co., Inc., 1946.

84. *Time,* February 11, 1946.

85. Maurice R. Davie, *Refugees in America.* New York: Harper & Brothers, 1947. Quoting *American Men of Science,* 1944.

86. *The New York Times,* February 9, 1947.

87. *The New York Times,* May 29, 1947.

88. *Universal Jewish Encyclopaedia,* Vol. 10 (1943).

INDEX

Abraham, Paul, 279
Academy of Natural Sciences of Philadelphia, 69, 70
Achim, András, 110
Ács, Gedeon, 62
Adamic, Louis, quoted, 229
Ady Endre Táraság (Ady Endry Society), 172
Agudath Israel, 191
Agriculture in Hungary. *See* Hungary
Aigner, Lucien, 289, 290
Alaska and the Klondike. *See* Heilprin, Angelo
Alexander, Dr. Franz, 242-45
Alvary, Lorenzo, 281
American Committee for Hungarian War Refugees, 168, 169
American Hungarian Catholic Society, 186
American Hungarian Engineer and Architect Association. See *Amerikai Magyar Mérnök és Epitész Egylet*
American Hungarian Federation, 175, 176
American Hungarian National Federation, 173, 174
American Hungarian People's Voice. See *Amerikai Magyar Népszava*
American Hungarian Relief, 169
American Hungarian Socialist Federation, 201
American Hungarian Student Association. See *Magyar Diák Egylet*
American in the Making. *See* Ravage, Marcus E.
American Jewish Congress, 193
American National Guard. See *Amerikai Nemzetőr*
American Reformed Church, 185
American Revolution, Hungarians serving in, 26-30
Amerikai Magyar Diák Egylet
Amerikai Magyar Mérnök és Epitész Egylet, 172
Amerikai Magyar Népszava, 198, 199, 201, 203
Amerikai Magyar Református Egyesület, 161-64
Amerikai Nemzetőr, 170 (quoted), 196, 197

Anatomy of Peace, The. See Reves, Emery
Angyal, Dr. Andras, 254
Anselm, Albert, 53
Antalffy-Zsiros, Dezső, 283
Anti-Semitism, 68, 222-24, 234
Arpád the Conqueror, 13, 14, 15
Art, Contributions to, 285-290
Aruch Hashalem. See Kohut, Rabbi Alexander
Asboth, Gen. Sándor, 67, 74, 76, 77, 82
Association Life. See Egyleti Élet
Atomic research. *See* Research
Auer, Leopold, 276
Ausgleigh (Compromise). *See* Habsburgs
Az Ember, 177, 203

Babri, Ignac, 63
Bagger, Eugene S., 234 (quoted), 257, 258
Bailey, Prof., quoted, 40
Bakcsy, Cornelius de, 301
Balance. See Heilprin, Michael
Balázs, Frigyes, 284
Balint, Emery, 270, 271
Balog, Ernő, 284
Balough, Charles, 237, 238
Bánát, Gábor, 274
Banky, Vilma, 272
Barothy, Charles, 82
Bartók, Béla, 274, 276-78, 279, 281
Beck, Martin, 291
Bédi-Schwimmer, Rosika. *See* Schwimmer, Rosika Bédi
Békássy, Stephan, 272
Béldy, Count Ferenc, 31
Belletristische Zeitung, 76
Bem, Gen. Jozef *(Bem Apó),* 79
Benedek, Dr. Terez, 245
Benesi, Oscar, 254
Beniczky, Cornel, 63
Bennett, James Gordon, 88
Benyowsky, Count Maurice Augustus, 29, 30
Benyowsky, Ferenc, 29
Berger, Oscar, 288
Berger, Victor, 292, 293
Berkó, Géza D., 201
Bethlen Otthon (Bethlen Home), 163, 164
Bettelheim, Bernát, 64

Binet, George, 300
Biró, Sári, 284
Bleuer, Lajos, 283
Bock, Martin, 31
Boehm, Father Károly, 181, 182
Bogardus, Prof. Emory S., 228
Bohem, Endre, 273
Bokor, Margit, 281
Borsodi, Ralph, 259
Bosnyák, Béla, quoted, 105
Box Office Attractions Film Rental Company, 214
Brandeis, Justice Louis D., 231
Bridgeporti (Bridgeport Association), 164, 165
Brown, Marcus, 298, 299
Brunauer, Stephen, 252
Brunner, Joseph, 300
Buchanan, James, 57
Budapest String Quartet, 284
Buena Vista, Cal., 35
Bus-Fekete, László, 273
Byng, Edward J., 266, 267

California, 34, 35
Campos, James W., 201
Campos, Stephen A., 201
Capa, Robert, 289
Cass, Gen. Lewis, 48, 49
Chabay, Leslie, 281
Chadwick, Rev. John W., 68
Civil War, Hungarians serving in, 53, 64, 73-83, 85, 86
Clayton, John M., 75
Cleveland, O., 158, 159, 181, 182
Cleveland Magyar Betegsegélyző, 158
Cobden, Richard, 38
Congress (U.S.), on Hungarian independence, 41-43, 48, 49
Csizmadia, Sándor, quoted, 104
Csoka, Stephen, 288
Cukor, George Dewey, 271
Cunard Line, 132
Curtiz, Michael, 271
Custer, George Armstrong, 86

Danburghy, Edward, 49
Dáncz, Lajos, 54
Darvas, Lili, 290
Davenport, Ia., 53, 54
Deák, Ferenc (signer of Ausgleich), 68
Deák, Ferenc (author), 269
Debs, Eugene V., 292, 293
Dembinszky, Ántal, 63
Depew, Chauncey M., quoted, 38, 39
Déri, Imre, quoted, 177
Déri, Otto, 284
"Dersq and Kelen," (Derzso, Alois, and Kelen, Imre), 288

Deutsch, Rozsika and Jancsika. See "Dolly Sisters"
Dienes, André de, 289
Dissolution of the Habsburg Monarchy, The. See Jászi, Oscar
Dobozy, Péter Pál, 82
Dohanos, Stevan, 288
"Dolly Sisters," 290
Doman, Nicholas, 270
Dömötör, János, 63
Dorati, Anton, 282

Eckhardt, Tibor von, 176
Eder, Gábor, 289
Edison, Thomas Alva, 208, 238
Eggerth, Marta, 281
Egyetemi Kör, 172
Egyleti Élet, 168
Eichhorn, Dr. Adolph, 252
Einstein, Prof. Albert, 247
Elizabeth, Queen, 22
Előre. See Magyar Jövő
Emergency Quota Act, 218
Emericus (St. Emeric), 21
Emerson, Ralph Waldo, quoted, 39
Emigration, causes of, 95, 96, 97, 125, 222; Home Government Policies on, 123, 130-33, 180, 182, 183, 221
Endresz, George, 173
Erdély, Ferenc, 287
Erdélyi, Gusztáv Sz., 196, 197
Erdos, Paul, 254
Ericson, Leif, 19-21
Ernster, Dezső, 281
Erster Ungarischer Kranken-Unterstuetzungsverein, 158
Escape to Life. See Körmendi, Ferenc
István, Béla, 82

Fabri, Ralph, 288
Fairchild, Henry Pratt, quoted, 229
Famous Players-Laski Corporation, 212
Farago, László, 269, 270
Faragoh, Francis Edward, 273
Farkas, Sándor Bölöni, 31-33
Farkas, Karl, 278
Farkas, Zoltán, 289
Federal Bureau of Immigration, 134
Federation of Hungarian Fraternal Societies. See Magyar Betegsegélyző Egyletek Szövetsége
Fejérváry, Miklos, 53
Fekete, István, 238
Fekete, Zoltán, 279
Feleky, Charles, 291
Fényes, László, 177
Ferber, Edna, 258, 259
Ferdinand I, 16
Feudal system in Hungary. See Hungary

Fight. See *Harc*
Figyelmessy, Fülöp, 81, 82
Fillmore, Millard, 42
Finali, Adolph, 300
Finta, Alexander, 288
First Hungarian Literary Society, 171
First Hungarian Sickness Benefit Association. See *Erster Ungarischer Kranken-Unterstuetzungsverein*
First New York Cavalry Regiment, 85
Fleischmann, Charles Louis, 300
Flesch, Ella, 281
Fodor, László, 270, 273
Fodor, Marcel William, 270
Fodor, Nandor, 270
Földes, Andor, 284
Foley, Capt. James L., 80
Fornet, Maj. Kornél, 48, 49, 52, 53, 80, 81
Fornet, Washington Béla, 53
Fox, Beauvaix, 261
Fox Film Corporation, 214
Fox, William, 206, 212, 213-15
Franklin, Benjamin, 27, 30
Franklin, Fabian, 72
Franz Joseph, Emperor, 49, 62, 298, 299
Frederick the Great, 26
Freeman, Jacob L., 300
Frémont, Gen. John Charles, 53, 75, 77, 79, 80, 81
Frémont's Body Guard, 79, 80
Freund, Dr. Jules, 253
Fülöp-Miller, René, 265
Füredi, Lily, 288

Gafni, Miklos, 280, 281
Galamb, Jozsef, 237
Galambos, G., 252
Gárdonyi, Géza, quoted, 197
Garibaldi Guard, 75
Garrick, Sidney, 272
Garvai, Andor, 257
Gedő, Lipot, 287
Gerster, Dr. Arpád, 170
Gilbert, Sir Humphrey, 22
Golden Book of Hungarians in America, 226
Golden Bull, 119
Goldmark, Karl, 275
Goldmark, Peter Carl, 252
Goldmark, Rubin, 276
Goldziher, D. Max, 253
Goltz, V. d., quoted, 96
Gomori, Andrew L., 300
Gompers, Samuel, quoted, 111, 112
Göndör, Emery, 288
Göndör, Ferenc, 203
Görög, László, 273
Grant, U. S., 77
Gratz, Gustav, quoted, 105

Greeley, Horace, 88
Griffin, D. R., 252
Gumpert, Martin, 228, 229
Gyenge, Anna. See Roselle, Anne
Gyoevoei, Ferenc, 303

Habe, Hans, 268
Habsburgs, rise of, to power in Hungary, 16, 18, 115, 116; revolt against, 37, 38, 63, 77, 81, 116, 162-164 (*see also* Hungarian War of Independence); exiles' denunciation of, 49; on emigration, 63; oppression under, 66, 84; 1867 compromise with *(Ausgleich),* 68, 84; political system under, 107-10, 112, 119, 120; relation of, with the Church, 190
Hacket, Gabriel D., 289
Hainer, Eugene, 52
Hainer, Ignatius, 51, 52
Hakluyt, Richard, *The Principal Navigations,* quoted, 22
Halasi, Albert, 269
Halász, George, 264
Halász, László, 282
Halmi, Arthur, 287
Halmos, Fred C., 301
Haraszthy, "Colonel" Agoston Mokcsai, 34, 35
Haraszthy, "General" Agoston Mokcsai, 33
Haraszti, Zoltan, 300
Harc, 177
Harmati, Sándor, 282
Harsányi, Alexander, 284
Harsányi, Rev. László, 186
Hatvany-Deutsch, Baroness Antonia, 269
Hatvany-Deutsch, Lily, 273
Havassy, Imre, 48, 49
Haydu Brothers, 300
Haz, Nicholas, 289
Heilperin, Michael A., 72
Heilprin, Angelo, 68-70
Heilprin, Henrietta, 66
Heilprin, Louis, 66
Heilprin, Michael, 65-68, 158
Hellinger, Mark, 272
Hennigsen, Mr., 63
Herceg, Géza, quoted, 298
Herz, Otto, 284
Herzl, Theodor, 192, 224
Herzog, George, 252
Himmler, Col. Martin, 303
Hirschl, Felix, 53
Hirschl, Samuel, 53
Hitler, Adolph, 174, 175
Hock, János, 179
Honti, Joseph, 282
Horner, Imre, 254
Horthy, Regent Nicholas, 174, 176
Horváth, Károly, 283

Howard, Leslie, 271
Hrdlička, Aleš, 62
Hubay, Jenő, 279
Heubsch, Ben, 271
Hülsemann, Chevalier, 37, 48, 49, 60
Hungarian America. See Magyar Amerika
Hungarian American Council for Democracy, 176, 177
Hungarian Association. See Magyar Társulat
Hungarian Club. See Magyar Klub
Hungarian Cultural Association of Philadelphia, 171
Hungarian Creek, Kan., 57
Hungarian Daily Journal. See Magyar Jövő
Hungarian Exiles Journal. See Magyar Számüzöttek Lapja
Hungarian Reformed Federation of America. See Amerikai Magyar Református Egyesület
Hungarian Sick Benefit Society, 158
Hungarian War of Independence, 18th century, 29, 164
Hungarian War of Independence, 1848, 17, 37, 38, 66, 75, 81; exiles from, 47-51, 52-63, 66, 73-82
Hungary, history of, 13-20, 21, 37, 38, 62, 174-76, 177; religion in, 15, 16, 24, 179, 180; feudal system in, 17, 18, 31, 106; languages of, 17, 18, 62, 84, 119, 162; land division in, 101-03; agriculture in, 101, 102, 105, 106; living conditions in, 102, 103-08, 112-14; 125, 127, 128; industry in, 111, 112, 236; social structure of, 114-20; population of, 120-22, social organizations in, 156, 157
Hunter, Gen. David, quoted, 76
Huszár, 59, 60
Huszár, George Bernard de, 270
Hunyadi, János, 16

Ignotus (nom de plume), 269
Immigration and Nationalization Service, report of, 220
Imrey, Frank, 287
Independent American Hungarian Church, 186
Independent Socialist Peasant Party, 110, 111
Indianapolis Journal, quoted, 78
Industrial expansion, 98, 99
Industry, in Hungary. See Hungary
Immigrants, prior to World War I, 94, 97, 98, 99, 122, 123-26; after World War I, 217-34; living conditions of, 126-29; restriction of, 217-21; location of, 225, 226; inter-marriage with, 226, 227; reaction of, to America, 228-34
Ingraham, Capt. Nathan Duncan, 60

Institutions and social organizations, for insurance, life and health, 158, 159-61, 164-67; Jewish, 158, 168, 169; nationalistic, 158, 173, 174-77; Protestant, 161-64; Catholic, 165, 166; for war relief, 168, 169; cultural, 62, 170-72
Insurance, life and health. See Institutions and social organizations
Inter-marriage. See Immigrants
Irion, Mrs. Yolanda Mero, 291

Jackson, Andrew, 32
Jámbor, Lajos, 287
Jászi, Oscar, 260, 261
Jewish Institute of Religion, 193
Johnson, Col. A. L., 303
Johnson, Dr. Joseph, Traditions and Reminiscences, quoted, 28
Jókai, Mór, 256
Journal of the American Exiles. See Tothvárady, Charles Kornis
Journey in North America. (1) See Farkas, Sándor Bölöni; (2) See also Haraszthy, "General" Agoston Mokcsai
Jozsa, Gyuri, 32

Kalapsza, Captain, 62
Kalassy, Sándor, 161, 162
Kálmán, Imre, 278
Kalnay, Francis, 303
Karasz, Mariska, 288
Kármán, Gen. Theodor von, 302
Kármán, Maurice von, 239, 240
Kármán, Theodor von, 239-42
Károly, Andrew, 287
Károlyi, Count Mihály, 102, 116, 177, 222
Kato, Kay, 288
Katona, Miklós, 54
Kaufman, Paul, 253
Kelemen, Pál, 267
Kelemen, Victor, 271
Kelen, Imre. See "Derso and Kelen"
Keleti, Juliska, 290
Kelp, John (Kelpius, Johannes), 24
Kemeny, John George, 249
Kerékjártó, Duci, 284
Kerényi, Paul, 51
Kereszturi, Dr. Camille, 253
Kertész, Andre, 289
Keszthelyi, Lt. Tibor K., 304
Kilényi, Edward, 284
Kilényi, Julio, 289
King, Mr., 32
Kinizsi, István, 62
Kiralfy, Bolossy, 207
Király, Mr. See King, Mr.
Klein, Rabbi Philip, 191
Knefler (Knoepfler), Gen. Frederick, 74, 78, 79

Kober, Leo, 288
Kocsis, Alexander, 62
Kodály, Zoltán, 274, 277, 279, 281
Koenigsberg, Gábor, 63
Kohányi, Tihamér, 165, 171, 197
Kohut, George Alexander, 191
Kohut, Rabbi Alexander (Sándor), 191
Kohut, Rebekah, 191, 256; quoted, 229
Konsag (Konschak), Father Ferdinand, 25
Koppanyi, Dr. Theodore, 252, 253
Korda family, 271, 272
Korda, Maria, 272
Körmendi, Erwin, 289
Körmendi, Ferenc, 265
Kornfeld, Baron, 182
Kossuth bankó (banknotes), 44
Kossuth, Emilia, 67
Kossuth, Ferenc, 162, 163
Kossuth, Lajos, as leader in War of Independence, 17, 37, 38, 66; in America, 38-46; army of, See Hungarian War of Independence, 1848, exiles from.
Kossuth, Lujza, 67
"Koszta Affair," See Koszta, Márton
Koszta, Iowa, 61
Koszta, Márton, 59-61
Kosztka, Lajos, 63
Kovács, Andreas, 230
Kovats, Col. Michael, 26-28
Kováts, Father Kalmán, 182
Köves, Tibor, 270
Kozlay, Gen. Eugene, 74
Kozlay, Odön, 63
Kozma, Tibor, 284
Kron, Gabor, 252
Kun, Béla, 222
Kun, László, 283
Kuthy, Zoltán, 184, 185
Kűrthy, Zoltán, 284

Labor, shortage of, 98, 133, 134; on selective immigration, 219
Ladd-Franklin, Christine, 72
Laemmle, Carl, 212
LaGuardia, Fiorello H., 299, 300
Land division in Hungary. See Hungary
Lang, Paul Henry, 269
Lányi, George, 193
László, Károly, 42
Langner, Dr. Ignac, 53
Lauzun, Duke de, 29
Lauzun's Foreign Volunteers, 29
Laytha, Edgar, 270
Lederer, Charlotte, 263, 295
Leidenfrost, Sándor, 287
Leimer, Mr., 32
Lener Quartets, 284
Lengyel, Emil, 261-63, 303
Lengyel, Melchior, 272, 273

Leroy-Beaulieu, Pierre Paul, quoted, 96
Lesznai, Anna, 288
Liberty. See Szabadság
Lichtman, Al, 211
Lilienthal, David E., 293-95
Ligonier, Pa., 163, 164
Liliom. See Molnár, Ferenc
Lincoln, Abraham, on Hungarian freedom, 37, 38; in Civil War, 73, 74, 75, 76
Lincoln, Gen. Benjamin, 28
Lincoln Riflemen, 74, 75
Liszt, Franz, 92
Literature, contributions to, 256-271
Lives of the Norse Kings. See Sturluson, Snorri
Living conditions in Hungary. See Hungary
Loew, Dr. Wilmos, 196
Loew, Marcus, 210
Loew, William Noah, 256, 257
Loewenthal, Jakab János, 63
Longfellow, Henry W., quoted, 40
Lopez, Narciso, 52
Loránd, Dr. Sándor, 245
Loránd, Edith, 284
Lorant, Stefan, 266, 267
Los Alamos, N.M., 249
Loveman, Adassa Heilprin, 72
Loveman, Amy, 72
Lowell, James Russell, quoted, 73
Lugosi, Béla, 177, 272
Lukas, Paul, 272, 290
Lulley, Manó, 63

McClellan, Gen. George B., 75
Madarász, László, 51
Madison, James, 30
Magyar, Alexander, 173
Magyar Amerika, 196
Magyar Betegsegélyző Egyletek Szövetsége, 166, 167
"Magyar Club" (Boston), 62
Magyar Klub (Detroit), 171, 172
Magyar Jövő, 201
Magyar Száműzöttek Lapja, 62, 158, 195, 196
Magyar Társulat, 170
Mailáth, Count J. de, quoted, 109
Majtényi, Baron Joseph, 53
Major, Henry, 285
Man, The. See Az Ember
Mandy, Gen. Charles. See Mundee, Gen. Charles
Mann, A. Dudley, 37
Marcy, William Learned, 61
Maria Theresa, Queen, 26, 27
Mark, Lajos, 287
Markowitz, Augusta, 300
Marshall, Louis, 192

Marton, Father Pan, 181
Maryland Historical Society, 28
Massey, Ilona, 272
Matzenauer, Margarete, 280
Mészáros, Lázár, 54, 55
Meszlényi, Mr., 46
Mezei, Frederick, 300
Mihalotzy, Col. Géza, 74
Mihalotzy, Fort, 74
Mihály, Kertész. See Curtiz, Michael
Mikszáth, Kálmán, 256
Mittelman, Dr. Béla, 245
Mogyorossy, Arkád, 196
Mohács Disaster, 13, 16
Moholy-Nagy, László, 286, 287
Molnár, Ferenc, 264, 265
Moody, Andrew, 184
Morgenstern, Dr. Oscar, 242
Motion Picture Patents Company, 210-12
Motion Pictures, 206-13, 252, 271-74
Moultrie, Gen. William, 28
Movement For a New Democratic Hungary. See Uj Demokratikus Magyarországért Inditott Mozgalom
Mueller, Ferenc, 31
Mundee (Mandy), Gen. Charles, 74
Munkácsy, Mihály, 91
Munkácsi, Martin, 289
Muray, Arthur, 289
Muray, Nickolas, 289
Music, contributions to, 62, 92, 129, 130, 274-84
Mussolini, Benito, 219
My Portion. See Kohut, Rebekah

Nagy, Frank, 289
Nation, The. See Heilprin, Michael
National Bureau for Economic Research, 125
Nationalism, 158, 159, 195, 217, 235; see also Institutions and organizations
Neumann, Prof. John von, 242
New Buda, Iowa, 50, 51, 52
New Orleans, La., 56, 62
New York Council of Hungarian Americans for Victory, 177
New York Evening Post, 61 (quoted), 72
New York Evening World. See Pulitzer, Joseph
New York Herald, 37 (quoted), 88
New York Times, quoted, 242, 281
New York Tribune. See Greeley, Horace
New Yorki Magyar Egylet (New York Hungarian Association), 158-60
New Yorki Magyar Nóegylet (New York Hungarian Women's Association), 158
Newspapers. See Press, the Hungarian
Nordau, Max, 96 (quoted), 193

Northward Over the Great Ice. See Peary, Robert E.
Nyiregyházi, Erwin, 284

Oliphant, Dr., 248
Oppenheimer, J. R., 249
Oppenheimer, Prof. Franz, quoted, 96, 101
Orban, Dr. Balint, 254
Oregon State Conference of Charities and Correction, 192
Organizations. See Institutions and social organizations
Ormándy, Eugene, 281
Our Age of Unreason. See Alexander, Dr. Franz

Pal, George, 300
Papp, David, quoted, 109
Pálinkás, Mihály, 159, 160
Paramount Pictures, 212
Parmenius, Stephen, of Buda, 22, 23
Pastorius, Francis Daniel, 25
Partos, Ferenc, 273
Pasternak, Joseph, 271
Patterson, Robert P., quoted, 295
Pauncz, Dr. Arpad, 245
Peary, Robert E., 69, 70
Pen, John, 268, 269
Perry, Commodore Matthew Calbraith, 64
Perczel, Col. Miklós, 158
Petersham, Maud and Miska, 288
Petőfi, Sandor, 54, 76, 257
Philharmonic Society of New York, 92
Pierce, Franklin, 61
Pivány, Dr. Eugene, quoted, 20, 21, 22, 28, 29
Pogány, Willy, 287
Póka-Pivny, Aladár, 26
Polachek, John, 300
Polereczky, Maj. John, 29
Polereczky, Maj. Matthias, 29
Polier, Justine Wise, 193
Political system in Hungary. See Hungary
Politzer, József. See Pulitzer, Joseph
Pollak, Celia Heilprin, 72
Pollak, Walter, 72
Pollak, Walter Heilprin, 72
Polya, George, 253, 254
Pomucz, George, 74
Prágay, János, 49
Prágay, John, 52
Press, the Hungarian, nationalism of, 195, 196, 197; reaction of, to World War I, 199, 200;—to World War II, 201-03; publishing centers of, 203, circulation of, 203
Prevost, General Augustine, 28
Pulaski, Count Casimir, 27, 28
Pulaski Legion, 28.

Pulitzer, Joseph, background of, 84, 85; in Civil War, 85, 86; as journalist, 87; as crusader, 87, 88, 89, 90; editorial policies of, 89, 90, 91; as publisher of *New York World* and *New York Evening World,* 90, 91; as founder of Columbia University School of Journalism and Pulitzer Prizes, 92
Puskás, Tivadar, 238

Queen Elizabeth, 210, 211

"Racial structure." *See* Immigrants, restriction of
Rácz, Gyula, quoted, 102
Radnich, Stephen, 52
Radó, Sándor, 245
Rado, Tibor, 253
Raisz, Erwin, 253
Rákóczi, Prince Ferenc, 29, 164
Rákóczi Segélyző Egyesület. See Bridgeporti
Rapée, Ernő, 282
Raskó, Aurel, 287
Rátkai, George and Helen, 288
Rátkay, Baron John, 25
Ravage, Marcus E., quoted, 229
Ray, Oscar, 270
Reformed Church in the United States, 185
Rednich, Imre, 48, 49
Reiner, Catherine, 281
Reiner, Fritz, 282
Reinhardt, Max, 207, 290
Reiss, Dr. Frederick S., 253
Rejtő, Gábor, 284
Religion, as family link, 174, 187, 188; under Hungarian Government supervision, 180, 182, 183-85, 190; Catholic, 181-83; Protestant, 183-86; Greek Catholic, 189, 190; Jewish, 191-93; *see also* Hungary
Reményi, Ede, 48
Reményi, Edward, 275
Reményi, Joseph, 258
Research and discovery, scientific, 57, 58, 69, 90, 236-54, 267; Atomic, 245-51, 294, 295
Reves, Emery, 267, 268
Rittenberg, Louis, 263, 264
Rogers, Hugo E., 300
Roheim, Dr. Géza, 245
Rombauer, Camp, 74
Romberg, Sigmund, 278
Roosevelt, Franklin D., 175, 247, 248, 294
Roosevelt, Theodore, 134, 298, 299
Roselle, Anne, 280
Rosenberg, Mrs. Anna M., 295
Rosenberg, Anna, 263
Rosenak, Dr. Stephen, 253

Roth, Feri, 284
Roth Quartet, 284
Rózsa, Lajos, 279
Rózsa, Miklos, 273, 279
Rózsa, Sándor, 168
Rubinek, Gyula, 117
Ruttkay, Mrs. Louise, 46

Sachs, Alexander, 247, 248
Samson, Maria, 229
St. Ignatius, Mission of, Cal., 25
St. Louis, 60
St. Louis Post-Dispatch. See Pulitzer, Joseph
Sandor, Arpád, 284
Sandor, György, 284
Sándor Rózsa General Aid Association, 168
Sárossy, Isák Nándor de, 24, 25
Sauk City, Wis., 34
Schick, Dr. Béla, 238, 239
Schoepf, Gen. Albin, 74, 77, 78
Scholz, János, 284
School of Journalism, Columbia University. *See* Pulitzer, Joseph
School of Living, 259
Schorr, Friedrich, 279
Schumberg, Prof. Tobias, 25
Schwalb, Miklos, 284
Schwimmer, Rosika Bédi-, 296, 298
Sebastian, George, 282
Seidl, Anton, 276
Sepeshy, Zoltán, 285, 286
Serly, Lajos, 276
Serly, Tibor, 279
Seward, William H., 49, 81
Sheridan, Gen. P. H., 86
Sigel, General Franz, 53
Silbermann, E. and A., 300
Simon, Louis, 284
Sinclair, Upton, 214, 215
Sirmay, Dr. Albert. *See* Szirmai, Dr. Albert
Skelly, Major F., quoted, 28
Slavs, 121, 122, 180, 181, 183, 197
Smith, Alfred E., 231
Smith, John, 23, 24
Smyth, Prof. Henry D., quoted, 246
Social structure of Hungary. *See* Hungary
Socialism, 293
Societies. *See* Institutions and social organizations
Soter, Bishop Stephen Ortinszky, 190
Stahel (Számvald), Gen. Julius H., 67, 74, 76
Stasney, Joseph, 254
Stearns, George Luther, 61
Steiner, Arpád. *See* Howard, Leslie
Steuben, Baron Frederick von, 30

Sturluson, Snorri, *Heimskringla (Lives of the Norse Kings)*, quoted, 19, 20
Sumner, Charles, quoted, 39
Surgeon's World, A. See Thorek, Dr. Max
Svéd, Alexander, 280, 281
Szabadság, 165, 197, 198, 199, 203, 226
Szabó, Sándor, 63
Szabós, Janos, family of, (hypothetical characters), 135-55
Szakáll, Szőke, 272
Szálay, László, 49
Számvald, Gen. Julius H. See Stahel, Gen. Julius H.
Szánthó, Enid, 281
Szántó, Lajos, 287
Szarvas, Theodore. See "Theodore of the Ritz"
Szego, Gabor, 253
Szekely, Michael, 281
Szekely, Mrs. George S. See Kato, Kay
Szekula, Bela, 300
Szell, George, 281, 282
Szemelényi, Ernő, 63
Szigeti, Joseph, 283, 284
Széptáj, Wis. See Sauk City
Széptáj, Cal. See Buena Vista
Szilárd, Dr. Leo, 246-251
Szirmai (Sirmay), Dr. Albert, 278
Szold, Benjamin, 295
Szold, Henrietta, 295, 296
Szold, Robert, 296

Takaró, Rev. Géza, 185, 186
Taylor, Zachary, 37, 47, 48
Telkes, Maria, 253
Teller, Edward, 254
Teller, Prof. E., 246
Temptation. See Pen, John
"Theodore of the Ritz," 301
Thirty-ninth New York Infantry Regiment. See Garibaldi Guard
Thorek, Dr. Max, 253
Thoult, Col. Stephen, 62, 79
Tolnay, Beatrice, 264
Tolnay, Charles de, 269
Torda, Dr. Clara, 253
Toth, Capt. Julius J., 303
Toth, Elek, 189, 190
Toth, Prof. Louis, 177
Tothvárady, Charles Kornis, 62, 158, 195, 196
Traditions and Reminiscences. See Johnson, Dr. Joseph
Transatlantic Trust Company, 182, 183, 184, 185
Twenty-fourth Illinois Volunteer Infantry Regiment, 75
Two-Way Passage. See Adamic, Louis
Tyrker, 19-21

Tyrnauer, Fred, 270

United States Atomic Energy Commission, 294, 295
Uj Demokratikus Magyarországért Inditott Mozgalom, 177
Uj Fény, 193
Ujházy, László, 47-49, 50, 51
Ujházy, Mrs., 51
Ujházy, Tivadar, 48
United Hungarian Jews, 169
University Association. See *Egyetemi Kör*
Urnay, Captain, 35
Utazás Ejszak-Amerikában. (1) See Farkas, Sándor Bölöni. (2) See Haraszthy, "General" Agoston Moksai
Utassy, Camp, 74
Utassy, Col. Frederick George, 75

Vágó, Sándor, 287
Vajda, Ernest. See Garrick, Sidney
Vajna, George, 300
Vallas, Anthony, 62
Valyi, Felix, 266
Vámbéry, Prof. Rusztem, 177
Vámos, Alfred, 300
Várady, Frederic, 288
Várady, Anthony, 288
Varconi, Victor, 272
Varga, Ferenc, 51
Varga, Margit, 288
Várkonyi, Béla, 283
Vadnay, László, 273
Verbrecher und Seine Richter, Der. See Alexander, Dr. Franz
Verhovay, Gyula, 160
Verhovay Segély Egylet (Verhovay Fraternal Insurance Association), 159-161
Vertès, Marcel, 288
Victor Emmanuel II, 81
Virgin Mary, Patroness of Hungarians, Roman and Greek Catholic Federation, 166
Vurglics, Anton, 63

Wagner, Col. Gustav, 75
Wallace, Gen. Lewis (Lew), 78
Washington, George, 26-28, 30
Wass, "Count," 35
Wass, Samu, 48
Waterman, Louise Mayer, 192
Webb, Colonel, 48, 49
Webster, Daniel, 41; quoted, 37, 42, 43
Weckbecker, M. D., 59
Wells, Gabriel, 300
Western Department, 75
Westliche Post. See Pulitzer, Joseph
Wigner, Eugene P., 246, 247, 248
Wilde, Cornel, 272
Wimmer, G. A., 49

Wines, 20, 30, 31, 35, 36
Wise, James Waterman, 193
Wise, Rabbi Stephen S., 191, 192, 193
Womens' Peace Party, 297
Wood, Al, 291
World Hungarian Federation, 174-76
World Jewish Congress, 193
World War I, 199, 200
World War II, reaction to, of American Hungarians, 174, 175, 201-03; effect of, on immigration, 220; Hungarians serving in, 302-04
Wunderlich, Jakob Janos, 54

Xántus, János, 55-59

"Ylla," 289

Zágonyi, Maj. (Col.) Charles, 67, 75, 79, 80
Zechmeister, László Károly Ernő, 253, 254
Zerdahelyi, Károly, 62
Zinn, Dr. W., 246, 247
Zionism, 224, 295, 296
Zionist Organization of America, 192
Zsulavszky, Col. Ladislaus, 74, 82
Zsulavszky, Emil, 82
Zsulavszky, Zsigmond, 82
Zukor, Adolph, 206, 207-13
Zulavsky, Mr., 46